Moonshiners aı
Prohibitionists

NEW DIRECTIONS IN SOUTHERN HISTORY

SERIES EDITORS
Peter S. Carmichael, Gettysburg College
Michele Gillespie, Wake Forest University
William A. Link, University of Florida

MOONSHINERS
AND
PROHIBITIONISTS

The Battle over Alcohol in Southern Appalachia

BRUCE E. STEWART

THE UNIVERSITY PRESS OF KENTUCKY

Copyright © 2011 by The University Press of Kentucky

Scholarly publisher for the Commonwealth,
serving Bellarmine University, Berea College, Centre College of Kentucky,
Eastern Kentucky University, The Filson Historical Society, Georgetown
College, Kentucky Historical Society, Kentucky State University, Morehead
State University, Murray State University, Northern Kentucky University,
Transylvania University, University of Kentucky, University of Louisville,
and Western Kentucky University.

Editorial and Sales Offices: The University Press of Kentucky
663 South Limestone Street, Lexington, Kentucky 40508-4008
www.kentuckypress.com

15 14 13 12 11   5 4 3 2 1

Library of Congress Cataloging-in-Publication Data

Stewart, Bruce E.
  Moonshiners and prohibitionists : the battle over alcohol in southern
Appalachia / Bruce E. Stewart.
      p. cm. — (New directions in Southern history)
  Includes bibliographical references and index.
  ISBN 978-0-8131-3000-2 (hardcover : alk. paper)
  ISBN 978-0-8131-3017-0 (ebook)
  1. Distilling, Illicit—North Carolina.—History—18th century. 2. Distilling,
Illicit—North Carolina.—History—19th century. 3. Prohibition—North
Carolina—History—18th century. 4. Prohibition—North Carolina—
History—19th century. 5. North Carolina—Social conditions—18th century.
6. North Carolina—Social conditions—19th century. I. Title.
  HJ5021.S84 2011
  364.1'33209756—dc22   2010050374

This book is printed on acid-free recycled paper meeting
the requirements of the American National Standard
for Permanence in Paper for Printed Library Materials.

Manufactured in the United States of America.

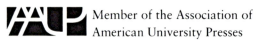 Member of the Association of
American University Presses

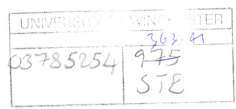

For Sunny

Contents

Tables and Illustrations

Tables

Illustrations

Preface

In the 1880s, Randolph Abbott Shotwell, a prominent Rutherford County resident, chastised the moonshiners of western North Carolina. He believed that these illegal alcohol distillers were a "distinct" branch of lower-class whites, "ignorant of even the first rudiments of education and wholly unable to give any account of the outside world." According to Shotwell, most of them had betrayed the South during Reconstruction by joining the Union League and bribing Bureau of Internal Revenue agents who enforced the federal liquor tax. The moonshiners, he explained, "were desperate characters . . . and the wealthy class, living in isolated farm houses, somewhat feared to incur their enmity." Nor did Shotwell approve of legal distillers. He insisted that these highlanders, along with their illegal counterparts, encouraged the widespread use of alcohol in mountain society, flooding "the country with liquor—'cheap as dirt,' and quite as filthy."

Shotwell's remarks must have disturbed distillers on both sides of the law in the Carolina highlands. As head of the Ku Klux Klan (KKK) in Rutherford, Cleveland, and Polk counties, Shotwell had been an early advocate of the moonshiners in their fight against the Bureau of Internal Revenue during Reconstruction. Like most other mountain whites, he feared that this agency promoted the expansion of federal authority. Moreover, Shotwell had befriended moonshiner Amos Owens and other illicit distillers who had joined the KKK to protect their economic interests. Despite his earlier positions, he refused to allow the KKK's legacy to be associated with such uncivilized and violent men. Legal distillers found Shotwell's comments disheartening as well. Before the Civil War, most highlanders, especially those living in more remote parts of the region, viewed these men—and women—as legitimate entrepreneurs. By the 1880s, that had changed. Portrayed as the purveyors of social discord, licit distillers discovered that the broad base of support they had enjoyed in western North Carolina was slowly diminishing.

This book explains why that change in attitude occurred. It probes the impact industrialization had on mountain society, examines how federal liquor taxation affected party politics in southern Appalachia, and describes the rise of the prohibition movement in western North Carolina during the nineteenth century. These phenomena, combined with mainstream media's negative portrayal of mountain society, helped spark a local movement against alcohol manufacturers. By the turn of the twentieth century, distillers had become a symbol of what was wrong with Appalachia, which provided local townspeople and "outsiders" with an excuse to "reform" rural western North Carolinians. More important, the antidistiller crusade helped remove the final barrier confronting temperance reformers in their quest for statewide prohibition: the belief that alcohol manufacturers had an inherent right to make a living.

Many friends and colleagues helped me write this book. Thanks must begin with the professors who guided me through graduate school. At the University of Georgia, I had the opportunity to study under the tutelage of John Inscoe. John is one of the best teachers and scholars I have ever known. He goes far beyond the call of duty to help his students succeed in academia and in life. Without his guidance, I would not be where I am today. I also want to express my gratitude to Peter Carmichael. Pete has always been there for me as both a mentor and a friend.

I first became interested in Appalachian history as a graduate student at Western Carolina University, where I worked with several talented historians. In particular, Richard Starnes helped me become a better scholar and person. I am indebted for the support I received from the faculty and my fellow graduate students at the University of Georgia. Steve Nash, Barton Myers, Judkin Browning, Robby Luckett, Frank Forts, Justin Nystrom, Bert Way, Ivy Holliman Way, and Paul Sutter, among many others, made my stay at Athens an enjoyable one.

Others have also helped out in a variety of ways. I am grateful to the *North Carolina Historical Review, Journal of Southern History,* and *Appalachian Journal.* Sections of the book draw on four articles that appeared in these journals and are used with the permission of their editors. I would like to thank John Bacon for giving me a place to stay while I conducted research at the University of North Carolina at Chapel Hill and Duke University. Throughout the years, Gordon McKinney, Durwood Dunn, and Dan Pierce have provided me with much-needed advice and encouragement. My editor Anne Dean Watkins offered timely enthusiasm to push me along. I would also like to thank my colleagues at Appalachian State University for their support.

Above all, love and thanks to my family. Sunny Townes, in particular, has been there for me as both a friend and an editor. This book is for her.

Introduction

On May 26, 1908, North Carolina voters approved a referendum ban-
ning the sale and manufacture of alcohol within state lines. Temperance crusaders had longed for this day, one that many felt would never
come. Throughout the nineteenth century, their calls for statewide prohibition had fallen on deaf ears because most North Carolinians, like
other Americans, believed that alcohol played an important role in
their everyday lives. But temperance advocates proved to be a stubborn
bunch. Even though they initially experienced widespread opposition
to their cause, they continued to write editorials in newspapers, deliver
speeches at churches and on street corners, and petition legislators to
take immediate action, arguing that alcohol impeded the state's moral
and economic prosperity. The enactment of statewide prohibition
in 1908 was the fruit of their lengthy and laborious struggle against
intemperance, and it would, they believed, allow North Carolina to at
last achieve "peace, prosperity, and happiness."[1]

North Carolina was among the first southern states to take such a
drastic approach in the fight to fully eradicate the influence of alcohol
in their communities. In 1907, Georgia became the first to "go dry,"
followed by Alabama, Oklahoma, Mississippi, and North Carolina.
By 1915, four other southern states had embraced statewide prohibition. A revolution had taken place in Dixie. Southerners, who had
historically opposed legal suasion on the grounds that it was unconstitutional, now emerged as the country's leading proponents of alcohol
reform. These crusaders soon joined their northern and western brethren in the fight for national prohibition, a campaign that ended successfully in January 1919 with the passage of the Eighteenth Amendment.

Most scholarship has credited the national Anti-Saloon League
(ASL) for convincing Americans in the early twentieth century to accept
legal prohibition. Following the Civil War, the saloon emerged as the
most popular public space to drink alcohol, especially beer, which had
surpassed whiskey as the beverage of choice for urban citizens. By
1900, nearly 300,000 saloons, most of which were controlled by large
breweries and sometimes housed gambling and other illegal businesses,
operated in the United States, doubling the number of those in existence twenty years earlier. Alarmed, temperance advocates viewed the

popularity of saloons as direct evidence of the alcohol industry's growing and corrupting influence over the American populace. Founded in 1895, the ASL, a coalition of antialcohol groups across the country, capitalized on these fears by focusing on the saloon—rather than the drinker—when advocating for prohibitory legislation. The only way to root out intemperance, supporters of prohibition believed, was to eliminate the institutional structures that promoted it. Using this argument, the ASL spearheaded the campaign that ultimately led to the adoption of prohibition, first at the local, then the state, and finally the national level.[2]

While the ASL demonized saloons, other reformers focused their attention on alcohol distillers, a group that scholars have overlooked when chronicling the rise of prohibition sentiment at the turn of the twentieth century. The great majority of saloons were concentrated in the urban Midwest and Northeast. As such, reformers elsewhere were forced to find other targets. In the South, where whiskey remained the most popular alcoholic beverage, prohibitionists increasingly blamed distillers—both legal and illegal—for the liquor problem and launched a campaign against them. The ultimate triumph of this crusade was significant. By overcoming the widespread belief that alcohol manufacturers had an inherent right to make a living, reformers removed the final barrier preventing most southerners from embracing legal prohibition.

This book chronicles the origins and expansion of the antidistiller movement in one section of the South during the nineteenth century: western North Carolina.[3] Predominantly rural and mountainous, the region was home to thousands of small distillers whose supporters often rallied against prohibitionists. The story begins in the late eighteenth century, when most Carolina highlanders still regarded alcohol manufacturers as well-respected members of the community, and it ends in 1908, when an overwhelming majority of mountain men, blaming distillers for perpetuating intemperance, crime, and violence, voted to enact statewide prohibition. In between, it illustrates how reformers capitalized on and perpetuated existing stereotypes of Appalachia to garner support in their fight against King Alcohol and, more importantly, those who made it.

By focusing on the antialcohol crusade in western North Carolina, this book grapples with several critical questions about rural southern society and how it changed throughout the nineteenth century. Three issues are at stake. First, the nature of social conflict in Appalachia remains a matter of controversy. Some scholars have characterized it as an insider-outsider phenomenon that developed at the turn of the twentieth century. According to them, struggles for economic and cultural dominance pitted mountain residents against northern capitalists and missionaries.[4] Other scholars have argued that this "us and them" dichotomy overlooks internal class strife. They insist that local elites, wanting to create an economically progressive "New South," sought to exploit the region's working classes.[5]

This book reveals that the earliest conflict over alcohol in the region was indeed locally driven and predates the Civil War. Beginning in the 1830s, the antialcohol crusade was both a reflection and a function of a class-differentiated society. Viewing themselves as refined and cultivated, middle-class townspeople embraced temperance because they feared that alcohol stymied the region both economically and morally. Many mountain residents, especially those in more rural parts of western North Carolina, disagreed, arguing that drinking and distilling were their right. This conflict over alcohol reform ultimately heightened preexisting social tensions within the region and sparked a cultural divide between urban and rural highlanders that would widen following the Civil War.

The second issue deals with the origins and development of the "myth" of Appalachia. Perhaps no other region in the United States has been subject to as much misconception and stereotyping as has the mountain South.[6] For many Americans, southern Appalachia was—and still is—a land of backwardness, poverty, hopelessness, and violence. It is—to use the words of journalist Dan Rather—"a place that seems like something out of another country."[7] Appalachia often evokes images of drunken hillbillies, rednecks, feudists, and moonshiners. Its denizens are supposedly eccentric, illiterate, lazy, and hard-drinking. They are "a different breed of people."[8]

Over the past thirty years, scholars have demonstrated that such negative images of Appalachia and its residents were largely a post–Civil War construct, "invented" by late-nineteenth-century missionaries, journalists, and local color novelists from outside the region who "discovered" an isolated people still living like America's pioneer ancestors. The nation's rapid advancements in communication, industry, and transportation following the Civil War seemed to have bypassed the southern mountains, creating a citizenry that remained backward, ignorant, and uncivilized. It appeared that time had stood still in Appalachia.[9] Although there were bits of truth in these observations, they were often exaggerated to serve the "economic opportunism, political creativity, or passing fancy of urban elites."[10] The resulting myths provided outsiders with an excuse to intervene in the lives of mountain residents, whom they viewed as crude and unrefined, in order to modernize—and capitalize on—the region. It also fulfilled the need of middle-class Americans to project their own fears onto a people perceived as different. In short, Appalachia became the "other," a place that reminded Victorian Americans why they had embraced industrialization and "progress."

While deconstructing these stereotypes, historians have assumed that they originated from outside the mountain region. This should come as no surprise. Most studies of Appalachian industrialism have emphasized "its exterior origins and its imposition upon a population whose own actions had little effect in the creation of a new economy."[11] According to this narrative, mountain residents became the victims of outside forces beyond their control at the turn of the twentieth century. Northern capitalists, absentee owners, and land speculators monopolized power by manipulating local governments and overwhelming "regional cultures with the legacies of industrialization." Such an understanding renders mountain residents powerless to stop these unwanted changes, much less shape the discourse of Appalachia.[12]

Recently, several scholars have begun to challenge such assumptions. They have argued that mountain residents played an active role in the development of Appalachian stereotypes. In his study of upper east Tennessee between the late eighteenth and mid-nineteenth centuries, for instance, David C. Hsiung discovered that negative images about Appalachia and its people began in the region long before local color novelists arrived on the scene following the Civil War. According to Hsiung, as early as 1800, mountain town dwellers and nearby farmers, eager for economic development and wider connections to the outside world, began to emphasize differences between themselves and the more isolated (and poorer) country folk. Chastising their rural counterparts as backward and ignorant, these "outward-oriented" urban inhabitants forged the negative images about the region that local colorists and missionaries popularized at the turn of the twentieth century.[13]

In studying the crusade against alcohol and the men who distilled it, this book also reveals that the origins of many Appalachian stereotypes lay in the antebellum period. In their quest for national legitimacy, urban middle-class highlanders began to identify their neighbors in rural western North Carolina as a backward people who adhered to "traditional" drinking mores and failed to meet the standards of "mainstream" American society. Tourists and writers would later tap into these perceptions, laying the foundation for negative images that persist today. Local townspeople, having already embraced temperance, continued to reinforce and perpetuate this mythology. Echoing the views of local colorists and missionaries, they undertook the mission of reforming these "traditional" country folk.

The third issue is the expansion of prohibition's support base to rural communities in the South. Townspeople were the earliest advocates of alcohol reform during the antebellum period. Embracing the middle-class virtues of self-control, frugality, and sobriety, they argued that temperance would make society more productive. These reformers were often labeled as radicals by their rural neighbors, who viewed alcohol as an integral part of their economy and culture and resented the attempts to limit their freedom. Following the Civil War, however, rural southerners increasingly championed temperance and joined forces with their urban counterparts. This alliance ultimately paved the way for the enactment of statewide prohibition in North Carolina and other southern states at the turn of the twentieth century.

Many scholars have credited the rise of the evangelical movement for sparking this change of opinion in the countryside. Wanting to shield their communities from the "sins" and "impurities" of an urbanizing New South, they argue, evangelicals embraced prohibition to stamp out important elements of "male" culture, such as drinking, that corrupted the morals of society at large.[14] Other historians have posited that middle-class townspeople, led by northern missionaries, stimulated rural support for prohibition by broadening their critique of alcohol during the 1880s. Unlike their antebellum counterparts, who emphasized liquor's negative impact on an individual's character, these reformers accentuated the danger alcohol posed to society as a whole. By stressing the systemic consequences of alcohol culture, they convinced rural southerners to embrace legal prohibition.[15]

This book focuses on the role that industrialization—rather than religious groups—played in galvanizing rural support for local and statewide prohibition. Beginning in the 1880s, a growing number of "traditional" communities in western North Carolina became more connected to the national economy, largely due to the rise of capitalism and urbanization that followed the extension of the Western North Carolina Railroad. Mountain evangelicals, unable to protect the home and church from the male culture in town centers, responded by embracing antialcohol reform. But their appeal for prohibition would not have gained widespread support without the emergence of new economic forces. The same was true of movements led by northern missionaries and local reformers. Their critique of alcohol culture and distilling was finally accepted because it made practical sense to many rural denizens who, adapting to a changing economic environment, discovered that preindustrial drinking mores fit poorly with the demands of life and labor in the New South. Unfortunately for alcohol distillers and their clientele, once these Tar Heel highlanders embraced temperance, the movement was strong enough to achieve statewide prohibition in 1908.

Taken as a whole, this book chronicles the social tensions that accompanied the beginnings of western North Carolina's transition from a rural to an urban-industrial economy during the nineteenth century. As such, it is part of a larger story about the origins and development of conflict within not only Appalachia but also rural America in general. Largely a product of industrialization and urbanization, the antialcohol crusade played an important role in this drama, one that often pitted town "progressives" against rural "traditionalists." In the middle of this battle for social control and cultural hegemony stood the alcohol distiller, whose decline in reputation ultimately reflected rural America's integration into "mainstream" society and helped paved the way for prohibition's triumph during the early twentieth century.

Part I

The Beginnings
of Antialcohol Reform,
1790–1860

1

"This Country Improves in Cultivation, Wickedness, Mills, and Still"

Distilling and Drinking during the Antebellum Period

Here's to Old Corn Likker,
Whitens the teeth,
Perfumes the breath,
And makes childbirth a pleasure.

Bluford McGee was born in 1832 and raised on the bank of Beaver Creek in Wilkes County, located on the eastern slopes of North Carolina's Blue Ridge Mountains. In 1850, McGee and several neighbors left the county for the California goldfields. There, he found nothing but hardship. He discovered little gold and developed severe rheumatism, which left him unable to walk. McGee spent the next twelve years at a San Francisco hospital, where he wrote an autobiography of his early life in Wilkes County.[1]

McGee's father, also named Bluford, was a central figure in his autobiography. The elder McGee farmed and made extra money by distilling his surplus apples into brandy and selling it to his neighbors. McGee wrote that his father made the best apple brandy in Wilkes County. His customers eagerly awaited the first taste of McGee brandy each season. To signal that a run, or batch, of brandy was complete, McGee's father would "go out in front of the still house and blow" on the still cap "as loud as he could." People from miles around would hear this noise and, knowing what it meant, head off to the still to enjoy the first run of the season. McGee remembered that his teacher, a brandy connoisseur, would even cancel class upon hearing the high-pitched sound. "The school house was as quiet as a tomb," McGee recalled, "when all of a sudden a deafening blast from my father's still cap came crashing in at the door." McGee saw the corners of his teacher's mouth begin "to twitch and glow with radiance, till they spread from ear to ear in a broad smile." The teacher dismissed class, put on his hat, and walked out, "leaving a clear streak of sunshine behind him that made the heart feel glad."[2]

Like those in Wilkes County, most antebellum Americans enjoyed drinking alcohol. For them, whiskey, brandy, cider, and other intoxicants were staples of their daily diets. They consumed these beverages as medicine, imbibed them in large amounts during social gatherings, and often used them as a substitute for water, which many considered too "low class" to serve to guests. By 1830, the average American drank nearly five gallons of liquor per year.[3] Most of the domestic spirits that these denizens consumed were manufactured in the backcountry, where farmers found it easier and often more profitable to distill some of their crops into alcohol. Between 1792 and 1810, as frontiersmen and other entrepreneurs capitalized on their fellow citizens' thirst for intoxicants, liquor production tripled in the United States, while the number of distilleries increased sixfold.[4]

One of Appalachian North Carolina's first industries, alcohol manufacturing enabled market-oriented farmers like McGee's father to obtain cash, a scarce commodity in the southern backcountry. Most highlanders accepted liquor distillers as respected members of the community. As elsewhere in the antebellum United States, whiskey flowed at dances, barn raisings, and militia musters in the region. Alcohol producers supplied their communities with a product that promoted social cohesion. Wilkes County residents, for instance, embraced the elder McGee's brandy enterprise as a legitimate business. His first run of the season gave citizens an opportunity to escape their normal routines and strengthen community bonds. Farmers and schoolteachers alike congregated near McGee's still to drink, gossip, and debate politics. For most antebellum mountain residents, McGee and other distillers were not marginalized criminals but entrepreneurs providing a service and meeting the demands of their clientele.[5]

America's First Frontier: A Cultural Synthesis

Western North Carolina is a land of mountains, valleys, and plateaus. Extending from Surry County in the north to Cleveland County in the south are the North Carolina foothills that make up the eastern slopes of the Blue Ridge range. The Blue Ridge mountains, part of the Appalachian chain stretching from eastern Canada to northern Georgia, divide the rest of western North Carolina from the foothills and piedmont to the east. Beyond these mountains in North Carolina lies a high plateau, traversed by several short, high ranges. Rivers flow between these ranges, creating fertile valleys across the plateau. Higher in the northwestern part of the state, and gradually lowering as it runs southward into Georgia, the plateau is bordered on the west by the Great Smoky Mountains. This range divides North Carolina from Tennessee and touts some of the highest mountains east of the Mississippi River.[6]

A diverse group of immigrants trickled into the region during the mid-eighteenth century. English, German, African, and Scots-Irish migrants, among others, traveled down the Great Wagon Road, a transportation artery linking western Pennsylvania to the southern colonies, and settled in the piedmont of North Carolina. They believed that the backcountry offered them limitless opportunity. Land was cheaper and more abundant there than in Pennsylvania or western Virginia. Some stopped in the foothill region, where they settled along the rich bottomlands of the Catawba and Yadkin rivers. Later, many of them, along with their slaves, pushed westward, ignoring the British government's Proclamation of 1763, which prohibited white migration west of the southern Appalachian divide.[7] Ascending the lofty ridges of the Blue Ridge mountains, they began to encroach on the hunting grounds of the Cherokees. "The number of families that have come from North Carolina and Virginia," one Cherokee Native American complained in 1766, "are circumstances very alarming to us . . . we were promised quiet possession of our lands and redress for our grievances."[8] This initial influx of Europeans to the region was only a sign of things to come.

At the close of the American Revolution in 1783, the North Carolina General Assembly allowed whites to legally settle in the territory west of the Blue Ridge. There, fertile valleys offered strong inducements to those seeking productive land. In 1802, French botanist Francois Michaux commented on the region: "These mountains begin to be populated rapidly. The salubrity of the air, the excellence of the water, and more especially the pasturage of these wild peas for the cattle, are so many causes that induce new inhabitants to settle there."[9] By foot, in wagons, and on horseback, thousands of whites from the piedmont and foothills ventured onto the high plateau lying between the Blue Ridge and Great Smoky mountains. The earliest settlers acquired land on the rich bottomlands of the New, Toe, French Broad, Catawba, and Swannanoa rivers. Many of them, possessing the most fertile and accessible lands, emerged as the region's economic, social, and political leaders. Latecomers occupied less desirable lands along smaller rivers and creek beds. It was not until the early nineteenth century that settlers moved farther up the hillsides into hollows and coves, remote areas that isolated residents from the outside world.[10]

During the eighteenth and early nineteenth centuries, western North Carolina was part of the American frontier. It was a land of migrants, some of whom used the region as a temporary home before moving to Tennessee, Kentucky, Alabama, or Georgia. Others stayed. These settlers transported some of their native culture with them to the mountains. They survived by borrowing traditions from one another and the Native Americans they encountered, creating a hybrid frontier culture.[11] Adapting to the new environment, settlers shifted from oats, barley, and sheep to an economy that relied on corn, rye, and pigs.[12] They constructed log cabins and barns based on German and Swiss carpentry designs and methods. The English, one of the largest ethnic groups to settle in the mountains, heavily influenced political organization, "as the system of English law was transplanted, basically intact, to the region."[13]

The Roots of Alcohol Distilling

The Scots-Irish added the tradition of making alcohol to this new mountain culture. Most of these immigrants were originally from the northern Irish province of Ulster. They had arrived in Pennsylvania during the early eighteenth century, and pressures from population growth soon pushed them to the backcountry.[14] Beginning in the 1740s, soil exhaustion and the quest for cheaper land encouraged a significant number of Ulstermen (as they preferred to be called) to migrate southward via the Great Wagon Road. Some settled in the piedmont of North Carolina, where they lived on the river bottoms and creeks west of the Yadkin River. From there, Ulstermen moved deeper into the foothills and, after the American Revolution, crossed the Blue Ridge mountains. By 1800, families of Ulster origin accounted for 43 percent of the population in southwestern North Carolina.[15] Along with cattle herding and Presbyterian churches, Ulstermen introduced the art of whiskey distilling to southern Appalachia.[16]

As early as the eleventh century, the Gaels of old Ireland had developed a method to manufacture whiskey from barley.[17] The Scots soon adopted Irish distilling methods. By the seventeenth century, the Irish and Scots began to combine their knowledge of the distilling process. In 1610, England's King James I, hoping to consolidate his control over the ten counties of Catholic Northern Ireland (Ulster), enticed Protestants from Scotland to settle there. These so-called Scots-Irish, or Ulster Scots, exchanged their skills with the older Irish inhabitants, thereby perfecting the process of whiskey distilling.[18]

The Scots-Irish continued to manufacture alcohol after migrating to Pennsylvania during the eighteenth century, although instead of barley they used the readily available corn and rye in their stills. The ingredients may have changed, but the finished product remained in high demand. Philadelphian Benjamin Rush complained about Scots-Irish distillers on the Pennsylvania frontier in the 1780s, stating, "The quantity of rye destroyed and of whiskey drunk in these places is immense, and its effects upon their industry, health and morals are terrible." This love of making whiskey did not dissipate when the Ulster Scots journeyed to western North Carolina and other southern backcountry regions. By the late eighteenth century, "columns of steel blue smoke poured from hundreds of stills over the six-hundred-mile backcountry along the Appalachian mountain chain."[19]

The Manufacture of Corn Whiskey

The antebellum whiskey-making process varied among distillers, depending on the quantity of spirits desired, the ingredients used, and the speed of manufacturing needed. Through trial and error, distillers created their own recipes and passed them on to their children or neighbors. A recipe book that William Lenoir of Caldwell County wrote during the 1790s reveals some of the debates surrounding the best way to manufacture alcohol. For example, Lenoir discovered that whereas some mountain distillers preferred to use rye malt to speed up the fermenting process, others cautioned against it.[20]

Although the recipes may have differed, the actual techniques utilized to distill alcohol in the American backcountry remained similar to those in Ulster. Antebellum distillers used the common pot still, a cop-

Early-twentieth-century distillers in the process of making whiskey. From John C. Campbell, *The Southern Highlander and His Homeland* (New York: Russell Sage Foundation, 1921), facing 110.

per container shaped liked a "large teakettle with a round lid and an extra-long spout." These stills proved extremely practical because they were light and easy to transport over rugged terrain.[21] By the 1790s, the demand was so high that merchants traveling the countryside added pot stills to their inventory. In 1794, for instance, Buncombe County merchant Zebulon Baird executed a bill of sale to William Lenoir "in consideration of one hundred and thirty pounds, for a still and other items of personal property."[22] The less affluent often built their own stills, a skill they learned from the Scots-Irish. Distillers made this primitive variation of the pot still by sawing a hollow log in two and running a copper pipe from one end to the other. With the halves reconnected, "beer [was] poured in at the top, steam [was] sent through the pipe, and alcohol was taken off through another pipe."[23] The finished product: corn whiskey.

Once in possession of a still, the pioneer distiller had to find a proper site to operate it. Since alcohol manufacturing required water, Ulstermen and other antebellum distillers preferred to set up their stills near streams—not a difficult task in western North Carolina.[24] But before selecting a stream, distillers had to make sure it was a "soft" water source, which they believed produced the best whiskey. Some examined the flora that surrounded the branch. Yellow root or red horsemint indicated that the water was soft. Others collected stream water in a jar, shook the jar, and tilted it on its side. If bubbles appeared in the water, it was soft, and the stream was suitable for operating a still.[25] Distillers' preference for soft water would later backfire. When the federal government attempted to enforce liquor taxation following the Civil War, Bureau of Internal Revenue agents often searched for illegal stills by studying the plants surrounding creeks and streams. If touch-me-nots grew along the banks, revenuers bypassed it, knowing "that moonshin[ers] wouldn't think of putting their still on a branch with touch-me-nots. For touch-me-nots along a branch means hard water and hard water won't make corn whiskey. It takes soft water."[26]

After finding a proper site, the pioneer distiller selected corn to make the whiskey (to make brandy, the distiller used peaches or apples).[27] The distiller would examine each kernel of corn by hand and discard any discolored or rotten ones. In order to change the corn's starch into sugar through fermentation, the distiller first made corn malt. The process involved placing unground kernels in a container with several holes in the bottom and pouring warm water into the container. If all went well, the corn would sprout in three or four days.[28] The distiller sometimes accelerated the sprouting process by burying the corn in manure.[29] The sprouts were then dried in the sun or before a fire.

Once the grains were dry, the distiller ground them into a coarse meal known as corn grits using a tubmill, which he could borrow from a neighbor or a miller if necessary.[30] When placed in an oak barrel and mixed with hot water, the meal became a mush called sweet mash. One bushel of mash stirred into thirty gallons of water produced one to one and a half gallons of whiskey.[31] The distiller then covered the barrel to keep its contents clean and placed it in the sun to dry. After four or five days, he uncovered the barrel and thinned out the sweet mash with warm water. Before re-covering the barrel, the whiskey maker sometimes added rye malt, made like corn malt, to speed up the fermenting process. The malt rose to "the top in a layer from one to two inches thick, sealed off the air, and sealed in the flavor."[32] During this time, the sugar in the sweet mash changed to carbonic acid and alcohol—a soupy yellow mixture known as sour mash.[33]

A moonshine still. From Margaret W. Morley, *The Carolina Mountains* (Boston: Houghton Mifflin, 1913), facing 206.

When fermentation was completed five to ten days later, the whiskey maker separated the mash from the water through the distillation process.[34] To ensure that the mash did not lose its 10 percent alcohol content at this stage, the alcohol manufacturer had to distill it promptly.[35] He first dipped the mash into buckets and strained it into the still through a piece of cloth. He then heated the pot still over a wood fire and cooked the mash at 176 degrees Fahrenheit, the temperature at which alcohol becomes vapor. The resulting vapor traveled up the neck of the still and into the worm, a copper coil connected to the pot still. The distiller then set the worm in a cooler barrel under a waterfall. The cold coil turned the alcohol vapor back into alcohol, which traveled out through a pipe directly into a pail, keg, or jug.[36]

This first batch, or run, of whiskey was not the finished product. Singlings, as the initial run was called, still contained excess water and, among other poisonous substances, fusel oil. To purify this murky liquid, the distiller made a second run—doublings—at a lower temperature. Some used the same still to make doublings, while others used two stills to speed up the process. If he was using one still, the distiller had to remove the spent mash and "wash it out with some unstrained 'beer' left in the mash barrel, a technique said to make the whiskey extra smooth and mellow." He then cleaned the pot with a rag and began to make doublings.[37]

Instruments that measured the strength, or proof, of alcohol were not available until the 1820s. Therefore, to estimate the proof of their whiskey, skilled pioneer distillers studied the "bead" that formed at the top of clear bottles filled with alcohol. If the bead was full of big, loose, collapsing bubbles ("rabbit eyes" or "frog eyes") after shaking the bottle, the whiskey was not the sought-after 100 proof (50 percent alcohol). However, if "the foam rose and remained in bubbles about the size of a No. 5 shot, the proof was right."[38] Other distillers used oil or lye to test whiskey's proof. An early-twentieth-century Georgia moonshiner described how pioneers used this method: "You put the oil in when the likker first comes out of the still. The way you tell . . . when the bead hops all the way out and sits on top of the surface, it's false. A true bead will stop half in the likker and half out on top."[39]

The Market Value of Distilled Spirits

As in other parts of the American backcountry, diversity was the key to mountain agriculture during the late eighteenth and early nineteenth centuries. Farmers cultivated fruits, vegetables, and other crops to feed their families and sometimes to satisfy market demands. All farmers grew corn, which usually made up at least half of their total output.[40] This grain thrived in western North Carolina's cool climate and fed its residents and their livestock. Mountain women and men served it three times a day as corn mush or Indian pudding. The most popular food item was cornbread, a dish that highlanders cooked over an open hearth and served with pork, vegetables, and wild berries.[41] Pioneers discarded little. They often made mattresses from leftover cornhusks; used corncobs as fuel, fertilizer, and stoppers in jugs; and created corn-cob and cornhusk dolls for their children.[42]

Beyond its many household uses, corn provided Carolina highlanders with a viable product that connected them to the national economy. Most Appalachian farming households were neither completely self-sufficient nor isolated from the outside world.[43] Pioneer and antebellum farmers produced at least a small surplus of livestock or grain, which

A view of the French Broad River above Asheville, n.d. Courtesy of the North Carolina State Archives.

they bartered to their neighbors or sold to storekeepers, itinerant merchants, and drovers. Merchants like James Patton, an Ulster Scot who migrated to western North Carolina in the 1790s, traveled throughout the mountain countryside, buying corn and other local commodities and selling manufactured goods from the North.[44] A vast network of trails in western Carolina gave the earliest migrants access to the larger market economy. During the 1790s, settlers began to build roads along the region's largest and most important river, the French Broad, which "flows northwestward from near the South Carolina border, through Asheville, into northeast Tennessee." These trails and roads allowed farmers to transport their crops to market or join their livestock with those being driven from Tennessee and Kentucky through the North Carolina mountains.[45]

The 1828 creation of the Buncombe Turnpike, running from Tennessee through Madison, Buncombe, and Henderson counties into South Carolina, increased Appalachian North Carolina's already thriving livestock trade. Each October, farmers and merchants from Kentucky, Tennessee, and North Carolina gathered up hogs and other livestock to sell to drovers, who then transported these animals to South Carolina and Georgia. Farmers who owned land near the Buncombe Turnpike, through which an estimated 150,000 to 175,000 hogs passed each year between 1828 and the Civil War, benefited from this trade. The enormous amounts of grain needed to feed these animals encouraged farmers to raise corn as a cash crop. In Madison, Buncombe, and Henderson counties, farmers grew one and a half times more corn than was grown by those in other mountain communities. Most sold or bartered their crop to merchants who established inns or stands along the turnpike.[46]

Not all farmers had such an accessible outlet for their crops. In remote counties, mountain residents found it more difficult to transport their corn crop to market. Transportation and trade routes could not accommodate the demands of these market-oriented farmers. In 1770, mapmaker John Collet described the roads of western North Carolina as "widened bridle-paths."[47] Nineteenth-century historian Eli W. Caruthers reported that during the 1790s, mountain roads were "almost impassable half of the year."[48] Methodist Bishop Francis Asbury, who included western North Carolina in his annual tours of the Southeast during the late eighteenth and early nineteenth centuries, would have agreed. After leaving Asheville in 1800, he gave up a carriage for his more reliable horse. "This mode of conveyance by no means suits the roads of this wilderness," Asbury wrote in his journal.[49] Many farmers discovered that it was impossible to transport bulk grain over such poor arteries. Trips to the market took so long that the crops often spoiled en route. "Under such disadvantages," Caruthers explained, "a load of grain of whatever kind w[oul]d be eat up before they c[oul]d get it to market."[50] Despite new roads like the Buncombe Turnpike, this problem continued to plague the region well into the nineteenth century. As late as 1849, traveler Charles Lanman lamented that "the roads have consumed all the corn that can be transported."[51] Mountain farmers needed cash to pay debts or to buy goods they could not produce at home. The economic independence that many of them sought remained elusive.[52]

Given the difficulties of travel, farmers in western North Carolina found a more efficient way to market their corn and fruit. A mule could carry about four bushels of corn on the long journey to market during

A farm on the French Broad River, ca. 1860. Courtesy of the North Carolina State Archives.

the antebellum period. After it was distilled into whiskey, however, a mule could haul the equivalent of twenty-four bushels of corn.[53] Distilling liquor was also a way to profit from excess yields of their crops. By turning their leftover corn, apples, and peaches into whiskey and brandy, they could sell or barter it to neighbors or merchants, supplementing other sources of income. During the 1790s, these Carolina highlanders likely produced as much alcohol as did residents in nearby Blount County, Tennessee, where the average farmer-distiller produced fifty gallons a year, or "one fourth to one half of the total corn harvest."[54]

Farmers often found that distilling was not only a more productive use of their crops but also more profitable. Account books from various stores in western North Carolina and neighboring states show that a bushel of corn and a gallon of whiskey sold for approximately the same amount—between 40¢ and 50¢—throughout the late eighteenth and early nineteenth centuries.[55] When the price of both commodities was comparable, farmers could make more money by distilling corn into alcohol.[56] In 1850, for instance, an Alexander County farmer could sell twenty bushels of corn for $10. Converted into whiskey, those twenty bushels sold for $25.[57]

Many western North Carolinians testified to the financial advantages offered by whiskey and brandy distillation. In 1810, William B. Lenoir wrote to his father, Gen. William Lenoir, who operated a still on his plantation in Caldwell County, that his "money will soon be gone, and I must move my saw mill, buy a saw, buy stills & set up a distillery, before I can make any money."[58] Life on the frontier was hard, and one of the quickest ways to earn money was to invest in a still. Lenoir's brother-in-law, Isaac T. Avery of Burke County, agreed that corn was most lucrative in liquid form. In 1824, Avery wrote that he had "made enough corn to do me, perhaps can make whisky enough to pay for my salt, sugar and coffee and perhaps pay my taxes, but money is as scarce as ever."[59] Avery demanded cash for his product, but other farmers used their homemade alcohol to barter. Caldwell County residents often exchanged whiskey and brandy for items such as shoes and horse collars in a local store.[60]

Census enumerators recorded only stills with capacities large enough to be classified as manufacturing plants, so the data are incomplete. However, the available data suggest that whiskey production increased in Appalachian North Carolina during the early nineteenth

Table 1.1. Comparison of Population and Gallons of Whiskey Produced in Western North Carolina and in North Carolina as a Whole, 1810 and 1840

	1810			1840		
	NC Total	Western NC Total	Western NC %	NC Total	Western NC Total	Western NC %
Population	555,500	59,380	11	753,419	104,570	14
Gallons	1,386,691	238,400	17	1,051,979	328,389	31

Sources: U.S. Census Office, *Aggregate Amount of Each Description of Persons within the United States of America and the Territories thereof . . . 1810* (Washington, DC, 1811), 75–76; U.S. Census Office, *A Statement of the Arts and Manufacturers of the United States . . . 1810 . . .* (Philadelphia, 1814), 133–34; U.S. Census Office, *Compendium of the Enumeration of the Inhabitants and Statistics of the United States . . . Sixth Census . . .* (Washington, DC, 1841), 43, 186.

century, as it did elsewhere in the southern backcountry. For instance, the per capita percentage of alcohol manufactured between 1810 and 1840 increased at a faster rate in the mountain region than in the rest of the state (see table 1.1). In 1810, western North Carolina accounted for 11 percent of the state's population and manufactured 17 percent of the state's whiskey. Thirty years later, the mountain region produced 31 percent of the state's whiskey and was home to 14 percent of the state's population.

In western North Carolina, some counties produced more whiskey than others (see table 1.2). The top four whiskey-manufacturing counties in 1840 (Surry, Burke, Wilkes, and Ashe) together accounted for 48 percent of the mountain population and 89 percent of the alcohol distilled in the region. All are located in the northeastern portion of western North Carolina. Several counties with a lower percentage of whiskey production (Buncombe, Henderson, and Haywood) were situated closer to the Buncombe Turnpike and other trade routes connecting the mountain region to livestock markets in Georgia and South Carolina. Farmers near these roads sold their corn to drovers, stand owners, or itinerant merchants instead of distilling it into alcohol. Together, Buncombe and Rutherford counties manufactured 7 percent of the region's alcohol and accounted for 28 percent of western North Carolina's population. Since census enumerators recorded only whiskey production, it is impossible to gauge the amount of brandy manufactured in the region during the antebellum period. Farmers who grew an abundance of peaches and apples in Henderson, Haywood, and other counties near the Buncombe Turnpike may well have distilled brandy more often than whiskey.[61]

Table 1.2. Percentage of Population and Per Capita Gallons of Whiskey Produced in Western North Carolina, 1840

County	Percentage of Population*/Rank	Gallons Produced/Rank
Rutherford	18/1	4/5
Burke	15/2	25/2
Surry	14/3	39/1
Wilkes	12/4	18/3
Buncombe	10/5	3/6
Ashe	7/6	7/4
Yancey	6/7	2/7
Haywood	5/8	1/8
Henderson	5/8	0.4/10
Macon	5/8	0.3/11
Cherokee	3/11	1/8

* Percentages were rounded off.
Source: U.S. Census Office, Compendium of the Enumeration of the Inhabitants and Statistics of the United States . . . Sixth Census . . . (Washington, DC, 1841), 43, 186.

Despite the existence of large distilleries, alcohol manufacturing remained an important cottage industry in western North Carolina and other parts of the American backcountry before the Civil War. Wills and inventories disclose that small farmers often left their families stills when they died, knowing that this would allow them to earn money.[62] Several of the region's elite operated stills, suggesting that the profession was not limited to the lower class and that the community deemed it a legitimate business. Caldwell County's foremost citizen, Gen. William Lenoir, operated a still on his large plantation at the turn of the nineteenth century. Lenoir, along with his overseer George Taylor, distilled excess yields of "fruit trees" into brandy and sold it to neighbors and travelers. This still must have been profitable because Taylor demanded that he receive "a twelfth part of the brandy" that he and Lenoir manufactured.[63]

Pioneer and antebellum distillers found various ways to market their product. Like Bluford McGee from Wilkes County, they often sold homemade alcohol to their neighbors.[64] Tenant farmers sometimes used their distilled spirits to pay the rent.[65] Young men, especially those without the means to own land or a still, were able to capitalize on their knowledge of the alcohol manufacturing process, a specialized skill they most likely learned in childhood from relatives or neighbors. Some of them may well have responded to this newspaper ad from nearby eastern Tennessee in 1825: "Wanted immediately, a first rate distiller. A young man without family, who understands the art of distilling corn and rye mixed, and all rye. He must be a man of sober habits. To such a one constant employment and good wages will be given."[66] Ambitious distillers could earn a substantial income. Entrepreneur Henry Reid made a small fortune operating a distillery in Burke County during the 1790s. Not satisfied, Reid expanded his liquor enterprise by purchasing a store, where he sold whiskey to neighbors and travelers and bought corn from nearby farmers to supply his distillery.[67]

Although most distilled spirits were consumed locally, some mountain residents tapped into more distant markets. In 1813, distiller John Welch, along with other Haywood County farmers, sold more than 4,000 gallons of barreled whiskey to Philip Hoodenpile, who had left the mountains to operate a tavern on the Mississippi frontier.[68] Yearly during the 1830s, Buncombe County farmer and distiller Else Burnett collected goods, including homemade alcohol, and traveled by wagon to Augusta, Georgia, where he traded the liquor to merchants in exchange for cash, gunpowder, calico, sewing thread, or other manufactured goods.[69] Whether using their homemade brew as a barter item or to make extra money, mountain farmers distilled alcohol because they knew that a market existed for it.

The Social Value of Distilled Spirits

Between 1790 and 1840, alcohol consumption in the United States increased dramatically. During those years, the average American imbibed more distilled spirits than at any other time in the country's history.[70] Americans were enjoying a "spectacular binge," and many Carolina highlanders joined in. Travelers remarked on the drinking habits of mountain residents and wondered why so many of them drank alcohol. Bishop Asbury often complained that the mountain residents he visited had a fondness for alcohol and observed that frontier life made them more prone to drinking and distilling. "This country improves in cultivation, wickedness, mills, and still; a prophet of strong drink would be acceptable to many of these people," Asbury wrote from Wilkes County in 1795. Five years later, he traveled to Warm Springs in Madison County, where drinking was just as prevalent. "My company," Asbury stated, "was not agreeable here—there were too many

The Rev. Francis Asbury, 1814. Courtesy of the Prints and Photographs Division, Library of Congress, Washington, D.C.

subjects of the two great potentates of this western world, whisky—brandy."[71] Other visitors commented on the availability and high consumption rate of liquor in the mountains, noting that most Carolina highlanders preferred whiskey to wine, rum, and brandy during the antebellum period.[72]

As elsewhere in the antebellum United States, homemade whiskey became popular in western North Carolina because it was readily available and cheap. Some mountain residents, especially those living in or near commercial centers, had access to beverages such as wine and rum. Yet because they were imported from Europe and the West Indies, these drinks were more expensive than whiskey. In the 1790s, wine and rum cost six pounds per gallon at William Tucker's tavern in Caldwell County, compared with three pounds per gallon for whiskey.[73] Mountain elites often bought imported spirits in bulk from local merchants or retailers in Charleston, South Carolina, to consume at dinner parties and ballroom dances.[74] But since its price seldom rose above 50¢ a gallon, corn whiskey proved the cheapest and most popular alcoholic drink in Appalachian North Carolina.[75] It remained affordable for two reasons. First, because merchants and tavern owners could always buy directly from nearby distillers, the demand for whiskey seldom eclipsed its supply. Second, improvements in the distilling process during the early nineteenth century kept the price of whiskey low. James C. Crow, a Scots-Irish chemist and distiller who moved to the southern back-country in 1825, was the first person to manufacture alcohol using scientific methods. Crow was known for "stressing almost clinical cleanliness and introducing the use of hydrometer, saccharometer, and thermometer for water, sugar, and temperature control." Antebellum distillers who could afford these instruments and understand how to use them "could . . . distill 3½ gallons of whiskey from a single bushel of corn, whereas their fathers had obtained only 2 gallons."[76]

Mountain residents did not have to travel far to buy spirituous liquors. Communities often had a still house where inhabitants and travelers could buy or barter alcohol.[77] Those who did not live near a distiller could purchase alcohol from retail establishments. By the 1790s, taverns dotted the mountain countryside and kept alcohol in stock throughout the year. Tax lists reveal that at least one legal tavern operated in every mountain county by 1815.[78] The earliest taverns, according the historian Guion Johnson, were probably crude weather-boarded buildings or log huts at best. "The more prosperous ones," Johnson explained, "consisted of several rooms, but most of them had only one large room with no interior division."[79] After 1800, entre-preneurs accommodated drovers and tourists by establishing stands and taverns at close intervals along the Buncombe Turnpike and other transportation routes. Hotels in resort communities such as Warm Springs in Madison County and Flat Rock in Henderson County sold an assortment of fine wines as well as domestic whiskey and brandy. These establishments were far superior to earlier ones, and they often catered to the rich. Small farmers did not drink at these establishments, but hotel owners were more than willing to purchase alcohol from them.[80]

The drinking habits and mores of mountain society resembled those of other rural communities in the United States before the Civil War. Not needing the discipline demanded by factory work, farmers often made little distinction between work and leisure. They freely mixed the two, turning some elements of their work lives into social events.[81] The

Logrolling. From John C. Campbell, *The Southern Highlander and His Homeland* (New York: Russell Sage Foundation, 1921), facing 90.

barn raising, a rural folkway practiced in many parts of the South, was one way Carolina highlanders combined work and leisure. Like logrolling and corn shucking, barn raising helped mountain residents maintain communal ties while providing farmers with much-appreciated labor. Easy access to whiskey enlivened these events.[82] In 1848, Charles Lanman witnessed a barn raising at a Buncombe County farm. Lanman's host "and some twenty . . . neighbors were assembled for the purpose of raising the framework of its [the barn's] position." Due to the men's jovial dispositions, Lanman figured that "an abundance of whiskey had already been imbibed" by most of them.[83] Occasionally, these cooperative undertakings did more harm than good. When neighbors helped Wilkes County resident Benjamin Cleveland harvest his crop in the 1790s, they became so intoxicated that they never completed the work.[84]

The demand for alcohol increased as communal binge drinking grew more prevalent during the early nineteenth century. This public drinking to the point of intoxication, common throughout antebellum America, prevailed when western Carolinians met at social events. In 1815, for instance, Bishop Asbury journeyed to Barnard's Station in Madison County, where residents celebrated his arrival with a nighttime dance. Far from being impressed, Asbury saw the dance as simply an opportunity to drink alcohol and play the fiddle, an instrument associated with the devil. Asbury quickly delivered a sermon to the drunken crowd against "such fiddling and drinking."[85]

Militia musters were another opportunity for mountain men to meet and drink together. Musters involved military drills, athletic contests, fighting, and often drinking, giving local distillers a chance to make extra money. Surry County distiller Hamp Hudson tried to sell his whiskey on militia day in 1829. But to his dismay, militia members hesitated to buy his product because of rumors that Hamp had distilled the liquor "from a mash-tub in which [his dog] Famus [had been] drowned." No one wanted to "drink one drap uv Hamp's nasty old Famus licker." Nonetheless, as the men stood in formation under the hot sun, their lips and tongues became parched, and Hamp's whiskey grew increasingly tempting. "Famus or no Famus," one of them finally declared, "I must take a little." The barrel of whiskey was soon dry. Thirty years later, Surry County resident H. E. Taliaferro showed how whiskey could be a distraction at militia gatherings. "'Cap'en,' 'leftenant,' and 'sargint' forgot their hard day's work," he remembered. "The 'litia and others fell to discussing questions of great moment; but the whole affair ended in skinned noses, gouged eyes, and bruised heads."[86]

As it did elsewhere in the United States, binge drinking in western North Carolina occurred most often during election and court days. In 1848, traveler Kemp Plummer Battle witnessed a politician in Yancey County furnishing alcohol to men, hoping to persuade them to vote correctly. He described the following situation: "I saw at Burnsville a specimen of mountain canvassing for the General Assembly. The candidate, a man named Flemming, spoke from a goods-box in front of a grog-shop most animatedly and effectively for about an hour with a tin quart-pot in his right hand. Then he went into the shop inviting the crowd to follow him to partake of whiskey. He was elected."[87]

During court week, mountain denizens assembled in their county seats, where they bought and sold goods, met friends, and drank liquor. In 1854, Asheville lawyer Augustus Merrimon complained about citizens' heavy drinking during court week in the Yancey County town of Burnsville: "There has been quite a crowd in attendance today and they have tried to see how badly they could behave themselves. . . . At different times I noticed groups about over the Court Yard and in the center stood a large gawky looking fellow with a fiddle and he would saw off some silly ditty[.] [T]wo or three drunken fools would dance

to the same."[88] Although it was a common outcome, communal drinking was not solely about getting inebriated. The custom had ideological
overtones. Regardless of their economic standing, men demonstrated
their worth and loyalty to the community by consuming large amounts
of alcohol together. Politicians also had to participate in this ritual.
Drinking with the people of their community was a display of egalitari-
anism and a necessity for election.[89]

Drinking served a more practical purpose as well. Like other antebellum Americans, western North Carolinians argued that spirituous liquors were healthful and nutritious. The belief that alcohol was
"good for what ails you" alarmed some mountain practitioners who
had trained in medical schools and rejected folk medicine. "Instead
of being lectured with regard to improper diet," an Asheville physician complained in 1852, "the patient is rejoiced to hear that brandy
is an antidote for all his ills, and that by the daily use of this beverage
he can still indulge in his favorite viands."[90] Mountain residents considered whiskey essential for protection against the exposure of out-
door work. In 1853, Merrimon wrote that rural farmers thought "that
to drink [whiskey] in damp and cold weather will warm them and
to drink in hot weather it will cool them."[91] Other highlanders pronounced distilled spirits a cure for colds, consumption, snakebites, and
other ailments.[92] Randolph County Methodist preacher Brantley York
remembered that in mid-nineteenth-century North Carolina, mothers soothed colicky babies by feeding them a teaspoonful of diluted
liquor.[93]

A lack of options could have been another reason why mountain
residents turned to alcohol. Antebellum western Carolinians sometimes refused to drink milk for fear of contracting "milk sickness," an
often fatal disease that afflicted people who consumed dairy products
from a cow that had fed on white snakeroot. To avoid this fate, they
may well have decided to drink a "safer" beverage such as whiskey
or brandy.[94] Fear of this disease continued well after the antebellum
period. Physician Benjamin Earle Washburn remembered that when he
arrived in Rutherford County in 1910, older residents refused to drink
milk. "Fear of milk sickness may have been the cause," he reasoned,
"for I was told that the disease had been much more prevalent a generation before."[95]

Alcohol played an important role in the social and economic lives
of antebellum highlanders. Before the Civil War, no stigma had yet

been attached to mountain residents who made alcohol. Whiskey and brandy were widely consumed at barn raisings, militia musters, and social events throughout the early nineteenth century. Many people believed in the medicinal qualities of these distilled spirits, and the region's rugged terrain and relatively poor roads made it easier and sometimes more profitable for farmers to manufacture some of their crops into whiskey and sell or barter it to neighbors and merchants. Mountaineers' demand for and acceptance of alcohol ensured that distillers could always find buyers. The federal government had not yet levied a permanent liquor tax on antebellum distillers, who were therefore not marginalized criminals but entrepreneurs responding to the demands of the marketplace.[96] As such, they gained the appreciation of mountain residents, who regarded drinking—and distilling—as a vital element of their economy and culture. As elsewhere in the United States, however, new economic and social forces would soon conspire against the mountain distiller and his clientele.

2

Select Men of Sober and Industrious Habits

Alcohol Reform and Social Conflict during the Late Antebellum Period

> They drink nor cider, rum, nor beer
> No brandy, gin, nor wine
> But water sparkling pure and clear
> And this is all a sign
> The sign of the Sons of Temperance.

"No other institutions in our opinion, can have a more salutary influence in checking vice, and giving a right direction to our various passions and appetites, than Temperance Societies." So wrote physician Jason F. E. Hardy, explaining why he and other middle-class reformers had founded the Asheville Auxiliary Temperance Society in April 1831. One of the first of its kind in western North Carolina, this organization was initially a success. Forty mountain residents, mostly from Asheville, joined the society that April because they believed that alcohol impeded the community's moral and economic prosperity. Two months later, the number of members had increased to sixty-five. But support for the Asheville Auxiliary Temperance Society was far from universal, especially in more remote parts of Buncombe County. Many farmers argued that the society and its desire to eradicate King Alcohol—as temperance advocates often termed alcoholic beverages—were "a scheme to deprive the people of their liberty." Several mountain churches joined the chorus of opposition, threatening to expel congregants who joined the organization. By 1832, the Asheville Auxiliary Temperance Society faced an uncertain future, as "enem[ies]" reduced its membership "to a bare majority." To the dismay of Hardy and other Asheville reformers, King Alcohol proved to be a formidable adversary.[1]

In the decades preceding the Civil War, countless Americans attempted to improve society through reform. Influenced by the Second Great Awakening and the expansion of market capitalism, these men and women embraced, among other social movements, the temperance cause.[2] Although this antialcohol crusade originated and thrived in the North, it achieved moderate success in the antebellum South. Like their cohorts above the Mason-Dixon Line, most southern reformers were middle-class professionals who tended to reside in towns with a thousand or more inhabitants. There, members of the urban middle class were numerous enough to influence local politics, and they supported the temperance movement, believing that it would improve their communities both morally and economically. These towns, mostly situated in the lowland South, also tended to have large African American populations, whose presence further encouraged whites to promote alcohol as an instrument of social control.[3]

Despite its rural character, the absence of large towns, and its small slave population, Appalachia was not impervious to the temperance reformation that swept across the nation during the antebellum period. In western North Carolina, the forces shaping antialcohol sentiment elsewhere in the United States—expansion of the market economy, growth of urban centers, and rise of a middle class—encouraged many highlanders to reject the drinking mores of American society.[4] Beginning in the 1830s, mountain crusaders founded organizations such as the Asheville Auxiliary Temperance Society to reform their rural neighbors and demonized the makers and sellers of distilled spirits. Alcohol, they charged, impeded the region's economic and moral potential. As Hardy and other urbanites quickly discovered, however, many rural residents remained skeptical of the antialcohol movement, believing that they had the right to drink and distill liquor and labeling reformers as fanatics.

This conflict over alcohol reform ultimately suggests that the potential fault line in antebellum white society was not between elite slaveholders and the yeomen but between the parochial "plain folk" and the burgeoning urban middle class.[5] In western North Carolina, it heightened social tensions, weakened important local institutions such as churches, and further polarized urban and rural residents. Temperance became a badge of respectability, one that helped delineate differences between middle-class residents of towns and rural mountain whites. Alcohol reform exacerbated a cultural divide that widened following the Civil War. Though it had humble beginnings, the antebellum temperance movement became a powerful force that shaped social relations in Appalachian North Carolina and other rural communities across the Old South.

Two Worlds in Western North Carolina

"This town . . . is very thin and the[y] live But very indifferently," land speculator John Brown noted of Asheville, North Carolina, in 1795.[6] Brown was not impressed, and for good reason. The "thin" settlement consisted of only a store, a hatter's shop, a small inn, and a gristmill.[7] Asheville, however, soon emerged as the center of political, economic, and social life in western North Carolina. Situated in the French Broad Valley and along the Buncombe Turnpike after 1828, it quickly became a crossroads for most travel and trade west of the Blue Ridge. It also served as a resort community, catering to wealthy South Carolinians and Georgians who journeyed there in the summer to enjoy the cool climate and scenic beauty. By the late antebellum period, according to a Macon County girl in 1847, Asheville was "a place *unsurpassed* in the known world for the *intelligence, refinement, correct taste, generosity* and *hospitality* of its inhabitants."[8] Along with three hotels and more than twenty stores, the town by then supported three churches, several schools, a women's college, a jail, a courthouse, and a population of 800.[9] John Brown would have been amazed.

Other communities flourished in western North Carolina in the late antebellum period. In the foothills east of the Blue Ridge, Morganton, Rutherfordton, and Wilkesboro, among other villages and hamlets, developed a thriving commerce, serving as gateways into and out of the highlands.[10] West of the Blue Ridge in the French Broad Valley, summer tourism played a major role in the development of Hendersonville, Flat Rock, and Warm Springs, whose residents supported lavish hotels and other businesses to accommodate their affluent guests. North and west of the French Broad Valley, county seats such as Boone, Murphy, and Franklin, though less developed than those to the east, emerged as important trading centers that linked nearby farmers to the larger market economy.[11] By the 1850s, ten mountain communities had a population of 150 or more inhabitants and functioned as urban centers in this overwhelmingly rural environment.[12] It was from these towns, largely situated in the French Broad Valley and east of the Blue Ridge, that the antebellum temperance movement garnered most of its support.

Regardless of their size or primary function, these communities attracted enterprising men and facilitated the growth of an urban elite and a professional middle class. Sons from well-to-do mountain land-holding families lived in or migrated to these communities, where, already possessing capital and influential family names, many of them emerged as leading businessmen and political figures. Since most of these towns served as county seats, they attracted lawyers, judges, and other officeholders. The arrival of these men and their families created a need for teachers, ministers, doctors, and other professionals. Realizing the economic opportunities offered by commercial centers, merchants, innkeepers, and artisans soon followed. Some of these professionals, because they had enough capital to purchase slaves, became the region's largest slaveholders.[13]

While towns helped link residents and nearby farmers to the market economy, a number of other Carolina highlanders found themselves more isolated—though not completely—from the outside world. The region's most fertile and accessible lands, located in the larger valleys, had been completely settled by the 1830s. Migrants thereafter had to move farther up the hillsides into hollows and coves to find available land, making communication difficult. As trade routes changed and migration dwindled, the Toe River Valley and other regions in western North Carolina that had been fairly accessible and well traveled during the late 1790s and early 1800s also became more isolated, thereby cutting more highland residents off from major trade and communication linkages.[14]

This influx of settlers into marginal regions, coinciding with the rise of urban centers, created a sense of difference within the population of western North Carolina by the late antebellum period.[15] Town residents and commercial farmers living in more open valleys increasingly defined themselves in opposition to their rural—and often poorer—counterparts.[16] During a political campaign in 1840, James Graham of Rutherford County advised his brother, William, to modify his dress when he visited rural voters. "If a Candidate be dressed Farmer-like," Graham wrote, "he is well received and kindly remembered by the inmates of the Log Cabin."[17] Town dwellers began to identify rural western North Carolina as a backward place where inhabitants failed to meet the standards of middle-class society. While traveling through Cherokee, Jackson, Haywood, Henderson, and Yancey counties during the early 1850s, for instance, Asheville lawyer Augustus Merrimon sometimes chastised rural farmers, labeling them as "dirty, impolite, and ungenteel."[18] Fellow Asheville resident Mary Gash agreed. In 1853, she and several visiting relatives attended a Christmas party in rural Buncombe County. Writing to her aunt after the engagement, the young woman complained that "to tell you the plain truth there was only a few young ladies there that I thought proper to introduce them to, and I managed that admirably, as it was rather a mixed multitude, mountain *boomers* and backwoods folks in abundance. It reminded one of the 'poor man's dinner' and it was given for the purpose [of] encouraging that class."[19]

Like Gash, urban middle-class highlanders wanted to be refined, cultivated, and fashionable. Having greater access to railroads and other communication linkages, these men and women frequently interacted with outsiders and were more attuned to cultural trends. They subscribed to and read national periodicals such as *Godey's Lady's Book, Harper's Magazine,* and the *Saturday Evening Post.* Influenced by these publications, mountain townspeople formed debating societies where they discussed such questions as "Is dueling commendable in any case?" and "Whether it be not unjust to exclude ministers of the Gospel from legislative bodies under our form of government?"[20] As one enthusiastic Wilkesboro woman wrote in 1843, "The Young gentlemen of the borough formed a debating society last week which I am in hopes will afford us quite a *literary treat* this winter."[21] These societies not only served as popular forms of entertainment but also allowed urban residents to meet and forge a common identity, one that stressed the middle-class virtues of industry, self-restraint, and temperance.

More so than their rural neighbors, mountain urban professionals also embraced education reform and economic development. To enhance their children's ability to succeed in the "modern" world, they funded the construction of primary and secondary schools throughout the region. By the 1840s, village residents, mostly from the middle class, could enroll in local seminaries and colleges such as the Wilkesboro Male Academy and Taylorsville Female Academy.[22] These students, along with their parents, hoped to improve their communities both economically and aesthetically. One Asheville resident in the 1850s explained that town dwellers, "in the spirit of improvement, a love of the beautiful, and a taste for the refined," desired to "make gardens of waste places, and turn barren hillsides into blooming undulations."[23] Even those living in smaller, less developed hamlets promoted economic growth and remained optimistic about the future. "We are making roads, building bridges, rearing dwelling houses and churches at a rate that would astonish you," Mollie Carrie from Macon County's Oak Hill community boasted to a friend in Asheville in 1855.[24] Priding themselves on being civilized, Carrie and others did not want outsiders to think of the region as a backward place. In their quest for respectability, moral improvement, and economic progress, mountain professionals made efforts to reform their rural counterparts. Influenced by the American Benevolence campaign—a middle-class evangelical movement that relied on extralocal bodies to improve society—many of the highland townspeople participated in the antebellum antialcohol crusade with the hope of lifting up the backwoods farmer from poverty and ignorance.

The Church Speaks

In June 1802, Methodist itinerant James Jenkins wrote a letter to Bishop Francis Asbury that described the first revival held in Rutherford County. "Thousands were present," Jenkins rejoiced. "Many poor sinners felt the power of God and were raised up to testify that He had forgiven their sins."[25] This news must have pleased Asbury, who, during his annual missionary tours of western North Carolina in the 1790s, had complained of enduring "filth, fleas, rattlesnakes, hills, mountains, rocks, and rivers." Now, however, the "encamping places" of the Baptists, Methodists, and Presbyterians made the mountain region "look like the Holy Land."[26] The Great Awakening, which had swept through the Eastern Seaboard during the mid-eighteenth century, had finally arrived in the Carolina highlands and other parts of the southern backcountry.[27]

Adapting to the rural landscape, Baptists, Methodists, and, to a lesser extent, Presbyterian churches established circuits, whereby a small number of clergy could serve wider geographic areas.[28] They also organized camp meetings or revivals. These social gatherings usually lasted for several days and helped circuit riders spread religion in regions where churches were widely scattered. "By calling persons away from worldly matters for several days of uninterrupted religious exercises," concludes Anne Loveland, camp meetings provided an opportunity "both for the conversion of sinners and the spiritual growth of professors."[29] According to historian Loyal Jones, the revivals "won many to the hope that all may achieve salvation and, beyond that, may improve human nature through sanctification."[30] Moreover, these meetings allowed settlers to maintain and strengthen community bonds. In between the daily services, singing sessions, and prayer meetings, revivalists met with neighbors and kinfolk, gossiped, and debated politics.[31] Hundreds of churches, the products of this evangelical movement, dotted the mountain countryside by the late antebellum period, providing moral guidance to their members and acting as centers of neighborhood activities.[32]

Religious leaders expressed their concern about the perceived prevalence of intemperance in the region. Gabriel Phillips of the Broad River Baptist Association in Rutherford and Cleveland counties wrote in 1827: "The present age might emphatically be styled the drunken age, so much does inebriety prevail."[33] But this was not a new phenomenon. At their 1801 inaugural meeting at Green's Creek in Rutherford County, members of the association had exhorted their brethren to "keep their bodies in subjection, watch against unlawful desires, and oppose within themselves, all unlawful appetites and refrain from shameful and outbreaking practices."[34] Now, nearly twenty-six years later, the "demon of intemperance" continued to hold "high carnival throughout the entire bounds of the body." Phillips could do nothing but issue another stern warning. "Let us, dear brethren," he pleaded, "unite in earnest supplication to the great Creator, that his creatures may cease to defile the image of their Maker by brutal sensuality, as in that image they were created; and verily we unto them that in brutalizing the creature they heinously offend the Creator."[35] Phillips and other members of the Broad River Baptist Association were not alone in their fight against King Alcohol during the early antebellum period. As elsewhere in the South, Methodists and Presbyterians in western North Carolina believed that drunkenness was a sin. These denominations feared that excessive drinking undermined republican institutions, ruined families, and subverted the church.

The churches were particularly alarmed about the tradition of treating, or the providing of free drinks on election days, arguing that it encouraged public intoxication and undermined the "rights of freemen" by "reducing politics to bribery."[36] As early as 1789, members

The Tree of Temperance. Courtesy of the Prints and Photographs Division, Library of Congress, Washington, D.C.

of the Yadkin Baptist Association, many of whom resided in Wilkes County, protested the practice of treating because it created "disorder."[37] Despite growing opposition to such corruption, politicians continued to utilize the practice. In 1827, the Broad River Baptist Association implemented a more radical policy, adopting a resolution "to withhold their support from any candidate for office who may be found in the habit of treating with spirituous liquors to obtain votes."[38]

Mountain evangelicals were quick to argue that alcohol not only led to corruption in politics but also had a negative impact on the moral fabric of society. By the 1830s, many of them agreed that sobriety was in the best interest of society at large. Rev. Henry Kerr of Rutherford County believed that drunkenness "destroy[ed] the peace and happiness" of the family, made "cruel fathers," turned wives into "widows," and instigated "crime" and "deprivation."[39] Evangelicals feared that even the moderate use of ardent spirits impeded the progress of religion and led professing Christians away from God. In 1840, the Tuckaseegee Baptist Association in Haywood, Jackson, and Macon counties insisted that drunkenness encouraged men to leave the church. Without the gospel, which was "design[ed] to lead us from evil to holiness [and] from the love of sensual gratification to a desire for spiritual enjoyment," people would live "contrary to the spirit of Christ."[40]

Before the 1830s, most churches in western North Carolina had relied on moral suasion to combat public drunkenness and alcoholism. Ministers stood in front of congregations, waved their fists in the air, and warned of the "seducing and dangerous effects of [alcohol]."[41] Yet many churchgoers remained unconvinced. Church minutes reveal that "drinking to excess" was the most common sin that male members committed. In almost all cases, accused sinners had become inebriated in public, which explains why churches rarely charged women for being intoxicated. Mountain women drank alcohol, but, conforming to the social precepts of the day, they did so in the privacy of their own homes, where church members were less likely to see them imbibing.[42] Baptist, Methodist, and Presbyterian churches had harsh penalties for members accused of drinking. As early as 1798, the Three Fork Baptist Church in present-day Watauga County expelled a member for "drinking liquor to excess."[43] Mountain congregations continued to excommunicate accused "drunkards" well into the nineteenth century.[44] More often than not, however, churches forgave offenders who admitted their guilt and professed repentance.[45]

Mountain ministers might have preached the dangers and evils of drunkenness on Sundays, but they did not promote total abstinence from alcohol, largely because it played an important role in the lives and economy of western North Carolinians, including their own. Most mountain churches refused to attack alcohol manufacturers, many of whom contributed generously to the churches from their distilleries' profits.[46] Baptist preachers often operated stills, and although they declared drunkenness immoral, they approved of moderate drinking and even occasionally consumed alcohol themselves.[47] Before preaching to his congregation at North Fork Baptist Church in Buncombe County during the 1820s, Else Burnett drank "about three fingers of properly distilled apple brandy."[48] But over time, many local residents increasingly challenged such tolerant attitudes toward distilling and drinking.

The Origins of Temperance Reform

Rev. Henry Kerr formed one of the first temperance societies in western North Carolina at Brittain Presbyterian Church in Rutherford County on July 4, 1831. During his thirteen years at Brittain, Kerr had become a leading proponent of benevolent reform. In the late 1820s, he had organized Sunday school, Bible, and home mission societies throughout the county. In 1831, he turned his attention to alcohol reform.[49] Unlike earlier proponents of reform, Kerr disapproved of even modest drinking because he believed that it ultimately led to drunkenness. "The moderate use of [alcohol]," he charged, "by professors of religion and moral persons, encourages and emboldens the intemperate, and leads the unwary to the verge of danger and death." Wanting to prevent such "evils," Kerr organized the Little Brittain Temperance Society, an auxiliary to the North Carolina Temperance Society founded in Raleigh just a few months earlier.[50]

Influenced by the burgeoning antialcohol movement in the North, Presbyterians like Kerr played an important role in the founding of temperance societies in the Carolina highlands and other parts of the state. The Presbyterian Church was the first to urge its members not to consume, sell, or distill alcohol, reflecting the belief that moderate drinking leads to drunkenness. In 1815, the Presbyterian Synod of North Carolina met in Fayetteville and encouraged local congregations to form "Moral Associations for the Suppression of Vice and Immorality." That same year, Rev. James Hall, who had founded several Presbyterian churches in the Carolina highlands during the 1790s, called for a statewide meeting to create a "moral association" and "to promote the formation of auxiliary societies."[51] Their work paid off in 1831 with the founding of the North Carolina Temperance Society, an organization affiliated with the American Temperance Society, which had been created in Boston, Massachusetts, in 1826. The Temperance

Society hired agents to travel across the state and establish local auxiliaries. One of these agents likely contacted Kerr, who was already an opponent of alcohol and agreed to form the Little Brittain Temperance Society.

One of the first of its kind in western North Carolina, this organization quickly boasted a membership of eighty-seven. Not surprisingly, the society garnered most of its support from middle-class urban professionals, merchants, and artisans. Like those in Asheville and other communities, these reformers embraced the antebellum temperance movement because they believed that alcohol corrupted the morals of highlanders and made them unproductive.[52] The officers of the Little Brittain Temperance Society were all prominent men who reflected both religious and secular opposition to King Alcohol. The group's president was former county commissioner John Carson, who was also president of the local Bible society and vice president of the Rutherford Sunday School Union. The vice president was Joshua Forman, an entrepreneur who had moved to Rutherfordton in 1826 from New York, where he had helped found the town of Syracuse. Kerr was the society's secretary. The executive committee included a postmaster, a merchant, a former commissioner for the village of Irvinsville, and a future sheriff.[53]

Members of the white middle class were joined by local Native Americans in their quest to promote temperance during the antebellum period. Indeed, many Cherokees supported the antialcohol movement. In the early 1830s, Chief Yonaguska formed a temperance society in Quallatown because he believed that alcoholism was not only destroying the tribe but also giving whites an excuse to confiscate Cherokee land.[54] In 1836, Macon and Haywood residents wrote that Cherokee sobriety surpassed white sobriety in the region.[55] Two years later, William Holland Thomas, a white merchant who was Yonaguska's adopted son, remembered that every Native American in Quallatown had signed the temperance pledge.[56] In 1845, he insisted that only eight Cherokees in that community drank alcohol.[57] Although Thomas probably exaggerated the extent of Native American sobriety in order to portray the Cherokees as stable and worthy citizens, scholars agree that intemperance within the tribe subsided during the 1830s and 1840s.[58]

By the 1830s, many white Baptists and Methodists, strengthened by the growth of their churches during and after the Great Revival at the turn of the century, joined the Presbyterians in rejecting the prevailing drinking mores of antebellum Americans. This new standard of public morality resulted in part from evangelicals' fear that people were hopeless sinners living in a world that was inherently evil. To achieve personal salvation, people thus had to refuse "worldly temptations." Preachers used their growing influence to argue that moderate drinking would lead to iniquity.[59] Along with public drunkenness, they disapproved of the practice of treating and frowned on farmers' drinking whiskey after work. These sinners could find salvation, however, and it was the duty of the church to lend a helping hand and use moral persuasion to encourage alcohol drinkers to become sober.[60]

The formation of the North Carolina Temperance Society in 1831 further solidified the attitudes of white evangelicals on the subject of alcohol reform.[61] By 1830, Baptists and Methodists had become the largest denominations in the South and wanted to expand into the frontier. Finding themselves in competition with the older, more established denominations, Baptists and Methodists responded by creating new structures that centralized authority. They also moved away from "spirit-inspiration," a disorganized but effective method that had originally drawn large numbers of converts, and they codified standards for conducting camp meetings and ensuring proper decorum. As Deborah McCauley has demonstrated, "religious experience . . . was no longer considered the appropriate focus for denominations that had ceased drawing their leadership and much of their membership from the plain-folk, as they once had, but now cultivated a clergy of educated professionals who, in turn, tended to a growing middle—as well as upper—class church membership, much of it concentrated in towns and cities."[62]

Power now shifted from local congregations to centralized agencies such as the Baptist State Convention and the Methodist Conference, which catered to the interests of middle-class townspeople. Like the Presbyterians, these agencies embraced the ideas of the American Benevolence movement, which promoted missions, seminaries, and temperance. Thus, the Baptist State Convention, perhaps responding to the creation of the North Carolina Temperance Society, recommended in 1833 that its brethren organize societies "to put a stop to the destructive practice of intemperance." Shortly thereafter, Methodist quarterly conferences also formed temperance societies throughout the state and encouraged its members to "abstain from making, vending, or using ardent spirits."[63]

Although such societies were organized in Rutherford, Buncombe, and Wilkes counties, church support for temperance reform remained limited in western North Carolina during the 1830s.[64] This was largely due to the emergence of antimissionary sentiments among Baptists and Methodists living in more remote, sparsely populated areas.[65] When evangelicals began endorsing extralocal seminaries, missions, and temperance organizations, many congregations disapproved, viewing the new developments as a break with tradition. The antimission churches feared that these societies threatened to destroy local autonomy and denounced them as being "inventions of men" without spiritual authorization.[66] In 1830, when the Baptist State Convention endorsed the funding of missions, about half the associations in North Carolina split from the state convention and created a distinct "Primitive Baptist" body. That same year, "traditional" Methodists, seeking to strengthen local authority, followed suit by forming the Methodist Protestant Church.[67]

The conflict within mountain Baptist congregations was especially pronounced.[68] In 1840, when the Tuckaseegee Baptist Association announced its support for temperance reform, unified hostility from many of the churches forced the group to issue a circular letter defending its decision. Elder John Haynes first clarified the association's position. "By 'entire abstinence,'" he explained, "we mean abandonment not only of the use, but of the manufacture and traffic in the article as a beverage." This call for "entire abstinence" indicates that temperance reformers were becoming more radical. Whereas they had initially condemned immoderate drinking, reformers now denounced alcohol distillers for encouraging "the foul stain which has [been] cast upon our holy religion." Haynes then addressed "the prominent objections" among members of the association. Most rejected church-based temperance reform because they saw it as an "infringement on the rights, a violation of the liberty of our members." Haynes dismissed this as absurd. "If the objection be good for anything in this case," he countered, "it is equally good against every principle and precept of the gospel of Christ, for there is not one which does not deny every Christian the right to sin, and restrain him from an indulgence in evil, which in this case he miscalls liberty." Haynes further argued that the association had not exceeded its authority by prohibiting members from drinking, distilling, and selling alcohol. In his view, Jesus Christ granted churches "the judicial power" to make and enforce laws promoting "holiness" and "spiritual enjoyment." "It is by virtue of this authority," Haynes concluded, "that . . . sinful follies, in which men indulge, have been declared inconsistent with the Christian character, and incompatible with fellowship in the church."[69]

The Rise of the Sons of Temperance

In the midst of these theological disputes over alcohol reform, the Sons of Temperance arrived in western North Carolina. Founded in New York in 1842, the Sons was a fraternal order in which members pledged total abstinence from alcohol. In 1843, the order organized a branch in Raleigh and hired lecturers to recruit new members throughout the state.[70] The arrival of these lecturers occurred at an opportune time for mountain evangelicals. Many churchgoers believed that the secular nature of the Sons of Temperance could help churches repair the schisms that had emerged within the Tuckaseegee Baptist Association and other congregations. Church members could now join this organization, thereby freeing religious associations from issuing a universal ban on alcohol. And because the Sons of Temperance was not affiliated with an ecclesiastical body, it could reach out to the "unchurched" and make them "decent members of society."[71] In regions like the Carolina highlands, where only one in seven people was a church member, locals and outsiders alike agreed that the Sons of Temperance promised to bring great change.[72]

As elsewhere in the United States, the Sons of Temperance received its strongest support from urban middle-class western North Carolinians.[73] More so than previous church-based reform societies, it promoted the values that mountain professionals and commercial farmers had been advocating for decades. Drunkenness not only leads to personal ruin and destruction, the Sons charged, but also impedes commercial prosperity. Temperance, in contrast, would bring moral and material improvement. Prominent businessmen like James Patton in Asheville, who had urged his sons in 1845 to hire "young men" of "sober and industrious habits," found this message appealing.[74] Like their evangelical brethren, these reformers urged people to restrain their appetites in order to achieve balanced, happy lives. As one member of the Sons of Temperance, stressing the middle-class virtues of sobriety, self-control, and industry, wrote in 1854: "The difference between [Mr.] Smith sober and [Mr.] Smith drunk is this—Smith drunk

Certificate for the Sons of Temperance, 1857. Courtesy of the Prints and Photographs Division, Library of Congress, Washington, D.C.

was rummy, ragged, and riotous—Smith sober is joyful, jovial, and jolly. Smith drunk was stuttering, stupid, and staggering; Smith sober is clear-headed and cautious; Smith drunk was sick, sore, and sorry; Smith sober is hearty, healthy, and, happy; Smith drunk was ill-read, ill-bred, and ill-led; Smith sober is well saved, well behaved, and well shaved."[75]

Augustus Merrimon, a future senator from Asheville who joined the Sons of Temperance in the early 1850s, agreed. "It is strange to me, however common a thing it is, that men, rational, intelligent men, will drink and become intoxicated," he wrote in 1853. "Why men get drunk, degrade themselves, destroy their physical system, ruin their minds, blast all their hopes and prospects, disgrace themselves, their family, their friends and neighborhood is something that I cannot account for."[76] For Merrimon and other middle-class townspeople, the Sons promised to help men who were "in the habit of lying drunk about the streets" redeem themselves and "hold respectable stations in society."[77]

Of the nineteen known societies affiliated with the Sons of Temper-

Augustus S. Merrimon, ca. 1870. Courtesy of the North Carolina State Archives.

ance in western North Carolina, twelve were in county seats and fifteen were either in the French Broad Valley or east of the Blue Ridge, suggesting that the order thrived in communities that were becoming more involved with the larger market economy.[78] Having greater access to railroads and other major transportation arteries such as the Buncombe Turnpike, farmers there could profit from selling their corn to drovers, stand owners, and itinerant merchants. These denizens were therefore less motivated to distill alcohol and more receptive to temperance reform. Only four temperance societies were located in the far northeastern and southwestern parts of the region, where farmers had limited access to major transportation arteries and often relied on distilling as a means of survival.[79]

An examination of the socioeconomic status of officers in local divisions reinforces the link between the temperance movement and urban middle-class mountain residents. Like their predecessors in the Little Brittain Temperance Society, leaders in the Rutherford Sons of Temperance, which boasted a membership of fifty in 1850, were successful businessmen or professionals and represented both secular and religious interests. The "Worthy Patriarch" was William Tanner, a merchant who employed two clerks. The remaining officials consisted of two carpenters, two Methodist ministers, a physician, a carriage maker, a blacksmith, a hatter, a saddler, and a lawyer.[80] With the exception of H. M. Corbitt, who lived in the nearby settlement of Mountain Creek, these officials resided in Rutherfordton, the county seat.[81]

Because the Sons of Temperance was a secret society, it is difficult to determine the socioeconomic status of its other members. Ian R. Tyrrell discovered a membership list in Rowan County in piedmont North Carolina that bolstered his argument that the temperance movement in the South was generally supported by small-town middle-class and artisan groups.[82] Although no such membership lists exist for western North Carolina, the makeup can be inferred through other means. For example, in 1854, a number of Ashe County farmers signed a petition calling for statewide prohibition.[83] Since the Sons of Temperance organized this campaign, these petitioners were likely members or supporters of that society. Two years earlier, farmers in nearby and economically comparable Yancey County signed an antiprohibition petition presumably in opposition to the Sons of Temperance.[84]

A comparison of these two groups is revealing. Of the twenty-three Ashe County prohibitionists positively identified in the 1850 agricultural census, seven who were listed as owning farms also had other professions.[85] Three of them were mechanics, two were merchants, and two were Baptist preachers.[86] In contrast, the twenty-six Yancey County antiprohibitionists who were positively identified reported only farming as their occupation.[87] More importantly, the Ashe County prohibitionists were wealthier in terms of property holdings than their counterparts in Yancey County. The average cash value of the prohibitionists' land ($762) exceeded that of the Yancey County antiprohibitionists ($397), while the average landholding of the Ashe County farms was double the size of the Yancey County farms.[88] These data suggest that professionals and more entrepreneurial-minded agriculturalists were more likely to support the Sons of Temperance than were simple farmers.[89]

Mountain Patriots and Women

As it had done for nearly a decade, the Asheville Sons of Temperance celebrated George Washington's birthday on February 22, 1855. William M. Hardy, whose father had organized Asheville's first temperance society in 1831, began the ceremony by reading a portion of Washington's Farewell Address. Rev. Chapman then walked on stage, where he delivered "a very eloquent and able" sermon that praised "the Father of His Country" and warned the crowd of the dangers of King Alcohol. Following Chapman's speech, members of the Sons of Temperance partook in a "Celebration Supper at the Court House." The ladies of Asheville had worked hard to prepare this meal, and the Sons were not disappointed. "The table was richly laden with the choicest viands, which would have done honor to princely pomp or regal splendor. It was a banquet no less pleasing to the eye than palatable to taste, and was discussed with a relish that was increased in intensity in proportion to the beauty and grace of their fair committee of arrangements who acted in the capacity of 'waiting maids' to the 'Sons.'" After the meal, Worthy Patriarch William Rankin raised his glass of water and toasted the memory of President Washington and his wife, Martha.[90]

This ceremony sheds further light on why the Sons of Temperance endured in western North Carolina and other parts of the South during the antebellum period. To a greater extent than previous temperance societies, the Sons specialized in public pageantry. It organized sign pledges, barbecues, and parades on important national holidays.

These elaborate affairs, which often received press coverage, helped the Sons of Temperance link their cause with the founding fathers' struggle for American independence. The symbolism was explicit, as shown by a society-sponsored Fourth of July celebration in Wilkesboro in 1851. Residents there heard a stirring speech by state lecturer C. C. Hackett. As one participant, calling himself "Independence," remembered, "[Hackett] improved the time very aptly and clearly, pointing out the propriety of employing our national anniversary in concerting plans for removing those national evils and vices which so much prevent the blessings and privileges achieved by our fore-fathers and still perpetuated to us by a kind Providence." After Hackett's speech, another member of the Wilkesboro Sons of Temperance read a "Parody on the Declaration of Independence" to the crowd, comparing the "repeated injuries" of King Alcohol to those committed by the English Crown on American colonists during the 1770s.[91] Throughout the mountain region, local orders organized similar celebrations where they condemned King Alcohol for, among other things, the "establishment of an absolute tyranny over the moral, civil, and religious rights of the people of these United States."[92]

Along with satisfying the "patriotic longings" of men, the Sons also appealed to mountain females, who were often sympathetic to the movement.[93] Women in Wilkes County, for instance, quickly joined the John's River Temperance Society in 1831, one of the first organizations of its kind in western North Carolina, outnumbering male members sixty-five to forty.[94] Early reformers, aware that women wanted to protect the domestic sphere, stressed alcohol's negative impact on the family.[95] As Jason Hardy, founder of the Asheville Auxiliary Temperance Society, explained in 1831, "[Drunkenness] destroys the fond hopes of kind and benevolent parents, and involves in gloom and misery the lives of tender and affectionate wives." Many Asheville women must have agreed. A short time later, Hardy reported that sixty-five people had become members, "a number of whom [were] Ladies."[96]

Although the Sons of Temperance excluded women from full membership, it considered them indispensable allies and supported the Daughters of Temperance, a national society founded in 1848. The men appreciated the work of their female counterparts, who played an important role in organizing and catering events, and women were welcome to attend meetings.[97] On at least one occasion, the Sons even allowed a woman to publicly speak on the subject of temperance. In

Advertisement for the Daughters of Temperance, ca. 1835–1856. Courtesy of the Prints and Photographs Division, Library of Congress, Washington, D.C.

1851, the "Ladies of Shelby" gave a Bible to the Sons of Temperance in Cleveland County. Cordelia Hamrick then addressed the crowd of 120 with "our best wishes and fervent desires, that the ruling hand of a kind Providence will continue to roll on the Temperance Car, until all the sons of earth shall be engaged in bearing aloft the Banner of Temperance, and shall take shelter under the branches of the Tree of Life."[98]

Behind the scenes, mountain women encouraged their husbands, relatives, and friends to embrace temperance. Writing to her son, Isaac Theodore Avery, in 1852, Elizabeth Avery from Burke County reminded him of the dangers of drunkenness, citing the death of Sherwood Branch, an alcoholic who had drowned in a nearby river. "When you see any of your friends and acquaintances falling into temptations, you can warn them of the[ir] danger," she pleaded. "Call to the[ir] minds the anxiety of the[ir] friends here . . . to hear that they are falling into all kinds of vices and wickedness—the very thought is too distressing to think of."[99] Other women tried to persuade their loved ones to become active members of the Sons and Daughters of Temperance. As one Buncombe County woman wrote to her cousin in 1852, "I was somewhat sorry to learn that you did not hear Mr. Hewlett, for if you had heard him I think from that hour you would have been a real strong, hot headed, fiery footed, run mad, deep down, dyed in the wool, Daughter of Temperance."[100] For mountain woman reformers, the temperance movement allowed them not only to protect the domestic sphere but also to serve as "representatives of virtue" in the public sphere.[101] From the experience, they gained a sense of self-worth and a political voice.

Temperance and Stereotypes

Female and male reformers were also responding to emerging stereotypes regarding the drinking mores of Appalachian society. Since the 1790s, outsiders had commented often on the extensive use of alcohol among mountain residents. But these early travelers, mostly evangelical circuit riders, did not view the drinking habits of highlanders as different from those elsewhere in the South.[102] By the 1830s, however, evangelicals began to single out western North Carolinians, believing that life on the frontier made them more prone to drink alcohol. In 1835, Baptist agent James Thomas referred to the western part of the state when he wrote: "The Temperance reform is evidently on the decline, and the use of strong drink is taking deep root, more or less in all

this fruitful country. I have seen not less than 17 distilleries in operation this fall in my field of labour; and woeful to tell, many professors
of religion, who say they desire the prosperity of Zion, to do good,
eschew evil, and abhor drunkenness in all its forms, make, sell, use,
give, and send abroad this awful evil, and they often quote the Scrip-
tures to justify their course."[103]

This perception of the region continued during the 1840s and
1850s. British geologist George W. Featherstonhaugh attributed the
intemperance of Haywood County residents to their lack of school-
ing. "Here was a village most beautifully situated," he said of Franklin in 1847, "but I could not learn that there was a man of education
in the place disposed to set an example of the value of sobriety to the
community."[104] Commenting on the abundance of stills in the Carolina
highlands in 1849, an unnamed Salisbury resident in Rowan County
believed that mountain neighbors "with few, very few exceptions, sit
still in ignorance and stupidity."[105] Six years later, a Fayetteville journalist, appealing to eastern prejudices against mountain residents, claimed
that "in almost every ravine and mountain gorge of Western North Carolina you will find a still house and an apple mill, placed there for the
purpose of turning the healthy grains and fruits of the earth into mad-
dening and killing beverage."[106] Perhaps the harshest remarks occurred
in 1852, when a writer for *Spirit of the Age,* the official organ of the
state's Sons of Temperance, described his travels in the Carolina highlands. Although praising the region for its fertile lands, scenic beauty,
and commercial prosperity, he saw "one object, in all the way to and
from the mountain, which I looked upon as a disgrace to the age in
which we live and a complete breach upon the natural creation of the
Christians' God. The object is a little dirty looking distillery."[107]

These negative images reinforced a preexisting interstate sectionalism that had resulted in damaging stereotypes about the mountain
region. As Calvin H. Wiley, editor of the *North Carolina Journal
of Education,* explained in 1857, "Our Eastern friends are much of
the notion that the West is a nation of semi-barbarians, destitute of
good breeding, politeness and everything else like refinement, living
in the woods and subsisting on roots and berries."[108] Two years later,
a Raleigh journalist returned from a trip to Asheville, where he had
been surprised to discover that "the people of the West are neither sav-
ages nor ignoramuses; but on the contrary, they are intelligent, high-
minded, hospitable, and civilized."[109]

Such misconceptions encouraged many Carolina highlanders to embrace the antebellum temperance movement. More likely than not, the image of the backward, drunken highlander insulted mountain residents, especially those living in urban areas who considered themselves refined and cultivated. This stereotype also threatened to impede enterprise and weakened the argument for an extension of the state railroad into the mountain counties.[110] Fearing that businessmen would not invest money in a region where intemperance prevailed, mountain reformers insisted that the liquor problem was improving. "Hurra for Madison," J. M. Scales wrote to *Spirit of the Age* in February 1851. "She has always had a bad name, but she has retrieved it now. She can look up now, as proud as any village, and say I am for cold water." That same year, residents of a mining village in McDowell County reassured "outsiders" that they were doing everything possible to combat King Alcohol. "In fact," they pointed out, "the house that the [Sons of Temperance] Division was organized in, was built and used for the purpose of dealing out that all-pervading destroyer of health, morals and property." Other mountain denizens wrote to state newspapers, bragging about their communities. "If you will allow us to indulge a little in County pride," Taylorsville reformers in Alexander County reported to *Spirit of the Age* in 1851, "we would say that we have the neatest and most quiet little village we have ever seen . . . we have no tippling Shop here." By 1853, the local division boasted a membership of 156. Members of the Asheville Sons of Temperance, which numbered 180, were just as confident. "We challenge the State to show us a town that has done better for itself and the cause," they declared.[111]

Ironically, middle-class mountain residents helped create the stereotypes that outsiders popularized during the late antebellum period. Most antebellum journalists and tourists likely rarely witnessed the stills and drunkenness that they reported. Instead, outsiders talked to the more accessible town residents during their travels.[112] But these local men (and women) voiced concern about the intemperance of their neighbors, especially those living in more remote areas. "I presume that you think that our mountain people here are not much in favor of reading temperance newspapers," an unnamed Hendersonville resident wrote to *Spirit of the Age* in 1851. "This I must confess is too much the case."[113] An anonymous Franklin resident agreed, blaming the lack of temperance reform on "the *hard-headed* opposition of some of our mountaineers."[114]

Even local politicians and professionals had little contact with country folk, who came to town only on court and election days. This limited interaction was all they needed to conclude that drunkenness prevailed in rural mountain society. Asheville lawyer Augustus Merrimon, for instance, often complained that rural Carolina highlanders would "see how badly they could behave themselves" during court week by "drinking and cursing." "I do not know any rival of this place in regard to drunkenness, ignorance, superstition and the most brutal debauchery," he complained about Jewell City farmers in Madison County in 1853. Their wives were also guilty. "I saw two women drunk and one cursed and swore desperately and proposed to whip some of her male friends that did not please her," Merrimon wrote of the Yancey County court in Burnsville. "Oh, what a shocking sight to see a woman drunk. A woman! Ah, a woman drunk! Shame on the unfortunate wretch!"[115] Other mountain reformers even requested help from outsiders, pointing out that no other "section of the country so much needs light, knowledge, and action stirred up among the people upon the Temperance Reform."[116] Tourists and writers tapped into these local perceptions, spreading the tales of the mountain folk to the lowlands and beyond. More importantly, reformers acted on their own misconceptions and began to advocate for statewide prohibition during the 1850s, believing perhaps that local control was impossible. The shift in tactics brought to a climax the social tensions that had been brewing in western North Carolina society for decades, and the mountain distiller found himself the central figure in this drama.

The Antidistiller Crusade

Like those elsewhere in antebellum America, North Carolina politicians considered liquor manufacturing an important cottage industry and rejected legislation that impinged on the rights of small distillers. Laws requiring retailers to purchase licenses did not extend to producers of ardent spirits. During the colonial period, regulatory measures had included clauses that allowed small distillers to freely sell their own alcohol. State officials continued these policies, permitting liquor producers to sell a quart or more of their whiskey without a license. Legislators knew that most North Carolinians, especially those living in the western part of the state, regarded liquor manufacturing as an inalienable right and an economic necessity.[117] These attitudes prevailed during the 1790s, when the national government levied taxes on imported and domestically manufactured alcohol. Western North Carolinians vehemently opposed these duties and ignored the law.[118]

Distillers had also escaped the wrath of alcohol reformers during the early nineteenth century. Temperance societies limited their protests mainly to the practice of treating and the consumption of alcohol near churches and colleges.[119] In North Carolina, legislators responded by passing a law in 1801 that made treating a crime punishable by a fine of 100 pounds.[120] Reformers voiced dissatisfaction with the license system, arguing that it had done little to solve the liquor problem.[121] Despite laws that required retailers to be "of Good Character" and to purchase an alcohol license, crusaders insisted that taverns remained a public nuisance, a source of "drunkenness, crime, and infamy."[122] Again, their efforts paid off. The General Assembly, hoping to eliminate less responsible retailers, "raised the license fee from forty-eight shillings in 1816, to ten dollars in 1850, and to thirty dollars in 1858."[123]

Despite their early legislative success, temperance advocates believed that these laws had failed to reduce alcohol consumption. They became more radical, blaming tavern owners and other retailers—licensed or not—for continuing to sell a "degrading vice" that had already "beggard thousands of families, broken the hearts of multitudes of wives and mothers, and sent many a hapless victim to a premature grave!!" Liquor did more than discourage productivity and stability. Temperance supporters feared that America was in great peril. "Should this vice continue to increase," Henry Kerr from Rutherford County warned in 1832, "it will destroy our national character. It will hurl us from the proud eminence on which we stand among the nations of the earth, to the depth of degradation and infamy."[124] Kerr and other mountain reformers would soon shift responsibility for the liquor problem to alcohol manufacturers. After all, these men and women were producing most of the spirits that taverns and other retail establishments sold.

In 1832, Kerr launched a series of attacks on liquor manufacturers, insisting that they, along with tavern owners, encouraged intemperance. "We would ask the conscientious distiller," the reverend wrote, "how he reconciles it to his feelings, to contribute to this great evil and misery. It may be said, that by his means, the bread of the needy is literally converted into a poison."[125] That same year, Jason Hardy from Buncombe County accused distillers of emanating "every species of crime, wickedness, and abandonment" throughout the Carolina highlands.[126] Thomas Lenoir, the son of a late-eighteenth-century mountain distiller and a leading planter, continued where Hardy had left off. Delivering a speech to a local temperance society in Lenoir in Caldwell County on Christmas Day 1843, he chastised: "There are those among us who are daily converting the bread; the staff of life into a slow and deadly poison, to destroy the mind and morals of the father and the peace and happiness of the family circle!! . . . Unfortunate man! It is never too late to do better, come now and make a last resolve, that you will assume your proper station in life."[127]

By the early 1850s, members of the Sons of Temperance had begun condemning alcohol distillers for promoting drunkenness and immorality.[128] For these reformers, distillers became a symbol of what was wrong with rural society. They were products of a "frontier" environment, one that needed civilizing.

Missionary Baptists and Methodists joined this chorus of opposition. As early as 1840, the Tuckaseegee Baptist Association recommended that churches "use their influence to arrest the evil of . . . making, vending, and using intoxicating drinks as a beverage."[129] Methodists followed suit. By the late 1840s, some Baptist and Methodist ministers could even excommunicate members who distilled alcohol.[130] These expulsions quickly sparked conflict within congregations. Although sympathetic to temperance reform, many mountain churchgoers, especially Primitive Baptists and "traditional" Methodists who lived in more remote, sparsely populated areas, denounced these resolutions as an infringement on the rights of distillers. Methodist circuit rider Augustine F. Shannon, for instance, encountered hostility from rural Haywood County residents in the late 1840s when he announced that the Holston Conference "disapproved [of] Stilling in the Church." "Some got mad and some was well pleased," Shannon wrote in 1849. "Some Sinners then said I was right & some Methodist Said that we lived in a free Country & that one had a right to do with his own as he pleases."[131] After the King's Mountain Baptist Association agreed to exclude distillers from membership in 1859, several rural churches withdrew, "forming themselves into a separate association with anti-temperance proclivities." These churches then expelled members who had supported the association's resolution. A "rebellious faction" of Walls Baptist Church in Cleveland County even refused "to surrender the church book" and fastened "three additional locks" to keep their opponents from entering the church.[132]

Welcomed by evangelicals in the 1840s as an organization that could help them avoid the schisms that had occurred over church-based reform, the Sons of Temperance ultimately heightened tensions within rural mountain congregations. In 1851, the Old Fields Baptist Church in Ashe County expelled several members of the Sons of Temperance.[133] These expulsions would not have surprised most western North Carolinians. The rift between temperance and antitemperance forces had been growing since the late 1820s, empowered by the American Benevolence movement of the middle class. Rural Baptist churches in Alleghany, Alexander, Cleveland, Rutherford, and Wilkes counties soon followed the example set by the Old Fields Baptist Church and dismissed members who joined the Sons of Temperance.[134]

Although arguing that drunkenness was immoral, antitemperance churches believed that neither the church nor the state had the right to prohibit the use, sale, or manufacture of alcohol, and antebellum distillers could rely on them for support.[135] In 1857, Squire Gouge, a distiller from Buncombe County, claimed that God had given farmers "the ingredients and the smartness to make what [they] wanted." "God gin us these things to be used," Gouge continued. "Now scripter says God looked upon all he had made and said it was good, and ef so be he hadn't intended us to drink licker, he wouldn't ha' gin it to us."[136] Rural Carolina highlanders also sympathized with liquor manufacturers, pointing out that "no man is, by any means compelled to drink to excess, and that stills [were] harmless in themselves." Others labeled temperance advocates as "fanatics," "Wolves in Sheep's clothing," and "followers of false Prophets." As one member of the Asheville Sons of Temperance complained to *Spirit of the Age* in 1851, "I can assure you everything has been said of us that the *miscreant* can concoct and set in motion."[137] On at least one occasion, farmers threatened reformers with violence. In 1852, twelve armed men from the countryside, led by a deacon of a local Primitive Baptist church, disrupted a temperance rally in Taylor's Spring in the far northwestern portion of Iredell County by firing "their war-like instruments into the air" and cursing at the crowd before returning "to the nearest distillery."[138] The conflict between these two groups intensified during the 1850s with the campaign for statewide prohibition.

Prohibition and the Decline of Temperance Reform

In July 1853, J. R. Weaver from Madison County "sat in the Jury Box to try issues between the State and some of the citizens [of that county], for

Assaults and Batteries, hog stealing, & c." Reviewing the cases, Weaver, a member of the Sons of Temperance, was appalled. "In every instance," he believed, "it was proven that *Alcohol* was the prompter, except one case of hog stealing, and in that, one of the witnesses said the prisoner was '*toxicate*' when he started to the mountains, the morning he killed the hog." To make matters worse, Weaver argued that local politicians were responsible for these crimes by promoting drunkenness. "We have six Candidates for the Clerkships in Madison County; five of whom are treating with a vengeance," he wrote to *Spirit of the Age.* "They have their regular appointments over the County for the citizens to meet and drink *a treat*—they meet and drink, and fight!" Despite their efforts, the Sons and local churches had failed to defeat King Alcohol. "Legal suasion," Weaver concluded, "is the only hope for Madison."[139]

During the 1850s, the antebellum temperance movement reached its final stage with efforts to enact statewide prohibition. Like Weaver, many northern and southern reformers concluded that the government should assist their crusade. For decades, they had relied on moral suasion to combat intemperance, but to no avail. Whiskey and brandy continued to flow at militia musters and other social events. Taverns still dotted the countryside, which temperance advocates believed encouraged disorder and crime.[140] And although legislators in North Carolina and other states had labored to regulate the distribution of alcohol, they had ignored the root of the problem: the distillers who manufactured "the staff of life" into "an article of death."[141] King Alcohol, crusaders feared, controlled their General Assemblies, "forbidding [them] to pass laws of immediate and pressing importance."[142] As one Carolina highlander explained in 1853:

> Of the many Traps that are set to catch men and money, I will mention a few. The counterfeiter has his trap—the highway man, the gambler, the Abolitionist, each have theirs; but the Legislature has wisely provided for the protection of our citizens from their wiles, and for the punishment of those who may be convicted of being guilty of setting any of the above Traps—but strange to say, it has made provision for set[t]ing other Traps, which have caused the loss of more lives—the waste of more property—filled the Jails with more inmates—the penitentiary with more convicts—the poor-house with more Paupers . . . than all the Traps that have ever been set beside! I

allude to the *license* grog-shop, and the dealers in intoxicating liquors in general.[143]

Believing that local laws prohibiting the sale of alcohol near churches and schools had proved beneficial and that moral suasion had failed, northern and southern crusaders began to demand that their General Assemblies enact statewide prohibition. In 1851, reformers achieved their first victory in Maine, where legislators agreed to ban alcohol from that state.[144] Emboldened by passage of the Maine bill, the Sons of Temperance in North Carolina launched a campaign calling for statewide prohibition in 1852. Almost 3,000 highlanders, nearly a third of whom were women, joined the cause.[145] These mountain reformers signed petitions, sent letters to the General Assembly, and wrote editorials in local newspapers. They insisted that prohibition was necessary to end pauperism, crime, and moral decay.[146] The General Assembly disagreed. In 1852 and 1854, North Carolina legislators, like those in every other slave state except Delaware, decided that legal prohibition was unconstitutional because it infringed on the rights of citizens, and they castigated the reformers as being "reckless of results."[147] Concluding its report in 1854, the House committee declared that prohibition was "a species of fanaticism, which has its parallel only in the insane desire, of those, who would deprive, at one fell blow, every planter of his slaves, and turn loose upon the land, without a moment's warning, millions of human beings."[148]

Opponents of alcohol reform could not have been more pleased. In 1852, Yancey County farmers feared that prohibitionists, much like northern abolitionists, were a "minority" group "attempting to control a majority." "What good can result from any law forced on an unwilling people," they asked the General Assembly in a petition. "Majorities should govern."[149] Like Gouge and other mountain distillers, these Yancey County residents believed that prohibition would increase alcohol consumption.[150] "Pass this law," they warned, "and . . . the unhappy Ireland will soon be ours that is; that our whole country will soon be covered with illicit stills and every community filled with spies and informers."[151] For many western North Carolinians, especially those being targeted by antiliquor agitators, the Sons of Temperance became a radical group on the fringes of society. Denounced as "a society of Infidels," the Sons of Temperance, although it continued to exist, never again received the mountain support it had enjoyed in the late 1840s and early

1850s.[152] As elsewhere in the South, the forces conspiring against the Sons—antimissionism, farmers' continued dependence on distilling, and rural residents' acceptance of preindustrial drinking mores—encouraged most Carolina highlanders to reject the antialcohol crusade.

On November 22, 1855, the *Asheville News* announced that S. F. Cary, a "distinguished temperance lecturer," would deliver a series of speeches in Rutherford, Henderson, Buncombe, and Burke counties during the month of December. In times past, the *News* would have reported Cary's every move and word as he traveled throughout the region. But this year was different. The newspaper failed to give its readers even a weekly update on Cary's whereabouts. Finally, on January 17, 1856, a month after Cary visited Buncombe County, the *News* broke its silence. Issuing an apology, the editors explained that the "paper was pre-occupied with other matter[s], and our engagements prevented us from attending and hearing his [speeches]."[153]

Like other newspapers in the South, the *Asheville News* had become preoccupied with national events. The conflict between North and South over the issue of extending slavery into the territories was not subsiding. In such uncertain times, why advocate for legislation that threatened to divide white mountain society? After advising readers not to make statewide prohibition "a party test, paramount to all others," the editors of the *News* put the issue to rest, never mentioning it again.[154] Many churches also welcomed the end of prohibition agitation. To weather the storm ahead, southern Baptists and Methodists believed that they needed to appear united and avoid issues that had disrupted their congregations for decades. Their efforts were largely a failure as congregations remained divided along class, geographic, and theological lines that the temperance movement had helped create.[155]

The cultural values of western North Carolinians also conspired against alcohol reformers during the antebellum period. As in other parts of the South, the mountain region remained predominantly rural, and farmers continued to adhere to a preindustrial ideology that tolerated alcohol consumption both during and after work. Businessmen and professionals might have been held in high regard among townspeople, but they were not yet a culturally influential force in rural mountain society. Reformers would have to wait until the late nineteenth century, when the region began to feel the full impact of industrialization and urbanization, before they could gain the support of rural communities on this issue.

Part II

The Golden Age of Moonshining, 1861–1876

3

"Is There Any Way to Get at the Distillers?"

The Fall and Rise of the Moonshiners, 1861–1868

There was an old Mountaineer
Who loved his Moon Shine dear.
He spent night and day
Thinking of a way,
To improve his Moon Shine still.

On March 18, 1862, a group of angry women, armed with axes, marched through the streets of Newton in Catawba County, North Carolina, determined to do something to rid their town of the influence of alcohol. They were headed toward the train deport, where local distillers had brought large quantities of homemade whiskey. Two weeks earlier, these "Ladies of Catawba" had demanded that the distillers stop manufacturing alcohol, arguing that it deprived the poor of corn. Those distillers now sat astride their barrels of liquor and faced an angry mob. Some of them tried to diffuse the situation by pointing out that they had an inalienable right to manufacture alcohol. But the women were unmoved. "While you are crying, 'law,'" one woman responded, "our little ones will cry, 'bread'—'bread.'" As the women began hacking the barrels, the whiskey poured onto the ground. When the dust had settled, the Ladies of Catawba, standing ankle-deep in alcohol, raised their hands in celebration.[1]

During the Civil War, the temperance movement, already slowed by the secession crisis, reached a nadir in membership and activity throughout the United States. With attention diverted elsewhere, the issue of alcohol reform no longer garnered the support and publicity it had once enjoyed. In fact, by 1865, only five of the fourteen northern states that had passed statewide prohibition during the 1850s retained those laws. The national government further undercut temperance efforts by passing the 1862 Internal Revenue Act. This measure, enacted to raise money for the war, required that alcohol vendors purchase a federal license, placed a tax on liquor distillers, and created the Bureau of Internal Revenue to enforce these new regulations. Many temperance advocates denounced the legislation, arguing that it restored legitimacy to the alcohol trade and made the United States dependent on liquor sales for revenue.[2]

Despite these setbacks, the South witnessed a renewed interest in large-scale prohibitory legislation during the Civil War. Faced with serious food shortages, nine Confederate states, including North Carolina, implemented wartime bans on the production of alcohol for nonmedicinal purposes. These measures gained the approval of southerners suffering from the economic devastation of war.[3] In western North Carolina, many rural residents had begun to resent the distillers, who used corn and fruit to make liquor rather than to feed their hungry neighbors, and to the delight of the Ladies of Catawba and other urban reformers, these rural residents embraced the state government's prohibition on alcohol manufacturing as an economic necessity.

Widespread support for prohibition, however, declined in the South following the Civil War. As food became more available, many Carolina highlanders protested attempts by temperance advocates to reinstate the statewide ban on alcohol manufacturing. The reputations of distillers also improved as opposition to the Bureau of Internal Revenue intensified across the South. Most white southerners believed that the national government was using this agency and the "infernal" alcohol tax to expand its authority. In western North Carolina and other parts of the South, these men and women increasingly joined forces with distillers in their fight against federal liquor law enforcement. The golden age of moonshining had begun.

Civil War Liquor Distillation and Prohibition

When North Carolina seceded from the Union on May 20, 1861, most mountain residents embraced the Confederate cause. Many of them had longed for this day. "You ought to hear us girls talk about fighting," Amelia Gwyn of McDowell County told her sister that April.

"I believe we have all concluded to fight to the last and die before we'll give up to a Yankee."[4] Most were ready to fight and die for the Confederacy. "Death or victory is our motto," Ashe County denizen James Gentry informed his father-in-law in May 1861.[5] Encouraged by their mothers and wives, young men eagerly enlisted in the Confederate army or the state militia, believing that the conflict would not last long. "I have not brought myself to believe that there will be much fighting," Caldwell County resident Edmund Jones wrote in May. "The courage of the North will evaporate after awhile, and the Southern States permitted to go in peace."[6]

This optimism would soon give way to harsh reality. Food shortages, largely due to the departure of males for military service, and rising prices resulted in economic hardship for most Carolina highlanders during the Civil War. As early as October 1861, Jackson County resident Elizabeth Watson complained: "Times in our county is hard for the poor class of people for every thing is giting so deer that they cant by hardly a noughf to live on. Salt is from nine to ten dollars a sack her and evry other thing in proportion. Thier is good crops in our county I think corn can be bought at 50 cts. all through the winter and now the people is . . . halling off thier meet. I don't now how we will git our nessaryes for money is scarce here."[7]

By 1862, the problems that Watson described—food and cash shortages, speculation, and disruption of the market economy—became widespread in western North Carolina. That December, a Waynesville woman complained to her aunt: "When the war broke out all I thought about was our friends going off & getting killed. I did not think about the small pox and evry kind of disease getting all over the country, and people starving to death and all that. . . . As I heard an old woman say the other day, 'seems like this country is might nigh tore up!'"[8] Others wrote to Governor Zebulon B. Vance, begging for economic relief. Many of them echoed the sentiments of Burke County resident Robert L. Abernethy, who in November 1862 implored Vance: "If it is Constitutional, and if your position as Governor of N. Carolina gives you the power to do so, in the name of God, of suffering humanity, of the cries of widows and orphans, do put down the Speculation and extortion in this part of the State."[9]

State and local officials scrambled to meet the growing needs of the poor. Governor Vance issued several proclamations forbidding the interstate trade of made food and domestic goods in an attempt

Zebulon B. Vance. From John Preston Arthur, *Western North Carolina: A History* (Raleigh: Edwards and Broughton Printing Company, 1914), facing 628.

to reduce speculation and conserve scarce items. In December 1862, the state legislature passed "An Act for the Purchase of Provisions," which appropriated $400,000 to buy corn and other provisions to feed the poor. By the spring of 1863, several mountain counties, like those elsewhere in North Carolina, had appointed commissioners and sub-commissioners to oversee the distribution of these funds to indigent residents.[10] Local elites also lent a helping hand by giving donations and lowering rents. Caldwell County landlord Joseph C. Norwood, for instance, noted in the fall of 1863: "The women begged to retain their rent, expecting to get it at a low rate. I thought it was best to give it to them, as a low price in Confedte money woult amt. to nothing—& we find it necessary here to be very liberal with the soldier's families."[11]

Another popular option for reducing economic distress was to curtail the distillation of alcohol. By 1862, many mountain residents, like others throughout the state, had begun to pressure government officials to suppress liquor manufacturing because they believed it contributed to food shortages. In February, Wilkes County denizen James Gwyn charged that distilling was one of the leading causes of "the great scarcity of corn" in the region.[12] One month later, Catawba County residents complained that alcohol manufacturing not only hurt the poor but also threatened to destroy the Confederacy. "Stop the stills, or ruin is our certain doom," they demanded. "We must make our bread, or perish for the want of it. A bountiful Providence has given us enough for man and beast; but distillers have already converted so much corn into poison, that prices look like famine ahead."[13] Many mountain churches reinstated their no-tolerance policies. In the spring of 1862, for instance, the King's Mountain Baptist Association voted once again to expel any member who distilled spirits.[14]

On February 21, 1862, North Carolina legislators unanimously passed the state's first tax on alcohol manufacturing, hoping to force distillers to cut back on production. Regardless of the size of their stills, alcohol makers now had to pay a tax of 30¢ on each gallon of liquor they produced. Careful not to overstep its legal authority and provoke cries of governmental oppression, the General Assembly made sure that local communities retained a degree of autonomy. On May 2, it enacted an ordinance that gave sheriffs the power to enforce and collect the tax. Before operating their stills, alcohol makers had to sign an oath to the sheriff that specified the quantity of alcohol they planned to manufacture. Upon conviction by local juries, violators of the ordinance had to pay a double tax and additional fines, the amounts determined by the county court judge.[15]

This tax, however, did little to satisfy alcohol opponents, especially the Sons of Temperance. Although it had lost support during the late 1850s, the order capitalized on the economic stresses of the war to resume its fight against King Alcohol. In 1861, reformers throughout the state worked to disassociate the Sons from its northern roots, publicly embracing the Confederacy and assuring worried citizens that they were doing everything possible to aid the cause. "Nearly all of our officers have laid aside their badges and put on soldier's uniform," the Swannanoa Sons of Temperance in Buncombe County proclaimed that June. "[They] have left their pens to corrode in the ink till they would dip their swords in tyrants' blood to write freedom for the sunny South."[16] The Sons attempted to use the conflict to its advantage by linking Confederate victory with alcohol reform. The *Spirit of the Age* claimed in 1862: "The whole Southern Confederacy is sustaining heavier damage from whiskey, than will ever be inflicted by the whole northern army, who come to subjugate and enslave us."[17]

The Sons of Temperance dismissed the proposed state liquor tax and launched a campaign against it. "We fear, nay, we know," Alexander Gorman, editor of *Spirit of the Age,* explained two weeks before state legislators enacted the tax, "that the love of money is so strong in the minds of many men, that they will disregard the most wholesome admonitions of the press, the pulpit, and betray their country to destruction for filthy lucre." According to Gorman, the state liquor tax was a compromise, one that "will be found futile and fail to accomplish the end designed." He emphatically believed that the General Assembly needed to prohibit liquor manufacturing in order to stop the "absolute destitution and suffering" of the poor and aid the Confederacy in its fight for independence. Prohibition, Gorman insisted, "is emphatically 'a military necessity,' because unless some relief of the kind is afforded, our soldiers, and those who are dearer to them than life itself—their families at home—must suffer for the necessaries of life."[18] Many mountain Confederates, especially those living in economically depressed areas, would find these arguments for prohibition appealing.

State legislators responded to the demands of their constituents. On December 7, 1862, the General Assembly passed a law that prohibited the distillation of corn and other crops into liquor until the conclusion of the Civil War.[19] Although taverns could remain open and residents could still consume alcohol, North Carolina distillers were shut out. Like the state liquor tax, county officials enforced the prohibition ordinance, thereby allowing local communities to retain control of alcohol production. Penalties were severe: a $100 fine or thirty days in prison.[20] Although state legislators passed the law for economic rather than moral reasons, Gorman and other antebellum reformers would have counted it as a victory. Never before had the state imposed such stringent ordinances against those who distilled alcohol.

Food shortages and subsequent rising prices continued to plague the region through the next year. In February 1863, Rutherford County resident E. D. Hawkins complained that corn could "hardly be had at all." "Grain," he lamented, "is badly needed for the support of the wives and children of the soldiers who are in the field."[21] According to one study on inflation in the mountain region, "the price of eggs increased 1666%, . . . bacon 2272%, flour 2777%, . . . and corn and potatoes shot up 3000%."[22] The extraordinary cost of these essential items made it difficult for most highlanders to survive. The threat of starvation became quite real in many sections of western North Carolina. In a letter to Governor Vance in November 1863, Henderson

County resident Maryann Arrowood pleaded, "Thare will have to be something don for us or we will all perish to death."[23]

Mountain residents increasingly blamed alcohol manufacturing for draining the food supply and embraced prohibition as an economic necessity. These men and women, many of whom were poor and resided in the countryside, had lost their sympathy for distillers and no longer viewed them as legitimate entrepreneurs. In February 1863, Hawkins chastised Rutherford County whiskey makers for continuing to deprive the local community of grain.[24] J. F. Eller also noted that several Wilkes County farmers were defying the prohibition law. "These men have so far went unmolested," he complained, "and are getting rich selling whiskey at $3 per quart, while they are also raising the price of corn so that if the poor class could obtain any they are not able to follow the prices."[25] Two months later, Wilkes County farmer T. J. Bicknell denounced distillers as "greedy" men and "lowdown females" who were "not responsible for any thing." He then asked Governor Vance to add an amendment to the prohibition law that would fine farmers who sold their corn to distillers.[26] These protests against alcohol manufacturing continued until the end of the Civil War.[27]

Mountain residents might not have wanted distillers to use local crops for liquor, but they still needed a supply of it for household uses. Like other Americans, highlanders relied on alcohol to cure colds, consumption, snakebites, and other ailments. As the war progressed, the Richmond government desperately needed whiskey to treat Confederate soldiers wounded in battle. Although North Carolina's prohibition created a shortage of medicinal alcohol, many mountain residents were hesitant to distill it, suggesting that most had accepted the law. Even with the blessing of the local community, men often sought permission from state authorities before making alcohol. Mountain farmers and physicians in Rutherford, Cherokee, Jackson, and Burke counties asked Governor Vance to allow them to distill whiskey. "We can not get any kind of spirits here for medical purposes," doctors J. A. Goode and J. W. Harris from Rutherford County explained in March 1863, "but [we] can get it done if you will give [us] a permit to do so." One month later, Goode and Harris wrote to the governor again, pointing out that "not one drop [of the alcohol] will be used as a beverage."[28] Although they wanted to distill and use alcohol for legitimate reasons, these men were unwilling to do so without the approval of state authorities.

Convincing Governor Vance was likely a difficult task. The Buncombe County native was fully aware of the economic difficulties highlanders faced and was a fervent supporter of the antidistilling law. This position was not popular with the Confederate government, especially Secretary of War James A. Seddon. In 1863, the War Department began to operate distilleries in North Carolina to alleviate the shortage of medicinal alcohol. This policy sparked a states' rights battle between Vance and Seddon.[29] That December, upon learning that the Richmond government was attempting to use tax-in-kind grain to manufacture liquor in Salisbury, Vance lashed out at Seddon and the War Department. He pointed out that North Carolina law "positively forbid[s] the distillation of any kind of grain within its borders under heavy penalties" and threatened to arrest the operators of the still. "It seems to me," he wrote to Seddon, "if spirits are so absolutely requisite for the Medical Department, that grain sufficient might be found in remote and plentiful districts, and leave for the use of the people every grain which is accessible. Be this as it may, I am sure you will agree with me in saying that no person can under authority of the Confederate Government violate State laws with impunity."[30]

Seddon moved the distillery out of the state but continued to hire North Carolinians to run the Confederacy's stills, arguing that the Richmond government had the constitutional authority to "raise and support armies." In 1864, Seddon reminded Vance that Confederate attorney general S. H. Rogers had ruled that "a State has no power to interfere with the Confederate government in the manufacture or even contracting for such supplies."[31] The conflict climaxed in February 1865, when the War Department employed several Burke County farmers to make whiskey. An outraged Vance threatened to use the state militia to uphold the prohibition law and protect the region's food supply. "Knowing as I do the wants of the community whose interest is there to be effected," Vance concluded, "I must earnestly insist that if such permission has been granted [which it had been] that it be immediately revoked."[32]

Mountain residents who received a Confederate contract were reluctant to manufacture alcohol without receiving the consent of state authorities. In April 1863, Mitchell County distiller A. D. Childs received a Confederate contract to distill 2,000 gallons of rye whiskey. Before starting the first batch, he explained to Governor Vance that the rye was "so much injured in the stocks that it cant be Eaten for Bread

& only useful for stock Whisky." Childs remained hesitant to break the prohibition law—even for the good of the Confederate cause—because he believed that most members of the local community supported it.[33] Nearly two years later, in January 1865, James Sloan considered resigning as "Chief Commissary" if Richmond officials ordered him to allow "certain parties in the western counties of the state" to distill alcohol. "I most respectfully request that you advise me what course I should follow," he wrote to Vance. "Shall I resign my position as Chief Commissary, or shall I obey orders which are repugnant to my better judgment and injurious alike to the best interest of the State and Confederate Governments?"[34] The following month, many Burke County residents were appalled when the War Department hired several local farmers to distill whiskey. Though they feared starvation, they had not lost their commitment to the cause. The community had sent its young men off to battle and now needed to provide for their families: "We respectfully protest against this for the reason, that grain is very scarce in this community and the families of soldiers and the poor & needy will require all the surplus which can be spared from the army, for their maintenance and support."[35]

There were some Carolina highlanders who refused to comply with the state's prohibitory law. These illicit distillers, who would become known as moonshiners in the 1870s, continued to argue that they had the right to make a living unmolested by the state government and declined to adhere to the local community's new standards. In February 1863, Cleveland County distiller Jesse M. Scruggs, when confronted by his brother-in-law, defended his actions. "Hit is," he said, "no harm for no won to make money when tha can if . . . whiskey is selling for the most profit of every thing."[36] Like Scruggs, other mountain farmers broke the law because distilling remained a profitable enterprise. In 1863, for instance, a Wilkes County farmer could earn a $2 profit if he distilled his corn into five gallons of alcohol.[37] The law merely added to the cost, and merchants quickly took advantage of the lucrative illegal trade. In February 1863, Macon County resident Alfred W. Bell reported that H. W. Nolen, a Massachusetts native who had migrated to the region just before the war, was transporting "some 2 or 3 hundred bushels of dried fruit across state lines into Ga. to be distilled into brandy."[38] Illicit distillers found various ways to market their product. Although most of them continued to sell it to neighbors, some farmers may have found buyers outside the region, where the price of alcohol was sometimes higher.[39] Others discovered that Confederate soldiers stationed in the Carolina highlands were eager to buy alcohol from them. This sometimes led to violence among troops and intensified the local community's disapproval of illicit distilling. According to Robert L. Abernethy in February 1863, soldiers in Burke County were "frequently breaking open granaries, drinking . . . insulting citizens, and making themselves a terror to the whole population."[40] Nine months later, complaining about the drunken behavior of several members of the Fifty-Sixth North Carolina Regiment in Wilkes County, Calvin Cowles wrote to Vance: "There is too much Brandy in the county for them and not enough corn."[41]

The resentment engendered by this black market distilling further strained community and kinship ties. Struggling to feed their families, mountain residents often assisted state and county law enforcement officials. In February 1863, E. D. Hawkins asked Governor Vance to arrest his brother-in-law, Jesse Scruggs. "I dont rite this to you because I have any harm at the man at all for he is my brother in law," he wrote. "[But] thare is families that cant git bread to eat hardly and he is not [caring] for hit."[42] One month later, Wilkes County residents published the names of their neighbors who refused to stop distilling and demanded that the state government prosecute these men to the fullest extent of the law.[43] In April 1864, James Simmons and several home guardsmen seized fifteen illegal stills in Rutherford County but were unable to apprehend the perpetrators, who had fled to South Carolina. "I ernistly pray . . . that we may have the right to take all the Stills we can find in operation and put them under lock," he explained to Vance. "Unless that is dun . . . tha [moonshiners] will still not respecting the Law nor the wants of the poor."[44] Later that same year, E. R. Norton of Horse Cove in Transylvania County confiscated a still and some fixtures hidden in a hollow tree from a South Carolina moonshiner.[45]

Although the majority had initially been willing to abide by the ban on distilling, the impending northern victory led many highlanders to fire up their stills again. By 1865, officials noted the resurgence of locally made liquor. In Surry County, one official reported that a farmer had "offered a certain number of gallons of 'Nick Williams' *new* whiskey in trade for a negro."[46] The four years of war had unraveled community ties, dividing mountain residents along political, racial, and class lines. The market for alcohol grew as civilian morale declined, making it hard for some farmers to resist the temptation to capitalize on the opportunity for profit. Conversely, the state could no longer count on the weary public to unify behind the antidistilling cause.[47]

The success of statewide prohibition against distilling was short-lived, but it gave reformers hope. The Civil War experience demonstrated that government officials could limit and control illegal distillation when local communities deemed it necessary. As Governor Vance remembered in 1886, most western North Carolinians complied with the prohibition policy during the Civil War. "'Old Rye' grew to be worth its weight in silver, and 'Mountain Dew' became as the nectar of the gods," Vance bragged. "Yet, true to their character as the most law abiding people on the continent, all respected the act of Assembly."[48] These Carolina highlanders, most of whom were poor and resided in the countryside, denounced distillers not necessarily because they disapproved of alcohol consumption but because its production was a threat to the community's food supply. The General Assembly also encouraged compliance with prohibition by allowing local communities to enforce it. Economic circumstances had temporarily brought rural residents to the side of middle-class reformers and turned the public against local distillers. The prohibition movement learned from this experience and, over the next four decades, would shift its focus from the dangers of King Alcohol to the men who made it.

Post–Civil War Reactions to State Liquor Taxation and Prohibition

Like the rest of the South, western North Carolinians struggled to rebuild their shattered communities following the Civil War. Soldiers returned home to find their fields fallow, their families starving, and their bills unpaid. Most of them quickly discovered that the poverty of wartime could not be quickly remedied. Food scarcities and speculation continued to plague the region. The depreciation of state bonds and labor shortages exacerbated the situation by forcing mountain residents to depend on an inflationary open market to buy food.[49] To make matters worse, violence stemming from wartime personal vendettas continued in many mountain counties long after the Confederate defeat in April 1865.[50] Survival was on everyone's mind. "What a humiliated and degraded people we are," William Tate, a prominent planter, businessman, and former slaveholder from Morganton, wrote to his daughter in August 1865. "It is as much as I can do to get enough for us to eat. We are living from hand to mouth."[51]

Since the ban on manufacturing liquor had ended with the Confederate defeat, state legislators quickly returned to the debate over regulating its production. On October 18, 1865, the General Assembly unanimously agreed to reinstate a tax on alcohol manufacturing, hoping once again that this would increase the food supply by forcing distillers to cut back on production. Regardless of the size of their stills, liquor manufacturers now had to pay a 25¢ tax on each gallon of alcohol they produced. Like its predecessor during the Civil War, the new state liquor tax left the local community in control of alcohol production, which helps explain its popularity among many mountain residents. The law required distillers to obtain a license from the clerk of the county court and pay the tax to the local sheriff, who had the authority to arrest violators. Upon conviction in county court, distillers were fined $10 for every day they had unlawfully manufactured alcohol. If the moonshiner refused to cooperate, the sheriff could confiscate the still, fixtures, and "any other personal property" of the distiller.[52]

Temperance activists continued to be the most ardent supporters of alcohol regulation, and they believed state taxation would raise the price of liquor and thus reduce consumption. This was of the utmost importance, because they also feared that alcoholism had increased throughout the state. According to the North Carolina Methodist Conference in 1866, four years of war had ruined "the morals and piety of the land." "Many old men pressed with their increased burdens have sought relief in the insensibility of drunkenness," the conference's Committee on Temperance complained, "while the young men, amid the strange associations incident to disrupted society, have formed habits of dissipation ruinous to their usefulness and the good of society."[53] Although it is impossible to confirm this claim, it seems possible that veterans—Union and Confederate alike—began to drink heavily to forget the trauma of battle.

The demand for temperance reform remained strongest in county seats, where residents noted an increase in binge drinking and criminal activity. In February 1866, residents of Franklin in Macon County protested distiller D. A. McConnell's decision to convert his new home into a tavern. They requested that William Holland Thomas, who had sold the house to McConnell, revoke the contract: "Now Col. [Thomas], you know what a blight it is on any civil community to have such an establishment among them . . . where our children would be constantly in contact with all the incivilities and obscene and degrading language so often practiced at such an establishment."[54] One month later, residents in Lenoir petitioned the General Assembly to enact a law prohibiting retailers from selling liquor within corporate limits. "We are impelled to petition for this amendment," they wrote, "because . . . vicious persons . . . [are] making our village the scene of brawling and drunkenness."[55] Many of these Lenoir reformers soon joined the Friends of Temperance, a reform society founded in Virginia in 1865. Largely due to its southern origins, this organization quickly became more popular than the Sons of Temperance, which, despite its best efforts, remained associated with northern abolitionists and disbanded in North Carolina shortly after the Civil War. Like the Sons, however, most Friends of Temperance lodges were located in county seats, suggesting that the temperance movement remained a largely urban phenomenon in western North Carolina.[56]

But community support for state liquor taxation proved fleeting. Many reformers and other North Carolinians increasingly believed that the tax had neither curtailed liquor manufacturing nor reduced drunkenness. As early as December 1865, the *Raleigh Sentinel* complained that alcohol distillers continued to consume a "very large quantity of grain" and sell their product to neighbors. The following month, the *Sentinel* argued that the only effective solution was a return to a statewide ban on manufacturing. "The Legislature can attain no higher position," the editors declared, "than when it rises above the clamors of personal interest, to guard society against a positive evil, and to protect the masses of the people from absolute want suffering." This would not only stabilize the food supply, the paper argued, but also reduce alcoholism. "The moral aspects of this question are alarming," it concluded. "One half or one third of this whiskey, instead of being eaten up in the form of bread by our people, will be drank by them, until many are made drunkards." In the eyes of the *Sentinel*, alcohol distilling remained an "evil," and state liquor taxation had failed to curtail it.[57]

In late January 1866, the General Assembly debated the passage of a bill outlawing alcohol manufacturing in North Carolina. But in the three years since passage of the first legislation, the antidistiller movement had lost unified support. In fact, many mountain residents actively opposed the bill. Representatives of the region's top four ante-bellum whiskey-producing counties (Surry, Burke, Wilkes, and Ashe) rejected prohibition because they feared its impact on both their reputations and an important local industry (see table 1.2). Legislators in Cherokee, Macon, Jackson, and Haywood counties also protested against the bill, and for good reason. Farmers in these more remote counties continued to find transportation to markets difficult. Many of them had resumed the practice of distilling alcohol after the Civil War, and they pressured their representatives to reject the bill. On February 7, 1866, the North Carolina Senate voted against prohibition.[58]

The following month, still facing a statewide food shortage, legislators, led by western North Carolinian Leander S. Gash, proposed doubling the taxes on both domestic and imported liquor.[59] Perhaps to his surprise, Gash received little support from his colleagues. In fact, the strong opposition of representatives of mountain districts helped secure the bill's defeat.[60] What had changed in the five months since the unanimous approval of the first liquor tax legislation? By 1866, food was becoming more available, and many Carolina highlanders had begun to tolerate alcohol distilling. Even churches relaxed their stance on liquor manufacturing. That spring, for instance, the King's Mountain Baptist Association overturned its 1859 and 1862 resolutions prohibiting members from distilling alcohol. Congregants likely believed that distilling would allow them to make extra money, and they pressured the association to change its policy.[61] Gash's proposed bill also garnered support for alcohol producers by reigniting intrastate sectional tensions. According to Gash in March 1867, mountain politicians had opposed the tax increase because it placed an "unequal" financial burden on their constituents. Because they believed that western North Carolina had more stills than other parts of the state, these men demanded that the General Assembly find an alternative way to raise revenue and augment food supplies.[62]

Many Carolina highlanders continued to support the original excise tax of 25¢ per gallon for two reasons. First, this tax did not significantly reduce the distiller's profit margin. By 1866, the price of a bushel of corn had dropped to $1.50, while a gallon of whiskey retailed at $3.00. Even with the tax, a farmer distilling five gallons of whiskey could earn a profit of $10.75.[63] Perhaps more importantly, the General Assembly allowed the local community to retain control of alcohol production. Sheriffs and other county officials enforced the state liquor tax, thereby reducing cries of governmental oppression. Federal liquor taxation, however, proved to be a different story.

The Administrative Structure of the Bureau of Internal Revenue

During the Civil War, the U.S. Congress levied duties on liquor, tobacco, and other "luxuries" to raise revenue. The Tax Act of 1862 established the Office of the Commissioner of Internal Revenue (commonly known as the Bureau of Internal Revenue) and divided each Union state into several collection districts.[64] The commissioner of internal revenue, a political appointee who headed the bureau, supervised hundreds of federal workers. A collector headed each district and appointed assessors to monitor output and determine the taxes of distilleries and inspectors to ensure compliance with the law. In 1863, the bureau began to hire additional internal revenue agents (or revenuers) to aid collectors in the North and Midwest.[65]

Northern congressmen initially believed that liquor taxation was an effective and "painless" way to raise revenue for the Union war effort. According to Rep. Justin Morrill of Vermont in March 1862, "a tax dependent upon the habits or vices of men is the most reliable of all taxes, as it takes centuries to change or eradicate one or the other."[66] Nor did Morrill and other legislators anticipate widespread resistance to the liquor law. "There is a considerable quantity of apple and peach brandy or whiskey manufactured in the State of New Jersey," Representative Stratton declared, "and neither the Representatives of that State nor the people of that State are disposed to ask that they shall be relieved from the payment of their fair share of the taxes necessary for the support of the Government."[67] Congressmen from the Midwest, however, whose constituents produced the Union's largest corn crops, rejected the proposed annual tax of $100 on each distillery because they feared it would drive small producers out of business. Led by Illinois Republican William Kellogg, these legislators convinced Congress to levy a liquor tax of 60¢ per gallon on all alcohol manufacturers instead.[68]

It appeared that northern distillers and their clientele were, as Morrill had predicted, "patriotic on the subject of taxation, and [would] never quarrel about the price of the article."[69] In 1864, the liquor tax generated $28,431,797.83 in revenue, and Commissioner of Internal

Revenue Joseph Lewis reported minimal resistance to the law. At the end of 1864, the U.S. Congress, hoping to accumulate more revenue, raised the tax from 60¢ to $2 a gallon.[70] Midwesterners were livid, arguing that the new duty was "unfair" to small farmers who relied on their distilleries for extra income. Ohio Democrat S. S. Cox complained: "New England manufacturers are getting richer every day. They . . . are becoming the owners of this country. . . . They are getting all the protection of the Government. . . . I claim for the farmers of the West, in absolute self-defense, some little regard."[71] By 1865, illicit distillers in Brooklyn, New York, and cities in New England joined the voices of dissent and refused to pay the levy.[72] Commissioner Lewis noted in 1866: "Great numbers of small stills, for the illicit manufacture of rum for molasses, were secreted in the garrets and cellars of the most populous cities, while many of the recognized and licensed distilleries were run by night, their proprietors keeping fraudulent accounts of their consumption of grain and other vegetable substances, and their production of spirits and the sale or removal thereof to bonded warehouses." To the dismay of congressmen, revenues dropped from more than $28 million in 1864 to $15,995,701.66 in 1865, as high taxes encouraged evasion.[73]

In the summer of 1865, Congress divided each former Confederate state into several collection districts. In North Carolina, the mountain counties fell in the Sixth and Seventh Collection Districts.[74] Over the next three years, congressmen, faced with enforcing the law throughout the reunified nation, created additional positions in the Bureau of Internal Revenue.[75] The Tax Act of 1868 further systemized the inspection of distillers by introducing gaugers, who tested and recorded "the amount and proof of each barrel of liquor distilled," and storekeepers, who "measured and recorded other phases of the distillery's production."[76]

Unlike the previous Confederate legislation, the Bureau of Internal Revenue relied heavily on federal officials to enforce the liquor law at the local level. Many white southerners detested these district attorneys, marshals, and soldiers, many of whom were former Unionists. District attorneys often faced ostracism, physical danger, and hostile juries as they prosecuted illicit distillers and retailers in the federal courts. Marshals, who arrested the violators, confronted similar obstacles and lacked funds to compensate deputies or informers. Until 1878, district attorneys and marshals could request federal troops to assist them in the capture of illegal stills and moonshiners. Southern-ers resented these tactics, especially the use of the military, calling it "bayonet rule."[77] Underpaid and overworked, these officials faced the daunting task of enforcing the federal liquor tax in an increasingly pro-distiller and anti–federal government South.

Beginnings of Moonshiner Resistance

When North Carolina reentered the Union at the end of the war, Presi-dent Andrew Johnson halfheartedly attempted to implement federal liquor law enforcement in the South.[78] The Bureau of Internal Rev-enue, lacking the manpower and the full support of Johnson, struggled to enforce liquor taxation throughout the South during Presidential Reconstruction. In 1866, Commissioner Lewis reported that agents had collected $25,654.67 from North Carolina distillers.[79] Compared with tax receipts during the remainder of the 1860s, that number was exceedingly low (see table 3.1). In March 1867, however, Congress passed the first Reconstruction Act, which divided the still recalci-trant South into twelve military districts.[80] As the military commanders restored political order, they were finally able to turn their attention to the moonshiners.

This new attention often took distillers by surprise. As Mitchell County farmer Zack McHone recalled: "I got married in '67 . . . and I got to studying how to get hold of some money. Hit seemed like stillin' would be about the best I could, so I rigged me out an outfit. I didn't think I was breakin' the law because there wa'n't no law. . . . Then after awhile talk riz about a Revenue and sure enough they come on me,

Table 3.1. Liquor Tax Revenue Collected by the Bureau of Internal Revenue in North Carolina, 1866–1869

Year	Revenue Collected ($)
1866	25,654.67
1867	172,255.34
1868	225,632.13
1869	180,519.36

Sources: Annual Report of the Commissioner of Internal Revenue, 1866–1867, 39th Cong., 2nd sess., 28; ibid., *1867–1868*, 40th Cong., 2nd sess., 81; ibid., *1868*, 40th Cong., 2nd sess., 69; ibid., *1870*, 41st Cong., 3rd sess., 40.

just as I was workin' in a place I'd picked below the house, and carried me down to Raleigh to be tried."[81] Revenuers had arrived in western North Carolina, but they quickly discovered that they faced a formidable opponent.[82]

Just over two months after passage of the first Reconstruction Act, Seventh Collection District collector J. B. Weaver reported that moonshiners had threatened him and other revenuers with violence.[83] Another frustrated revenuer in Wilkes County wrote to the Second Military District headquarters: "Is there any way to get at the distillers?"[84] In late April, newly appointed Commissioner of Internal Revenue E. A. Rollins requested federal troops be sent to protect and aid revenue agents enforcing the liquor law in the region.[85] Maj. Gen. Daniel E. Sickles, commander of the Second Military District, deployed a company of the Fifth U.S. Cavalry Regiment, stationed in Morganton, to the counties west of the Blue Ridge. Shortly thereafter, he permitted bureau agents to carry firearms when conducting raids.[86]

Many local residents, believing that distilling was essential to mountain economies, often joined the moonshiners' cause, further impeding the progress of federal liquor law enforcement. In May 1867, J. B. Weaver complained that he could not hire anyone in Caldwell County to collect the liquor tax. "The disposition of the community was such that I could not find any person willing to accept the position of distraining officer," he wrote to Rollins.[87] That same month, the *New York Times* reported that moonshiners enjoyed a broad base of support in western North Carolina. According to its editors, even when distillers were captured, agents found it nearly impossible to find residents willing to indict or convict them. "The officers of the Internal Revenue service are frequently treated with disrespect," the *Times* noted, "and when offenders are prosecuted in the civil Courts and violations of the internal revenue laws indisputably proved, juries fail to convict the parties."[88]

From the beginning, mountain residents—even those who did not manufacture alcohol—challenged the legitimacy of the Bureau of Internal Revenue. These Carolina highlanders insisted that the federal liquor tax (which remained at $2 a gallon) placed a heavy burden on small producers. This was a valid complaint. In 1867, a bushel of corn sold for $1 and whiskey retailed at $3 a gallon. Without paying a tax, mountain farmers who manufactured two bushels of corn into five gallons of alcohol earned a $13 profit, whereas legal distillers netted only

$5.[89] Farmers who ran small distilling operations argued that they simply could not afford to pay the tax. "We venture to say there will be but few distilleries continued in this State," the *Hendersonville Pioneer* reported in May 1867, predicting that liquor taxation would drive small farmers out of the distilling business.[90]

Other western North Carolinians embraced the moonshiners' fight against the Bureau of Internal Revenue because they saw federal liquor law enforcement as an attack on local autonomy. The U.S. government, rather than local and regional agencies, was now driving policy on the distillation of alcohol in their communities. This resistance was not an isolated historical development. When the federal government levied taxes on imported and domestically manufactured alcohol in 1791 and 1814, mountain residents vehemently opposed these duties and ignored the law. Because of this resistance, the federal government retreated from its first attempt to collect the liquor tax.[91] The Confederate tax-in-kind (or tithe tax) also left a bitter taste in the mouths of many highlanders. Levied in 1863, this "national" tax required farmers to give 10 percent of their produce to Confederate authorities. Many farmers denounced the Confederate tax-in-kind because they believed it placed too heavy a burden on food surpluses. Mountain resistance intensified when Confederate authorities used force to collect it. Several farmers armed themselves and attacked tax collectors, while others agreed not to support any politician who endorsed this tax. Mountain whites would remain suspicious of any new direct tax imposed by the national government and continue their tradition of active opposition.[92]

Revenuers' history of Unionism did not help their cause with the mountain populace. Wartime Unionism was often a prerequisite for southerners hired by the Bureau of Internal Revenue. A revenuer in North Carolina's Seventh Collection District, William Dedman, had edited a Unionist newspaper, the *Hendersonville Times,* during the Civil War.[93] Sixth Collection District agent Jesse Wheeler had to relocate from North Carolina to Indiana after he circulated copies of Hinton Rowan Helper's subversive antislavery tract *The Impending Crisis of the South* in 1859.[94] Agents also angered Confederate sympathizers by protesting the hiring of men of questionable Union loyalty. After being removed as assessor in North Carolina's Sixth Collection District, Hardie Hogan Helper, the brother of Hinton, was furious because "he, a good and reliable union man" had been fired, insinuating that his replacement, W. J. Henderson, was not.[95] Former Confederates quickly developed a deep hatred for revenue agents, whom they labeled as Unionists and purveyors of radical change in the post–Civil War South.

The federal government received some support from residents, both urban and rural, who continued to blame distillers for food shortages and price inflation.[96] E. A. Rollins wrote to Major General Sickles in April 1867: "There is every reason to believe that if the illicit distilleries are closed those parties now holding the grain will put it upon the market at such prices as will bring it within the reach of many who are now suffering for want of bread."[97] Sickles concurred. On May 20, 1867, he issued General Order Number 25, which prohibited residents in the Second Military District from converting their grain into alcohol. This order remained in effect until January 1868 and drastically enhanced the federal government's authority to combat distilling. Alcohol manufacturers, who had often relied on local juries to acquit them, were now tried before a military tribunal.[98]

Most support for General Order Number 25 came from residents in mountain communities where moonshining continued to diminish food supplies. In September 1867, several Polk County farmers testified against moonshiner John Huntzinger, who was subsequently fined $100 and sentenced to four months in prison by the commanding officer at Morganton, Bvt. Col. William Bedford Royall. Three months later, Wilkes County residents informed military officials that William Aiken was distilling corn into whiskey.[99] The cooperation of these mountain residents helped make General Order Number 25 a success. According to newly appointed Second Military District commander Edward R. S. Canby in September, this decree had forced many distillers to cease manufacturing alcohol and subsequently reduced the price of corn by 50 percent in western North Carolina.[100] But based on extant reports from revenuers and other federal officials in 1867 and early 1868, moonshiners continued to operate frequently in the counties of Ashe, Burke, Caldwell, Cleveland, Haywood, Jackson, Macon, and Wilkes.[101] Five of these counties (Ashe, Haywood, Burke, Caldwell, and Jackson) had experienced the lowest percentage decreases in corn production between 1860 and 1870, revealing that widespread opposition to federal alcohol control occurred most often in communities where food was more readily available (see table 3.2). Many residents there believed that distillers no longer posed a threat to the local com-

Table 3.2. Top Ten Counties with the Lowest Percentage Decrease in Corn Production in Western North Carolina, 1860 and 1870

County	Corn Production (Bushels)		Decrease (%)
	1860	1870	
Ashe	122,080	120,545	1
Haywood	229,001	206,998	10
Burke	254,650	217,049	15
Caldwell	259,457	207,731	20
Jackson	203,269	156,050	23
Madison	235,276	167,971	29
Buncombe	462,190	324,566	30
Wilkes	305,899	202,590	34
Alexander	209,182	137,207	34
Macon	248,202	162,199	34
Average for western NC	312,002	173,693	44

Sources: U.S. Census Office, *Agriculture of the United States in 1860 . . . The Eighth Census* (Washington, DC: Government Printing Office, 1864), 105, 109; U.S. Census Office, *A Compendium of the Ninth Census: 1870* (Washington, DC: Government Printing Office, 1872), 766–69.

munity's survival and increasingly resented the federal government's attempt to regulate liquor production.

Ultimately, support for General Order Number 25 proved short-lived. By the fall of 1867, improving economic conditions prompted western North Carolinians to distill alcohol and demand that Sickles revoke the prohibition decree. In November, residents in Yancey and Madison counties argued that there was now "an abundance of grain" in their communities and asked the federal government to allow them to manufacture whiskey.[102] That same month, thirty-two farmers from Wilkes County sent a petition requesting that Second Military District headquarters void General Order Number 25. "The only way that we have ever been able to get money to pay our taxes," they complained, "has been by distilling our corn into whiskey, and thus making it portable to market." Forty miles from the rail line in Wilkesboro, these farmers explained that it cost 50¢ per bushel to transport their corn to the depot, making it difficult for them to earn a profit. "Unless distilling is allowed," they concluded, "it will be impossible for the People to pay their taxes without bringing their Lands under the hammer."[103]

By the winter of 1867, many mountain residents stopped asking

for permission to distill their corn into alcohol and started to manufacture it illegally. In December, *New York Times* correspondent A. H.
Guernsey reported that moonshining in western North Carolina had
increased. "The stills are located in unfrequented districts, sometimes
in the midst of an impenetrable jungle, and carefully concealed when
not in operation," he wrote. "The liquor is stored in kegs, and carried
down the mountains on sleds; as there are no roads. . . . After reaching the confines of civilization—if the region where it is vended and
consumed can be called civilization—it is sold in small quantities to
the country grocers."[104] Later that same month, agent Edward Jennings
explained the situation in Cleveland and Burke counties:

> Despite all I can do as an official, who exercise himself at all
> times, it seems to be impossible to stop the distillation of grain
> into whiskey. . . . My division being a rural one of large scope
> of course I cannot be omnipresent, when in one county, the
> citizens of the other, fabricate a rumor that the restrictions are
> withdrawn so as to allow distillers to manufacture whiskey.
> Upon no one am I able to [capture] because no one directly
> can be found whom I can force as a witness. There is . . . under
> ground work going on that no expert can detect.[105]

Engraving of "Illicit Distilling of Liquors—Southern Mode of Making Whiskey,"
Harper's Weekly 11 (December 7, 1867): 733. Courtesy of the Prints and Photographs Division, Library of Congress, Washington, D.C.

Canby revoked General Order Number 25 in January 1868, but distillers remained defiant. When Canby deployed more troops into the region to enforce the law, mountain distillers argued that the Bureau of Internal Revenue was using excessive force and condemned the agency for allowing "bayonet rule" to continue. On March 12, the first documented gun-fight between moonshiners and revenuers in western North Carolina occurred in Macon County. Three days earlier, E. R. Hampton and six federal soldiers seized two stills and captured one moonshiner in Deep Creek in Jackson County. They continued into Macon County, where they arrested another illicit distiller. On the morning of the twelfth, Hampton and his men marched to Cowee Creek and confiscated one still and twenty-five gallons of brandy. That night, the party set up camp. Sergeant John Mulby recalled what happened next: "At about Twelve O'clock . . . we were attacked by a party of thirteen men who fired into the camp. We returned their fire until our ammunition was almost exhausted when by advice of [Hampton] we destroyed the Still and emptied the liquor which we had seized upon and abandoned the Camp."[106] Violent clashes like this one between revenuers and moonshiners would multiply in the future.

By 1868, most western North Carolina distillers must have felt fortunate. Condemned by many mountain residents as "soulless scoundrels" during the Civil War, their reputation had improved considerably. As food became more available, many highlanders no longer feared that alcohol manufacturing threatened their community's survival, and they rejected reformers' call for statewide prohibition. Viewed once again as legitimate entrepreneurs, distillers increasingly garnered the support of mountain residents who resented the Bureau of Internal Revenue, an agency that promoted the expansion of federal authority. This was only a sign of things to come. To the delight of illicit distillers, mountain Conservatives soon followed suit by linking the issue of liquor taxation with opposition to broader Reconstruction policies. In this atmosphere, the moonshiner emerged as a celebrated figure in the region, a "hero" who valiantly fought against what many mountain whites saw as an "oppressive" federal government.

4

"They Tax Us and Give Us Negro Civil Rights"

Moonshiner Violence and the Politics of Federal Liquor Taxation, 1868–1876

Come, all you booze-fighters, if you want to hear,
About the kind o' booze that they sell around here.
It's made a-way back in the lonesome hills
Where there's plenty of moonshine stills.

Conservative Zebulon B. Vance from Buncombe County smiled when news reached him of his triumph over Republican Thomas Settle in the 1876 November gubernatorial election. For the first time since the Civil War's end, a Conservative was governor of North Carolina. Throughout the state, Conservatives, who shortly thereafter renamed themselves Democrats, celebrated Vance's victory and the defeat of Congressional Reconstruction. One newspaper declared that North Carolina was "now a white man's state and white men intend to govern it hereafter."[1]

North Carolina Republicans were livid over the news, and many blamed the state's western counties for their defeat. Henderson County denizen Hamilton Ewart complained that "had the gain in the West been proportional to that in the East, the Republican victory would have been a magnificent one."[2] Republican O. H. Dockery observed that "western counties that had voted solidly Republican in 1868 were Democratic by 1877."[3] What had gone wrong? Many Republicans believed that their national party's support of African American political equality had forced mountain whites to vote Conservative. Other party members disagreed. Ewart argued that "the direct cause" of Republican defeat in western North Carolina "was the odium which existed against the Internal Revenue law, and the hatred and contempt entertained by the people for its execution." He noted that Conservatives had capitalized on mountain whites' opposition to federal liquor taxation by "saddling the responsibility of its passage upon the Republican Party." Ewart concluded that mountain Republicans did little to refute this charge, resulting in a political failure that crushed the local party in 1876.[4]

Scholars have overlooked Ewart's explanation for the Republican defeat in western North Carolina during Reconstruction.[5] Most have emphasized that the greatest challenge to mountain Republicans was their national party's promotion of African American political equality. Gordon B. McKinney, for instance, argues that the local leadership's association with Radical Republicans drove thousands of mountain whites, resentful of African American suffrage, from the party of Lincoln.[6] Historians following McKinney have also emphasized racism as the defining characteristic among whites in western North Carolina. Eric J. Olson posits that the black experience in Asheville, North Carolina, differed little from elsewhere in the South, while John C. Inscoe asserts that western North Carolina adhered to the racial sentiment of the South during Reconstruction.[7]

Although these scholars stress mountain racism as the key to understanding the Republican Party's decline in western North Carolina, they often do so at the expense of other factors. During Reconstruction, white southerners also waged an often overlooked war against the Bureau of Internal Revenue, an agency that promoted the expansion of the federal government and its "infernal" alcohol tax. In the end, Democrats capitalized on whites' opposition to both black political equality and federal liquor law enforcement to build support against the Republican Party. While they did restore "home rule" at Reconstruction's end, they ultimately failed to defeat the Bureau of Internal Revenue.[8]

As in other parts of the South, the issues of African American civil rights and federal liquor taxation conspired against Republicans in western North Carolina.[9] During Reconstruction, most highlanders, believing that the Bureau of Internal Revenue undermined local autonomy, joined forces with the moonshiners in their fight to "make a little licker." Consequently, the illicit distiller became a folk hero, an outlaw who supposedly killed in self-defense and for a noble cause: to protect his community from an "oppressive" national government. As such, North Carolina politicians appeased mountain voters by protesting the

revenue law. Conservatives linked liquor taxation with Radical Republicanism and the question of "home rule."[10] Republicans counterat-
tacked by dissociating themselves from their national party's support
of the liquor law, but they were unable to change the public's negative perception of liquor taxation and its association with the party of
Lincoln.

The Emergence of Mountain Republicanism

Following the Civil War, North Carolina politics changed dramatically.
The Reconstruction Act of March 1867, which restored military rule
in the South and gave African American males the right to vote, convinced William W. Holden, leader of the state peace movement during
the Civil War, and his followers that the Republican Party represented
their most direct avenue to political power. That month, Holden allied
with African Americans, white Unionists, and "carpetbaggers" to organize the North Carolina Republican Party. Most Republicans supported
black suffrage, internal improvements, and free enterprise. Conservatives, mostly former slaveholders and white Confederates, joined the
Conservative Party, a reconfigured version of what had been the Democratic Party; they denounced African American political equality and
portrayed themselves as the defenders of states' rights.[11]

Western North Carolina Republicans found themselves in a precarious situation. Unlike the residents of eastern Tennessee, most Carolina highlanders had supported the Confederacy and were inclined
to join the Conservative Party. Most mountain denizens also opposed
African American suffrage and feared that emancipation would lead
to racial amalgamation.[12] The unwillingness of white highlanders to
accept black equality sometimes led to violence, as evident in a race riot
that erupted in Asheville on the day of the 1868 presidential election,
resulting in the death of an African American.[13]

Despite these setbacks, the party of Lincoln established itself in
western North Carolina. It appealed to blacks, who, although con-
stituting only 14 percent of the region's populace, were an important
political ally. In the 1868 gubernatorial election, for instance, all five
mountain counties with the highest percentage of African Americans
(Burke, McDowell, Polk, Rutherford, and Henderson) went Republican.[14] Black Republicans further deflated racial fears by deferring their
efforts at political activism to white party leaders. In 1871, Madison

County African Americans thanked Republican William L. Scott for the "gratifying and praise worthy way" he had treated them. "Having so lately escaped from slavery," they wrote, "we know that our state and condition are backward, yet we are not so far back as to be ungrateful for kindness. We hope that 'ere long we may rise upward and testify to the friends of the colored man we are and have improved sufficiently to merit their praise."[15] From all outward appearances, these blacks posed little threat to the white leadership of the mountain Republican Party.[16]

Republicans in western North Carolina also adjusted their platform to local conditions. Many mountain residents, struggling to gain equal political footing with those living in the eastern part of the state, embraced the Republican call for democratic reform. Republicans' endorsement of internal improvements also appealed to Carolina highlanders, who, since the antebellum period, had demanded that the state government build a railroad in the region.[17] Although mountain Republicans portrayed themselves as the region's economic protectors, their national party's support of federal liquor taxation would tarnish this image and cause them to lose the support of most white highlanders.

The Politics of Federal Liquor Taxation

The gubernatorial election of April 1868 was the first test for Republicans in North Carolina. Running on the Republican ticket, Holden supported the passage of a new constitution that promised to reform North Carolina's aristocratic sociopolitical system. The constitution would, among other changes, abolish property qualifications for the governor and legislators, guarantee manhood suffrage, and allow voters, rather than the General Assembly, to elect judges.[18] Conservatives were outraged. Identifying themselves as the "white man's party," they nominated Samuel S. Ashe for governor and denounced the Republican-sponsored constitution.[19]

As the election approached, Conservatives and Republicans scrambled to gain support in western North Carolina. Conservatives, hoping to benefit from mountain racism, "appealed to the white people to stand up for their race."[20] In March, the *Asheville News* warned Buncombe County residents that black suffrage would ultimately lead to racial amalgamation. "If you would save your State from Negro rule, the DAUGHTERS of our poor white people [would not be] forced into

Tod R. Caldwell, ca. 1872.
Courtesy of the North Carolina
State Archives.

social equality with Negro BOYS at School," the *News* read. "WHITE MEN
OF BUNCOMBE, your political and social rights are invaded."[21] That same
month, an estimated 2,000 whites gathered in Rutherford County to
denounce "the negro vote" and rally sympathy for the Conservative
Party. Former governor Zebulon Vance addressed the crowd, telling
them to "stand up for their birth right, and crush this negro equality
doctrine with the force of an avalanche."[22] Meanwhile, Republicans
attempted to appease mountain voters by nominating Tod Caldwell, a
prominent Burke County politician, for lieutenant governor and by promoting the construction of railroads in the western part of the state.[23]
The Republican *Asheville Pioneer* issued an attack on the "insidious"
Conservative Party: "Under cover of an outcry against high taxes,
oppression, corruption and unconstitutional appropriations, the prin-
cipal property holders of the middle and eastern counties who have
taxed us for twenty years to furnish themselves with the conveniences
of railroads and canals, are determined . . . to annihilate all hope of an
extension of railroad facilities to the West."[24]

　　The Republican platform was effective. The majority of Carolina
highlanders voted for Holden and agreed to adopt the new state con-

stitution.[25] For these men, having been shut out of politics for generations, the Republican Party offered a new and vibrant democracy.[26]
Conservatives were shocked. Their call for white supremacy had failed
to recruit a sufficient number of mountain whites. Turning their attention to the November presidential election pitting Republican Ulysses
S. Grant against Democrat Horatio Seymour, Conservatives realized
that they had to stress local issues other than race to gain the allegiance
of western Carolinians.

The opposition to federal liquor taxation was just what the Conservatives needed. That September, the *Raleigh Sentinel* blamed Republicans for the law and insisted that Radicals enforced liquor taxation
"to prevent poorer citizens from distilling and to create a *monopoly,*
for the benefit of *wealthy capitalists,* who make distilling spirits a
great business." The paper threatened that this "whiskey ring" would
destroy western Carolinians who relied on whiskey distillation for a
living. "All this partial and oppressive legislation," the editorial concluded, "is the fruits of corrupt Radicalism, and let the people hold
the 'Carpet-bag,' 'scalawag' members of Congress from this state, to a
strict account about this oppressive and unjust way of building up the
'Whiskey Ring.'" This represented a shift from the previous support of
whiskey and brandy taxation. Sensing a growing hostility among "the
Western people," Conservatives saw this as an opportunity to link revenue taxation with charges of Republican corruption.[27]

This approach was particularly successful in the mountains. In a
letter to the *Asheville News* that September, Buncombe County lawyer and politician Thomas Clingman wrote: "The recent charge in the
tax on spirits shows the motive which governs the Radical Party now
controlling both branches of Congress."[28] Conservative James Gwyn
from Wilkes County argued that the Republican presidential candidate
"was not the man to break" the corrupt whiskey rings that supposedly
controlled the national government. "This country has no great man
engaged in politics," he complained in February 1868, "no second rate
great man, no third rate great man, no fourth rate great man."[29] For
Gwyn and other mountain Conservatives, liquor taxation and Reconstruction had become inseparable issues.

Trying to salvage their image in western North Carolina, state
Republicans defended the U.S. Congress and blamed President Andrew
Johnson for the liquor legislation. That September, the Republican
Raleigh Standard argued that Johnson was "the head and the heart

of the whiskey ring." Though acknowledging that the liquor tax was so great that many distillers in the Carolina highlands were "forced to close up," the *Standard* promised its readers that Congress would "review the revenue laws." It then reminded mountain voters that Republicans had always supported the poor man's interest and that "the rebel secession Democracy was responsible" for the liquor law. "By giving the vote of the State to Grant," the *Standard* read, "the people of North Carolina will be far more likely to receive favorable legislation at the hands of Congress than by electing secessionists and rebels."[30]

In the mountains, Republicans tried to shift the blame for the unpopular tax to the Conservative Party. In October 1868, the Republican *Asheville Pioneer* argued that Conservatives were "endeavoring to make capital; just now, out of the revenue tax upon distilled spirits." The newspaper pointed out that it was Secretary of Treasury Hugh McCulloch, a Democrat, who had prevented Republican governor Holden and Bureau of Internal Revenue commissioner E. A. Rollins from reducing the federal liquor tax. The *Pioneer* explained that the Republican Party had always protected the poor man's regional economic interests.[31]

On the eve of the 1868 presidential election, many mountain Republicans feared that the issue of federal liquor taxation was hurting the party's chances for victory. Just to the east, several Rowan County lawyers suggested that it would be "a wise policy for the Republicans to allow what few distillers who have complied with the law of Congress to continue the business."[32] Madison County Republican William L. Scott went so far as to admit that federal liquor taxation was "generally believed as a sham."[33] Meanwhile, Burke County Republicans faced a political crisis when eight illicit distillers, all party members, were arraigned for failure to pay the federal tax. Writing to Lieutenant Governor Tod R. Caldwell, a Burke County Republican observed that Conservatives had "made capital out of the affair by making our friends believe that their arraignment and probable ruin is owing to Radical rule." The unidentified citizen warned that these moonshiners and their supporters would "never cast another Republican vote if the present liquor law is not modified" and noted that "it would be impossible to elect a Republican member in the present state of feeling." Much to the dismay of Burke County Republicans, Caldwell was unable to have the charges dropped.[34]

The 1868 election results reveal that mountain Conservatives had gained considerable ground. Democratic presidential candidate Horatio Seymour won a majority of the mountain votes, while both Republican incumbents running for Congress in the region lost.[35] Conservatives had hit mountain Republicans where it hurt. Having lost by using the race card, they portrayed themselves as the region's economic protectors by denouncing the federal liquor tax. Meanwhile, mountain Republicans were unable to disassociate themselves from the locally unpopular policies of the national government, such as African American political equality and federal liquor taxation. Republicans had learned a bitter political lesson, but moonshiners could not have been more pleased. As long as Reconstruction and federal liquor taxation remained inseparable issues, they enjoyed a broad base of mountain support in their fight against the Bureau of Internal Revenue, one that would soon take a violent turn.

The Anti–Liquor Tax Argument

In June 1868, head of the special revenue committee David A. Wells, Commissioner of Internal Revenue E. A. Rollins, and U.S. Secretary of Treasury Hugh McCulloch met in Washington, D.C., to discuss ways of improving federal liquor law enforcement. These officials "pointed out two causes as operating to reduce revenue: an excessively high rate, and the inefficiency and corruption of officials." While Rollins and McCulloch focused their attention on hiring more "honest and capable revenue men," Wells convinced Congress to lower the liquor tax from $2 to 50¢ a gallon, hoping that this would encourage moonshiners to become legitimate. "It is part of a civilized government," Wells explained, "in framing laws for the assessment and collection of taxes, to know when the maximum revenue point in the case of each tax is reached, and to recognize that beyond that point the government 'overreaches itself.'"[36]

Aided by this tax cut and wanting to ensure maximum collection, newly elected Republican president Ulysses S. Grant intensified federal regulation of liquor production by sending more military aid to bureau agents. But Grant's enforcement efforts would come at an inopportune time for many Carolina highlanders. By 1869, farmers in Rutherford, Buncombe, and other mountain counties were producing surpluses, which alleviated their fear that alcohol manufacturing deprived the

local community of corn.[37] In Surry County, for instance, corn became
so abundant that its value dropped from $1.50 a bushel in 1868 to 50¢
a year later. As a result, many mountain residents, especially those living in more remote areas, opted to once again convert a portion of their
crops into alcohol. The growing market value of liquor further motivated farmers to uncover their stills. While the price of corn continued
to decline, whiskey remained at $4.00 a gallon in 1869. By distilling
rather than selling his corn, a farmer could increase his profit margin
twentyfold.[38] Mountain residents believed that the federal liquor tax—
even after it was reduced to 50¢ a gallon—promoted the expansion
of federal power and threatened an important local industry. Moonshiners and their communities joined forces in the fight for the right to
"make a little licker."[39]

The "language of natural rights" and "localistic republicanism"
garnered political support for the moonshiners following the 1868
election. As long as distillation did not deprive their communities of
foodstuffs, mountain residents who did not produce alcohol regarded
liquor manufacturing as an inalienable right. Moonshiners gained sympathy among these residents by claiming that they had the right, just
as their fathers did, to make a living unmolested by the federal government. "Those people [illicit distillers]," revenue agent D. C. Pearson from Burke County remembered in 1882, "had been in the habit
of making whisky all their lives; from after the war they thought they
could do as heretofore."[40] Alexander Stephens, a resident of the mountains of Georgia, shared the views of his Carolina brethren. He wrote:
"A farmer should have the same right to boil his corn into 'sweet mash'
as to boil it into hominy."[41] The ideal of republican virtue also helped
moonshiners win support in their fight against the Bureau of Internal
Revenue. As they had insisted during the antebellum period, alcohol
distillers and their supporters argued that a republican government had
no right to interfere with the rights of law-abiding citizens. Federal revenue enforcement, they strongly believed, had violated this pact.[42]

Moonshiners and their supporters also viewed liquor taxation as
a tool used by the federal government to prevent them from restoring
"home rule." For many former mountain Confederates, liquor taxation
reaffirmed their fears of Yankee centralization. Amos Owens, a moonshiner and ex-Confederate from Rutherford County, vowed never to
pay the liquor tax. "Why in tarnation," he questioned, "should he
share the yield from his blockading labors with Washington?"[43] After

1868, the Republican *Raleigh Standard* reinforced this fear of federal tyranny by comparing the liquor tax with taxes imposed on American colonists by the English Crown during the 1770s. "Taxation without representation is not carrying out in good faith, the policy inaugurated by the Revolutionists," the *Standard* explained. "The genius of our government has become wholly deformed."[44] Many highlanders felt that liquor taxation signaled the beginning of an abusive federal government that could impose dominance over its citizens at will.

There was a litany of other complaints as well. Farmers who had just recently turned to distillation argued that this tax reduced their profit margin. Regardless of the amount of liquor produced, all distillers were required to purchase licenses and pay a 50¢ tax on each gallon. By 1869, however, this tax was probably not as burdensome to alcohol manufacturers as critics portrayed it. Even when the price of whiskey dropped from $4.00 a gallon in 1869 to $2.00 in 1871, a farmer could still make a profit of $5.50 by legally distilling his corn into whiskey.[45] But many mountain residents, even those who did not manufacture alcohol, still believed that this tax placed a heavy burden on small local producers. One Caldwell County farmer, who had never "made a drop of liquor" and drank only a "wee bit," protested "the unjust and oppressive operation of the internal revenue laws of the national government." Since distillers in the mountain counties had little means and lived in one of the "most inaccessible regions," this resident understood the necessity of distilling. With the burden of paying a liquor tax, the "plain countrymen" would be unable to provide for their families.[46]

Supporters of the moonshiners insisted that liquor taxation benefited wealthy distillers who produced alcohol in bulk, while hurting smaller distillers. In September 1869, one mountain resident complained that this tax made "no distinction between the man who simply distills for his own use and the distiller who makes thousands of barrels for sale." How could these farmers regain economic prosperity, the author questioned, "if every dollar they make is wrung from them by the tax-collectors?"[47] That same month, the Conservative *Raleigh Sentinel* argued that the liquor tax created "a *monopoly,* for the benefit of *wealthy capitalists,* who make distilling spirits a *great business.*"[48] Many Carolina highlanders, aware of the economic importance of the local liquor industry, sympathized with small distillers and demanded the liquor tax's repeal.

Faced with such widespread opposition, the Bureau of Internal Revenue looked to the military for support. By 1870, both the Fifth and Seventh U.S. Cavalries, stationed in Morganton, Asheville, and Shelby, and the Fourth U.S. Artillery, headquartered in Rutherfordton, protected bureau agents conducting raids in western North Carolina.[49] Revenuers' authority to summon federal soldiers increased with passage of the Force Act of 1871. Though aimed at combating the Ku Klux Klan (KKK) by giving federal officials the power to use troops for protection when making arrests, this act also granted Internal Revenue agents the same authority.[50] The use of troops prompted further cries of "bayonet rule" among mountain whites and amplified the potential for violence.

The Rise of Moonshiner Violence

During the late 1860s, moonshiner resistance to federal liquor law enforcement occurred sporadically. Conservatives and Republicans tried to minimize violence by asking alcohol distillers and their supporters to remain patient for the liquor tax's repeal. "In accepting Reconstruction," the Conservative *Asheville News* explained in 1869,

A moonshine still house hidden in the laurel. From Horace Kephart, *Our Southern Highlanders: A Narrative of Adventure in the Southern Appalachians and a Study of Life among the Mountaineers* (New York: Macmillan, 1922), facing 112.

"we have accepted its concomitant evils, and shall bear with them until the conservative people all over the land shall become strong enough to abolish them by that sure but peaceful remedy—the ballot-box."[51] Republicans also urged moonshiners not to violently resist the liquor tax "but [to] ask for its repeal." "Let petition after petition be drawn up and sent to our representatives in Congress," the Republican *Raleigh Standard* advised North Carolinians opposed to the revenue law.[52] Hopes for a peaceful resolution were soon shattered when the Grant administration intensified federal regulation.

Outbreaks of violence did occur, but most moonshiners used their wits rather than a Winchester rifle to evade revenuers.[53] Instead of fighting, illicit distillers tried to avoid fines and possible prison sentences by locating their stills "in unfrequented districts, sometimes in the midst of an impenetrable jungle or laurel brake, and carefully concealed when not in operation."[54] Others devised more elaborate hiding places. North Carolina moonshiner Charles Folias evaded revenuers by digging "a tunnel leading to the cave where his still was hidden."[55] During the 1870s, Haywood County illicit distiller Arthur Rathbone hid his illegal cargo in a nearby pond. "Back when I was distillin'," Rathbone recalled years later, "that Fern Pond was all swampy and sort of like quick-sand. I hid a lot of likker there. Kept the revenooers from gettin' it when they come a-easin' around. Trouble was, that swamp just sucked up them cans and I couldn't reclaim them."[56] Moonshiners also avoided violent confrontation by posting pickets to give ample warning of a posse's approach. Revenuer William Ball complained that agents hunting down illicit stills in Ashe County often heard "the blowing of horns and the peculiar hoots employed as signals of coming danger. Throughout the sections where these violations of the law take place, the whole country is patrolled and picketed. So complete is the system of signals that no stranger can be seen without instantaneous alarm being given all through the neighborhood."[57]

Mountain residents sometimes discouraged revenuers from collecting the liquor tax by issuing threats of violence. In March 1871, several men stopped revenuer W. H. Deaver outside his office in Marshall in Madison County. Deaver remembered what happened next: "They asked me if I knew the way to Asheville [in Buncombe County]. I told them I did. They pointed the road out to me and said it was only so many miles, and for me to take it, and get out of this county with my damned Revenue."[58] Cleveland and Rutherford county residents

A moonshine still under the mountains. From Arthur Talmage Abernethy, *Moonshine: Being Appalachia's Arabian Nights* (Asheville: Dixie Publishing Company, 1924), frontispiece.

greeted John B. Eaves with similar threats. "I felt that in some localities there I would be unsafe because of my position as a revenue officer," he explained in 1872.[59]

When threats proved ineffective, some moonshiners tried to kill troublesome federal agents. Four months after his encounter with hostile Marshall residents, Deaver was attacked by Joseph A. Thompson, a Republican moonshiner from McDowell County who had complained "that his own party had turned against him and [he] intended to kill some of them."[60] Events did not go according to Thompson's plan: his rifle initially misfired, Deaver was able to return fire, and Thompson died in the gunfight. Other Internal Revenue agents were not as fortunate. In 1872, the *Asheville Pioneer* reported that moonshiners from Cherokee and Clay counties fatally wounded revenuer C. C. Vest in a shoot-out in Union County, Georgia.[61] Two years later, the paper described an altercation between illicit distiller William R. Dills and federal agent N. H. Burns in Swain County: "On Sunday, the 15th, as [Burns] was traveling on the road 12 miles from Charleston on the Tennessee border, he was shot through the heart and killed instantly by William R. Dills. The shooting was done with a rifle-gun, and at such close quarters that the patching of the bullet was found in the hole where the ball penetrated the body. . . . The section of the country in which the killing was done, is cursed with some wild and lawless men."[62]

Communities often supported these assaults on revenuers. In 1870, a "group of forty to fifty armed men" forced revenuers to release a Rutherford County moonshiner from jail.[63] The moonshiners who killed Vest in 1872 "received large additions to their party from the neighborhood."[64] Conservatives also defended illicit distillers by downplaying the level of violence directed at Internal Revenue agents. When rumors began circulating that moonshiners had killed two revenuers in western North Carolina, the *Asheville News* responded: "We dare say that when these *reports* come to be investigated they will be found to consist of more fuss than fire."[65]

Moonshiners on trial for violence against the federal government often found sanctuary in local courts.[66] In 1874, a mountain jury acquitted several Swain County moonshiners charged with the murder of federal agent N. H. Burns.[67] Upon hearing the verdict, Judge Robert Dick was shocked that the jury had exonerated these men "from a clear case of murder." He concluded that revenuers who ended up in mountain courts faced almost certain conviction, due to the "great prejudice against the Government."[68] Federal agents in western North Carolina agreed. When U.S. Marshal W. H. Deaver, who had just recently survived an attempt on his life, was indicted for murder and assault in Madison County in 1873, he asked Attorney General Charles Devens to transfer his case to federal court. "I am safe in saying," Deaver pleaded, "that no officer of Internal Revenue or Marshal could obtain

Engraving of "Moonshiners," *Harper's Weekly* 22 (November 2, 1878): 865. Courtesy of the Prints and Photographs Division, Library of Congress, Washington, D.C.

a fair and impartial trial in the state courts."[69] Republican district attorney Virgil Lusk from Asheville sometimes complied with Deaver's and other mountain agents' requests to remove their cases from state courts.[70] This led supporters of the moonshiners to charge that revenue officials had become immune from punishment.[71]

The moonshiners found additional support from the Reconstruction-era Ku Klux Klan.[72] Following the Republican victory in the 1868 gubernatorial election, North Carolina Conservatives organized a state Klan, hoping to launch a violent counteroffensive against the party of Lincoln.[73] Like those elsewhere in the South, Klansmen in western North Carolina sought to restore "home rule" and white supremacy by assaulting white Republicans and African Americans.[74] Believing that they were protecting the local community from "outsiders," mountain Klansmen, many of whom were illicit distillers, also targeted Internal Revenue agents. In April 1868, collector William Dedman returned to his hotel room in Waynesville in Haywood County to find a coffin-shaped letter pinned to his door. Observing the letters "K.K.K." inscribed on top, a startled Dedman read the warning: "Baker's Tomb—Western Division—Windy Month—Cloudy Day—Bloody Hour. Ku Klux Klan, the hour approacheth. Shake up dry bones and meet on the Mysterious Circle of the Hollow Sphere. From East and West, from North and South, we come to measure justice for the traitor's doom. When darkness reigns then is the hour to strike." Dedman took the letter down and discovered a white mask resting on a post near his door.[75] The letter's message was clear: leave Haywood County immediately.

During the early 1870s, Klan violence in western North Carolina intensified. Having already established themselves in Buncombe, Rutherford, Madison, and Cleveland counties, Klansmen organized two dens in Polk and McDowell counties, and three in Burke.[76] By the spring of 1871, the KKK also emerged in Catawba, Clay, Haywood, and Yancey counties.[77] Extralegal retribution in these mountain counties was brutal. In 1871, a "band of Kuklux" ransacked the house of Yancey County resident W. C. Brackins. The Republican *Asheville Pioneer* did not indicate why Brackins had been targeted but reported, "They seized Mr. Brackins and dragged him out into the yard, stripping off his clothing, and beat him upon his naked back and over the head with pistols until he was covered with blood from head to foot." However, the assailants were not satisfied. They reentered the house, hurled Mr. Brackins's baby "across the room," and raped his wife.[78]

Like the issue of black suffrage, Klan members used the liquor tax as a rallying point to unify mountain whites against the Republican Party and Congressional Reconstruction. In 1871, collector Pinkney Rollins reported that illicit distillers in Polk, Burke, and other mountain counties were "under a kind of protectorship of that secret organization called 'the Ku Klux Klan.'"[79] That same year, agent C. C. Vest recalled that "squads of men claiming to be the K.K.'s" in Cherokee and Macon counties had sworn "that the law shall not be executed in this county, that they will make whiskey, sell whiskey whenever they please and in defiance of the revenue authority of the United States."[80] Assessor J. B. Eaves indicated that the Klan's efforts in Cleveland County were successful, reporting that M. H. Berry and other revenuers "dare not attempt to collect any taxes" for fear of being "Ku-kluxed."[81] In August 1871, Klansmen attacked bureau agents who had confiscated several barrels of whiskey. Berry remembered, "They inquired where those damned Yankee revenue officers were. They swore they were going to have them out and kill the last son of a bitch. . . . I have fought Indians on the plains, and heard them give many a war-hoop, but those Kuklux that night left Mr. Indian in the shade."[82]

Moonshiners often used the KKK to assault suspected informants, whether Republican or Conservative. In Cleveland County, illicit distiller Amos Owens and other Klansmen ransacked Mr. McGahey's house on a cold February night in 1870. McGahey was a Republican who had given revenue agents the names of several moonshiners. This den also whipped a white Conservative, Almon Owens (no relation to Amos), that same night. Congressman Luke P. Poland would later ask Klansman Julius Fortune why he and others had attacked Owens. Fortune answered, "Because he talked too much and worked too little." "Reported some distillery, did he not," Poland then inquired. "Yes, sir," Fortune replied, "I think he did."[83] Klansmen believed that McGahey and Owens had betrayed the local community by helping the Bureau of Internal Revenue—in their eyes, the worst of crimes. In 1871, Rollins pointed out that fear of physical retribution from the Klan was largely responsible for the reluctance to collaborate with revenue agents. "The doings of this Klan," he wrote, "have filled many people with such terror that they are afraid to say or do anything that might bring its vengeance upon them."[84] Cleveland County revenuer J. B. Eaves agreed. "It is nearly impossible to get any positive information as to where these distilleries are located. Citizens are afraid to reveal anything they may know, for fear they will be visited by the K.K.K."[85] Frightened residents refused to cooperate with bureau officials, and as a result, revenuers found it hard to capture, let alone convict, illicit distillers.

The fight against the revenuers united Conservatives and Republicans, and many Republican moonshiners joined the Ku Klux Klan. One Conservative Klansmen from Rutherford County, James L. Grant, testified that many Republican distillers both opposed the liquor tax and supported the Klan. "They consider that they can run their stills without paying taxes, if the Ku-Klux Party would be in power," Grant stated, "that they would put down the revenue, so that they could just run their stills publicly."[86] And according to Conservative Marcus M. Wells from Cleveland County, Republican moonshiner Mr. Hambrick had enlisted in the Klan to "protect him in distilling." The Ku Klux Klan and the moonshining business, he explained, "seemed to cooperate together."[87]

The Klan courted this type of support by assisting Republican moonshiners in retrieving property confiscated by the Bureau of Internal Revenue. For Joseph Thornburg, a Republican moonshiner from Gaston County, the KKK in nearby Cleveland County was a blessing. In August 1871, Klansmen from this den surrounded agent S. H. Wiley and other revenuers after they had confiscated Thornburg's whiskey. Wiley remembered: "About two o'clock we were aroused by one of the clerks, who stated that about fifty masked men, all armed with muskets and rifles, had surrounded the premises, demanding that both the liquor and the revenue officers should be delivered to them." Wiley feared that these Klansmen would attack his group, so he turned the whiskey over to them.[88] The Ku Klux Klan was a valuable ally to illicit distillers, Conservative and Republican alike.

As Klan violence intensified in western North Carolina during the early 1870s, Conservative leaders began to believe that they had created a political liability. They feared that this violence would provoke the federal government to send in more troops, and they reassured Republican governor Tod Caldwell (who assumed the governorship in 1871, after Holden was impeached) that they did not support these outlaws. As Conservatives withdrew their support and made no effort to protect Klan members, the terrorist organization deteriorated as arrests mounted and Klansmen testified in court against one another.[89] By 1872, Klan activity had ceased in western North Carolina and other parts of the South. But Conservatives did not completely abandon the moonshiners. They still shared a common enemy: the Bureau of Internal Revenue.

Politics and Federal Liquor Taxation

While moonshiners and Klansmen battled revenuers, the issue of federal liquor taxation remained a major issue in state politics. Following the 1868 elections, North Carolina Conservatives, resentful that the Bureau of Internal Revenue provided Republicans with more than 300 patronage jobs, intensified their attack on liquor law enforcement.[90] In 1869, the *Raleigh Sentinel* blamed Radical congressmen for this "oppressive, difficult, and costly" tax on small local producers. "We call upon the plain, honest, hardworking men of the country, to remember what persons and what party have inflicted these wrongs upon them," the *Sentinel* concluded.[91] Mountain Conservatives agreed. That June, the *Asheville News* vehemently protested the use of federal troops to enforce the revenue law, a painful reminder of the failure to overthrow Congressional Reconstruction. The newspaper warned its readers: "When Federal taxes are collected at the point of the bayonet, then our people will witness what has not occurred in our State since the days King George was master here."[92] In October, another Conservative mountain newspaper, the *Rutherfordton Western Vindicator,* used a lighthearted play on words to criticize what was for its editors a serious matter. "All Englishmen by the name of Hale," it read, "who are engaged in the business of pronouncing the name without the H shall be considered manufacturers of 'ale and must pay the license required of all brewers and distillers."[93] Through such rhetoric, Conservatives hoped to profit from mountain whites' fear that the federal government would impose stringent control over their communities via revenue enforcement.

In 1870, Governor Holden created a militia to protect African Americans and white Republicans in the piedmont from Klan violence. This decision provoked a popular outcry against the Republican Party in the Carolina highlands and other parts of the state. Yancey County residents considered Holden's use of the militia "a declaration of war." The governor's selection of former Union colonel George W. Kirk—remembered for his raids on western North Carolina during the Civil War—to lead the militia also drove many former Confederates from the Republican Party. Editors of the Republican *Rutherford Star,* for instance, viewed the so-called Kirk-Holden war as evidence of the governor's "tyranny, usurption, treachery, and corruption."[94]

The party's esteem fell further in the eyes of many western Carolinians when President Grant endorsed federal liquor law enforcement during the late 1860s. To convince mountain voters that the local party was not responsible for these "outrages," the Republican-controlled General Assembly approved a resolution in 1869 that exempted all distillers who manufactured less than 300 gallons of alcohol annually from paying the state liquor tax.[95] By doing so, Republicans attempted to appeal to small producers, the group most vehemently opposed to liquor taxation. One year later, Senator Alexander H. Jones from Henderson County, one of the state's largest peach and apple producers, requested that Congress lower the tax on fruit brandy. This proposal appealed to many mountain residents. One Polk County farmer observed that Jones, who would be reelected to office, was "gaining friends daily" due to his "recent activity and energy, in having the Brandy distilling modified so that all can still."[96]

No matter how hard local Republicans tried to distance themselves from liquor taxation, however, mountain whites typically saw them as the purveyors of big government and the agents of radical change. Most agreed with a Caldwell County farmer who pointed out in 1869 that the Republican Party was in power nationally and "responsible for all laws good, bad, and indifferent." Because the national party had failed to modify or repeal the tax, this farmer concluded that mountain Republicans would suffer politically.[97] Others placed the blame solely on the local Republican Party. A Wilkes County distiller believed that Republican politicians had betrayed him. "Republicans speakers for party purposes and to carry the election, stated that the revenue laws had been repealed," he wrote in 1869. "Under their influence and word, poor men stilled their fruit and will now be sold out of house and home."[98]

By the early 1870s, mountain Republicans conceded that their constituency resented the national party's support of the Bureau of Internal Revenue. In 1871, a federal official admitted that "hostility to revenue laws [was] not confined to [Conservatives] but [was] general."[99] One year later, Republican Hardie Hogan Helper argued that President Grant and Governor Holden should "remove every Internal Revenue officer in the State."[100] Burke County Republicans agreed. Writing to Grant in September 1872, they asked him "to banish from its service the officials that had charge of the Collection of the Revenue in this District."[101] The U.S. Congress ignored these concerns and instead raised the liquor tax from 50¢ to 70¢ a gallon in December 1872. Mountain Republican C. R. Thomas feared that the party of Lincoln was in serious trouble. "Our people," he explained to James Ramsay, "do not wish to be annoyed any longer with both Federal and State tax gatherers."[102]

North Carolina Conservatives were happy to see discord within the Republican ranks, and they continued to link liquor law enforcement with opposition to broader Reconstruction policies. In 1872, the *Raleigh Sentinel* charged that the Republican Party had manufactured stories about moonshiners attacking revenuers to create an excuse to send more troops into the state and secure its political dominance.[103] Mountain residents came forward with their own accusations of corruption. Distillers claimed that revenuers carried blank search warrants, which were "filled in whenever they found a property they wanted to search."[104] The *Asheville Citizen* and *Rutherfordton Western Vindicator* singled out federal official W. H. Deaver, accusing him of "persecuting good and law-abiding citizens."[105] Conservatives promised mountain voters that they would do everything possible to end revenue corruption and liquor taxation. In April 1872, they introduced a bill in Congress calling for a repeal of the brandy tax and a decrease of the tax on whiskey manufacturing.[106] Later that year, the Conservative state platform demanded that the federal government completely and immediately abolish the "inequitable, vexatious, and tyrannical" revenue system.[107]

In 1873, the Bureau of Internal Revenue's reputation plummeted further when reporters exposed a massive scandal involving large distillers and revenue officials in the Midwest. These revenuers had allegedly allowed several distillers to evade the liquor tax in exchange for bribes used to finance Grant's 1872 reelection campaign.[108] For many mountain whites, this incident confirmed Conservatives' charges of corruption. One Buncombe County resident explained, "It is now thought there is a combined ring to harass and distress the people and it is thought that a majority of the officials are concerned, hence their retention in office."[109] Democrats were quick to point out that many of these alleged corrupt agents were Republican. Several Conservative moonshiners argued that revenuers treated them more harshly than their Republican counterparts. "Should Conservatives be persecuted and shot at," one Wilkes County farmer complained in 1873, "because they are not the supporters of such dogs [Republicans]?"[110]

The issue of corruption among bureau agents proved to be a divisive one for mountain Republicans. In 1873, agent James G. Ramsay, hoping to gain control of revenue patronage in western North Carolina, charged Sixth District collector John J. Mott with malfeasance.[111] Mott fought back by writing an angry letter to his adversary: "I understand information is volunteered to you upon which it is expected that charges of mal-administration in office are to be prepared against me with a view of ousting me and your taking my place. Men have enough to bear holding like public stations to this, without receiving assault at the hands of those who ought to be their friends."[112] Undeterred, Ramsay wrote to newly appointed Commissioner of Internal Revenue J. W. Douglas, insisting that his appointment as collector of North Carolina's Sixth Collection District would be good for the party. "I beg leave to say that [Mott] has never done or effected more for the Republican cause, than I have," he assured Douglas.[113]

Although Republican leaders endorsed Ramsay, Mott gained the support of the party's rank and file, largely due to his ability to cooperate with illicit distillers.[114] In January 1873, A. C. Bryan from Wilkes County pointed out that Mott, "in a quiet and gentlemanly way, has started quite a number of lawful distilleries in this district which have proved a success, thus convincing the peoples, that the Law can be complied with and more money made than could be otherwise. In my opinion, we will be able to carry the district in August next unless Mott should be thrown out, or superseded by someone obnoxious to these mountain peoples."[115] George H. Brown, secretary of the Union Republican Executive Committee in Wilkes County, agreed. "Dr. Mott," Brown insisted in 1874, "is certainly the strongest stake in the Republican Party in this district, he has done more than any other man to keep up the party, and for him to be thrown over board it looks like giving up every thing."[116] Despite this strong support, Grant appointed Ramsay to head North Carolina's Sixth Collection District in November 1874.[117] After hearing the news, a disappointed Mott wrote to Judge Thomas Settle: "It is not because I am involved that I say so, but the party in North Carolina is receiving injury in this removal and the appointment of R[amsay] that it cannot recover from."[118]

Meanwhile, mountain Conservatives continued to hit Republi-

Robert Vance, ca. 1860s. Courtesy of the North Carolina State Archives.

cans where it hurt. In 1874, Robert Vance, a member of the Friends of Temperance and the brother of Zebulon Vance, ran for Congress in western North Carolina's Eighth District, denouncing African American suffrage and the Bureau of Internal Revenue.[119] He charged that federal liquor taxation violated mountain whites' inalienable rights and proposed a bill in Congress making penalties against moonshiners less stringent.[120] Mountain Republicans responded by calling for lower whiskey taxes, but to no avail.[121] Vance defeated the incumbent Republican, receiving 62 percent of the vote.[122] With such widespread hostility toward federal liquor taxation and black political equality, the Conservatives set their sights on the 1876 gubernatorial election.

The End of Reconstruction

Conservative candidate Zebulon B. Vance led his party in attacks against the Republican campaign for African American political equality. In 1875, Republican congressmen had proposed a civil rights bill to safeguard what remained of blacks' rights and Reconstruction. Furious, North Carolina Conservatives pledged to save the state "from the thralldom of niggerism."[123] Vance immediately toured the western counties, denouncing the bill.[124] Worried local Republicans scrambled to assure mountain whites that the bill only called for separate but equal facilities. Other party members opted to ignore the civil rights controversy altogether. Highlanders, however, remained unconvinced and voted in favor of a new Conservative-sponsored state constitution that discriminated against blacks.[125]

Vance did not limit his criticism to the issue of civil rights. He also seized the opportunity to link Republicans to the much-hated Bureau of Internal Revenue. Mountain Conservatives quickly embraced the former governor. The Conservative *Asheville Citizen* wrote that Vance had defended white highlanders by addressing the "great issues involved in the present—the interests of the people contrasting with the selfish conduct of the Grant Revenue office-holders." The newspaper then agreed with Vance that revenuers controlled the Republican Party, warning voters that "revenue office holders" worked "only for their big offices." "Such is radical revenuism," the *Citizen* concluded.[126]

The incompetence and poor judgment of some federal agents strengthened the Conservative charges of revenue corruption and further discredited the Bureau of Internal Revenue.[127] In 1875, North Carolina's Western District Federal Court contemplated prosecuting agent William S. Pearson of Buncombe County and five gaugers from the Sixth Collection District for falsely recording the amount of whiskey distilled at several stills, an illegal practice known as "spreading the account."[128] Pearson and some of the other gaugers were members of prominent mountain Republican families, and many party members feared the political repercussions their trials might have in the upcoming gubernatorial election.[129] Republican governor Curtis H. Brogden and other high-ranking state officials asked U.S. Attorney General George Williams not to prosecute the men. "We are satisfied," they wrote, "that you will not allow the character of a young man [Pearson] of so much promise and one who has so ably defended the principles of our party . . . to be ruined."[130] District Attorney Lusk, an Asheville native, advised the commissioner of Internal Revenue and U.S. attorney general to drop the charges. "I would respectfully suggest," he wrote to the attorney general, "that no further good would result to the government by a continuation of these prosecutions."[131] The federal court's failure to hear the case against Pearson and the other agents heightened the fears of mountain whites that Republicans had conspired to undermine local autonomy via revenue enforcement.

As the election grew closer, Vance continued his assault on the Bureau of Internal Revenue. He condemned the entire system as corrupt and called agents "red-legged grasshoppers." Holding up to his mountain audience a grasshopper preserved in alcohol, Vance proclaimed: "This fellow . . . eats up every green thing that God ever gave to man, and he only serves the universal dissolution. The time has come when an honest man can't take an honest drink without having a gang of revenue officers after him."[132] Conservatives rallied behind Vance. In February 1876, the *Asheville Citizen* accused revenuers of monopolizing local political offices. "Corrupt" revenue agents in Buncombe County, the paper charged, were "determined to rule the party, and keep all the big offices, and all funds in the family."[133]

Republicans realized that the issue of federal liquor taxation and Grant's support of the Bureau of Internal Revenue threatened to destroy the party in western North Carolina. They feared that highlanders believed that Grant was using "corrupt" revenuers to expand federal power. In June 1876, W. S. Tate complained: "The management of the Internal Revenue Service in this district, Republicans tell me, is not only odious but infamous and many have become lukewarm."[134] Republican Robert Dick sided with Tate, pointing out that he "had heard from some counties in the mountains that some of the [Internal Revenue officials] are doing damage by an improper execution of the Revenue Laws."[135]

The actions of the national Republicans only exacerbated the situation. In 1873, Wilkes County Republican A. C. Bryan told Thomas Settle "that an overwhelming majority of the people" in the Carolina mountains were "fittingly opposed" to any increase in liquor taxation. "If Congress does increase the tax," he predicted, "it will be a heavy load for us [Republicans] to carry."[136] The Republican-controlled Congress did not heed the warnings of its mountain constituents, raising the federal liquor tax from 70¢ to 90¢ a gallon in March 1875.[137] This tax increase accompanied a drop in whiskey prices, which, as usual, hurt small-scale law-abiding distillers the hardest.[138] Whereas they had earned a $5.50 profit on every five gallons of alcohol they produced in 1871, legal whiskey makers now netted only $1.00.[139] As such, this tax increase encouraged both legal and illegal distillers to be receptive to Vance's political rhetoric.

Mountain Republicans did make a last-ditch effort to improve the federal agency's reputation in the Carolina highlands before the gubernatorial election. Judge Dick, for instance, "put deputy marshals on notice that they would be dismissed for excessive rudeness, force, or obtaining confessions by promise or threat."[140] J. J. Mott, whom President Grant had recently reinstated as collector of the Sixth Collection District, implemented a more radical policy.[141] He simply refused to collect the liquor tax in the months preceding the gubernatorial election. "It would have been a hardship upon the distillers," Mott explained in October 1876, "to have made payment before this time [because it] would have caused bad feeling and injury to us [Republicans] *politically.*"[142] The Republican *New Regime* in Rutherford County suggested that the federal government stop prosecuting Amos Owens and other small illicit distillers "for some little irregularity concerning the revenue law." Instead, the newspaper argued, national authorities should focus their attention on convicting revenue officials and large distillers in the Midwest who had participated in the whiskey ring scandal of 1873.[143] These efforts to alleviate mountain opposition to federal liquor taxation, however, arrived too late to save the Republicans. Vance defeated Settle, receiving 63 percent of mountain votes.[144]

Following the 1876 election, disgruntled Republicans admitted that Conservatives had capitalized on local issues to gain the allegiance of mountain whites. "I have no doubt," agent D. C. Pearson from Burke County recalled in 1882, "that many men who voted for the Republican ticket prior to that time were induced to vote the Democratic Party, thinking they would be relieved of the [federal liquor] law and its operations by the Democratic administration coming into power."[145] J. J. Mott concurred. Testifying before a congressional inquiry on revenue corruption in western North Carolina, he argued in 1882:

> The purpose of the Democratic Party, as I understood it and felt it, was to make capital by traduction of the Revenue laws and officers. This was done by the public speakers and newspapers throughout the State. That system of abuse and traduction grew, and was taken from the speakers and the press by the populace. . . . It subjected the officers to insult and suspicion, and incensed those who were engaged in illicit distilling, and

encouraged them to stand out against the law, and to go on in the face of the law.[146]

As they had with the issue of African American political equality, Conservatives successfully used federal liquor taxation as a rallying point to unify mountain whites against the party of Lincoln and Congressional Reconstruction. Many highlanders believed that the road to redemption lay with both the eradication of black suffrage and the destruction of the Bureau of Internal Revenue, an agency promoting the expansion of federal power. Mountain Republicans, unable to distance themselves from the national party's support of liquor law enforcement, could do nothing but watch their support wane. Ironically, however, Vance's victory in 1876 would mark the beginning of the end for the moonshiners in western North Carolina.

Part III

The Road
to Prohibition,
1870–1908

5

Civilization Requires Prohibition

The Beginning of the End for the Moonshiners, 1870–1882

> All the drunkards will never be dead,
> I can tell you the reason why;
> The young ones always grow up
> Before the old ones die.

When President Ulysses S. Grant appointed Green B. Raum as commissioner of the Bureau of Internal Revenue in August 1876, moonshiner resistance to federal liquor taxation was increasing throughout the mountain South. In western North Carolina, J. J. Mott and other agents informed the new commissioner that conditions there were bleak. The moonshiners were well armed and ready to fight, and they had the support of most communities. Even county sheriffs and state attorneys lent a helping hand, detaining and prosecuting revenuers "on trumped up charges, alleged to have been committed while these officers were in the discharge of official duty."[1] To make matters worse, Zebulon Vance and other prominent mountain Democrats championed the moonshiners as heroes. Raum was infuriated. "It is well known that numerous persons are engaged in the illicit manufacture and sale of spirits in your district," he scolded Mott in June 1877, "and I desire that you shall take immediate steps to suppress the same with a strong hand."[2]

By the early 1880s, however, Raum believed that the situation in western North Carolina and other parts of southern Appalachia had improved. Testifying before a congressional inquiry on revenue corruption in 1882, he bragged that North Carolina's Sixth Collection

District "has been lifted up from the attitude of fraud and resistance to authority into an observance of the law; and officers now can ride from one end of [Mott's] district to the other, without danger of being bushwhacked, whereas, five years ago, a private citizen passing through that country with 'store' clothes on, and who was unknown to the people, was in danger of being suspected as a revenue officer and shot."[3] Indeed, Mott reported that "the people have become more reconciled to the law and many good people have engaged in distilling under the law."[4] Revenuers and mountain residents alike concurred that the illicit distillers now found themselves under attack from Democrats and other former allies. The broad base of support they had enjoyed in the region was quickly deteriorating.

Following Reconstruction, many southerners increasingly advocated for a New South, one in which industry, agricultural efficiency, and cheap labor would become the backbone of the region's economy.[5] These men and women emphasized economic development and welcomed the expansion of railroads across Dixie. Materially, middle-class townspeople benefited the most from this shift and gradually replaced the planter elite as the South's dominant economic and political figures. Wanting to create a new industrial social order, many of them resumed the crusade to reform the drinking habits of their brethren. By the end of the nineteenth century, they had organized thousands of temperance societies throughout the region. Having lagged behind the North in its support for temperance reform, the South now emerged as the leading champion in the nation's fight against King Alcohol.

In western North Carolina, the arrival of the railroad—and along with it, "civilization"—encouraged many townspeople to embrace New South rhetoric and the amenities of urban America. These highlanders, believing that alcohol consumption and other preindustrial practices stymied the region's economic potential, once again embraced the temperance movement. Scholars have failed to recognize the central role that the moonshiner played in the revival of this antialcohol crusade. For mountain reformers and their cohorts outside the region, he epitomized what was wrong with rural society. He was an unwanted remnant of the colonial past, a rugged individualist who rejected modernity and promoted intemperance. Like other rural "traditionalists," the alcohol distiller had no place in the New South.

The Beginning of Western North Carolina's Industrial Revolution

In 1868, Asheville resident and former congressman Thomas Clingman wrote a pamphlet published by the American Agricultural and Mineral Land Company, an organization owned jointly by northern capitalists and local entrepreneurs. In it, Clingman attempted to attract northerners with capital to invest and settle in western North Carolina by extolling the region's scenic beauty and fertile soils. "The air," he wrote, "is almost always bracing and exhilarating in a high degree, while no country is more healthy, being not only free from all miasmatic diseases, but favorable even in winter." Clingman bragged that the region's vast timber resources, abundant minerals, plentiful waterways, and hardworking white population made it ideal for manufacturing. In short, there was "no country more inviting to industrious emigrants."[6]

Following the Civil War, Clingman and other local leaders, most of whom resided in commercial centers, increasingly believed that the

Thomas Clingman, ca. 1865–1880. Courtesy of the Prints and Photographs Division, Library of Congress, Washington, D.C.

future of western North Carolina (and of the South) lay in northern investment and economic modernization. Prominent among these men was physician H. P. Gatchell, owner of a tuberculosis sanitarium at Forest Hill, just south of Asheville. In 1870, he penned the first of many pamphlets that celebrated the region's healthful climate and promoted tourism as a catalyst for other forms of economic development. Gatchell insisted that only in western North Carolina could a "Northern man, who wishes to rear a healthful, industrious, and energetic family," find a "desirable home." "There can the white race maintain the health and vigor which are essential to preserving labor and to great results," he concluded.[7]

Whether promoting the region's climate, agricultural potential, or untapped mineral resources, men like Gatchell and Clingman insisted that "capital and enterprise" would allow western North Carolina to become "one of the most prosperous sections of the country."[8] They believed that economic development depended on completion of the Western North Carolina Railroad (WNCRR), and as many mountain residents had done for decades, they argued for its extension into the counties west of the Blue Ridge.[9] Railroads promised to link the region to other parts of the South, increase commercial traffic, and advance tourism. "I am willing to be taxed well on my little property to have a railroad in the county," wrote a Hendersonville African American in an 1873 letter in which he demanded that state legislators fund the construction of the Asheville-Spartanburg Railroad. "We want a railroad—we need one, as everybody knows. And I believe if we all knew our interests and go to work, like we ought to do, we will have one, and that soon." The *Asheville Citizen* also lauded the benefits of the railroads. "Our old colored friend," the newspaper stated, "knows that his property will more than double in value if a railroad goes to his place, besides bringing numberless new ways for the people to make money."[10]

Despite local support, internal scandals and mountain topography hampered railroad construction throughout the 1870s. Work on the WNCRR stopped at Old Fort in McDowell County in 1873 after directors Milton S. Littlefield and George Swepson embezzled $1 million in bond proceeds that were supposed to be used to expand the railroad to Asheville. Meanwhile, rugged terrain in Polk County slowed construction of the Asheville-Spartanburg Railroad. The lack of progress alarmed many western North Carolinians. "Enterprising men will not remain in a section remote from railroad and telegraphic communication," Caldwell County's *Lenoir Topic* reported in 1878. "They find no market for their produce, and become disheartened at the prices they are compelled to sell the same for—and receive their pay in merchandise."[11] By 1879, Old Fort remained the western terminus of the WNCRR, and work on the Asheville-Spartanburg Railroad continued to lag in Polk County.[12]

While little progress was being made on the railroads, mountain residents were somewhat successful in their attempts to entice outside investment. In 1870, the New York–based Cooper Institute purchased 1,500 acres of land in Madison County and sold it to a group of northern settlers who founded the Western North Carolina Manufacturing and Agricultural Association.[13] Two years later, B. B. Babington Sr. from Pittsburgh, Pennsylvania, and Massachusetts inventor M. S. Worthington moved to Shelby in Cleveland County, where, hoping to capitalize on the region's cheap labor, they formed the Carolina Sewing Machine Company.[14] In 1873, intending to float timber down the Yadkin and Pee Dee rivers to South Carolina, a Canadian company purchased large tracts of land in Watauga and Wilkes counties.[15] That same year, S. S. and J. E. Clayton from Baltimore, Maryland, bought the Ore Knob copper mine in Ashe County. This particular business venture was a huge success. By 1878, the mine employed more than 700 workers and was the leading producer of copper in the United States.[16] In 1879, northerner John Wilder, owner of the famous Cloudland Hotel on Roan Mountain in Mitchell County near the Tennessee–North Carolina border, also invested in the region's raw materials, purchasing a portion of the Cranberry mica mine in Watauga County.[17] But overall, most northern capitalists remained hesitant to invest in western North Carolina, largely due to the absence of railroads west of the Blue Ridge.

Mountain entrepreneurs, most of whom had belonged to the antebellum elite and urban middle class, seized the opportunity to profit from the changing economy. Former slaveholding families in Ashe County, for instance, retained their elite social status after the Civil War by turning away from agriculture to pursue industrial enterprise, investing mostly in copper mines.[18] Jackson County businessmen in Webster scrambled to acquire lands rich in copper, corundum, mica, and gold deposits, while Thomas Clingman, who saw such promise in the region, purchased a mica mine on Beech Creek in Watauga

County.[19] Other local residents opted to invest in the region's above-ground resource: timber. Even without having access to a railroad line, a Madison County lumberman reported that "he had spent $4,000 and had reaped $10,000 worth of marketable lumber" in nine months of operation.[20] East of the Blue Ridge, in Catawba, Cleveland, Burke, Surry, and Rutherford counties, mountain entrepreneurs founded several textile plants and iron forges, hoping that these manufacturing industries would stimulate economic growth.[21]

Although western North Carolinians would not feel the full impact of industrialization until the 1880s, local entrepreneurs laid the groundwork for it in the 1870s. Capital invested in manufacturing increased dramatically in the region during this decade. Out of the eighteen mountain counties that reported manufacturing investment in 1870 and 1880, fifteen had an increased industrial product.[22] Topping that list were Alexander, Yancey, Haywood, and Cherokee counties, all of which had invested little capital in manufacturing before the Civil War. Industrial development in the Carolina highlands was slowly expanding beyond the dominant antebellum commercial centers located in Buncombe, Caldwell, Catawba, Cleveland, and Surry counties.[23] With the advance of modernization, however, came a widening of the cultural gap between town and countryside, a phenomenon that occurred across the post–Civil War South.

Temperance, Local Option, and the Creation of a New Social Order

For many mountain denizens, economic progress went hand in hand with cultural reform. Local business leaders believed that it was imperative for residents to conform to the new demands of the New South. For the capitalist experiment to succeed, men and women who had left their farms for jobs in towns had to quickly adapt to the rhythms of wage labor, ruled by the time clock and the factory whistle, and embrace the Victorian middle-class virtues of self-restraint and hard work. Those who remained on farms would also need to make adjustments. According to Clingman in 1877, the "two vices yet to over-come" in rural society were "ignorance and laziness."[24] Reformers encouraged mountain farmers to practice scientific farming and participate more in the market economy in order to increase agricultural productivity. Above all, they wanted people to stop drinking alcohol, a tradition that allegedly threatened to impede the region's economic and moral prosperity.

During the early 1870s, local missionary Baptists, most of whom had remained silent on the issue for nearly a decade, resumed their campaign against intemperance. In 1871, members of the Broad River Baptist Association claimed that crime and violence had multiplied in western North Carolina since the end of the Civil War. According to J. R. Logan, the association's chairman, increased alcohol consumption, especially among young men, was responsible for this apparent breakdown in law and order. "We often witness with sadness," he explained, "the evil genius of intemperance in many things, disturbing the peace and quiet of the churches, and even whole communities, poisoning the very foundation of morality." In 1872, the King's Mountain Baptist Association called on members "to arouse from their slumbers and try to do their whole duty [to eradicate the excessive use of alcohol]. . . . We see very many of our young men and old men too alike steeped in the foul sinks of intemperance, perverting the cause of Christian progress."[25]

It is impossible to determine whether alcohol consumption was actually increasing in western North Carolina during the 1870s. Nationwide, the crusaders' work seems to have paid off, as the per capita consumption of absolute alcohol remained well below its antebellum levels.[26] Nonetheless, mountain temperance agitators complained that farmers in more remote parts of the region continued to drink whiskey at barn raisings, dances, and other social events.[27] The persistence of these traditions does not necessarily mean that rural highlanders were drinking more alcohol than they had in the past, although declining economic prosperity may have led to a rise in alcohol consumption by the early 1870s. The average size of a farm in western North Carolina had shrunk from 365 acres in 1860 to 139 acres in 1880.[28] Hardest hit were young men, who, unable to inherit enough land to sustain a livelihood, migrated to towns looking for work. Unemployed and disheartened, some of these men might have turned to alcohol to lighten their spirits.

Whether or not alcohol consumption increased, many town residents believed that it had, and they noted the appearance of "dangerous" young men who allegedly engaged in drunken brawls and criminal activity. New town ordinances prohibiting the retail sale of alcohol reflected these fears. In 1871, the county seat of Marshall forbade the sale of alcohol within one mile of corporate limits, and Asheville politicians prohibited retailers from vending liquor on Sundays. Both these ordinances included clauses that made it illegal for residents to fight and "curse" within corporate limits.[29] Two years later, commissioners in Wilkesboro, declaring that drunkenness had become "a source of annoyance to the citizens," announced that they would no longer grant alcohol licenses to venders operating within one mile of the town.[30]

The Order of Good Templars was one of the leading organizations in this renewed crusade for temperance.[31] Founded in New York in 1872, the Good Templars was a fraternal order whose members pledged total abstinence from alcohol. Like the Sons of Temperance before the Civil War and the Friends of Temperance during the 1860s, the Good Templars organized most of its lodges in western North Carolina villages and towns, suggesting that the temperance movement remained a largely urban phenomenon. In 1875, nineteen of its twenty-nine mountain councils were located in county seats.[32] Of the ten remaining lodges, three were located in burgeoning commercial centers: one in Nebo, a busy depot on the WNCRR in McDowell County, and two in Mount Airy in Surry County, which was quickly becoming a major textile manufacturing center.[33]

The pressures of industrialization and urbanization that took place in western North Carolina in the 1870s were particularly hard on county seats. More so than other mountain settlements, county seats, which already possessed a larger number of businesses and job opportunities, experienced rapid population growth during this decade. These community centers, most of which had been hamlets during the antebellum period, evolved into towns that housed hundreds of residents. By 1880, with the exception of Robbinsville in Graham County and Dodson in Surry County, every mountain county seat had a population of at least 100.[34]

With the economic benefits of urbanization came social disruption. Many people believed that the influx of rural populations—and the alcohol they drank—had increased violence in their towns. "Intemperance is growing in our midst to an alarming extent," Shelby residents in Cleveland County complained in 1873, "and has a very bad effect upon the men."[35] Morganton reformers in Burke County concurred, explaining: "The sale, use, and traffic of spirituous liquor is a growing evil in our community. To such extent does this evil abound, especially

Certificate for the Order of Good Templars, n.d. Courtesy of the Prints and Photographs Division, Library of Congress, Washington, D.C.

on all public times, that our females cannot walk on the street without the fear of insults and molestations from the intemperate, that are to be found staggering on our streets . . . and indulging in language so revolting to decency."[36] Fearing that increased drinking was detrimental to the peace and order of their communities, many townspeople embraced the Good Templars, along with the Friends of Temperance, which continued to garner support in the French Broad Valley.

This antialcohol sentiment, however, was more than just a reaction to perceived increases in crime and violence in western North Carolina. Everywhere below the Mason-Dixon Line, the reemergence of temperance reform, especially within evangelical churches, constituted "part of a larger Lost Cause effort to sanctify society and re-create the antebellum southern apologists' notion of the especially religious South."[37] In 1872, for instance, the King's Mountain Baptist Association insisted that antebellum southerners were a sober people chosen by God to lead the nation. "It was once our boast that we could sit under our own vine and fig tree and worship our Maker according to the dictates of conscience," the association claimed. "How changed now is our condition at the present day!" The King's Mountain Baptist Association and other religious groups increasingly blamed intemperance on Congressional Reconstruction, arguing that "the Carpet Bag Government had failed to regulate the liquor evil."[38]

J. R. Logan, chairman of the Broad River Baptist Association, charged that northern "military domination or despotism" had supplanted "the great bulwark of civil liberty" by bringing into power an "intemperate administration of secular authority." "The instrumentalities used to carry out this vile system," he concluded, "are often of the lowest classes of society."[39] By embracing temperance, Logan and other mountain evangelicals argued, the South would remain God's chosen region.

More important, alcohol reform reflected the interests of middle-class townspeople who wanted economic and moral progress. Prominent among these reformers was Methodist preacher Robert L. Abernethy. Born in Lincoln County in 1822, Abernethy moved to Burke County in 1853, where he founded Rutherford College and served as its president until his death in 1894.[40] He joined the Friends of Temperance during the early 1870s and quickly emerged as one of the region's most outspoken proponents of the antialcohol movement. Like other crusaders, Abernethy stressed the middle-class virtues of industry, self-discipline, and sobriety. The drinking habits of rural mountain residents concerned him, and he chastised churches for not supporting the temperance crusade. "The outside world about Rutherford College," he complained in 1873, "does not believe much in Temperance Societies." The economic and moral future of western North Carolina was at stake, and religious leaders were not helping to improve the situation. Abernethy concluded: "I take these broad grounds upon the Temperance question, that in these days of progress and advanced education and development, the preacher, layman or Christian, who stands silently outside of the Temperance organization, is claimed upon the side of drunkenness; and the preacher, layman or Christian who openly opposes the Temperance organization, is guilty of making drunkards."[41]

In 1872, thousands of western North Carolinians, most of whom resided in county seats, followed Abernethy's lead and joined a statewide movement calling for the enactment of local-option laws that would prohibit the sale of alcohol near courthouses, churches, schools, and manufacturing facilities. Intemperance, several Asheville denizens complained to the General Assembly in 1873, "is detrimental to the peace, prosperity, good order, and good name of the community in which it is done."[42] One year later, Jefferson resident R. H. Gresham pleaded to the *Asheville Citizen:* "I wish you may drive the sin of intemperance from Western North Carolina, then you will prosper more than now."[43] Taking lessons from their failed attempts to enact statewide prohibition during the 1850s, reformers insisted that local-option laws were neither unconstitutional nor tyrannical because they allowed residents to ban alcohol within their own communities.[44] And although they believed that residents had every right to distill and sell alcohol, crusaders argued that it was the government's responsibility to help the region advance. As Morganton petitioners explained in 1873: "[We do not] disavow any disposition to hinder the trade and occupation of those engaged in the traffic and sale of spirituous liquors in our midst, yet such demoralization as connects with their trade demands legislation."[45]

Having already become popular elsewhere in the post–Civil War South, the local-option movement received the support of many western North Carolinians.[46] By 1880, seventy-two churches, twenty-five towns, fifteen schools, and two manufacturing plants had enacted prohibition within the mountain region.[47] Of these locales, sixty-one of them were situated in county seats, suggesting that local prohibition, much like temperance reform, remained largely an urban phenomenon.[48] But these laws were also passed in other mountain communities that were undergoing rapid economic and population growth. Of the thirty-five churches not situated in county seats, nine were located near the Buncombe Turnpike or the WNCRR.[49] Another church, Towns Creek, operated in Mount Airy in Surry County, which was becoming a major manufacturing center. And the burgeoning villages of Old Fort, Sulphur Springs, King's Mountain, and Snow Hill, along with the Hazel Green factory in Buncombe County and the Ore Knob copper mine in Ashe County, passed prohibition decrees. In all, nearly 75 percent of local-option prohibition mandates were in county seats or in developing mountain towns.

To the delight of reformers, local-option laws seemed to have immediate success. Touring the Carolina highlands in August 1873, M. M. McKenzie, a state lecturer for the Friends of Temperance, was amazed at the progress that had been made in such a short time. "Most of the western towns," he proudly wrote, "have prohibitory laws to protect them from the curse of grog shops, as the result of such laws you find but little drinking among the citizens."[50] One year later, journalist Edward King believed that Waynesville had become "as orderly as a Quaker community." "No liquor is sold within a mile of the town's boundary," he observed. "Some lonely and disreputable shanty, with the words 'BAR-ROOM' on a clearing along the highway, is the only resort for those who drink 'spirits.'"[51]

Mountain women played an important role in the enforcement of local-option laws. Embracing their status as "representatives of virtue" in the public sphere, they quickly endorsed the temperance movement when it made its resurgence in the 1870s, and they were instrumental in building grassroots support for local prohibition. They often sent petitions to the General Assembly demanding that it pass local-option legislation, and they encouraged their friends, family, and neighbors to reject King Alcohol.[52] Once such laws were passed, women reformers made sure that local officials promptly enforced them. In 1873, Edwin Chandler noted that Asheville "ladies will take the matter in hand [and] aid the law very much in preventing violations and protecting society."[53] According to R. H. Gresham the following year, women in Jefferson informed on residents who continued to sell alcohol illegally. "The ladies," he explained, "say that they have engaged in the war for life, that is to put down the evil traffic . . . and to keep it down."[54] In April 1874, the *Raleigh Sentinel* reported that alcohol consumption had declined in western North Carolina "under the crusades of the woman."[55] As elsewhere in the United States, the temperance movement gave mountain women, excluded from the political process, a sense of self-worth and a public voice.

The quick success of local-option laws heightened tensions between local prohibitionists and alcohol manufacturers. Reformers, knowing that moonshiners had the support of the Conservative Party and were considered heroes by many highlanders, made it clear that local option would not prohibit the manufacturing of distilled spirits. Instead, most prohibitionists sought to close down taverns, or grog shops, believing that these "places of sin" encouraged men (and women) to drink whiskey.[56] But while communities were passing local-option laws during the 1870s, many moonshiners and their legal counterparts continued to meet the local demand for alcohol. In 1876, the *New Regime* complained that intemperance was increasing in Rutherfordton, largely due to "mean men" who were "peddling whiskey through the country in a secret way."[57] Three years later, the *Blue Ridge Blade* revealed that nearby distillers had smuggled whiskey into the prohibition town of Morganton, where they made "a good many drunk" and caused "disorder and fights."[58] Consequently, mountain reformers increasingly turned their attention to distillers, whom they blamed for the continued use of alcohol in their communities.

Town-dwelling reformers began to intensify their efforts in rural areas and accused farmers who ran stills of encouraging traditional drinking mores in mountain society.[59] During the early post–Civil War period, the distillers had been the standard-bearers in the continued fight against the party of Lincoln and its Reconstruction policies. But by the late 1870s, middle-class townspeople saw the profession as harmful and an impediment to economic growth. In 1878, the *Webster Spectator* in Jackson County believed that liquor manufacturing was "a curse of the country." "Let it be put down," the editors demanded.[60] Waynesville resident W. W. Stringfield insisted in 1879 that "our beautiful mountain country will 'blossom as the rose,' and our mothers, wives, sweethearts and sisters, will sing anthems of praise" if farmers stopped distilling whiskey.[61] "Let the good work go," the *Hendersonville Independent Herald* read in 1882, praising the federal court's conviction of several moonshiners. "There is no

Randolph Shotwell, ca. 1870s.
Courtesy of the North Carolina
State Archives.

necessity for a single violation by illicit distilling in any of our mountain sections."[62]

As they had done briefly in the antebellum period, temperance
advocates were able to turn distillers, especially moonshiners, into
a symbol of what was wrong with rural society, rather than valiant
southerners protecting the local community from the federal government. They were, according to a Franklin resident in Macon County in
1878, unchurched and uncivilized.[63] Stringfield charged that illicit distillers were "willing to endanger their own and their neighbors' souls
and bodies to get a little of this 'hellfire' for 'campfire' or for sickness."[64] Rutherfordton resident Randolph Shotwell was just as harsh.
He characterized moonshiners as "thriftless, uneducated, unthinking

beings, who live little better than negroes."[65] Perhaps most indicative of the change in sentiment was Democrat A. T. Davidson from Asheville, who had once opposed federal liquor law enforcement but in 1882 insisted that illicit distillers had become "the worst part of the community."[66] Celebrated as heroes during Reconstruction, moonshiners now found themselves under attack from former allies like Davidson, who not only embraced alcohol reform but also changed their opinion about the Bureau of Internal Revenue and its once "infernal" liquor tax.

The Bureau of Internal Revenue Strikes Back

In 1876, Commissioner Raum found himself heading a federal agency with an uncertain future. In his first report to Congress, he reported that moonshiners were operating more than 2,000 stills throughout the mountain South, costing the Treasury $2.5 million annually.[67] Raum was particularly concerned by activity in North Carolina's Sixth Collection District, which encompassed nearly all the mountain counties in the state.[68] "I found [this] district filled with illicit distillers," the revenue commissioner remembered in 1882. "There seemed to be a spirit of opposition to the laws and to their enforcement. The illicit distillers were particularly difficult to handle, as they combined from time to time to resist the officers and to prevent them from enforcing the laws."[69]

Between 1878 and 1882, Raum launched a campaign against illicit distillers that would ultimately reduce resistance to liquor law enforcement and improve the reputation of the Bureau of Internal Revenue. He believed that effective enforcement required "a force of deputies, armed when necessary, as will demonstrate the ability and determination of the government to collect its revenues and enforce its laws."[70] Raum realized that the use of federal troops "was a constant irritation to the people" and "should not be long continued"; instead, he relied heavily on civilian raiding parties.[71] These posses usually consisted of twelve to twenty well-armed and well-equipped volunteers led by a paid deputy collector appointed by the district collector. Each unit also had a deputy marshal, who issued warrants and had the authority to arrest any distiller they caught in the act, even if no warrant had been processed.[72]

Using these civilian posses, Raum and Sixth District collector J. J.

Mott coordinated the first of many seasonal sweeps throughout the region in 1878, focusing on moonshine strongholds in Burke, Wilkes, and Polk counties.[73] That February, a group consisting of thirty men captured three stills and arrested seven moonshiners in the infamous South Mountains of Burke County.[74] Eight months later, revenuer A. C. Bryan and his raiding party confiscated 1,000 gallons of whiskey and brandy, while destroying 4,000 gallons of mash in Burke and neighboring counties.[75] Agents from South Carolina and Georgia helped drive moonshiners who had fled from the "Dark Corners" of North Carolina (Polk, Henderson, and Transylvania counties) back into the state, where revenuers were waiting to arrest them.[76] These raids proved effective. In 1877, revenue agents captured 122 illegal stills in western North Carolina. Two years later, that figure had jumped to 274. The number of moonshiners taken into custody also increased dramatically, from just 43 in 1877 to 343 in 1879.[77]

Despite these successes, many mountain distillers continued to resist government regulation. Most of them opted to hide themselves and their stills, though some assaulted raiding parties in carefully planned ambushes. In March 1878, a group of "concealed" moonshiners fired on three revenuers who had recently destroyed the stills of two men connected with a gang operating in the Brushy Mountains of Wilkes County. Although "bullets cut the trees and struck in the ground around the deputies, neither of them was injured," a relieved Mott informed Raum weeks after the ambush.[78] Other revenuers were not so lucky. One year earlier, in March 1877, a "band of armed men" from Polk County "seemed to rise up simultaneously from concealment in the woods" and rushed the courthouse near Hendersonville, attempting to free a fellow moonshiner from custody. Revenuers were able to drive the moonshiners away, but not before the "mob" had shot, stabbed, and beaten a deputy marshal to death.[79] During Reconstruction, violence directed at the Bureau of Internal Revenue was often fueled by a lingering resentment of the party of Lincoln. But an 1878 raid on the property of Burke County Republican James York, where twelve fellow party members opened fire on agents, indicates that the battle for the right to make liquor was no longer being fought along party lines.[80]

Between 1876 and 1880, when moonshine violence against the Bureau of Internal Revenue reached its climax in the mountain South, twenty-five agents were killed in the line of duty, an average of about six per year. When compared to the death rates of deputy marshals in the Wild West, which averaged twenty per year, those in southern Appalachia were low.[81] Agents often reported that illicit distillers seemed to be aiming too high during shoot-outs. Because many moonshiners were experienced hunters, their poor marksmanship suggests that they intended to only intimidate federal officials, not kill them. Nevertheless, with four agents wounded and one killed, North Carolina's Sixth Collection District was one of the South's most dangerous regions for revenuers during the late 1870s.[82]

Revenuers depended on information from local residents to identify and apprehend illegal distillers. As government efforts to enforce the liquor law garnered more support from mountain communities, moonshiners struck out at denizens who cooperated with agents.[83] In Burke County, an angry distiller knocked down a Mr. Ramsey, a suspected informer, with a rock "and then stamped him in the face." "These fellows accuse Ramsey of reporting them," Deputy Bryan reported to Mott in June 1878. "They killed his horse some weeks past; Ramsey then borrowed a mule from Amos Huffman to tend his crop, and last Tuesday night they shot the mule dead in Ramsey's stable."[84] In January 1879, an Alexander County resident who had been "both active and useful in breaking up" stills was "dragged from his house at night and severely beaten by six disguised men."[85] Legal distillers were also victims of the moonshiners' wrath. In Macon County, revenuer George Smathers revealed that "blockaders" had assaulted several legitimate distillers and forced them out of business.[86] Though successful in the short run, violence against community members ultimately undermined the moonshiners' already waning local support and left them more vulnerable to the Bureau of Internal Revenue.

Having demonstrated that the federal government was determined and able to enforce the liquor law, Raum initiated the second phase of his campaign against the moonshiners in 1878. "The plan was . . . to force violators of the law to the wall, so to speak," Raum remembered four years later, "and then after they had become satisfied of the determination of the government and its ability to enforce the laws . . . to extend to them leniency, on such conditions as should appeal to the best side of their nature, so as to induce them to cease committing frauds and resisting the officers."[87] While insisting that revenuers continue their "operations with increased vigor," Raum began to grant amnesty to moonshiners who pled guilty in federal court and pledged to stop illegally distilling alcohol.[88] Many western North Carolinians approved of the amnesty order. That August, editors of the Democratic *Lenoir Topic* in Caldwell County felt confident that distillers were "anxious to accept the terms" the federal government had offered.[89] Two months later, the grand jury for the Western District of North Carolina "most earnestly recommend[ed] fellow citizens to accept the clemency extended."[90] In November, the *Asheville Citizen,* a strong supporter of the moonshiners, reluctantly conceded that the federal government was now addressing "the gross injustice done [to] the people of North Carolina."[91] Hundreds of moonshiners turned themselves in to federal and state authorities. As such, the number of convictions for evading federal liquor taxation more than doubled in North Carolina's Western District, increasing from 308 in 1877 to 801 in 1879.[92]

While Raum was convincing moonshiners to abide by the law, officials at the local level worked to improve the Bureau of Internal Revenue's reputation in western North Carolina. Most prominent among these men were district judge Robert Dick and revenuer J. J. Mott. During Reconstruction, Dick had fired deputy marshals engaged in fraud and threatened to dismiss those who used "excessive rudeness, force, or obtain[ed] confessions by promise or threat."[93] In 1877, Dick, now known for his "kindly temper," reminded marshals that arrests "must be made in accordance with law, and only upon warrants duly issued." This pleased mountain Democrats. "A little law judiciously applied to these revenue officers," the *Asheville Citizen* commented on Dick's decree, "might have a happy effect, for that they have trampled upon justice with a lordly air is a notorious fact."[94] Like Raum, Judge Dick believed that leniency would reduce opposition to federal liquor taxation and often suspended the sentences of petty violators, "who paid reduced fines averaging about $20 instead of the minimum of $100 and a thirty-day jail term prescribed by law."[95]

As head collector of the Sixth District, Mott played a more instrumental role in improving the bureau's performance and reputation following Reconstruction. He first addressed complaints from local residents that most agents were dishonest and "ignorant."[96] In 1876, Mott issued a statement that he would fire any agent who drank alcohol excessively. He followed through on his threat, dismissing several revenuers after local citizens complained that they had become "addicted to drinking."[97] Shortly thereafter, Mott, attempting to reduce partisanship in the bureau, appointed several Democrats.[98] Finally, Mott responded to charges that resistance to revenue enforcement would continue until he appointed "men of character and honesty."[99] By 1882, he had heightened the qualifications for agents and required all applicants to receive an "endorsement from the citizens and well-known people of the neighborhood."[100]

The new agents claimed to be more efficient and well respected than their predecessors. Agent T. K. Bruner explained the secret of his success: "I took the oldest clothes I had, and colored shirts, and looked as ordinary as any countryman. I made my habits conform to theirs, and was generally liked in the neighborhood."[101] Burke County revenuer Tom Davis tried to get to know the local community. He "would shake hands with the people and be very friendly with them." Davis also refused to arrest moonshiners or seize stills without a search warrant, making him a model officer in the eyes of mountain residents.[102] In 1882, A. C. Avery, a Democrat and longtime critic of the Bureau of Internal Revenue, testified that Davis was "a very prudent sort of man, and after arresting them [illicit distillers] he would treat them with great kindness and consideration. If he had confidence in them he would let them off to go and hunt their bondsmen and never used rough or disagreeable language to them."[103]

In 1878, hoping to further encourage moonshiners to become legitimate, Mott convinced Raum to reduce the legal minimum capacity of distilleries in western North Carolina from six to three and a half bushels of corn.[104] The largest profits in manufacturing alcohol were in livestock rather than in the whiskey itself. Mountain distillers would often fatten their livestock (mostly hogs) on corn mash, popularly known as "still slops," throughout the year and then sell them to neighbors or merchants.[105] "A man that has a good farm and so on," revenuer W. M. Walker explained in 1882, "can pasture his stock for a month on his wheat pasture and oats. Outside of that they have to keep up the distillery, or the stock goes down."[106] Even if taxed, poorer farmers who were unable to purchase large stills could now afford to become legitimate because their main source of income was in livestock. North Carolina revenuer Tyre Green recalled in 1882: "I know the man I storekept for has made money; he had machinery and a good ordered distillery, and sold the whisky from $1.35 and $1.50 a gallon. The distiller told me he was making money at it, not making a large amount, but a living at it. He had a great many hogs and cattle."[107]

Between 1878 and 1879, the number of legal distilleries in North

Carolina's Sixth Collection District rose from 42 to 198, an increase of 371 percent. Of those 198 legal distilleries, 154 had a capacity of five gallons or less, suggesting that Mott's policy, along with Raum's carrot-and-stick approach, was convincing small distillers to become legitimate.[108] Moreover, the amount of revenue collected in the region grew from $259,076.24 in 1877 to $336,238.72 in 1879.[109] "The old 'moonshiners' are nearly all at work under the law," Mott bragged to Raum in January 1880, "and those who are not are intimidated and kept out by those who are."[110]

These policies may have significantly reduced moonshining, but they failed to eliminate it. Making illegal whiskey remained profitable for many Carolina highlanders, especially those without livestock who could not benefit from the legalization of small distilleries. In 1880, a bushel of corn sold for $1.00 and a gallon of whiskey for $1.40.[111] If a farmer decided to distill illegally, he earned a $5.00 profit on every five gallons of alcohol, while legal distillers netted only 50¢. The renewed vigilance surrounding the federal liquor tax led many mountain farmers to either legitimize their endeavors or give up distilling altogether. But some liquor manufacturers refused to give up so easily.

Based on the testimony of agents during a congressional inquiry on revenue corruption in 1882, there were three major moonshine pockets in western North Carolina during the late 1870s. The first centered on the Brushy Mountain region in Wilkes County, where, according to former revenuer James A. Ramsay, "the mountains were so steep that you had to get down and lead your horse."[112] Another lay in the South Mountains in southern Burke and northern Rutherford counties.[113] The third was the infamous "Dark Corners," made up of Polk, Henderson, and Transylvania counties, considered by revenuers to have the heaviest concentration of illegal stills in the state.[114] Its proximity to South Carolina and Georgia allowed moonshiners to slip across the state line and avoid capture. These regions also happened to be some of the poorest areas in western North Carolina, suggesting that economic necessity drove many mountain residents to distill alcohol illegally.

During the 1870s, traditional inheritance practices, land speculation, population growth, and a decrease in soil fertility had begun to undermine mountain farmers' quest for economic independence.[115] In western North Carolina, the average size of a farm shrank from 190 acres in 1870 to 139 in 1880. Hardest hit were farmers living in the "Dark Corners" region, helping to explain why it was the most active

Table 5.1. Top Ten Mountain Counties with the Greatest Decrease in the Cash Value of Farms, 1870 and 1880

County*	1870 Value ($)	1880 Value ($)	Change (%)
Transylvania	931.35	588.02	−37
Polk	1,001.75	655.30	−35
Henderson	1,017.23	722.48	−29
Burke	670.15	492.81	−26
Rutherford	663.59	509.24	−23
McDowell	808.52	634.59	−22
Madison	733.26	636.34	−13
Mitchell	563.77	502.36	−11
Wilkes	529.58	498.26	−6
Clay	782.52	741.44	−5
Average for western NC	673.56	745.61	+11

*Graham and Swain counties were not included in the 1870 and 1880 census reports. Sources: U.S. Census Office, *The Statistics of Wealth and Industry . . . Ninth Census: 1870* (Washington, DC: Government Printing Office, 1872), 214, 218; U.S. Census Office, *Report on the Productions of Agriculture . . . Tenth Census: 1880* (Washington, DC: Government Printing Office, 1883), 300–302.

moonshine enclave. The size of Transylvania County farms fell from 282 acres in 1870 to 137 in 1880, a decrease of 51 percent, while those in Polk County shrank 37 percent. Henderson County farmers were more fortunate but still experienced a 28 percent decline in farm acreage. The same was true for farmers living in Burke, Rutherford, and Wilkes counties.[116] To make matters worse, while the cash value of farms in western North Carolina rose 11 percent during the decade, the value of farms in the three regions with the heaviest moonshining activity actually decreased (see table 5.1).

Despite the economic hardships that motivated many moonshiners, local communities increasingly sided with revenuers. Raum's amnesty order played an important role in this reversal of public opinion. In December 1878, district attorney Virgil S. Lusk from Asheville reported hearing "frequent expressions extolling the Government for its liberality . . . coming from sources, a month since in sympathy with the violators of the law and condemning the Government for enforcing it."[117] Similarly, revenuer W. M. Walker observed in 1882, "It was very hard there a few years back. In fact, up to the amnesty we had no showing at all; since the amnesty we have been countenanced by the better part of the people of the district."[118] Webster residents in Jackson County confirmed that many highlanders, especially townspeople, believed that the revenue service was acting fairly and that distillers should obey the law. "Well, the Government offered an amnesty, to clear up old offenses," they wrote to the *Asheville Citizen* in 1878, "and those who go at it now, after having had fair warning, out to be taught to 'stand from under.'"[119]

Citizens increasingly began to see the Bureau of Internal Revenue as the defender of peace and legitimate enterprise rather than an oppressive tool of northern tyranny. Moonshiners had often used violence and intimidation to ensure local solidarity, but now these tactics were working against them. When illicit distillers assaulted an Asheville preacher whom they mistook for a revenuer, the *Bakersville Republican* and the *Lenoir Topic,* both former critics of the Bureau of Internal Revenue, were outraged. "It is high time that these violators of the law were brought to justice," the newspapers stated in June 1879. "When a peaceable citizen cannot travel the public road without being stopped by a desperado with pistol in hand, the law should be enforced with the utmost rigor."[120] Legal distillers, whose numbers had increased almost fivefold by 1879, also demanded that the federal government enforce the law, largely to protect their operations from moonshiners and to prevent inflation. These distillers, Mott observed, acted as "a sort of police in the neighborhood against illegal ones," informing on moonshiners and sometimes breaking up illicit stills themselves.[121]

Temperance reformers in mountain towns embraced the Bureau of Internal Revenue as an important ally, believing that the federal liquor tax would reduce consumption by raising the price of alcohol. In April 1879, Waynesville denizen William W. Stringfield encouraged his neighbors to join the temperance crusade and support revenuers in their fight against the moonshiners. "With the State [local-option] laws we have," he explained, "and with the aid and cooperation of the present U.S. revenue laws, enforced . . . by honest, faithful and vigilant officers, there is no reason why this vile monster [alcohol] may not be trampled beneath the feet."[122] To the delight of reformers, the legalization of many small distilleries in 1878 seemed to have discouraged drunkenness and improved public order. Revenuer Tyre Green explained:

> I will just tell you my opinion. Where there were so many of those blockading distilleries running, they [moonshiners] were

William W. Stringfield,
1908. Courtesy of the
North Carolina State
Archives.

always afraid of being reported, and the consequence was, the
people around the neighborhood, the men disposed to drink,
would lie around those distilleries and drink all the time. These
distillers were afraid to drive them off, for fear they would
report them. But now with these small distilleries, running
according to law, these men can't get anything to drink there,
and the distillers are at perfect liberty to order them off, and
they can't report them. That has been my idea.[123]

Although revenuers received most of their support from townspeople, rural western Carolinians were also becoming more hostile toward
the moonshiners. In 1880, residents of the Cleveland County countryside petitioned the federal government to offer a reward for the capture of Jake Mull, a "notorious blockader" who had "thousands of
gallons of Whiskey hid in the fastnesses of these mountains."[124] That
same year, Cherokee County citizens appealed "to all good citizens to

no longer shelter these violators of the law and disturbers of the public tranquility by their silence and indifference."[125] Many revenuers confirmed that public opinion was improving in the more remote parts of the region. W. M. Walker recalled that when traveling in the countryside during the early 1870s, "it was very difficult for a raiding force to get anywhere to stay or anything to eat in our district." Like other revenuers, he had to purchase supplies in towns where the residents would agree to conduct business with him. On one raid, Walker's force ran out of food and had "to hire a negro boy" to purchase "some chickens, flour, and bacon." By 1882, however, that had changed. Walker reported that whereas only a few years ago people had refused them food, "[revenuers] are treated now something like white folks, mostly, wherever we go."[126]

Even mountain Democrats admitted that the Bureau of Internal Revenue's reputation had improved. Testifying before a congressional inquiry on revenue corruption in 1882, Democrat A. T. Davidson conceded that opposition to federal liquor law enforcement had declined. "I will say, in justice to the service that the trouble has not been so great in the last two or three years," he explained. "It has quieted down somewhat, and the criminal dockets of the Federal courts have been much lessened within that time." What were the reasons behind this change of public opinion? According to Davidson, "familiarity with the law and a returning sense of right on the subject with the officers and the citizens . . . produced the better state of things now."[127] Unlike during Reconstruction, Democrats also insisted that most revenuers were now honest and efficient. "Up to 1876," lawyer J. M. Leach explained, "the system commenced badly, with improper, and in some instances, bad and corrupt men in office as subordinates, but it gradually grew better year by year."[128] A. C. Avery agreed. "Just after the war, a majority of the officers, collectors and deputy marshals, were thought to be imprudent and indiscreet men," he remembered. "At a later period, within the last

A. C. Avery. From John Preston Arthur, *Western North Carolina: A History* (Raleigh: Edwards and Broughton Printing Company, 1914), facing 356.

eight or ten years, we have had some deputy marshals and deputy collectors against who I have heard no charge."[129] Losing the support of Democrats forced illicit distillers to retreat. Things would get worse, however. In 1881, mountain reformers launched a campaign for statewide prohibition that would further alienate moonshiners from their former supporters in the Democratic Party.

The Politics of Prohibition

The *New York Times* and other national newspapers closely followed the political events unfolding in North Carolina during the summer of 1881. In March, the Democratic-controlled state legislature had ordered a general election to take place on the first Thursday of August to decide whether to enact statewide prohibition, forbidding both the sale and the manufacture of alcohol. As the August referendum approached, the issue of prohibition was on everyone's mind in the Tar Heel State. "The campaign has been in progress for more than two months," a *New York Times* correspondent wrote in late July, "and in every considerable town there are daily meetings of 'wets' and 'drys'— as the anti-prohibitionists and prohibitionists are laconically dubbed by some of the papers. . . . Sitting at a table in hotels your neighbors discuss nothing but the all-engrossing topic of whiskey or no whiskey, the arguments of enthusiastic editors, and the points made by the latest speakers in the neighborhood."[130] This election was gaining national exposure, for good reason. It was the first time a southern state had considered implementing a ban on both the retail and the production of alcohol since the antebellum period. Unlike during the 1850s, statewide prohibition had also become a partisan issue, one that threatened to destroy the Democratic Party in North Carolina.

Empowered by the success of local-option laws in their communities, religious groups and temperance organizations began to push for more drastic legislation during the late 1870s and early 1880s. In December 1879, the State Conference of the Methodist Episcopal Church–South issued a decree demanding that the state legislature prohibit the sale of "ardent spirits" in North Carolina. The following year, the North Carolina Methodist Conference and the Baptist State Convention argued that alcohol produced "poverty and crime throughout the country" and urged its followers to sign petitions asking the legislature to pass statewide prohibition. By February 1881, more than

100,000 voters, along with 50,000 women and children, had answered this call.[131] "The movement in favor of prohibition in North Carolina has proceeded until its proportions are beyond any reasonable anticipations," the *Asheville Citizen* reported. "Similar exertions in behalf of temperance have been made elsewhere, but in no other state have we known such monstrous petitions to be presented to the legislature."[132]

Despite the demands of these state and mountain reformers, Democrats remained hesitant to pass statewide prohibition. They had observed recent events in Virginia with great interest. During the late 1870s, the Readjusters, an independent political movement led by William Mahone, wanted to scale down Virginia's enormous debt but found their path blocked by the Democratic Party. Undeterred, they formed an alliance with local Republicans in 1879. In 1880, Republicans gained control of the state legislature and elected Mahone to the U.S. Senate, where he appointed his supporters and Republicans to important committees and offices. This left the Democratic Party in Virginia in shambles.[133] North Carolina Democrats did not want to suffer the same fate.[134] In March 1881, the *Asheville Citizen* warned that the issue of prohibition had generated "great excitement" in the Carolina highlands and that, if passed, enforcement would evoke "the same indignation as accorded" to the Bureau of Internal Revenue and the Republican Party during Reconstruction.[135] Lawmakers feared that western North Carolinians, many of whom continued to regard alcohol as an integral part of their social existence and economy, would blame the Democratic-controlled state legislature for the law and abandon the party.[136] Senator Zebulon Vance realized the potential political repercussions of prohibition on the Democratic Party and refused to endorse the bill. An 1887 letter to Theodore Davidson concerning the rise of the Prohibition Party in North Carolina helps explain why Vance may have chosen this course of action. Although "determined never to stand one moment in the way of the moral welfare of the state," Vance insisted that there were "considerations here that zealots [were] likely to overlook if not disregard." The issue of statewide prohibition included "so many legal rights involved, so much capital invested in the trafficking and the change proposed [was] so radical" that Vance could not consent to it. Neither would he publicly denounce it, arguing that the issue was a "purely social question."[137]

Mountain reformers tried to reassure Democratic politicians that statewide prohibition would not harm the party. In January 1881,

Augustus Merrimon, a former member of the Asheville Sons of Temperance, told the prohibition convention in Raleigh that the question would remain apolitical.[138] The Rev. S. V. Hoyle of Morganton suggested to Burke County representative Samuel Tate that the Democrats could survive a prohibition bill and prevent a mass exodus from the party by calling for a general election and allowing voters to make the final decision.[139] Democratic lawyer W. S. Pearson of Morganton concurred. He assured Tate in February that prohibition "will not as I am told you think injure the Democratic Party." In fact, Pearson believed the Democrats would actually benefit from the measure because it would eliminate the need for the Bureau of Internal Revenue, thereby weakening the Republican Party in the mountains. "This whiskey," Pearson explained to Tate, "has played the devil with all of our people on both sides of the fence—the Revenue officers whose business will now be taken from them have played the devil with our State."[140]

Tate was not convinced, but the majority of state legislators were. In March, they agreed on a prohibition bill to present to the voters. The proposed law would ban entirely the sale and manufacture of alcohol (cider and wines excepted) within North Carolina. Only druggists, physicians, and apothecaries could vend alcohol for medical, mechanical, and chemical purposes after obtaining a license from a county commissioner. Customers would be allowed to purchase up to a gallon of alcohol, as long as they had a certificate from a practicing physician. Violators of the law would be fined $100 or $500. If voters approved prohibition, the law would go into effect on October 1, 1881.[141]

J. J. Mott, chairman of the Republican state executive committee, did what he could to use the issue to divide the Democratic Party. In May, he formed an alliance with antiprohibition forces in the hope of gaining the support of Democrats who resented governmental intrusion into their private affairs.[142] Not wanting to lose the support of Republican prohibitionists, Mott defended his position: "Republicans in every township must organize and poll a full vote against this bill as the only means of condemning class legislation and to prevent the creation of a powerful monopoly of druggists, apothecaries and physicians, which is always dangerous in a government like ours. . . . When this has been done, Republicans will be ready to aid in regulating the sale of liquor in such manner as will remedy and correct as many abuses growing out of the use of liquor, as can be remedied and corrected by legislation."[143] Most Republicans in western North Carolina, whatever their views on temperance, accepted this alliance with antiprohibitionists because they realized that their survival depended on it. Prohibition threatened to destroy the Bureau of Internal Revenue and the hundreds of patronage jobs it provided to party members.[144]

Ironically, mountain distillers on both sides of the law conveniently overlooked the fact that revenue officials were leading the movement, and they joined the ranks of antiprohibitionists. Although some "cynically calculated how much it would improve their business," most "moonshiners themselves were not likely to vote for prohibition."[145] They sided with revenuers like Mott, who argued that prohibition threatened to do irreparable damage to the economy. As Mott explained to Raum in July 1881, prohibition "strikes at the industry of manufacturing spirits in North Carolina, and . . . would [break] up the business of distilling to the great injury of a people who have engaged in that business . . . for more than a hundred years."[146] The proposed law also threatened to make it harder for the moonshiners to evade the law because it would have added yet another set of officials attempting to break up stills and haul people into court.[147] It made sense for distillers to risk alienating themselves from local Democrats by siding with the Republicans and the Bureau of Internal Revenue to fight statewide prohibition.

"Wet" and "dry" forces scrambled to gain the support of Carolina highlanders. In every mountain county, both groups organized barbecues, rallies, and meetings where members of the community discussed the arguments for or against prohibition.[148] As they had done in the past, "wets" argued that prohibition was a "radical" piece of legislation that threatened to deprive citizens of their "personal liberties" and insisted that the August referendum was unconstitutional. According to an unnamed "law student" from Caldwell County, the North Carolina and U.S. Constitutions stated that legislators had the sole responsibility of passing all laws. "This government," he explained in June, "is a democracy, but it is a representative democracy in which the people by their construction have divested themselves of the power to make laws, and transferred it to their agents in legislature assembled."[149]

Hoping to appeal to temperance supporters, "wets" broadened their critique of statewide prohibition beyond the legal arguments. They warned that prohibition would ultimately promote disorder and intemperance. "I fully believe," a Caldwell County man explained in July, "if [prohibition] should become the law of the state it will result in bitterness and constant litigation to the great prejudice of the country."[150] When speaking at a rally in Watauga County that same month, local farmer Christian Moretz cautioned reformers that prohibition would encourage moonshining and resistance to state authority. He warned that "there would be a blockade still at the head of every branch, and that whiskey would be brought here from Tennessee in abundance" if prohibition became law.[151] A McDowell County resident added that the law would weaken public schools, which had been largely funded by a state tax on alcohol retail licenses.[152] Antiprohibitionists also capitalized on intrastate sectionalism by arguing that prohibition would benefit wine makers in eastern North Carolina. Moretz, for instance, insisted that "eastern men" had originated "the bill in order to force us to buy their wines [which would have been exempt from the prohibition law]."[153]

Supporters of the ban were not intimidated. Responding to the Caldwell County "law student," a Mr. "Lex" pointed out that the student "was too young to know the fact that eight millions of dollars are carried out of the State yearly to enrich northern liquor dealers, while our poor suffer for bread, and their children grow up in ignorance."[154] Another Caldwell County resident confronted the "personal liberties" argument: "Let us come nearer home and examine the law against carrying concealed deadly weapons. Is it not generally admitted to be a good one? But it infringes upon our rights and liberties, and it must be done away with! Then, to be 'free as the air we breathe,' we must allow drunken bullies to go at large, armed to the teeth, and a big canteen of whiskey strapped to their backs." He also rebuked the assertion that the law would create a monopoly of druggists who would sell liquor at exorbitant prices, thereby making it harder for the "common people" to obtain alcohol for medicinal purposes. He dismissed this charge as "too absurd to credit." He concluded by asking, "Which places the most venom in the bodies of our race, the teeth of poisonous serpents or the worm of the still?"[155]

Prohibitionists continued to reassure mountain Democrats that the issue would not divide the party. "It is not a political movement," a Macon County resident explained, "but is the combined wisdom of the best men of all political creeds, and deserves the hearty co-operation of every citizen of North Carolina."[156] Robert Abernethy from Burke County pointed out that prominent mountain Democrats, including Zebulon Vance, endorsed the bill's passage. Abernethy urged voters not to support the antiprohibitionist coalition, which he believed was a "morally stunted breed" composed of revenuers, large distillers from the North, and African Americans. "Such men as the Vances, Merrimons, and others who have been produced amid the cloud-capped mountains of North Carolina," he declared, "can never condescend so low as to affiliate with such a dirty, filthy set of men."[157]

Prohibitionists argued that the region's numerous distilleries were not a valuable part of the mountain economy, as their opponents suggested, but a hindrance to its expansion. The law, they said, would help bring order, industry, and economic growth to western North Carolina. "Let me ask," a Caldwell County resident wrote in July, "what branch of human industry would not be advanced by abstinence from spirituous liquors?" Prohibition would force farmers to grow commercial crops and raise livestock, he answered, thereby "enabling those who have not enough of the 'staff of life' to live in much more comfort." And he believed the region would benefit from the ban because it would "be a powerful stimulus towards railroad building in order to dispose of the surplus grain."[158] The Executive Committee of Prohibition in Caldwell County insisted that outlawing distilled spirits would "promote the best interests of society and increase the prosperity and happiness of the whole country."[159] Again, the editors of the *Asheville Citizen* showed how far sympathies had shifted when they sided with the prohibitionists. They accused opponents of hindering the region's "moral and social advancement" out of greed. "You should vote for prohibition," they exhorted readers, "because of the results upon the coming generation, to whom we are to look for the preservation of our institutions, and the perpetuation of our liberties. In these the hopes of our Country are centered."[160]

As the August referendum approached, the outcome of the vote remained uncertain. That June, a Watauga County farmer reported that "our people seem divided on this great question."[161] "Next to the Normal school in point of interest to the people of Macon County," another mountain resident wrote in July, "is the subject of prohibition." He felt that the vote in Macon County was "about equally enough divided to make matters interesting."[162] According to the *Newton Enterprise*, public opinion in Catawba County seemed to favor prohibition.[163] But many prohibitionists feared that they had not gained the support of enough rural residents. "The farmers of the mountains and coves have made up their minds how they will vote," a Buncombe County man wrote in July, "and most of them . . . propose to worship under their own vines and fruit trees." He concluded: "All that [we]

Table 5.2. Vote on Prohibition in Western North Carolina, 1881

County	For Prohibition		Against Prohibition	
	Number	Percent	Number	Percent
Yancey	502	60	329	40
Transylvania	230	53	202	47
Clay	149	53	133	47
Cherokee	270	51	262	49
Cleveland	1,142	49	1,144	51
Haywood	655	49	676	51
Mitchell	366	49	381	51
Buncombe	1,606	48	1,745	52
Madison	719	44	917	56
Catawba	876	40	1,305	60
Graham	79	39	125	61
Swain	116	36	204	64
Jackson	258	35	476	65
Alexander	337	34	652	66
McDowell	383	33	786	67
Macon	257	32	558	68
Henderson	328	28	824	72
Rutherford	602	26	1,699	74
Polk	142	24	460	76
Watauga	228	24	731	76
Burke	348	22	1,238	78
Caldwell	245	22	871	78
Ashe	266	17	1,328	83
Surry	314	13	2,067	87
Wilkes	337	12	2,429	88
Alleghany	49	6	720	94
Western NC total	10,804	33	22,262	67

Source: Daniel J. Whitener, *Prohibition in North Carolina, 1715–1945* (Chapel Hill: University of North Carolina Press, 1946), appendix.

can say to [prohibitionists] is to keep cool and not trifle with our liberties. [We] will do like Putnam of old at the battle of Bunker Hill."[164]

The prohibitionists indeed fell short of their goal, as 71 percent of North Carolina voters rejected the bill in August.[165] "Dry" forces received a higher percentage of the vote in western North Carolina than elsewhere in the state.[166] Support for prohibition appears to have been strongest in the mountain counties that underwent rapid industrial change during the 1870s. In the western part of the state, prohibitionists won in four counties and received more than 48 percent of the vote in four others (see table 5.2). Two of the mountain counties that favored prohibition, Yancey and Cherokee, experienced the second and fourth highest percentage increase in capital invested in manufacturing between 1870 and 1880. The 1870 census did not include the amount of capital invested in Transylvania and Clay counties, making it impossible to determine the effect of industrialization on the vote there. But considering the high rate of moonshiner violence in Transylvania County and its reputation as part of the troublesome "Dark Corners," highlanders there may have supported prohibition in an attempt to end lawlessness.[167]

Despite losing the election, mountain prohibitionists remained optimistic about the future. Convincing a third of highlanders to vote in favor of the ban was certainly a victory. Chastised as radicals during the antebellum period, prohibitionists were slowing garnering the support of thousands of western North Carolinians. Their popularity would continue to increase during the last two decades of the nineteenth century, when the region underwent rapid economic expansion. The arrival of the Western North Carolina Railroad would further transform mountain society and encourage more denizens to embrace the amenities and philosophies of urban America. These highlanders would argue that the New South had no place for alcohol or the men who made it.

6

"These Big-Boned, Semi-Barbarian People"

Creation of the Myth of Violent Appalachia and Its Consequences, 1878–1890

I'll tune up my fiddle and rosin my bow,
And make myself welcome wherever I go.
I'll buy my own whiskey and make my own stew;
If it does make me drunk it is nothing to you.

"It is a good deal the fashion to ascribe to this transmontane country an undue share of that moral and intellectual darkness . . . characteristic of the back woods settlement." So wrote an anonymous mountain resident to the *Asheville Citizen* in 1883, angry over the media's portrayal of western North Carolina as a violent and uneducated region. "The error begins with ignorance of facts," the writer pleaded. "The mountain people are neither so ignorant nor so irreligious as careless persons pronounce them." Nor were most of them violent moonshiners. "While there is occasional violence," he explained, "it is so exceptional as to justify the assertion that there is no more peaceful, law abiding and moral people than those of Western North Carolina."[1] This plea for understanding would fall on deaf ears. Captivated by the national media's coverage of the "Moonshine Wars" in the late 1870s, Victorian middle-class Americans had already accepted the stereotype of Appalachia as "the home of the hunter, the moonshiner, and the beasts of the forest."[2]

Although negative images of Appalachia and its people originated during the antebellum period, it was not until after the Civil War that these misconceptions gained widespread acceptance among northern and southern townspeople. This was largely due to the emergence of local color writing, a literary genre that grew out of new American literary magazines and catered to a burgeoning urban, middle-class readership in the 1870s. The goal of these writings was to increase magazine sales by focusing on the peculiarities of Appalachian people.[3] Local colorists ultimately "discovered" a distinct but noble white "race" out of step with modern society.[4] Beginning in the late 1870s, however, writers forged another conception of mountain whites, one that portrayed them as both violent and savage. The moonshiner played an important role in the creation of this stereotype, epitomizing a mountain populace that Americans came to fear as a threat to civilization.

Since the 1970s, historians have devoted considerable attention to the images of mountain residents produced by local color novelists, journalists, and missionaries at the turn of the twentieth century. They have demonstrated conclusively that negative stereotypes about the region often reflected middle-class America's desire to stress the benefits of industrialization and "progress." "In an age of faith in American, and more generally Western, intellectual, cultural, and social superiority over the other 'races' of the world," historian Anthony Harkins explains, "these [stereotypes] were designed to show not cultural difference so much as cultural hierarchy—to celebrate modernity and 'mainstream' progress."[5] Urban, middle-class Victorians perceived southern Appalachia as an unwanted remnant of the colonial era. They believed that the region and its people were economically, geographically, and culturally at odds with modern America.

Hoping to reaffirm their cultural superiority, among other reasons, Victorian whites also depicted Appalachia as a region where lawlessness and violence prevailed. Most historians have emphasized the role of feuding in the construction of the myth of violent Appalachia. During the late 1880s, they agree, the national media's coverage of the Hatfield-McCoy feud and others convinced middle-class citizens that mountain whites were inherently more violent than other Americans. Although correct, these scholars have underestimated the impact of moonshiner violence on the formation of such misconceptions. Published nearly a decade before the emergence of Victorian America's fascination with feuding, local color and newspaper accounts of illicit distilling, whether sympathetic to the moonshiners or not, portrayed southern Appalachia as a lawless region that needed civilizing.[6]

Many urban highlanders in western North Carolina, however,

responded unfavorably to the negative images of the region popular-ized by journalists and local colorists. During the 1880s, the arrival of the Western North Carolina Railroad and other transportation arter-ies had ushered in an era of rapid industrial growth in the western part of the state. Northern and local entrepreneurs built textile factories, mines, and lumber camps, while residents in Asheville and other grow-ing communities embraced the philosophies of urban, middle-class America. These townspeople, who were becoming a politically and cul-turally powerful force, believed themselves to be civilized and whole-heartedly rejected the myth of violent Appalachia. But their actions ultimately helped reinforce and perpetuate this stereotype. In their haste to differentiate themselves from mountain country folk, they identified their rural neighbors as a group of ignorant, drunk moonshiners. In the end, urban mountain residents attempted to salvage their own image by embracing the reform-minded "uplift movement" of the 1890s.

Moonshining and the Creation of Violent Western North Carolina

In October 1869, *Appleton's Journal* published a three-part series called "Novelties of Southern Scenery" by landscape artist and travel writer Charles Lanman. This illustrated work introduced middle-class Americans to western North Carolina (and other parts of southern Appalachia), portraying it as a land of "grand and beautiful scenery." Lanman believed that the Civil War had prevented "modern civiliza-tion" from "rapidly developing" in the mountains. Western North Carolina's landscape remained pristine because it had not been cut up to make way for "cumbersome coaches and the railway trains." The mountain peaks, he reported, rose higher than Mount Washington in New Hampshire and offered abundant resources, blue skies, and diverse flora and fauna, all "glories beyond compare." "The Roan and the Bald, the Grandfather, and the Whiteside Mountains, each and all of them, and hundreds of others afford charms and delightful associa-tion without number," Lanman praised.[7]

"Novelties of Southern Scenery" was the first of several illustrated works on Appalachia's mountain landscape published in *Appleton's, Harper's,* and other literary magazines during Reconstruction. Spurred by technological advances in the mass production of images, increas-ing literacy, and the growth of advertising, these articles appealed to urban, middle-class northerners who, adopting British aesthetics, wanted to enjoy "picturesque" scenes that contained elements both beautiful and sublime.[8] These illustrated works also served to reunite the North with the South.[9] War-weary northern urbanites were eager to reconcile with their former adversaries, learn about the southern landscape, and invest in its unexploited raw materials.[10] *Appleton's* and other urban-based magazines met this demand by providing their readership with a glimpse of a "strange and peculiar" world.

Like "Novelties of Southern Scenery," subsequent illustrated pieces portrayed western North Carolina's landscape as pristine and untamed. Henry E. Colton, another *Appleton's* writer who penned a series of short features on the region in 1870 and 1871, declared that the Carolina highlands was "nature's gallery of the queer, the beautiful and grand." Set amid "lofty mountains, majestic and fatherly, standing with a saintly presence like a benediction over the gentle valley," it was a land undisturbed by modern society.[11] In *The Land of the Sky; or Adventures in Mountain By-ways*, Frances Fisher Tiernan, using the pen name Christian Reid, continues where Colton left off. This novel, serialized in *Appleton's* during the autumn of 1875 and based on a trip Tiernan made to the region, chronicles the adventures of four young northerners spending a summer in western North Carolina. These Victorian youths encounter a land "so boundless and so beautiful, that the imagination is for a time overwhelmed." They also discover a pristine mountain landscape. When traveling from Asheville to Warm Springs, the characters feel that they are "leaving civilization altogether behind, plunging deeper and deeper into the heart of primeval Nature." The narrator describes what the group observes: "[The mountains] rise over our heads hundreds of feet . . . in every interstice of which great pines grow, and thickets of rhododendron flourish. In the dark shade, ferns, flowers, and mosses abound, together with trees of every variety, while down the hill-sides and over the rocks countless streams come leaping in foam and spray."[12]

Focusing on the "curiosities" of the landscape, Colton, Tiernan, and other scenic entrepreneurs mostly ignore the mountain inhabitants.[13] In *Land of the Sky*, for instance, Tiernan mentions only one Carolina highlander by name: John Pence, "a spare, sinewy man, dark as an Indian, with the eyes of a hawk, who wears a pair of the brownest and dirtiest corduroy trousers."[14] When local characters did appear in literature, writers often portrayed them as the product of an isolated environment. In 1872, David Hunter Strother wrote that the high-lander was "born and nurtured in poverty and seclusion. He [had] no set pattern to grow up by, with none of the slop-shops of civiliza-tion at hand to furnish him ready-made clothing, manners, or opin-ions."[15] Two years later, author Edward King described western North Carolinians as noble people out of step with modern America. "They were neatly dressed in home-made clothes, and their hair was combed straight down over their cheeks and knotted into 'pugs' behind," King explained. "There were none of the modern conventionalities of dress visible about them. The men were cavalier enough; their jean trou-sers were thrust into their boots, and their slouch hats cocked on their heads with bravado air."[16] For the most part, however, the mountain landscape remained the central character in the narratives of scenic entrepreneurs. It was a world different from that in which they and their urban readership lived, a fantasy of an unspoiled wilderness devoid of civilization.

Beginning in the mid-1870s, a new literary genre emerged that would further shape how middle-class Victorians perceived southern Appalachia and its people. More so than earlier authors, local color-ists began to focus considerable attention on the dialect and culture of mountain people. Building on the works of Lanman, Strother, and King, they portrayed white mountain inhabitants as a noble "race" uncorrupted by the evils of modern civilization. In "Qualla," published in 1875, Rebecca Harding Davis praises Carolina highlanders for their primitive lifestyle:

> They were not cumbered with dishes, knives, forks, beds, or any other impediments of civilization: they slept in hollow logs or in a hole filled with straw under loose boards of the floor. But they were contented and good-natured: they took life, leaky roof, opossum, and all, as a huge joke, and were honest gentlefolk despite their dirty and bedless condition. . . . Money, indeed, appeared throughout this region to be one of the unknown luxuries of civilization; and it's startling (if any-thing could be startling up yonder) to find how easily and com-fortably life resolves itself to its primitive conditions without.[17]

In "The French Broad," published in *Harper's Monthly* that same year, Constance Fenimore Woolson expresses a similar admiration for mountain whites. "There are noble hearts under those gaunt, ungraceful exteriors that excite your mirth," one of Woolson's characters explains. "Those very women will come over the mountains from miles away, when you are ill, and nurse you tenderly for pure charity's sake. They will spin their wool and dye and weave, and make you clothes from the cloth."[18] These characterizations of mountain folk served to differentiate middle-class townspeople from the rural, primitive "other" and helped satisfy urbanites' longing for a simpler past. Southern Appalachia became a refuge, a place where these Victorians could escape from the hustle and bustle of city life.[19]

By the late 1870s, the depiction of southern Appalachia in literature had become less of an idyllic escape from the realities of the modern world and more of a region full of violence and lawlessness. In 1879, Louise Coffin Jones claimed that most Carolina highlanders belonged to "the lower class, composed of 'poor white trash,'" and "the civilities, courtesies, even some of the decencies, of life were dispensed with; and as a relapse from culture is always more degrading in its influence and tendencies than a corresponding state of ignorance among a people who have never been elevated, so these degenerate Anglo-Saxons compared unfavorably with the native Indians, a few of whom still lingered in the mountains."[20] For local colorists like Jones, this was a primitive people who had willingly rejected modernity. The mountain moonshiner played an important role in the creation of this stereotype. Even though illicit distilling persisted in many northern cities and in other parts of the South, it would become synonymous with the mountain region, largely due to the national media's coverage of the conflict between the Bureau of Internal Revenue and moonshiners following the end of Reconstruction. These accounts helped convince many outsiders that mountain residents were inherently more ignorant and violent than other Americans. They perpetuated the idea that all highlanders—not just moonshiners—were products of a "frontier" environment, a "big-boned, semi-barbarian people" who needed civilizing.

Although conflicts between illicit distillers and revenue agents were reported as early as 1867, it was not until the late 1870s that northern newspapers and magazines depicted moonshining as one of the "peculiarities" of southern Appalachia.[21] By 1877, the New York Times was offering extensive coverage of the Moonshine Wars, noting that illicit distilling occurred most frequently in the mountains of Tennessee,

Georgia, and the Carolinas. The *Times* first argued that the Democratic Party encouraged "densely, ignorant men of the up-country" to evade the federal liquor law. It stated in July 1878:

> At one time, during the rule of Republican Governors . . . an earnest and what promised to be a successful effort to break up the rapidly-growing traffic was made by the Federal officers, aided by United States troops. The return of the Democracy to power brought other methods, however; the State courts did everything in their power to shield the still-owners against the officers of the National Government, until, some time after the inauguration of the present Administration, the distillers in many cases began to openly defy the Marshals, and to publicly break the laws which they had previously violated in secret.[22]

By 1880, however, influenced by descriptions of the region in local color literature, the newspaper had begun to downplay the role of politics, instead blaming geographic isolation for the violence surrounding moonshining. "They [illicit distillers] live in districts remote from railroads and from markets, where they could sell surplus grain," the *Times* explained. Like most highlanders, these moonshiners "were illiterate and ignorant. They scarcely ever read a book or a newspaper, and know very little of what is going on in the world." This, combined with their supposed natural fondness for whiskey and distrust of federal authority, encouraged mountain farmers to manufacture alcohol illegally. The best way to end illicit distilling and improve the region, the paper argued, was to introduce mountain inhabitants to civilization by building free schools and railroads. "So long as they remain isolated," the *Times* concluded, "they will defy the laws."[23]

As the national media coverage of moonshiners intensified in the late 1870s and 1880s, local color writers also began to include them as central characters in their stories. During those years, illicit distilling became virtually a requirement in descriptive pieces dealing with the mountain region. Writers used the moonshiner as a symbol of what was wrong with Appalachia and, like the media, proposed that only industrialization could change the behavior of mountain residents.

In 1877, *Harper's* published "The Moonshine Man: A Peep into His Haunts and Hiding Places," the first of several pieces that focused on illicit distilling in southern Appalachia. This work contains two themes that journalists and local colorists would build on as they developed the image of both moonshiners and highlanders. First, it characterizes illicit distilling as the product of geographic isolation. Second, it uses the distiller to epitomize tensions between urban America and savage Appalachia. The anonymous author explains: "The moonshiner in a large city is as mild-looking a man as is ever seen. The sudden change from horseback to a seat in the [train] cars, on which nine-tenths of them have never ridden until captured, and the startling effect produced by sudden entry into a city after long years of life in rural regions, so overcome the illicit distiller that his appearance on the streets would picture him to the observer as meek and mild-mannered in the extreme." The story's message is that illicit distillers were unable and unwilling to adapt to civilization and felt out of place when forced out of their natural habitat. They were members of "the poorest and most ignorant classes," the unwanted remnants of the colonial past.[24]

Woolson further develops these themes in the short story "Up in the Blue Ridge," published in *Appleton's* in 1878. Woolson, who just three years earlier had extolled highlanders for their simplicity in "The French Broad," now expresses the fear that most of them will never adjust to modern society. The story chronicles the adventures of Stephen Wainwright, a northerner who visits North Carolina and falls in love with a mountain girl. Wainwright, however, soon discovers that his life is in danger because many local residents, including a Baptist preacher, believe he is a revenue agent attempting to capture the notorious moonshiner Richard Eliot. According to Woolson, Eliot is a typical highlander: he turned to illegal distilling because he was unable to "adapt" to modern society and find a "civilized" profession. Wainwright convinces the locals that he is not a revenuer, but his cousin and fellow New Yorker John Royce pledges to capture Eliot, who has murdered a revenue agent named Allison. In a battle of the civilized versus the savage, Royce and Eliot square off in a gunfight. Eliot wounds Royce and escapes, vowing to continue his illegal activities. "The moonlight-whiskey is made up in the mountain, and still the revenue-detectives are shot," Woolson concludes. "The wild, beautiful region is not yet conquered."[25]

Following the publication of "Up in the Blue Ridge," journalists and local colorists devoted considerable attention to illicit distilling in the Carolina highlands, which they considered to be one of the most dangerous moonshine enclaves in the United States.[26] Edward Critten-

Engraving of "The Moonshine Man," *Harper's Weekly* 21 (October 20, 1877): 820. Courtesy of the Prints and Photographs Division, Library of Congress, Washington, D.C.

den's 1879 dime novel about Lewis Redmond, an actual moonshiner whose exploits against revenuers in South Carolina had gained him national notoriety, helped solidify this perception.[27] Published in Philadelphia, this tale of romance, betrayal, and murder must have thrilled its Victorian audience. In it, Redmond kidnaps and falls in love with the angelic Gabrielle Austin, who has the misfortune of riding in a carriage attacked by Redmond's gang. Gabrielle soon discovers that her captor is a tormented man. Although educated and refined, he lives only to avenge his father's death at the hands of Internal Revenue agents. "One night a body of Federal troops surrounded our house, and demanded my father's surrender," he explains to Gabrielle. "Like a brave man he refused, and gave up his life rather than sacrifice his liberty. The shock of that terrible night's occurrence killed my mother, and I, a boy in years and in experience with the rugged side of life's journey, was an orphan." Although Redmond ultimately allows Gabrielle and her fiancé, who attempts to rescue her, to leave unscathed, he refuses to abandon his way of life. "Redmond the outlaw," Crittenden concludes, "still defies the authority of the law, daily commits crimes unparalleled in history, has startling adventures and hairbreadth escapes."[28]

In August 1879, *Harper's Weekly* printed "Law and Moonshine," an exposé on illicit distillers in western North Carolina. The piece agrees that moonshiners are the products of geographic isolation, but it adds a new explanation: genetics. According to the anonymous author, most mountain whites are not only illicit distillers but also naturally "wild" and "grotesque." They are social misfits dedicated to kinfolk and predisposed to reject authority. "It is impossible," the author explains, "to convince these big-boned, semi-barbarian people that the revenue official who comes with an armed posse into their haunts, searching for and destroying their stills, is not an emissary of a tyrannical and unjust government, for whom the sly bullet is but too good a welcome."[29] Unlike "Up in the Blue Ridge," "Law and Moonshine" places the blame for moonshiner violence squarely on the shoulders of highlanders, whose culture and genetic makeup encourage them to act irrationally.

By the 1880s, many journalists and local colorists had adopted the view that moonshining was the result of both geographic isolation and genetics.[30] In 1882, *Atlantic Monthly* reported that illicit distilling was "partly a feature of the old warfare of the mountaineers against the civilization and the people of the towns." These "tall, finely-built,

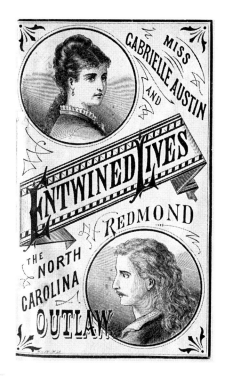

Cover of Edward Crittenden's dime novel *The Entwined Lives of Miss Gabrielle Austin, Daughter of the Late Rev. Ellis C. Austin, and of Redmond, the Outlaw, Leader of the North Carolina "Moonshiners"* (Philadelphia: Barclay and Co., 1879).

Engraving of "Law and Moonshine— Crooked Whisky in North Carolina," *Harper's Weekly* 24 (August 23, 1879): 667. Courtesy of the Prints and Photographs Division, Library of Congress, Washington, D.C.

powerful, loose-jointed" men were supposedly a breed apart, a distinct, racialized "other" genetically and culturally predisposed to break
the law.[31] According to Donald Baines, writing in 1885, illegal distillers in Macon County remained "semi-barbarians" and, as such, knew
"no law of right and justice."[32] Baines and other writers also linked the
highlanders' alleged genetic inferiority, inherent violence, and fondness
for alcohol to feuding, a practice that became synonymous with the
region during the late 1880s.[33] Kentucky journalist James Lane Allen
explained in 1886: "The special origins of [feuding] are various: blood
heated and temper lost under the influence of 'moonshine'; reporting
on the places and manufacturers of this; local politics; the survival of
resentment engendered during the civil war—these, together with all
causes that lie in the passions of the human heart and spring from the
constitution of all human society, often make the remote and insulated
life of these people turbulent, reckless, and distressing."[34]

Journalists and fiction writers continued to promote industrialization as the solution to the economic and social ills of the southern Appalachian Mountains. By improving education, introducing new religious
groups, and modernizing the region's economy, the moonshiner—who
was both a product and a cause of his environment—would be eliminated. Railroads, factories, and other industrial projects would usher
in a new era of "progress" by discouraging highlanders from engaging
in illicit distilling, binge drinking, and violence.[35] As Baines concludes:
"In a few more years, when the march of progress shall have sounded
through these woods and dales the 'moonshiners' occupation will be
gone, and in his stead we shall find industrious, hard-working farmers,
cultivating the rich soil that is now running to waste; the hum of the
spindle shall succeed the bubbling of the still, and where now is nought
but desolation, squalor and ignorance, there shall be cultivation and
plenty, happiness and wealth, education and intelligence."[36]

The myth of violent Appalachia and its moonshiners was embraced
by two groups. Northern capitalists could rationalize their activity in
the region because they were, in effect, saving the people of Appalachia
as much as they were profiting off them. It also allowed middle-class
Americans to project their own fears about economic modernization onto a people they perceived to be different. The illicit distiller
reminded these Victorians why they had embraced industrialization
and "progress." Moreover, northerners' embrace of violent Appalachia
permitted them to reunite with the South following Reconstruction.

Engraving of "The Moonshiner's Home," *Harper's Weekly* 30 (October 23, 1886): 687. From the Shirley Stipp Ephemera Collection, D. H. Ramsey Library, Special Collections, University of North Carolina at Asheville.

By focusing their attention on moonshining and later feuding in the mountains, middle-class northerners were able to overlook the racial violence that accompanied "redemption" elsewhere in South, thereby making it easier for them to reconcile with their former adversaries.[37]

Perhaps more significantly, the myth of violent Appalachia ultimately encouraged northern, middle-class Victorians to launch the uplift movement of the 1890s. These reformers, disappointed over their failure to empower African Americans in the South during Reconstruction, increasingly focused their attention on reforming mountain whites, whom they believed were "Americans-in-the-making." Although primitive and violent, highlanders had supposedly rejected slavery, been loyal to the Union during the Civil War, and remained racially pure, the embodiment of Anglo-Saxonism. In other words, they possessed "qualities which made them capable of uplift and improvement." These myths helped open "a new path for northern humanitarianism that was far removed from the disturbing racial and social conflicts that held the South in its grip" during the last two decades of the nineteenth century.[38] But this northern-based reform crusade would not have been possible without the support of mountain townspeople, who, ironically, helped create and perpetuate the myth of violent Appalachia. Wanting to create a New South, these urban residents denounced the drinking mores of their rural neighbors and embraced the uplift movement with the hope of ridding their communities of alcohol distilling, which they believed was a backward practice that had no place in the burgeoning industrial social order.

Industrialization, Full Speed Ahead

On March 11, 1879, an enthusiastic James W. Wilson, chief engineer and president of the Western North Carolina Railroad, wired Governor Thomas J. Jarvis: "Daylight has entered Buncombe County today: grade and center met exactly."[39] After two long years and the loss of some 400 lives, workers—mostly African American convicts—had finally completed the eleven-mile stretch of railroad over and through the mountain from Old Fort to Swannanoa, a village nestled along the western slopes of the Blue Ridge in Buncombe County. On October 3, 1880, the WNCRR reached Asheville, where the next phase of construction carried track in two directions—west toward Waynesville in Haywood County, and north to Marshall in Madison County.

Arrival of a stage at Warms Springs Motel in Madison, North Carolina, 1875. Courtesy of the North Carolina State Archives.

The arrival of the WNCRR ushered in an unprecedented era of economic growth in the Carolina highlands, starting with the tourism industry. The railroad made it easier for middle-class Americans to vacation at mountain resorts. Thousands of wealthy tourists, including George Washington Vanderbilt, the grandson of industrial tycoon Cornelius Vanderbilt, journeyed to the region, where they vacationed and sometimes purchased land for the construction of large country estates. Resort communities sprang up in Cashiers in Jackson County, Highlands in Macon County, and other small towns throughout western North Carolina as well.[40] Asheville benefited most from the burgeoning tourist business. Between 1800 and 1885, the city's population increased from 2,610 to 5,000, and its property values more than quadrupled from $904,428 in 1880 to $4,453,234 in 1889.[41]

Seeing the prosperity it brought their neighbors, Carolina highlanders pushed for the further expansion of the railroad. According to a Haywood County entrepreneur in 1882, the completion of the WNCRR would allow Waynesville to "compete with Asheville in this unmistakable herald of civilization and sign of progress."[42] Railroads promised to create what most local boosters now called a New South, one in which tourism, industry, and cheap labor would become the backbone of the region's economy. "When these lines are completed," a Jackson County resident explained in 1882, "the attention of Northern capitalists will be attracted, and I predict that in twenty five years millions of capital will be invested in Western North Carolina in manufacturing enterprises."[43] Other highlanders argued that the railroad would become a panacea for the economic woes of their communities. In the rural Burke County township of Lower Fork, farmer N. L. Chapman insisted that "all we need is a railroad through this part of the county, to ship our lumber to market, to make the South Mountain section second to none for its moneyed productions."[44]

Western North Carolinians got their wish. By 1890, the western branch of the WNCRR traveled through parts of Haywood, Jackson, Macon, Swain, Graham, and Cherokee counties, while its northern branch extended from Asheville through Marshall in Madison County, ending at Paint Rock on the North Carolina–Tennessee border. In 1886, Polk, Henderson, and Buncombe county residents celebrated completion of the Asheville-Spartanburg Railroad, which linked the region to Columbia, South Carolina. Meanwhile, east of the Blue Ridge, subsidiary railroads reached into the mountain counties of Rutherford, Caldwell, Alexander, Mitchell, Surry, and Wilkes, connecting them to important commercial centers such as Lincolnton, Statesville, Charlotte, and Winston in the piedmont.[45] The *Charleston News and Courier* reported in 1886 that the completion of these railways had fulfilled the "dream of the dwellers by the seaside and of their friends by the snow line."[46] Industrialization, and with it "civilization," could at last permeate the mountain countryside.

Local promoters once again insisted that the region abounded in timber and mineral resources, with the hope of enticing outsiders to invest capital. "I will say we have good mountain country," a Graham County entrepreneur explained in 1882, "well timbered and watered of all countries . . . . Our lands will produce almost anything that is common to a mountain country."[47] Two years later, a real estate agent wrote that "Ashe County [is] near the centre of a region rich in minerals—especially mica, copper and silver—timber and water power."[48] Perhaps more important, boosters insisted that manufacturing would prove profitable due to the "abundance and cheapness of white labor" in western North Carolina.[49] "Our water power is unlimited, fuel for the steam engine, both wood and coal, are cheap, the cost of living is small and wages, consequently, low—the very conditions necessary to a thriving manufacturing community," editors of the *Morganton Mountaineer* argued in 1883. The paper encouraged northern business-men to act quickly, guaranteeing that their efforts in the region would most certainly prosper. "Manufacturing in . . . Western North Caro-lina is no longer an experiment," the *Mountaineer* declared. "Numer-ous examples of large returns from the capital invested are to be had in neighboring towns and counties, and the capitalist may now enter the manufacturing field with every confidence of success."[50]

These efforts to recruit industrialists were successful. Whereas capital invested in manufacturing increased 54 percent in western North Carolina between 1870 and 1880, it rose 186 percent during the 1880s. Specifically, industrial expansion in the region occurred in mountain counties that had access to rail lines before or during the early 1880s. Out of the sixteen counties that experienced an increase in capital invested in manufacturing, fourteen of them had a railroad before 1886.[51] In contrast, six of the eight mountain counties where industrial output declined were without rail service until the late 1880s or 1890s.[52]

This new wave of investors from New Jersey, Ohio, Pennsylvania, and Tennessee built manufacturing facilities and purchased (sometimes illegally) land from mountain residents.[53] West of the Blue Ridge, com-panies were attracted to the area's rich mineral and timber resources in Jackson, Mitchell, Yancey, and Swain counties.[54] East of the Blue Ridge, in Burke, Caldwell, Catawba, Cleveland, Rutherford, and Surry counties, textile and tobacco factories multiplied as entrepreneurs scrambled to capitalize on the region's cheap labor.[55]

The arrival of the railroad and subsequent industrialization trans-formed the lives of western North Carolinians, rural and urban alike. Industrial jobs increasingly drew mountain residents from their homes to towns, factories, and lumber camps. In 1889, for instance, the tex-tile manufacturer Belmont Mills in Shelby boasted more than 120 employees, most of whom had left their farms for jobs in the factory.[56] Although they would become dependent on the company that hired them, many of these men and women were eager to leave the country-side. During the 1880s, the average size of mountain farms declined 13 percent, making it more difficult for rural residents, especially young men unable to inherit a sizable amount of land, to achieve economic independence.[57] Factory, mine, and lumber work promised to give these highlanders a steady wage. By the mid-1880s, this movement away from the countryside had become so prevalent that observers worried about the future of farming. "Too many of our farmers . . . are . . . all the time looking for an opening into some other occupation however insignificant," editors of the *Morganton Star* bemoaned in 1885. "How many of our fathers' sons . . . are willing and eager to leave home and take a little humble position in town for about what they can eat and wear."[58] A Caldwell County farmer agreed. "There are too many bread eaters growing up and too few farmers," he complained to the *Lenoir Topic* that same year. "Too many want to [move to towns] and teach school, study law, go around where somebody has the headache and tell them, 'I'm a doctor and will cure you for so much.'"[59]

As was common, county seats were the chief beneficiaries of this migration. Population in these communities rose 101 percent between 1880 and 1890.[60] But by 1890, sixty other communities experienced significant population growth. These urbanizing centers were no longer concentrated in the foothills east of the Blue Ridge. In the French Broad Valley, Buncombe, Henderson, and Madison counties boasted eight non–county seat towns with 100 or more residents, while nineteen towns located in counties to the north and west of the valley reached or surpassed this number.[61]

Like elsewhere in the South, highlanders in these developing towns adopted the lifestyle and philosophies of urban America. With the railroad and industrialization came telegraph and telephone lines, technologies that enhanced existing businesses and allowed town folk to tune in to national cultural trends. Officials in Asheville, Waynesville, Jefferson, Lenoir, and other new commercial centers scrambled to build paved roads and improve sanitation. Power lines and electric streetcars became the symbols of "civilization," amenities that separated townspeople from their rural neighbors. To further illustrate their difference from country folk, towns prohibited hogs and other livestock. Businessmen believed that these animals had no place in towns because they posed a health risk and spoiled "the appearance of our streets." In 1886, for instance, Buncombe County politicians passed an ordinance prohibiting free-range livestock in Asheville, hoping, among other reasons, to rid the city of its rural character.[62]

Priding themselves on being refined and cultivated, mountain townspeople also responded unfavorably to the popular stereotypes about the region, which they had unintentionally helped create. By the 1880s, many, if not most, outsiders believed that Appalachia was at odds with modern America. According to an Asheville resident in 1882, this could not have been further from the truth, at least in the urban centers. "In the towns," he pointed out, "is a highly educated and intelligent class, some foreigners, some from other parts of the United States, and some the improved native stock." Indeed, some visitors found the reputation of mountain folk misleading. Editors of the *Asheville Semi-Weekly Citizen* proudly published a letter from an "intelligent visitor," who chastised "Yankees" for comparing Carolina highlanders to "illiterate" Africans. "I have been surprised to find a people," he wrote to the newspaper, "shut out from the world as they have been . . . so intelligent and intellectual. Many of them are brainy, and their faces would furnish as fine a picture of the Caucasian race . . . as can be found anywhere." Townspeople defended themselves, insisting that the region was neither unchurched nor uncivilized. "We venture to say . . . that among no people with whom we have had inter-course is the religious element so strong," the *Asheville Semi-Weekly Citizen* read in 1883. "The mountain people are neither so ignorant nor so irreligious as careless persons pronounce them."[63] T. K. Brown from Black Mountain in Buncombe County agreed. "We have a civi-lized community, we have churches, occasional preaching, and some refined Christian people."[64] Boone denizen "Old Hal" said it best in a letter to the *Lenoir Topic* in 1885: "The Watauga people are so quiet and civil. Who would not be proud of our county and her people?"[65]

Mountain townspeople accused the national media of slander. As early as 1878, the *Asheville Citizen* criticized the *Cincinnati Enquirer* and other northern newspapers for printing "lies" about the violent nature of mountain residents. The *Citizen* was most offended by the new assumption that most Carolina highlanders were moonshiners. In 1879, it scolded *Harper's Weekly* for printing "Law and Moonshine," which described highlanders "as big-boned, semi-barbarian people," and it chastised distillers for the damage they had done to the region's reputation. "We want the ignorant Republican moonshiners of our mountains," the *Citizen* admonished, "to know what their party friends up North think of them."[66] Two years later, R. A. Cobb from Morgan-ton denounced Crittenden's *Entwined Lives* for "grossly libel[ing] the people of my native mountains," calling Crittenden's characterization of Redmond and other mountain residents as murderers a "fraudulent hoax."[67] Upon reading *The Heart of the Alleghenies; or, Western North Carolina* in 1884, Franklin resident J. F. Ray expressed similar disgust at travel writers Wilbur Zeigler and Ben Grosscup's negative portrayal of mountain residents as ignorant "hillbillies" and moonshiners. "The authors themselves are continually getting in to the habit of expression supposed to be peculiar to the mountain people, such as 'riled,' 'biled,' 'toted,' 'jined,' 'shootin-irons,' &c," Ray concluded. "The only hope at present that I can see for the book is in the possibility that it may never be read and therefore never condemned."[68]

But their attempts to salvage their reputation just perpetuated the myths surrounding the region. Urban highlanders blamed their poor image on the people of the countryside, farmers who refused to adopt the new customs and mores of an industrial, modernized Appalachia. The *Asheville Citizen* claimed in 1880 that "the rural population" continued to spend "the spring and summer months in partial idleness working only to produce enough for their own consumption."[69] According to the *Rutherford Mountain Banner* one year later, farmers, supposedly reluctant to embrace the larger market economy, had failed "to take advantage of and improve the opportunities that are before them."[70] And although towns had improved technologies, some leaders believed that residents would have to work hard to overcome their tendency to lack the necessary "energy." In 1886, a Lenoir resident noted:

> Our young men are growing up in idleness. We, who should be setting before them a more worthy example, are alone to blame. If we wish to earn a reputation for being wide-awake, progressive citizens, we must do better than we have been doing. By means of the railroad, we have been brought into communication with the outside world, and before many months we shall have added another great factor, in the way of a telegraph line. But all these aids will do us no good if we do not support them.[71]

To become prosperous, western North Carolina needed "a population of intelligence, industry, and morality that honor their county and add to its wealth in their character as good and useful citizens." Its residents, rural and urban alike, would have to accept the values of self-control and hard work.[72]

Local leaders continued to argue that alcohol was the leading cause of highlanders' apparent inability to adapt to the new economic order. Despite their efforts, reforms had been unable to purge "traditional" drinking mores from mountain society. This led to the corruption of the "young generation" and the persistence of crime and violence.[73] For those trying to better the region's image, alcohol consumption discouraged men and women from embracing the virtues of industry and frugality. "When [young men] should be at work," a Lenoir resident complained in 1886, "they spend their time on the street corners, and very often are engaged in disreputable attempts at disturbing the public peace."[74] Many local denizens warned that the future of western North Carolina was in peril. "Let everyone remember," the *Blue Ridge Enterprise* read in 1884, "that the hope of the country rests on the rising generation; that its moral and intellectual culture is necessary to preservation of liberty; [and] that liquor is an open enemy to every virtue."[75] These critiques of alcohol consumption reflected town boosters' belief that the "traditional" culture of rural mountain residents impeded economic modernization.

Consequently, the fear of alcohol abuse reinvigorated the anti-moonshiner crusade in western North Carolina during the 1880s. Some argued that illicit distillers continued to defy local-option laws and that the resulting intemperance and lawlessness promised to be the ruin of the region. In 1885, for instance, Samuel T. Kelsey from the resort community of Highlands complained that Macon County moonshiners "come in and sell out their whiskey on the sly, make some of our people drunk, pick quarrels, yell and shoot around the streets after night. Highlands is the best town in the state west of Waynesville and has bright prospects unless the Govt. allows these 'moonshiners' to control the country and run good citizens off."[76] Two years later, Bakersville residents demanded that "respectable" folk unite to combat illicit distilling, a "curse" that threatened to destroy the community.[77] An unnamed Morganton citizen voiced a similar dislike for moonshiners in 1889. Illicit distillers, according to him, were "evil" men who "entrap our young men and draw them down to a drunkard's grave."[78] Morganton minister Robert Abernethy issued one of the harshest critiques. He chastised moonshiners as "low graded, unprincipled radicals [whom] decent, clean, white [men] should consider outside the pale of the human race."[79]

Distillers on both sides of the law continued to lose the support of their former allies. The *Lenoir Topic* and *Morganton Star,* both of which had historically opposed the Bureau of Internal Revenue and federal liquor taxation, quickly joined the reformers in their crusade against moonshiners. According to W. W. Scott, editor of the *Topic,* moonshiners in Alexander County, ruling "with an iron first" and intimidating local residents, had "ruined and debauched" the community of Duck Creek. "Good people and good citizens," he continued, "protest and recognize the injury done not only to them and their surroundings but also to the reputation of the locality in which they live."[80] Foreshadowing events to come, local reformers began to attack licit distillers as well, arguing that their trade—even though the federal and state governments deemed it legitimate—discouraged capitalists from investing money in the region because it promoted intemperance and lawlessness. As the *Morganton Star* explained in 1889: "We talk about developing the great resources of our grand old North State and invite capitalists to come into our midst and tell them all things are ready, yet when we take a calm survey of our State and find in nearly every locality a 'hell hole' [distillery] . . . we find that the ground is not fully prepared."[81]

By 1890, many local urban reformers concluded that conflict in western North Carolina was not the result of industrialization or the social changes that accompanied it but a product of the traditional culture of mountain residents. The alcohol distiller served as a scapegoat, a symbol of what was wrong with Appalachian society. Self-proclaimed "respectable" townspeople desperately wanted to create a New South and chastised outsiders for stereotyping the region as a place of violence—a myth they had unwittingly helped create and perpetuate. Like their northern counterparts, these denizens would embrace the uplift movement with the hope of eradicating distilling and the traditional culture that encouraged it. But the worst was yet to come for liquor manufacturers, who also found themselves under attack from the rural communities that reformers mistakenly believed supported them.

7

"Afloat on the Tide of Improvement"

The Uplift Movement and Rise of Prohibition Sentiment in Rural Communities, 1885–1900

One awful dark and stormy night
I heard and saw an awful sight
Lightning flashed and thunder rolled,
It made me think of my poor soul.
I dashed the drink down and left the place,
And went to seek redeeming grace.

During the last two decades of the nineteenth century, Appalachia became a center of mission outreach. Northern and—to a lesser extent—southern evangelicals journeyed to the region, where they discovered an impoverished rural culture in dire need of reform. Like journalists and novelists, missionaries believed that geographic isolation had prevented modern civilization from reaching mountain communities. As such, most highlanders remained "traditionalists" who refused to abandon folkways that impeded economic and moral progress, the most damaging of which, the missionaries believed, was the distillation and consumption of alcohol. With the help of local townspeople and the growing influence of the Woman's Christian Temperance Union, a national organization founded in Ohio in 1873, missionaries sought to "uplift" mountain whites by sobering them up.

But most highlanders were neither as ignorant nor as drunk as reformers portrayed them. In rural western North Carolina, a grass-roots temperance crusade that relied on local-option legislation to combat King Alcohol had already started before the arrival of most missionaries. By the 1880s, many country folk, having become more connected to the market economy and embracing New South rhetoric, increasingly yearned to "improve" themselves both economically and morally. In 1900, J. A. Bolden from Wilkes County's Roaring River district summed up the feelings of mountain residents living in smaller, more remote neighborhoods: "Old things are passing away and all things are becoming new. Evolution is evident on all hands. Progress is the watchword of the hour, and if we who are representing this great movement would move with the tide, we must keep in line. Our motto is 'onward and upward.'"[1] Rural reformers like Bolden wanted to build more schools, construct better roads, and entice capitalists to invest money in their communities. Their desire for "progress" also encouraged them to denounce traditional drinking mores and side with their urban counterparts in the fight against King Alcohol. Unfortunately for liquor manufacturers, these men and women, like those in towns, would embrace statewide prohibition at the turn of the twentieth century.

The Uplift Movement: Alcohol Reform from Above

"Whether this people shall arise to a level with the rest of our country depends largely upon our efforts," wrote Ellen Myers in "The Mountain Whites of the South," an 1885 treatise that pleaded with members of the American Missionary Association (AMA) to uplift the people of Appalachia. In 1882, Myers and her husband, both AMA missionaries, had arrived in eastern Kentucky, where they "discovered" a land of ignorance and violence. "More than half of the adult population cannot read and write," she explained. "The school-houses are the merest log-cabins, with puncheon benches without backs or desks." They witnessed mountain children "left to amuse themselves, and listen to idle men bragging about how they can 'drop [shoot] their man every time.'" Reformers like the Myerses believed that these stories perpetuated the cycle of violence. "They drink in these tales of brutality," Ellen continued, "mistaking them for chivalry, till their chief desire is to become the possessor of a revolver." The only solution, she concluded, was for organizations like the AMA to step in. "We hold in our own hands the answer to the problem," she wrote. "The children must be brought up differently from their parents. Education and practical religion must be gotten to the masses."[2]

Stereotypical photograph of an Appalachian family. From Margaret W. Morley, *The Carolina Mountains* (Boston: Houghton Mifflin, 1913), facing 182.

Myers's description of mountain whites was not very different from those of journalists and local color novelists. But more so than writers, she and other reformers, mostly northern missionaries and local middle-class townspeople, felt compelled to help assimilate rural Appalachians into "mainstream" society. These men and women believed that because mountain whites were of "pure Anglo-Saxon stock," they (unlike blacks) could be "modernized," "Christianized," and "Americanized." For Myers and other missionaries, it was their duty to reform mountain folk through education and social services.

After 1885, northern religious societies increasingly embraced this uplift movement. Along with the AMA, the Presbyterian Church (USA) played an important role in organizing schools and churches throughout southern Appalachia.[3] In 1877, the Rev. L. M. Pease, founder of the Five Points Mission in New York City, retired to Asheville. There, he became "interested in the plight of little mountaineer girls" and opened a school for their benefit. In 1887, he donated this school to the Presbyterian Board of Home Missions, which subsequently organized the Home Industrial School in Asheville.[4] That same year, Ohio native Luke Dorland founded a mission school at Hot Springs in Madison

County. Reverend Dorland, who had presided over the Scotia Seminary for African American women in Cabarrus County, North Carolina, for twenty years, moved to Hot Springs in 1886 and discovered that "a large portion of the adult population can neither read nor write." "There are grades of intelligence and refinement from the highest to the lowest," Dorland explained to friends in Ohio, "but the stranger passing through wonders how human beings can exist in so low and degraded a state." He concluded, "They have no hope and they need light." With the financial support of the Presbyterian Board of Home Missions, he established the Dorland Institute to improve "the low and degraded condition of the mountaineers."[5]

Mission work in western North Carolina (and other parts of southern Appalachia) accelerated during the 1890s. By the end of the decade, Presbyterians and Episcopalians had established churches and schools in Ashe, Buncombe, Henderson, Burke, Transylvania, Haywood, Cherokee, Jackson, Watauga, and Graham counties.[6] These northern missionaries also initiated the handicraft revival, hoping to make the lives of mountain women less "dull and monotonous." In 1895, Frances L. Goodrich received a handmade coverlet from a resident of Brittain's Cove in Madison County. Realizing that these coverlets would appeal to urban consumers, she founded Allenstand Cottage Industries in 1897. Goodrich believed that this mission would "save from extinction the old-time crafts" and impart the "habits of thrift and industry" to mountain women.[7] Meanwhile, nondenominational organizations lent a helping hand. By the early 1890s, the Philadelphia-based Needlework Guild of America and the Boston-based Flower Mission Association operated craft-based missions throughout the region.[8]

Susan Guion Chester was typical among these northern reformers. Born in 1868, Susan's father was Charles T. Chester, a warden of St. Paul's Episcopal Church in Englewood, New Jersey. In 1884, Chester entered Vassar College, where she served as president of her class and became active in the YMCA and Students' Association. Like many middle-class, college-educated women, she found employment opportunities in the burgeoning social service movement. Upon graduating in 1888, Chester worked at Bishop Whitaker's School for Girls in Nevada. She soon became interested in Appalachian mission work, however, after hearing of the "plight" of mountain whites. In the early 1890s, Chester moved to western North Carolina to work for an Episcopal mission in Grace in Buncombe County. In addition to her job, she joined local outreach groups, becoming president of the Flower Mission of Asheville and the Needlework Guild in 1892.[9]

Like other northern missionaries, Chester quickly became alarmed at the apparent lack of morals and civility among the rural mountain populace. Writing to the *Philadelphia Church Standard* in 1893, she claimed that more than 300,000 Carolina highlanders existed "in total ignorance of all that serves to make life really worth living and seemingly devoid of a desire to rise above the level of the animal." She continued, "Dark, far darker than I would willingly paint them, are the cabin homes of a vast number of mountaineers, but it is the vice of ignorance, the isolation of generations." Chester attempted to combat these "dark" conditions by founding the Log Cabin Settlement in Buncombe County, sometime before 1895. The first of its kind in southern Appalachia, this settlement school was intended to provide education and industrial training to "ignorant" mountain residents. "Let us keep in mind," Chester concluded, "that this [settlement] movement is but one phase of the great awakening of our times to the needs of humanity."[10]

Whether establishing social settlements, missionary churches, or industrial schools, reformers sought to alter the "traditional" culture of mountain whites, which they perceived as alien but malleable. These missionaries believed that alcohol was at least partially to blame for the idleness, ignorance, and heathenism of the Appalachian people. In 1891, the *American Missionary* reported that eastern Tennesseans often "ran off preachers" by "cuttin' up, drinkin' and shootin'" at evangelical revivals, and it claimed they profaned the Christmas holiday by becoming intoxicated. Even more disturbing for northern reformers was alcohol's negative impact on the mountain family. Throughout the 1890s, missionaries reported that mountain men frequently indulged in binge drinking, encouraged their children to consume alcohol "at a very tender age," and "unmercifully" beat their wives. According to one social worker, these drunken fathers "did not want their children to go to school lest they themselves would have to do a little work." "It is wonderful what these women and children can endure and yet live," the missionary concluded. "All this misery comes from ignorance and whiskey, neither of which could continue to exist if the Christian people of the country knew of these wretched conditions."[11]

Northern missionaries correlated highlanders' inherent fondness for alcohol to their inclination toward violence and moonshining. As missionary D. L. Pierson described Madison County's rural populace in 1897, "Extreme poverty and the fact that they look upon whiskey as one of the necessities of life, lead many mountaineers into the illicit and dangerous business of making 'blockade' whiskey." Like other reformers, Pierson believed that moonshining had destroyed the moral fabric of Appalachian society. She claimed that mountain residents had "their own peculiar criminal code" that praised tax evasion and the murder of revenue officers. Moreover, Pierson insisted that moonshining contributed to feuding, a supposed "traditional" mountain practice that had begun to capture the imagination of Victorian Americans during the late 1880s. "The betrayal of a secret 'still' is a heinous crime," she explained. "Feuds for generations arise from such betrayals."[12]

That Pierson and other reformers focused on alcohol and illicit distilling as leading causes for the inability of mountain whites to become "civilized" is not surprising. Journalists and local color novelists continued to shape middle-class Americans' perception of southern Appalachia as a land overrun by intemperance and moonshining. The 1893 publication of Mary N. Murfree's "The Moonshiners at Hoho-Hebee Falls" and similar stories fascinated urbanites and reinforced their belief that most mountain residents distilled and drank moonshine.[13] Much of this literature also served as propaganda for the uplift movement. Missionary Margaret Johann's "A Little Moonshiner," for instance, chronicles the rescue of a rural mountain girl from poverty and ignorance. The girl lives in a crude cabin "built of logs, and the branches of trees, and clay." One day, she accompanies her father, whom revenuers had arrested for illicit distilling, to the town of Marshall in Madison County. She is dumbfounded, having never seen windows, ceiled walls, and trains. A town resident helps the "poor little thing" by convincing the community to build a new cabin for her father. "The place is a little nearer to civilization than the old cabin, but yet it's wild enough to be homelike to them," the narrator concludes. "As for the father . . . he'll go at some legitimate work—tobacco raising perhaps."[14]

Stories like this reflected northern missionaries' views on the dangers of illicit distilling. Like journalists and local colorists, they feared that this profession prevented rural whites from embracing wage labor, commercial agriculture, and other "civilized" pursuits. Even more distressing, illicit distilling victimized mountain children, who, mired in poverty, remained ignorant of the outside world. But, as Johann emphasizes in "A Little Moonshiner," these unfortunate families can find salvation. Urban philanthropists set out to encourage moonshiners to go to school, embrace mainstream Christianity, learn new job skills, and participate in the larger market economy. Reformers sought the elimination of alcohol distilling, which they believed to be the downfall of mountain society.

Northern relief societies utilized education, "proper" religious instruction, and coercion to achieve their goals. Beginning in the early 1890s, the AMA instructed missionaries to help illicit distillers, most of whom lived in "wickedness" and "semi-barbarism," by setting up "outposts" and providing them with "spiritual" guidance.[15] Members of the Presbyterian Church (USA) soon joined the cause. During the late 1890s, the Rev. Mac E. Davis, a member of the Asheville Presbytery, traveled throughout western North Carolina and asked moonshiners to cease manufacturing alcohol. When these pleas fell on deaf ears, Davis took more drastic measures, accompanying revenue agents on raids and petitioning the General Assembly to ban whiskey distilling.[16]

Northern missionaries teamed up with highlanders, mostly middle-class townspeople, to promote antialcohol reform in Appalachia. Although they denied claims that the region was "uncivilized," many urban Carolina highlanders did admit that the "majority" of their rural neighbors were not "prosperous and cultured."[17] These reform-ers believed that if they could eliminate alcohol from the countryside, they could overcome the geographic isolation and "primitive" agricul-tural practices that had conspired against "this less fortunate class."[18] In 1892, Buncombe County native Cornelius Miller Pickens feared that the lack of "refinement" among highlanders was largely due to their inherent love of alcohol. "I don't believe the whiskey question has ever been talked much here," he wrote in his diary after delivering a tem-perance lecture in Polk County. "People need education on the subject . . . I don't understand why people get so far behind." He was also dis-turbed by the number of distilleries that persisted. "I am sorry to say this," Pickens complained, but "Polk County has seventeen govern-ment distilleries in it, and it is the smallest county in the state."[19]

The Rev. Robert F. Campbell of the First Presbyterian Church of Asheville, who counted himself a proud "mountain white," defended the region from "sweeping and indiscriminate statements" but acknowl-edged that a large number of rural denizens lived in "ignorance, misery, and vice." "Our evangelists found numbers of homes without a lamp, a candle, a comb, a looking-glass, and similar articles of civilized life," he admitted in 1899. "Many of the people had never seen a town, and the buggy in which the evangelists traveled was in some places considered a great curiosity." Campbell chastised the drinking habits of rural whites for encouraging poverty and indolence. He believed that most of the men lacked a work ethic and spent their time hunting, fishing, moonshining, and "imbibing the blood of John Barleycorn." Alcohol had also taken its toll on young men, most of whom had "reached the summit of [their] ambition" once they owned a dog and a gun, "learned to pick the banjo," and possessed "a bottle of whiskey."[20]

Campbell and other reformers both pitied and respected the mountain people. "We cannot fail to love this land of beauty nor to appreciate the high and noble qualities of its dear people," E. G. Prudden from Blowing Rock in Watauga County reminded missionaries in 1892. "Their patient endurance of deprivation and trial calls forth our warmest sympathies."[21] It was this sentiment that encouraged urban highlanders to embrace the uplift movement of the 1890s. They allied with northern missionaries and increasingly supported gun control and antiswearing legislation, which they believed would help rid the countryside of lawlessness.[22] These local reformers also agreed that King Alcohol was a central cause of ignorance and sought to eradicate it.

Many mountain townspeople saw the Woman's Christian Temperance Union (WCTU) as an important vehicle for promoting antialcohol reform throughout the region.[23] Founded in Ohio in the mid-1870s, the WCTU established its first chapter in western North Carolina in Asheville in 1883.[24] By the 1890s, mountain women had organized chapters in Dillsboro, Highlands, Newton, Wilkesboro, Waynesville, Hickory, and Morganton. These WCTU reformers prided themselves on their role in the uplift movement. They worked with the Flower Mission of Asheville and other northern-based benevolent societies by cosponsoring temperance speeches, picnics, and rallies.[25] WCTU workers, who often received financial support from local businessmen, blamed the drinking habits of mountain whites for perpetuating laziness, immorality, and lawlessness. "Having fought intemperance in [Ohio] for 2 years, we sought Highlands for rest, amidst its mountains, to find the peace befitting the grandeur and beauty of its scenery," northern migrant and WCTU member Mrs. Hunt explained in 1883. "But alas! The trail of the serpent is over even this sequestered spot, and the holy

Women crusaders pleading with a saloon keeper to stop selling alcohol, 1874. Courtesy of the Prints and Photographs Division, Library of Congress, Washington, D.C.

calm of Nature is rudely disturbed by the ribald song of the drunkard."[26] Lela Potts, a "native" mountain resident and secretary of the Dillsboro WCTU in Jackson County, agreed. In 1891, she feared that many highlanders were unwilling to part ways with "the greatest evil in our land" and had chosen "vice and immorality" over "a higher and nobler civilization."[27]

With local residents and northern missionaries united in the fight against alcohol, the WCTU sought to alter the behavior of mountain whites through education and religion. Believing that it was too late to reform adults, the society focused considerable attention on shaping the "intellectual develop" of young people. In Dillsboro and other communities, it sponsored essay-writing contests for girls, awarding prizes for the best essays on temperance, and encouraged mountain children to participate in temperance parades. At one such celebration in 1892, 150 boys and girls marched down the streets of Waynesville wearing temperance badges and carrying banners that read, "Tremble king alcohol, for we shall grow up."[28] The WCTU viewed the public schools as another vehicle for promoting antialcohol reform in rural communities. In 1887, members from Buncombe and Catawba counties petitioned legislators to require schools to teach students about the harmful "effects of alcohol upon the human system."[29] Their pleas were not in vain, and in 1891, the North Carolina General Assembly unanimously passed a law that required scientific temperance instruction in public schools.[30]

The WCTU, Presbyterian Church (USA), and other societies played a vital role in perpetuating antialcohol sentiment in western Carolina and other parts of the South. These missionaries enjoyed widespread support in mountain towns. Local manufacturers also joined the cause and refused to hire men who drank alcohol during and after work.[31] Many crusaders sincerely wanted to save mountain people from their perceived social ills. Others used temperance reform as a mechanism of social control, arguing that traditional drinking mores encouraged rural whites to resist wage labor and capitalism. Either way, reformers ultimately downplayed the negative impact of industrialization on mountain society. They insisted that conflict in Appalachia was not the product of economic exploitation but the result of a backward culture that required reforming.

Although the uplift movement did have an effect on Appalachian society, the region had already begun to change—to become more "civilized," as the reformers would call it—before the arrival of most missionaries in the 1890s. Capital invested in manufacturing, for instance, increased 186 percent during the 1880s, facilitating the expansion of industrial capitalism and urbanization throughout the Carolina highlands. Despite northern visitors' claims that the populace was "unchurched," the number of religious institutions actually grew by 104 percent between 1870 and 1890, while the population rose only 72 percent.[32] In fact, compared with the state as a whole, the mountain region's aggregate population-church ratio of 206:1 was slightly lower in 1890 (see table 7.1). Nor did western North Carolina lag behind the rest of the state in education. The number of children attending common schools in the Carolina highlands increased at a greater rate than elsewhere in the state between 1870 and 1890 (see table 7.2). And, more important, prohibition sentiment in the Carolina highlands had already shifted from urban centers to more rural parts of the region by 1890. Of the 175 known places that enacted local-option laws between 1881 and 1890, 101 (or 58 percent) of them were in non–county seat

Table 7.1. Aggregate Population-Church Ratio in Western North Carolina and in North Carolina as a Whole, 1890

	Population	Churches	Ratio
Western NC	336,940	1,634	206:1
NC total	1,281,007	5,190	247:1

Sources: Robert P. Porter, Report on Population of the United States at the Eleventh Census: 1890 (Washington, DC: Government Printing Office, 1895), 33–34; Henry K. Carroll, Report on Statistics of Churches in the United States at the Eleventh Census: 1890 (Washington, DC: Government Printing Office, 1894), 74–75.

Table 7.2. Percentage Increase in Children Attending Common Schools in Western North Carolina and in North Carolina as a Whole, 1870 and 1890

	1870	1890	Increase (%)
Western NC	13,855	68,313	393
NC total	40,013	138,521	246

Source: University of Virginia Geospatial and Statistical Data Center, United States Census Data Browser, 1870 and 1890 censuses.

townships or in communities with fewer than 100 residents, an increase of 248 percent from the previous decade.[33]

Northern and local missionaries ultimately exaggerated the extent to which most mountain denizens were without churches or schools before the 1890s. In other words, these reformers were not solely responsible for "civilizing" the region. Rapid increases in the number of mountain schools and churches had preceded their arrival. The same was true of prohibition sentiment. With the expansion of the market economy, the rise of urbanization, and the growth of churches and schools, many rural whites soon believed that traditional drinking mores were incompatible with the exigencies of life under the new industrial order. The same forces that galvanized middle-class townspeople to support temperance reform had begun to operate in more remote parts of western North Carolina. Adapting to a changing economic environment, many rural highlanders argued that alcohol impeded their communities' economic prosperity. The arrival of missionaries and benevolent societies merely advanced this grassroots movement. By the turn of the twentieth century, mountain residents would increasingly abandon distillers and embrace statewide prohibition.

The Rise of Antialcohol Reform in Rural Communities

Like other southerners, western North Carolinians witnessed an economic and social revolution during the last two decades of the nineteenth century. The arrival of the WNCRR and other railways in the 1880s ushered in an era of unprecedented change. During that decade, capital invested in manufacturing expanded 186 percent, while the population in county seats rose 101 percent. These trends continued into the 1890s. By the end of that decade, capital invested in manufacturing had increased an additional 178 percent.[34] County seats continued to grow, but by 1900, 113 other mountain communities had at least 100 residents, an increase of 88 percent from the previous decade.[35] These towns were not concentrated in the eastern foothills of the Blue Ridge but in counties in the French Broad Valley and beyond. There were twenty of these non–county seat commercial centers in Buncombe, Henderson, and Madison counties, and thirty-eight in counties north and west of the valley, which had historically been the most remote. By 1900, 22 percent of western North Carolinians lived in county seats and other urbanizing settlements with populations of over 100.[36]

Since the antebellum period, urbanization had widened the gap between urban and rural highlanders. But the growth of towns during the 1880s ultimately brought these two groups together.[37] With improved transportation, farmers found it easier to travel to towns, where they found a larger market for their products, purchased a variety of new consumer goods, and observed "mainstream" culture. Although numerically small, mountain villages and towns helped bridge the gap between rural and urban life.

Meanwhile, traditional agricultural practices had begun to work against many mountain farmers, sparking an economic crisis. The slash-and-burn technique of forest farming became counterproductive, as deforestation and soil exhaustion increased in the mountain region. Inheritance practices and population growth exacerbated the situation by decreasing farm acreage, and large amounts of land had to be left fallow to restore the fertility of the soil.[38] All this made it more difficult for western North Carolinians to produce enough food to both sustain their households and sell for a profit.

The industrialization of western North Carolina allowed some mountain farmers to adapt to these changes by migrating to commercial centers, where they often found employment in industrial factories, or to mining and lumber camps.[39] Many highlanders took up commercial agriculture. Tobacco was especially appealing. By the 1880s, a farmer with the help of "two small boys" could earn $900 for every acre and a half of tobacco harvested. Wealthy farmers benefited the most from this cash crop because they had the economic resources to purchase additional land and hire tenants.[40] But tobacco also held great promise for small landowners, a growing number of whom had access to the larger market economy because of urbanization and improved transportation. As a result, tobacco cultivation skyrocketed 181 percent in western North Carolina during the 1880s, while corn production increased only 12 percent. Several counties in the far southeastern and northeastern parts of the region, whose residents had historically been the most isolated, experienced the highest percentage increase in tobacco cultivation.[41] For these farmers, the introduction of commercial agriculture allowed them to compete with those residing east of the Blue Ridge and in the French Broad Valley.

Contrary to the claims of northern missionaries and local urban reformers, these rural whites embraced "progress" and "civilization." At the same time that railroads and urban development helped reduce the level of isolation in many mountain regions, Carolina highlanders confronted an agricultural crisis, as forest farming became an ineffective adaptation to the land. Industrial capitalism and urbanization offered rural whites new markets and opportunities. Many shifted from semisubsistence to commercial agriculture by cultivating tobacco and, in the far southeastern part of the mountain region, cotton.[42] These highlanders also abandoned traditional agricultural practices with the hope of maximizing their profit margins. One rural resident observed in 1890 that farmers around the small community of Emanuel in Caldwell County had become "a very progressive class of people." "Some are using improved farming implements, such as wheat drills, harvesting machines, mowers, sulky plows &c," he proclaimed, "and almost all of them make good progress improving their farms."[43] Census records confirm that a growing number of mountain farmers embraced economic modernization between 1880 and 1900. During those years, the cash value of farming implements and machinery in the region increased 71 percent.[44]

The expansion of commercial farming, industrial capitalism, and urbanization in more remote parts of western North Carolina sparked a social revolution. By the 1890s, rural residents shared many of the values of their urban counterparts. Having greater access to towns and becoming more entrenched in the larger market economy, they found themselves—to use the words of one rural highlander—"afloat on the tide of improvement."[45] Farmers adapted to the new environment not only by abandoning traditional agricultural techniques but also by stressing the importance of public education. "The day has arrived when uneducated people must take a rear position in the ranks of life," a rural resident from Transylvania County explained in 1891. "Let us hoist the banner of education west of the Blue Ridge till it can be seen all around."[46] A farmer from southeastern Caldwell County also called for reform. "We want better society and better schools," he wrote in 1890. "Society is what the neighborhood makes it. So we all should try to our utmost to make it good."[47] A growing number of rural whites believed that their communities could achieve prosperity through education reform, internal improvements, and participation in the national economy.

Echoing the opinions of their urban counterparts, rural highlanders also increasingly critiqued preindustrial drinking mores, fearing that liquor impeded the region's economic and moral potential. The Southern Farmers' Alliance offers a lens through which to view anti-alcohol sentiment among these mountain whites. Founded in Texas in 1878, this organization addressed the immediate concerns of farmers and tenants struggling to achieve economic independence during the late nineteenth century.[48] Like farmers elsewhere in the South, many Carolina highlanders, embracing commercial agriculture or becoming more dependent on the cash economy, fell victim to the crop-lien system, exorbitant shipping rates, and declining tobacco prices.[49] The Southern Farmers' Alliance called for cooperatives, credit reform, and railroad regulation, which appealed to these rural whites (and blacks) caught in a vicious circle of debt. By 1891, western North Carolinians had organized suballiances in at least sixteen of the twenty-six mountain counties.[50]

The Southern Farmers' Alliance succeeded in part because it worked within the prevailing rural culture.[51] Because this organization reflected the values of its members, it provides an opportunity to gauge rural whites' views on, among other things, market relations and temperance. The actions of the alliance in western North Carolina reveals that many mountain farmers had accepted capitalism by the turn of the twentieth century. Although they sponsored cooperatives, most highlanders ultimately refused to endorse the subtreasury plan, government control of railroads, and other radical reforms.[52] These farmers sought to protect themselves from bankers, merchants, and landlords, but they also wanted to continue to participate in the larger market economy. Their goal was to "humanize" capitalism, not to overthrow it.[53]

Moreover, rural highlanders in the Southern Farmers' Alliance desired to improve their communities both "mentally" and "morally."[54] These men were living in "a progressive age" and yearned to "keep up with the times." "Let your main object," the Watauga County Farmers' Alliance declared in 1890, "be to educate the agricultural people as the world moves onward and higher in the heights of civilization and intelligence . . . or we will always be behind."[55] Like their urban counterparts, alliance men advocated for education reform and gun-control laws with the hope of ridding the countryside of ignorance and lawlessness.[56] They also shared missionaries' views that temperance would bring moral and material improvement. According to the Caldwell County Farmers' Alliance, alcohol was "one of the greatest evils of our land," having "degraded mankind," "blighted our homes," and robbed "heaven of precious souls."[57] To achieve success in farming, alliance members urged people to become "modest, gentle, unassuming, moral, and temperate."[58] As one mountain farmer explained in 1891:

> The Alliance encourages honesty, industry, and morality. Its members are encouraged to live within their means, and to avoid debt as much as possible. . . . Indolence and down right laziness has affected us all more or less. We all eat too much idle bread. Too much precious time is wasted. . . . [Thus,] no lazy man should be admitted. . . . The fostering and encouraging of morality . . . will tend to lessen crime, elevate the membership, and indirectly benefit all the people. [As such,] no drunkard, liar, thief, openly profane man, fornicator, or dishonest man should be admitted or retained in the alliance.[59]

For these whites, alcohol had stymied the region's economic potential by breeding ignorance, idleness, and crime. As such, the drinking mores of their neighbors required reforming.

Rural Baptists and Methodists joined the alliance in the fight against intemperance in the countryside. During the early 1870s, these assemblies had revived the antialcohol struggle in part to re-create the deeply religious nature of the pre–Civil War South.[60] The end of Reconstruction helped persuade rural churchgoers to advocate for social reform because it lessened sectional tensions. "With little incentive to appear different from the northern, radical, political churches," Charles Israel argues, "southern Evangelicals could more safely enter politics on the side of moral questions."[61] The growth of the Good Templars and other secular temperance organizations further motivated congregants to increase their role in the antialcohol campaign during the 1880s.[62] Fearing that they were becoming irrelevant in modern society, religious groups in western North Carolina and other parts of the South insisted that churches, not secular organizations, should "lead in the great reform."[63] These phenomena—Lost Cause ideology, the end of Reconstruction, and increased competition from secular organizations—deepened the resolve of rural Baptists and Methodists to reform the behavior of all mountain residents by eliminating the influence of alcohol.[64]

As transportation improved, more rural residents were able to travel to towns, which church leaders believed exposed them to profanity, prostitution, and alcohol.[65] Like those elsewhere in the South, mountain evangelicals responded by forbidding congregants from drinking ardent spirits.[66] Overlooking the fact that local residents had been drinking alcohol long before the advent of industrialization, they passed local-option laws in an attempt to protect the home and church from the sins of urban America.[67] During the last two decades of the nineteenth century, rural highlanders emerged as ardent proponents of antialcohol legislation. Between 1881 and 1889, 101 mountain churches and schools located in non–county seat townships or in communities with fewer than 100 residents passed local-option laws, an increase of 248 percent from the previous decade. This trend continued into the 1890s. Of the 258 known places that enacted local option during that decade, 164 (or 64 percent) of them were situated in rural communities (or townships with no settlements larger than 100 residents).[68] The rise of prohibition sentiment in western North Carolina, then, was a reaction to urbanization. Mountain evangelicals increasingly turned to local option to combat the evils of town life and redefine their place in the changing world.

An examination of local-option legislation at the county level, however, reveals that the rise of prohibition sentiment was, in fact, as much

Table 7.3. Percentage Increase in and Rank of Capital Investment in Manufacturing in the Fifteen Mountain Counties with the Largest Number of Rural Communities Enacting Local Option, 1880 and 1900

County	Number of Communities with Local Option / Rank	Increase in Capital Investment in Manufacturing (%) / Rank
Madison	31/1	3151/3
Ashe	28/2	27/24
Caldwell	28/2	995/7
Mitchell	22/4	106/23
Polk	13/5	629/11
Surry	13/5	311/15
Wilkes	13/5	1827/4
Henderson	11/8	398/13
Cherokee	9/9	187/20
Alexander	8/10	142/22
Buncombe	8/10	912/8
Catawba	8/10	670/10
Haywood	8/10	1038/6
Rutherford	8/10	3913/2
Jackson	8/10	1729/5

Sources: U.S. Census Office, *Report on the Manufacturers . . . Tenth Census: 1880* (Washington, DC: Government Printing Office, 1883), 159–60; U.S. Census Office, *Twelfth Census . . . 1900 . . . Manufacturers, Part II: States and Territories* (Washington, DC: U.S. Census Office, 1902), 664–66.

a secular reaction to the transition to an industrial economy as it was an evangelical crusade against the evils of urban society. Between 1880 and 1900, for instance, local-option laws were more often enacted in rural districts undergoing industrial and economic growth. Of the fifteen mountain counties that had the highest percentage increase in capital investment in manufacturing during those years, eleven of them led the region in number of rural communities that passed local prohibition (see table 7.3). Rural highlanders living in counties where farming remained profitable were also more likely to support local-option legislation. Nine of the fifteen counties that experienced the highest percent-

Table 7.4. Percentage Change in and Rank of Cash Value of Farms in the Fifteen Mountain Counties with the Largest Number of Rural Communities Enacting Local Option, 1880 and 1900

County	Number of Communities with Local Option / Rank	Change in Cash Value of Farms (%) / Rank
Madison	31/1	–3/20
Ashe	28/2	+33/11
Caldwell	28/2	+24/14
Mitchell	22/4	+52/3
Polk	13/5	+20/16
Surry	13/5	+22/15
Wilkes	13/5	+30/13
Henderson	11/8	+48/5
Cherokee	9/9	–2/19
Alexander	8/10	–53/25
Buncombe	8/10	+39/8
Catawba	8/10	+4/18
Haywood	8/10	+36/9
Rutherford	8/10	+51/4
Jackson	8/10	–69/26

Sources: U.S. Census Office, Report on the Productions of Agriculture . . . Tenth Census: 1880 (Washington, DC: Government Printing Office, 1883), 300–302; U.S. Census Office, Twelfth Census . . . 1900 . . . Agriculture, Part I: Farms, Live Stock, and Animal Products (Washington, DC: U.S. Census Office, 1902), 464–66.

age increase in the cash value of farms led the region in the number of rural communities that enacted local prohibition (see table 7.4).

Expressing the sentiments of their urban counterparts, many rural Carolina highlanders increasingly believed that traditional drinking mores were a poor fit with the exigencies of life in the New South. This new worldview made it easier for them to support local-option legislation, although many highlanders were not yet ready to embrace the more radical statewide prohibition. Only when local-option and other antiliquor laws supposedly failed to reduce alcohol consumption would the reformers' call for statewide prohibition gain widespread currency in the region at the turn of the twentieth century. The moonshiner and his legal counterpart played a central role in this drama.

8

"Wilt Thou Send the Revenues Down upon the Distillers"

A Political History of Prohibition, 1882–1908

> Rise, ye men of North Carolina,
> Hear ye not the muffled roar
> Of the battle-drum resounding
> From the mountains to the shore?
> See the banner floating high.
> Bearing this sublime inscription:
> "North Carolina Will Go Dry."

On April 21, 1908, federal judge Jeter C. Pritchard, a Madison County resident and former Republican senator, arrived in North Wilkesboro to deliver a speech in favor of statewide prohibition. Four months earlier, the General Assembly had ordered a general election to take place on May 26 that would allow the voters to decide whether to ban the sale and manufacture of alcohol in North Carolina.[1] Pritchard, a proponent of legal prohibition since the 1890s, quickly agreed to canvass the state to rally support for the proposed law.[2] In his North Wilkesboro speech, the judge voiced the sentiments of thousands of mountain residents who had already concluded that King Alcohol "must go."[3] He began by reminding the audience that prohibition was a bipartisan issue and then condemned alcohol as a disease that plagued the region and impeded its progress. "Is there anyone among us here tonight who can tell me of a single good thing that whiskey has done here in Wilkes County?" he asked. "I have never heard of a town or county that tol-

erated a distillery or barroom that did not have more or less trouble."
Pritchard ended his speech by attacking alcohol manufacturers who
argued that the law would "deprive the people of their personal liberty." He concluded:

> Because you happen to have some men here who have fruit
> in the county, the idea of letting these men distill their fruit
> and thus destroy your boys and girls for their personal liberty
> is preposterous. Suppose I had a plan to manufacture yellow
> fever germs and I should come here to North Wilkesboro and
> should say to you here, "Gentlemen, I want to make a living
> and I want to [do so by] manufacturing yellow fever germs."
> Would you let me go on at a thing like that? You would have
> me arrested or else you would lynch me before I could get out
> of town.[4]

At the end of the nineteenth century, it appeared that the campaign
for statewide prohibition had run out of steam throughout the United
States. Despite the efforts of the Prohibition Party and the Woman's
Christian Temperance Union (WCTU), only Maine, Kansas, and North
Dakota supported bans on alcohol by the 1890s. And even in those
states, prohibitory statutes remained unpopular. "I have come to the
conclusion that public opinion will ultimately compel the repeal of the
law," Maine resident Noah Brooks explained in 1898. "In many parts
of the State [prohibition] is for all intents and purposes a dead letter, at
least, it is so far inoperative that the utter inefficiency tends to bring all
law into contempt."[5] To make matters worse, the subsequent collapse
of the Prohibition Party and the waning influence of the WCTU left
the prohibition movement without national leadership and in disarray.[6]

These failures encouraged many temperance organizations such as
the Anti-Saloon League to adopt a new strategy at the turn of the twentieth century. Instead of advocating for statewide prohibition, they
began to campaign for the enactment of local referenda that banned
the sale of alcohol. Crusaders believed that these laws would bring
their neighbors face-to-face with the obstinate saloon and eventually
convince them to accept prohibition on a broader scale. Like their
cohorts elsewhere in the United States, southern prohibitionists used
the policy of "local gradualism" to great effect.[7] By 1907, 825 of the
994 counties in the South had passed local-option legislation, solidify-

ing the region's new reputation as the leading champion for alcohol reform in the United States.[8]

Southern crusaders like Pritchard knew that the key to victory lay in focusing public attention on the "evils" of not only the saloon but alcohol manufacturing as well. In western North Carolina, reformers since the antebellum period had found the road to prohibition blocked by the supporters of the distillers. Although they increasingly embraced temperance during the last two decades of the nineteenth century, highlanders remained hesitant to infringe on the rights of alcohol producers by enacting statewide prohibition. Instead, they believed that local option would solve the liquor problem. Beginning with the Democratic Party's acceptance of federal liquor taxation and its subsequent abandonment of the moonshiners in the early 1880s, however, a series of events would convince them otherwise. During the 1890s, many alcohol manufacturers, including many that paid their taxes and were "legal" in the eyes of the federal government, continued to sell their product in communities that had enacted local-option ordinances. Infuriated, mountain reformers passed antidistiller laws, but to no avail. By 1908, it seemed that statewide prohibition was the only viable solution. For them, distillers were no longer legitimate businessmen, nor were moonshiners folk heroes; both were the purveyors of violence and crime. Reformers had finally witnessed the elimination of the final obstacle to statewide prohibition.

Democrats and Federal Liquor Taxation

Twenty-six years earlier, the success of the prohibition movement had by no means been certain. In January 1882, mountain Republican J. J. Mott, emboldened by his party's successful campaign to defeat the August 1881 referendum on statewide prohibition, quickly moved to consolidate his political power in North Carolina. Mott first secured the support of President Chester Arthur to limit opposition from within Republican ranks. He then resigned as collector of Internal Revenue to allow himself more freedom of action, nominating Tom Cooper, head of the North Carolina Anti-Prohibition Executive Committee, to replace him. Despite opposition from prohibitionist Republicans, Mott persuaded the U.S. Senate to confirm Cooper's nomination. By April, Mott was in complete control of the North Carolina Republican Party.[9]

Mott sought to gain the support of dissatisfied Democrats by opposing the state's undemocratic county government system. In 1876, Democrats had created a county government system that allowed the state legislature, rather than voters, to elect local officials. This system suppressed both Republicans and dissident Democrats, thereby providing Mott with an issue that appealed to a diverse group of voters, regardless of their stance on prohibition.[10] In June 1882, Republicans and so-called Liberal Democrats agreed that they would cooperate in races for the state legislature during the upcoming fall elections. Centering their attacks on county governments, coalition candidates ran strong races throughout the state and almost unseated the Democrats.[11] In North Carolina's Seventh Congressional District, Liberal Democrat Tyre York received 51 percent of the vote, while Democrat Robert Vance, challenged by C. L. Cooke, an independent candidate who advocated reform of the county government system, saw the percentage of his vote in the Eighth Congressional District fall 13 points between 1880 and 1882.[12] The mountain Democratic Party was in serious trouble.

Even before the 1882 elections, Senator Zebulon Vance feared the liberal movement and attempted to discredit it. He accused Republicans and dissident Democrats of being part of an allegedly corrupt Bureau of Internal Revenue.[13] Believing that several Republicans, resentful of Mott's tactics, would testify against their party leader, Vance convinced Congress to launch an investigation into the Bureau of Internal Revenue in western North Carolina.[14] Senate hearings were held in April 1882 and generated more than 450 pages of testimony. Vance, who served as chairman of the investigating committee, hoped these hearings would highlight the political abuses of federal revenue officials. Several witnesses, mostly Democrats, backed up Vance's changes that revenuers sometimes took bribes from legal and illegal distillers.[15] Vance also forced Mott to admit that he had solicited money from revenue officials to fund the 1880 state Republican campaign. Mott defended his actions, claiming that these donations were voluntary and that he had not punished any agent who refused to make a contribution.[16] Commissioner of Internal Revenue Green B. Raum quickly came to Mott's defense. He testified that the collector was "entitled to the approbation of the government for the manner in which he has administered the office."[17]

Although Vance was confident that his investigation had demonstrated the corruption of Mott and other revenue agents, it had little impact on the mountain Republican Party or the liberal movement. The committee failed to uncover any malfeasance that North Carolinians had not already suspected. "In fact," according to Gordon McKinney, "the argument can be made that the hearings gave men like Raum and Mott an opportunity to distinguish themselves from those who had clearly abused the system before them."[18] By the time Vance launched his investigation, liquor taxation had already become less of a political issue in western North Carolina. This was partially a result of the Bureau of Internal Revenue's efforts to reform its image. A balance of force and leniency, combined with more ethical behavior by agents, had helped when the Democratic Party took control of both houses of Congress in 1878.

Democrats could have dismantled the bureau, which they had denounced as tyrannical during Reconstruction. Instead, they left the agency intact.[19] That same year, Mott, then head collector of North Carolina's Sixth Collection District, reduced local Democratic opposition by appointing several highly qualified Democrats as agents. To the dismay of the moonshiners, these revenuers continued to enforce the law.[20] The national party's failure to abolish the federal liquor law ultimately forced many mountain Democrats to accept the system. Agent D. C. Pearson remembered in 1882: "Public sentiment [toward revenue enforcement in the mountain South improved], because the Democrats, getting control of Congress, made no change in the revenue laws, and those people became convinced that it would be the same, let them be in power or out of power, that those appeals that had been made to them on the part of the Democracy, to enable the Democracy to get into power, proved not to be true."[21]

By 1882, the mountain Democratic Party found itself in a precarious situation. Committed to reducing the national tariff, which its constituents believed would help raise the price of agricultural goods, Democrats remained reluctant to abolish the revenue service. If Congress eliminated internal taxation, the loss of the millions of dollars it generated in federal revenue, they feared, would lead most Republicans to refuse to reduce the tariff.[22] The increased collection that followed the reform of the Bureau of Internal Revenue had made the liquor tax the country's leading source of internal revenue, "rising from 30 percent of the collections in 1868 to 63 percent in 1884."[23] Many mountain Democrats admitted that abolishing the internal revenue system was "impractical" and that lawmakers should focus on reforming it instead.[24] Even Robert Vance, one of the most outspoken critics of the revenue service during the 1870s, agreed. "Perhaps it would be best to attempt only a readjustment of the system to the actual wants of the people," he told a *Charlotte Observer* reporter in 1883.[25] Democrats found it increasingly difficult to totally denounce federal liquor taxation. Although continuing to argue that the government should eliminate the Bureau of Internal Revenue, the Democratic *Morganton Mountaineer* favored a duty on distilled spirits. "[Democrats] demand the repeal of the system, not the tax," the newspaper read in January 1884. "They fully recognize the fact that it is but just and right that whiskey and tobacco should be taxed."[26] The Democratic *Mountain Banner* in Rutherford County wrote three months later, "Let the tax alone, but let free people pay it like freemen and then let it go to the U.S. Treasury instead of into the pockets of [revenuers]."[27]

When Democrat Grover Cleveland became president in 1885, mountain Democrats, who now had control of federal patronage, further embraced the Bureau of Internal Revenue. According to Raum, Democrats no longer held "up to contempt the hated internal-revenue officer [following Cleveland's victory]. This person is now a Democrat, and of course must be regarded as a gentlemen."[28] Letters from Democrats poured into the office of Zebulon Vance, asking the senator to nominate them for a revenue position.[29] Vance would not disappoint many of them. He gave his son Charles a revenue position and secured the appointment of his former law partner, Clement Dowd, as Sixth District collector.[30] Vance and other Democrats also protested Cleveland's decision to retain several Republican revenuers until their terms of office expired. In July, Dowd complained to Vance that only one out of the fifty men he had recommended for positions in the Bureau of Internal Revenue had been appointed.[31] Editors of the *Lenoir Topic* lashed out at President Cleveland that same month: "We know that the excuse is that these old deputies know the ropes and are re-appointed to show the new deputies around; but there has been plenty of time for that. And there are other men in Caldwell County than the Republican deputies who know the lay of the land and need no instruction from them in the work of hunting illicit distillers."[32] Vance and other Democrats now accepted the revenue system and demanded that they be allowed to participate in it. It provided them with patronage powers they had never held before.[33]

Many moonshiners believed the new Democratic revenue agents

would ignore them, or at least harass them less than the Republicans had. In Cherokee, Macon, and Jackson counties, where many farmers continued to have limited access to railroads and other transportation arteries, local citizens and revenuers reported an upsurge in illicit distilling following Cleveland's successful presidential campaign. In February 1885, Macon County resident Samuel T. Kelsey complained that moonshiners there and in the neighboring township of Moccasin in Rabun County, Georgia, had become "so bold that they think they can run over the community as they please."[34] On the night of March 11, these illicit distillers even launched an attack on the village of Highlands in Macon County, attempting to rescue two fellow lawbreakers from jail. Deputy Marshal T. B. Coward remembered:

> There were 12 or 13 of the raiders. They formed a line in front of us about 40 ft. from us, made a demand on us for the release of the prisoners at the peril of our lives, at the same time presenting their guns on us. I called to them if that was their only business the best thing for them to do would be to leave at once for they could not get the prisoners. At the close of my last words, they fired upon us. Came near getting me the first fire. We were ready for them and retuned the fire, I suppose there were about 60 shots fired from our side. They stood the fire until about the sixth round from our side, then retreated in the dark and were not seen anymore that night. One of their party William Ramsey was killed dead, 3 arrested, and from the best information I have been able to obtain 3 or four wounded, one perhaps fatally.[35]

This "Moccasin War" forced officials to take immediate action.[36] Democrat Joseph Miller, the newly appointed commissioner of Internal Revenue, blamed "the late disturbance" on the assumption that the Bureau of Internal Revenue would no longer enforce the federal liquor law. With the support of Zebulon Vance, Robert Vance, and other mountain Democrats, Miller authorized the creation of a "special force" to apprehend the "criminals who are terrorizing the law abiding citizens of [Highlands]" and instructed bureau agents in other parts of the Carolina highlands to suppress illicit distilling. Due to the "acts of violence and threats of the illicit distillers," Miller explained to U.S. Attorney General A. H. Garland in April 1885, he "deem[ed]

it highly important that there should be an early manifestation of the
intention of the Government to bring to punishment, at whatever costs,
all persons who so defy its laws and menace the lives of law-abiding
and peaceful citizens."[37]

These efforts were successful. In 1885, the first year in which the
Democrats controlled the Bureau of Internal Revenue, agents seized
196 stills in western North Carolina's Fifth and Sixth Collection Districts, an increase of 216 percent from 1884.[38] The number of convictions for evading federal liquor taxation also rose from 163 in 1884 to
357 in 1886.[39] These attempts to enforce the federal liquor law significantly hampered the moonshiners' ability to sustain a well-organized
resistance movement. By 1886, collector Clement Dowd believed that
three-man posses, which would have been considered insufficient during the 1870s, were adequate to conduct raids in western North Carolina. "The 'moonshiner' invariably runs on the approach of an officer,"
Dowd reported to Commissioner Miller that December. "They are as
utterly without organization, & almost as wild, as the foxes & wolves
which roam among the 'crags & crannies' of the Blue Ridge."[40]

The Democrats' acceptance of the Bureau of Internal Revenue
and their willingness to enforce liquor taxation, however, convinced
some highlanders that the party had betrayed them. "You now hear
the clamor of aspirants to be revenue collectors on the democratic side
of the house," a Watauga County resident complained in March 1885.
"The Radical party saw the folly of the system, why not the Democrats
see the folly of it likewise?"[41] Burke County Democrats were just as
furious. Following the news of Cleveland's victory in November 1884,
they had felt "like the children of Israel when they reached the Promised Land," believing that the party would eliminate the revenue system. But they would be disappointed. "No change will be made in the
law," residents complained six months later. "We see too many of our
leading Democrats fishing for the offices."[42] Chastising party politicians, the *Morganton Star* wrote in the fall of 1885, "The Democratic
Party will not do what it promised, namely, repeal the revenue law; and
this arises from the fact that so many Democrats are seeking revenue
offices. The odium of the Internal Revenue is now shifted from Republican to Democratic shoulders; and it is indeed an onerous burden,
wide-spread and far reaching in its ramifications."[43]

Mountain Democrats quickly scrambled to appeal to disgruntled
party members, and for good reason. They found themselves in the

same predicament that had plagued Republicans during Reconstruction. As the controlling party of the Bureau of Internal Revenue, and wanting to reduce the national tariff, they were forced to support a federal agency that many highlanders continued to oppose. Exacerbating the dilemma, North Carolina Republicans, predicting that Cleveland would win the presidential election, had adopted a plank in their platform that called for the abolition of the revenue service. Reviving claims that Republican—but not Democratic—revenuers were corrupt, the Democratic Party tried to reassure voters that it would reform the system. "The Republican men all drank whiskey," the *Shelby Aurora* in Cleveland County reported in July 1885, "but the Democrats are temperance and church members and will never take a smile or get crooked."[44] Meanwhile, the *Lenoir Topic* praised newly appointed collector Dowd's declaration that "no man who drinks whisky need apply to him." "Illicit distilling will go on now," the newspaper concluded, "but revenue officers will not be traveling politicians any longer. That is the difference."[45] The Bureau of Internal Revenue survived this round of criticism, and, based on the rising number of arrests and seizures, Democrats were determined to suppress moonshining, which most believed had no place in the New South.

As a result, by 1885, the Democratic Party had abandoned moonshiners. With the election of Grover Cleveland in 1884, mountain Democrats embraced the Bureau of Internal Revenue and the patronage powers it provided them. Responding to the demands of middle-class townspeople, who were becoming a powerful force in mountain politics, they intensified enforcement of the federal liquor laws and increasingly viewed those who resisted as a liability. These Democrats would soon endorse local-option legislation, further alienating legal and illegal distillers from mountain communities.

The Local-Option Crusade and Its Consequences

On December 10, 1885, eighty of North Carolina's leading prohibitionists met in Greensboro to discuss the possibility of organizing a state Prohibition Party. In 1869, the Good Templars and other northern-based temperance societies had founded the national Prohibition Party. Convinced that "wets" controlled Democrats and Republicans alike, they wanted to increase prohibition sentiment by educating voters on the evils of alcohol and providing them with a practical political alternative.[46] Following Reconstruction, this third-party movement began to garner support among southerners. By 1884, antialcohol proponents had established the Prohibition Party in Alabama, Texas, Tennessee, and Virginia.[47] Distraught over the failed statewide prohibition campaign of 1881, North Carolina reformers followed suit at Greensboro in 1885 and agreed to organize the Prohibition Party in their state. "We can no longer support either of these old parties [Democratic and Republican] . . . without endorsing the power of the saloon in politics and aiding to perpetuate that power," they concluded that December; therefore, "we . . . declare the imperative necessity for a new party, with Prohibition of the Liquor Traffic its prime object . . . and invite the votes of all who cast ballots and the sympathy of all others."[48]

State and mountain Democrats feared that this new political organization would weaken their party and greeted it with disdain. Just four years earlier, they remembered, more than 40,000 North Carolinians, most of whom were Democratic, had favored statewide prohibition. These voters were now being encouraged to join a party dedicated to its success. Democrats quickly lashed out at the Prohibition Party, arguing that its existence threatened to impede the progress of temperance. "We cannot see any good to come of such a party," the Democratic *Salisbury Watchman* read in December 1885. "There is reason to apprehend more damage to the temperance cause than benefit."[49] That same month, the *Lenoir Topic* revealed the true motive behind Democrats' denunciation of the Prohibition Party. It warned that the third-party movement would divide Democrats in the upcoming 1888 gubernatorial election and "give fresh hopes of reanimation to the Republican party which, but yesterday, was dead in North Carolina." "A Democrat naturally opposes any movement antagonistic to the success of the great and living principles of his party," the newspaper elaborated, "while a Republican just as naturally welcomes whatever tends to promote the disintegration of the great party of people."[50]

But Republicans were unable to capitalize on their adversaries' dilemma. By 1888, the rise of temperance sentiment within the party of Lincoln had made it dangerous for Republican leaders to embrace the antiprohibition cause. They remained unconvinced that a three-cornered gubernatorial election would result in a Republican victory, predicting (correctly) that Prohibitionists would fail to convince enough Democrats to defect from their party.[51] As such, Republicans

Advertisement for the Prohibition Party, 1888. Courtesy of the Prints and Photographs Division, Library of Congress, Washington, D.C.

and Democrats alike attempted to neutralize the appeal of the Prohibition Party. In the months leading up to the 1888 gubernatorial election, most Republicans downplayed their party's opposition to statewide prohibition seven years earlier. Meanwhile, Democrats labeled Prohibitionists as "radicals" and urged party members to "stand by the old ship of Democracy—the friend of the South and of white supremacy."[52] These efforts soundly quelled the Prohibition Party, as its candidate for governor received only 3,124 of the 285,556 votes cast.[53]

Despite the party's failure at the polls, its existence did have an impact. Before the 1888 gubernatorial election, Republicans and Democrats for the first time officially endorsed local option, with the hope of using it as a weapon against the Prohibition Party. By attacking the liquor trade in local areas along nonpartisan lines, they sought to placate opposition from within their parties and depoliticize the issue of prohibition. "The old political parties . . . have a chance to take the wind out of the sails of the third party movement by voting for local-option," the *Wilson Advance* explained in 1885. "This they can do without interfering with their old party relations."[54] Editor J. F. Murrell of the *Hickory Western Carolinian* agreed. "If [we] take an open and positive stand in favor of Prohibition under the operation of our

Local option laws," he argued in 1887, "there will be no disturbing element [Prohibition Party] in this State."[55]

Although this strategy succeeded in defeating the third-party movement, it ultimately encouraged prohibitionists to intensify their fight against King Alcohol. Emboldened by Republicans' and Democrats' endorsement of local prohibition, North Carolina reformers organized thousands of local-option elections following the 1888 gubernatorial campaign.[56] These elections sparked conflict within communities throughout the state and continued to make prohibition a political issue. Ironically, town boosters, once staunch advocates of prohibition, now became the leading opponents of local option in western North Carolina. These men feared that the fight against alcohol would stymie tourism, which had emerged as one of the region's most important industries.[57] A resident from the newly chartered town of Blowing Rock in Watauga County explained in 1889:

> The burning question is that of "beer or no beer"—whether or not a saloon to sell beer shall be opened. The argument begins upon the expediency of it, the advocates claiming that a saloon will be an attraction and draw visitors who would not come without it, while the opponents stoutly claim that the saloon would drive away many of the best class of visitors and would attract a very unsavory class. The advocates boldly assert that no prohibition summer resort has ever been a success and that Blowing Rock will never amount to anything until it has a saloon.[58]

The most publicized debate regarding the sale of alcohol occurred in Asheville in 1892, when the board of county commissioners attempted to appease both "drys" and "wets" by granting liquor licenses to several hotels on the condition that these establishments sell alcohol only to their guests. Outraged, supporters of local option organized a prohibition voting club and demanded that the commissioners overturn their decision to license barrooms in the city, but to no avail. Politicians feared that local option threatened to damage the economic interests of the community and refused to support it. Asheville, the birthplace of the temperance movement in western North Carolina, would remain a "wet" town until October 1907.[59]

Despite these setbacks, alcohol reformers enjoyed a broad base of mountain support. During the 1890s, 407 churches, schools, and towns passed local-option ordinances in western North Carolina, an increase of 60 percent from the previous decade.[60] Even if unsuccessful, reformers discovered that local prohibition elections provided them with a forum to educate citizens on the dangers of alcohol and build grassroots sentiment for antiliquor legislation. When an election was called, prohibition became the most important issue in local politics for months at a time.[61] Antialcohol advocates took the opportunity to form clubs, organize rallies, and endorse politicians who supported local prohibition.[62] Women often served as the backbone of this local-option crusade, holding prayer meetings and pledging voters against whiskey.[63] Reformers believed that local prohibition would bring peace and order to their communities.

Even when local-option laws were successful, residents were often disappointed to find that alcohol consumption and violence persevered.[64] Expectations were dashed and support for local prohibition diminished as alcohol continued to flow into "dry" communities. "The local option law . . . prevails in Lenoir and Lower Creek townships, yet liquor is sold in both townships," the *Lenoir Topic* complained in 1889. "Many good citizens, who have voted for local option and who abhor the sale and use of whiskey as a beverage, are debating whether it would not be better to license and control the liquor traffic."[65] In 1890, a *New York Times* reporter described western North Carolina as "'dry,' so 'dry' in fact that 100 gallons of blockade whisky serves a small town of 150 inhabitants of all ages and both sexes for a week's consumption . . . and 50 gallons provide for the festivities of the Fourth of July. The prevailing thirst due to the 'dryness' of the towns is amazing."[66] Burke, Caldwell, and Mitchell county residents believed that local-option laws had resulted in an increase in the number of illegal alcohol retail establishments. In 1899, the *Morganton Herald* complained that these so-called blind tigers arose like "a small pox epidemic" and proved that sheriffs were "powerless" to enforce the law.[67]

Unable to prevent the sale and consumption of alcohol in their communities, mountain prohibitionists increasingly lashed out at the liquor manufacturer. There were good reasons for this rise in antidistiller sentiment. Beginning in the early 1890s, several forces led many Carolina highlanders to produce alcohol (often illegally) and sell it in "dry" communities. In 1891, a nationwide depression began that would continue until 1897. This economic crisis hit many mountain residents hard, as the size of their farms declined 22 percent and their cash value dropped 17 percent during those years.[68] In 1894, the Democratic-controlled Congress, seeking to recover the federal government's own losses without raising the tariff, increased the federal liquor tax from 90¢ to $1.10 per gallon.[69] Meanwhile, hundreds of mountain communities enacted local-option laws.

These factors—agricultural depression, a higher alcohol tax, and local prohibition—made moonshining an attractive alternative for many western North Carolinians. The new tax encouraged evasion because it significantly reduced the small distiller's profit margin. By 1894, the price for a bushel of corn in western North Carolina was 40¢, while a gallon of whiskey sold for a $1.20. Without paying a tax, mountain farmers who turned two bushels of corn into five gallons of alcohol earned a $6.00 profit. Legal distillers, however, netted only 50¢.[70] The enactment of local-option laws further encouraged illicit distilling by providing a wider market for moonshiners, who, without legal competition, often raised the price of alcohol on thirsty mountain residents who did not appreciate the ban.[71]

As a result, moonshining in western North Carolina and other parts of the United States increased dramatically during the 1890s. The *New York Times* reported in 1895 that "there [was] more illicit distilling and trading of 'blockade' whisky in [the] country than ever before."[72] One year later, the federal government estimated that moonshiners produced between 5 million and 10 million gallons of alcohol annually.[73] Commissioner Miller refused to concede defeat, however. Appointed in 1893, he instructed revenuers to conduct more raids on suspected moonshine enclaves, which often proved successful.[74] Between 1890 and 1893, revenuers had confiscated 355 stills and arrested 130 people in western North Carolina. During the first three years of Miller's tenure, agents seized 1,065 distilleries and made 208 arrests.[75] None-theless, the great divergence between seizures and arrests suggests that illicit distillers remained an elusive lot. They continued to post pickets and, on at least one occasion, used a modern invention, the telephone, to give ample warning of a posse's approach.[76]

Other moonshiners responded by returning to organized resis-tance. Between 1891 and 1896, illicit distillers operated a "white cap" club in Wilkes County to protect their whiskey operations from fed-eral and local officials. Modeled partly on the Ku Klux Klan, white caps had appeared in Mississippi, Alabama, and Georgia in the late

A moonshine still seized by revenuers. From John C. Campbell, *The Southern Highlander and His Homeland* (New York: Russell Sage Foundation, 1921), facing 103.

1880s.[77] Like the Klan, these vigilantes wore disguises and terrorized African Americans in an attempt to maintain white supremacy. They also targeted local residents who worked with revenuers to eliminate moonshining. In March 1891, Wilkes County white cappers assaulted their first victim, a Hunting Creek farmer rumored to be an informer.[78] But it was not until the mid-1890s, when the Bureau of Internal Revenue cracked down on illicit distilling, that such violence occurred frequently in Wilkes County. Throughout 1895, white cappers often paid unwelcome visits to informers and fired on federal agents conducting raids.[79] In the Roaring River section of the county, these terrorists ruled with an iron fist. In March 1895, the *Wilkesboro Chronicle* reported that white caps there were "an energetic people in the cause of Satan." The newspaper elaborated: "Last Friday night a crowd went to Ansel Prevette's, and called him to the door and shot him through the thigh. They went to John Prevette's near by and tore down his dwelling house. They then went to an unoccupied house belonging to Mathew Prevette and burned it. John and Mathew are sons of Ansel, [who was a witness] a few days ago in a case again[st] W. C. Wiles, charged with blockading. . . . It is dangerous to be safe up there."[80]

Moonshiners throughout the region increasingly resorted to violence. Yancey County moonshiners also waged war against the Bureau of Internal Revenue. Most prominent among these desperadoes was George McCurry, who gained local notoriety after shooting two federal agents in 1896. The bloodshed did not stop after McCurry's arrest in 1897. His fellow illicit distillers continued to attack officials attempting to enforce federal liquor taxation and local-option laws in that county. Whether traditionalists who simply made alcohol for themselves and their neighbors or large-scale operators attempting to profit from prohibition laws, distillers remained convinced that federal and local liquor laws threatened to destroy their livelihood. Many of them insisted that they were not—to use the words of McCurry—"bad men."[81]

But the resurgence of moonshiner violence convinced a growing number of Carolina highlanders otherwise. Following the outbreak of brutality in Wilkes County in 1895, residents there denounced illicit distillers and argued that "about three fourths of them ought to be hung and be done with it."[82] "We hope these people will realize the fact that in taking up arms against these officers they are 'bucking,' and it will result disastrously to them," editors of the *North Wilkesboro News* explained in April 1895. "There are many ways of making a living other than blockading, and we hope the time will soon come when they will also realize this fact."[83] That November, an unnamed Wilkes County Democrat demanded that President Grover Cleveland send more revenue agents "upon the distillers of Wilkes and knock the everlasting stuffing out of them forever and forever."[84] Yancey County denizens joined this chorus of opposition. In 1897, after local officials captured moonshiners George McCurry, Moses Wilson, and Mac Webb, "three of the most desperate criminals that ever infested that or any other county in North Carolina," residents there were "determined to see that these desperadoes are properly punished."[85] "George [McCurry] has long been a terror, not only to Yancey county, but to many counties in western North Carolina and adjacent parts of Tennessee," one person wrote to the *Marion Messenger* in February 1898. "Deputy Sheriff Feltz deserves the gratitude of all good citizens [for capturing McCurry] and no doubt will receive it."[86] Legal distilleries were not immune from the wrath of mountain reformers. Many community members denounced these establishments as "places of vice and sin . . . , maelstroms of the neighborhoods which they infect, into which nearly all that is good is swallowed up."[87]

This increase in antidistiller sentiment forced the General Assembly to take action. In 1893, state legislators added a provision to local-option laws that allowed voters to outlaw the manufacturing of alcohol around schools, churches, and businesses. If convicted, illicit distillers would be subject to a fine or a prison sentence, the amount or length of which would be determined by the county court.[88] In 1899, the General Assembly went one step further, passing a statute that permitted voters to decide whether to ban the sale and production of liquor within entire counties. Violators of this law would be "fined or imprisoned for each and every offence or both, in discretion of the [county] court." The statute excluded druggists, however, who could purchase and sell alcohol to residents with a prescription from a practicing physician.[89]

Many western North Carolina reformers embraced these laws. Between 1893 and 1903, mountain voters agreed to prohibit the manufacture of alcohol around 369 schools, churches, and businesses. Of the 209 known locales that banned liquor production during those years, 145 (or 69 percent) of them were situated in non–county seat townships or in communities with fewer than 100 residents, indicating that the antidistiller movement had now shifted from urban centers to the countryside.[90] Voters in fourteen of the twenty-five mountain counties also passed total bans on the sale and manufacturing of alcohol.[91] However, the perceived failure of local-option laws led other state and mountain reformers to experiment with the dispensary system.

The Dispensary Movement and Its Consequences

In 1893, Governor Ben Tillman established the South Carolina Liquor Dispensary, allowing only government-operated stores to sell alcohol in that state. Proponents of this system believed that it would appease both "wets" and "drys" by eliminating saloons and their attendant evils without abolishing drinking. Unlike most saloons, dispensaries prohibited drinking on the premises, operated only during daylight hours, and refused to sell alcohol to minors. Profits from dispensaries went back to the state government, which used the money to build schools, roads, and other public works. Along with taming drunken misbehavior, Tillman and other reformers argued that this system would improve South Carolina's educational facilities and infrastructure.[92]

North Carolinians soon pressured the General Assembly to adopt a similar system, believing that local-option laws created more prob-

Ben Tillman, 1905. Courtesy of the Prints and Photographs Division, Library of Congress, Washington, D.C.

lems than they solved. In May 1895, the *Wilmington Review* in New Hanover County reported that dispensaries were preferable to "the regime having so called prohibition with its drug stores and blind tigers."[93] Many Carolina highlanders agreed. That January, a Burke County resident had insisted that a dispensary in Morganton would reduce public disorder and generate economic progress. He explained in the *Morganton Herald*: "The town needs waterworks and graded schools and we must have them soon if we expect our town to grow. Now, as to the 'sources of revenue' open to the town, the most sure and lucrative is to license bar rooms or put up a dispensary. . . . Why not try a [dispensary]? The town needs money and in what better way could we control the liquor traffic. Give this matter your most earnest attention, and remember that our town's interests and future welfare hangs in the balance."[94]

Townspeople in Lenoir, Hickory, and Marion also welcomed the establishment of a dispensary, hoping it would "put an end to personal bickerings and animosities over the subject of [local option]."[95] "The dispensary is better than the present system," the *Hickory Press and Carolinian* stated in February. "That is certain, and would be a proper solution of the liquor traffic."[96] The *Marion Messenger* expressed a similar opinion. "If the whiskey evil, the greatest in this land and State, cannot be subjugated," the paper warned, "then the next best thing is to regulate and restrict the evil workings and effects of the traffic upon the public."[97]

The North Carolina General Assembly quickly responded to these requests. In March 1895, it allowed Haywood County residents to outlaw all saloons and establish the state's first dispensary in Waynesville. Controlled by the county government, the dispensary forbade drinking on its premises, was closed on Sundays, and sold liquor in sealed packages of one-half pint or more. Vending alcohol contrary to the law became a misdemeanor, punishable by a fine of between $200 and $500 and imprisonment for thirty days or more, at the discretion of the court.[98] Although it sold only $35 of alcohol on its first day of operation, the dispensary proved to be a success. In 1897, it netted a profit of $3,112.91, which was divided equally between Haywood County and Waynesville.[99] James P. Cook, an editor of the *Concord Standard* who visited Waynesville that same year, claimed that the dispensary had also tamed main-street drinking behavior. According to Cook, the dispensary's lack of saloon attractions, such as billiards and gambling, had taken the fun out of drinking and forced men to seek other forms of entertainment.[100] Many local residents agreed. "The dispensary for Haywood county . . . has solved the liquor question to the satisfaction of the people, so far as this county is concerned," an unnamed Waynesville reformer wrote to the *Asheville Citizen* in February 1897.[101]

The success of the Waynesville dispensary mobilized antialcohol proponents who believed that local prohibition had failed.[102] By the late 1890s, hundreds of citizens from across the state bombarded the General Assembly with petitions demanding that it establish additional dispensaries and outlaw saloons. The Baptist Young People's Union of North Carolina, based in Raleigh, expressed the sentiments of these reformers, writing to the legislature in 1897:

> We, the Baptist young people of North Carolina, representing every county and section, do hereby most humbly and sincerely petition your honorable body, to use every lawful and reasonable means within your power to pass the bills now pending for the establishment of dispensaries in certain towns and counties in North Carolina, and to use every honorable means to suppress the traffic that is cursing our State, blighting her young manhood, weakening all her citizens, crippling her schools and impeding the progress and usefulness of every church and Christian enterprise in North Carolina.[103]

Legislators acted on these requests. In the western part of the state, dispensaries opened in the county seats of Rutherford (1897), Swain (1899), Burke (1899), Macon (1901), and Madison (1905).[104]

But support for this movement was far from universal. Hard-line prohibitionists and evangelicals made little distinction between dispensaries and saloons, and they denounced the county governments' use of "blood-money" to improve roads and build schools. "I believe we have as good a right to legalize murder as we have to legalize and endorse the sale of liquor as a beverage," C. M. Anderson wrote in 1895 to justify why he and several other Morganton ministers had refused to sign a pro-dispensary petition. "When we legalize the business and sanction of it [via the dispensary system], we become partners and are equally guilty with the salesman, and there formally withdraw ourselves by our rebellion from His provincial protection."[105] These complaints continued into the next century. In 1903, farmers in the small community of

Ferry explained why they wanted the dispensary in Rutherford County closed: "If it is wrong for a blind tiger to sell whiskey it is wrong for Rutherford County to legalize the sale of it and receive one-half the profits. Christians can't afford to legalize a business which will destroy peace and happiness in this world."[106]

Other highlanders charged that dispensaries, like local-option laws, had failed to solve the liquor problem. They pointed out that blind tigers continued to operate in mountain counties with established dispensaries. "The laws of the land are violated in every neck of the woods," Henrietta residents in Rutherford County complained in 1903. "There seems to be quite an array of dispensers of 'bug juice' in this locality, and it is evident from the signs of times that it is a very salable commodity there."[107] That same year, Burke County voters abolished the dispensary in Morganton. "While it was in operation," an unnamed Morganton resident remembered in 1905, "there was no appreciable falling off in drunkenness or crime, and as a source of revenue it fell far short of what its promoters claimed for it."[108] "Johnny Hopeful" from Waynesville believed that the dispensary there had actually increased alcohol consumption. In 1903, he complained: "There is nothing good ever comes in or goes out from [the dispensary]. There is where sin, and shame, and crime, and death, are sold lawfully. Here is where it is lawful and respectable to buy that which makes fiends of those who drink what is sold here."[109]

Reformers distraught over the perceived failure of the dispensary movement once again lashed out at the producers of alcohol. In March 1903, the *Lenoir Weekly News* charged that illicit distilling had bred "more crime than any other unlawful occupation men engage in."[110] Local businessmen blamed moonshiners for contributing to the moral and economic decline of their employees by selling alcohol to them. S. B. Tanner, owner of Henrietta Mills in Rutherford County, recalled in 1908: "When we built our mill villages, this vicinity was noted for its blockade distilleries, and we had no end of trouble among our operatives, which interfered seriously with the running of our mills, and it was difficult for us to retain decent and respectable people at our mills, on account of rowdyism, midnight brawls, etc."[111]

Legal distillers also incurred the wrath of mountain reformers. "The average country distillery is the loafing place of the most worthless characters of the surrounding country," editors of the *Wilkesboro Chronicle* complained in 1903. "There are more crimes committed near the still-houses and by reason of the influence of the stills than anybody supposes."[112] That same year, the *Henderson Hustler* insisted that legal distillers were destroying the region. "The scent of the distilleries is a stench in the nostrils of all decent people," the newspaper read. "Lives are being wrecked at home and the bad influence is spreading."[113]

In March 1903, state legislators responded by enacting the Watts Law, which prohibited both the sale and the manufacture of alcohol (wines and ciders excepted) outside of incorporated towns. North Carolinians who vended liquor contrary to the law had to pay "a fine of not more than $200 or imprisonment not exceeding six months." Penalties for manufacturing alcohol were harsher, reflecting the belief that distillers—legal and illegal—were largely to blame for intemperance. The county court charged first-time offenders with a misdemeanor and, if convicted, sentenced them to serve six months to two years in jail. Upon a second violation of this law, distillers were charged with a felony and imprisoned for one to four years and fined between $100 and $1,000.[114] The noose was tightening around the neck of alcohol manufacturers. The *Wilkesboro Chronicle* declared in 1905: "Every good citizen of all parties should hold up his hands in the heroic fight he is making to end the day when violators of the law conspire to defraud the government and make a reign of terror in the neighborhoods where they carry on their nefarious practice."[115]

Some vestiges of the region's lengthy history of distilling persisted. A dwindling percentage of the population continued to insist that neither the church nor the state had the authority to ban alcohol manufacturing. In 1894, the Brushy Mountain Baptist Association in Wilkes County issued a decree forbidding members to produce liquor. Several churches, however, refused to abide by the resolution, insisting that members had an inherent right to distill alcohol, and forced the association to reverse its position.[116] Opposition to antidistiller laws continued into the next century. Some, like S. M. McCall, a Caldwell County minister, even argued that the Bible sanctioned alcohol manufacturing. Denouncing statewide prohibition in 1908, he insisted that Jesus Christ himself had been a distiller, having performed his first miracle in Cana of Galilee by making water into wine. "If those interested in the effort to establish Prohibition prove to the satisfaction of the American people that Christ committed a sin, and that Christ set a bad example to future generations," McCall concluded, "then we fear that they will have succeeded in destroying the very foundation of the Christian Faith."[117]

Other mountain residents remained convinced for secular reasons that antidistiller laws were unconstitutional and threatened to destroy an important local industry. In 1903, seventeen Wilkes County farmers argued that the Watts Law "would be an unjust infringement upon the rights of our citizens, guaranteed to them under the constitution." These men then warned that the statute discriminated against "the poor class of people, who are entirely dependent upon their little fruit and corn crops for support." Petitioning the General Assembly, they explained: "Owing to the enormous crops of corn produced in the Western States of the country, we cannot enter the markets of the world in competition with these great corn producing States and owing to the cheapness of corn and other foodstuffs there we cannot compete with them in stockraising therefore without our cash market for corn furnished by the distillers here at home."[118] Baptist minister McCall agreed. "We want to elect legislators and members to congress pledged to do all in their power to bring about the repeal or judicious modification of all oppressive liquor legislation," he said, "so as to give North Carolina an equal chance with the sister States of the Republic."[119]

Viewing prohibition as a threat to their jobs, many revenuers became outspoken opponents of antidistiller legislation and often refused to cooperate with state officials. It was not in their best interest to eliminate the liquor trade.[120] Georgian T. C. Crenshaw explained: "I am a tax collector, not the guardian of the prohibition laws. I am not here to suppress liquor making or liquor selling."[121] Bureau agents argued that antidistiller statues would ultimately fail to reduce alcohol manufacturing and consumption. "Just wait until the brandy season is fairly open and you may expect to see no end of blockading," Rutherford County agent Vance Scoggin chastised after passage of the Watts Law in July 1903. "Available locations on the creeks and braches will be at a premium."[122] The continuation of the Bureau of Internal Revenue reinforced the position of highlanders who insisted that payment of the federal liquor tax exempted them from antidistiller laws, and they continued to manufacture alcohol.[123]

This infuriated state and mountain prohibitionists. "The federal authorities are not looking for any violations of the state law," Alexander County residents complained in 1903.[124] Two years later, D. H. Tuttle from Caldwell County accused revenuers of taking "hush money" from illicit distillers. "Let good citizens see to it that the U.S. Revenue officers do their duty," he pleaded. "Let good men of all creeds and parties put aside their fear and indifference in this matter and using law for all its worth, end this wickedness."[125] The antiprohibition stances of revenuers led to charges of leniency toward the moonshiners. In 1905, a Wilkes County resident angrily demanded that agents stop showing "tenderness" to blockaders. "Haven't they [revenuers] an oath to enforce the law and don't they make out their pay accounts for work done?" he asked. "We have never heard of an officer getting too 'tenderhearted and considerate' to send in his pay account at the regular time."[126] With such widespread opposition to distillers and other opponents of antialcohol legislation, the final obstacle preventing the enactment of statewide prohibition had been removed.

Prohibition's Triumph

At 6:30 A.M. on May 26, 1908, church bells rang out in Waynesville in Haywood County. Members of the local churches had awoken early that morning, eager to encourage their neighbors to vote for statewide prohibition as they walked to the courthouse. Even before the polls opened at 7:00 A.M., the "good women of the community" had assembled on the streets, pleading with voters to "deposit their ballots in favor of home and country." At 9:30 that morning, these women, accompanied by several children, marched down Main Street, where they sang temperance songs and waved prohibition banners in the air. They would not be disappointed. Although the first ballot cast in Waynesville was "wet," it "was soon overwhelmed by an avalanche of 'dry' ballots." By day's end, only one township in Haywood County had voted against statewide prohibition. "Old Haywood," the *Waynesville Courier* reported two days after the election, "had . . . covered herself with glory, and had gone 'dry' by nearly 2000 majority."[127]

Other counties reported similar outcomes. The final tally was 113,612 votes, or 62 percent of the state, in favor of statewide prohibition in 1908. "North Carolina first at Bethel, farthest at Appomattox, and the first State in the Union to banish the liquor traffic by popular vote," the *Washington Progress* in Beaufort County boasted on May 30. "Each man should record his vote in the family Bible."[128] Mountain reformers were especially elated. So often depicted as a land of intemperance and moonshining, western North Carolina had garnered a higher percentage of "dry" votes than elsewhere in the state, despite laws that had recently denied suffrage to African Americans.[129] With

the exception of Alexander, Surry, Alleghany, and Wilkes, every mountain county had voted in favor of statewide prohibition, a complete
reversal from the doomed campaign of 1881.[130] In the eyes of many
local urban reformers, their rural brethren had become members of
modern civilization by finally embracing "sobriety, morality, decency,
education, and progress." "We feel so proud of Jackson in this fearless
fight," editors of the *Jackson County Journal* wrote after 96 percent of
voters in that county endorsed prohibition. "It shows they are ready
to stand for right."[131] In 1919, these highlanders would again celebrate
when Congress passed the Eighteenth Amendment, outlawing the sale
and manufacture of alcohol in the entire country.[132] It appeared that
they had finally won their battle against King Alcohol.

Conclusion

Prohibitionists' legislative triumph over King Alcohol in the United States at the turn of the twentieth century was nothing short of amazing. They had managed to make illegal a product that Americans had enjoyed for generations. By centering its attention on the saloon, the Anti-Saloon League convinced countless Americans that the most efficient way to combat intemperance was to eliminate the businesses that sustained it. This strategy often led to statewide prohibition laws in the North and West, where the number of saloons had increased twofold since the Civil War. In western North Carolina and other parts of the rural South, however, saloons remained relatively few, and whiskey continued to prevail over beer. To build support for legal prohibition, southern reformers had to persuade residents that alcohol manufacturing was the root of the liquor problem.

This proved difficult. Throughout the nineteenth century, most western North Carolinians believed that citizens had an inherent right to manufacture alcohol. Although they often supported laws that regulated taverns and criminalized public drunkenness, they insisted that the government—local, state, and federal—had no legal authority to deprive their neighbors of the opportunity to make a living by distilling liquor. For them, alcohol manufacturing was a respectable profession that played an important role in the region's economy and culture. The advent of federal liquor tax enforcement following the Civil War strengthened highlanders' devotion to the distillers, especially those who did not bend to pressure from Washington and continued to produce it illegally. Many mountain residents viewed moonshiners as valiant southerners protecting the community from an abusive federal government, and they scoffed at reformers' claims that these men were troublemakers.

Despite such widespread sympathy for alcohol and those who distilled it, southern prohibitionists were able to establish support for their cause well before the arrival of northern reformers and the Anti-Saloon League at the turn of the twentieth century. In western North Carolina, antiliquor proponents found moderation to be an effective tool. Most of them were not extremists who demanded immediate statewide prohibition, a tactic that had been ineffective in the 1850s. Instead, mountain reformers began to build grassroots support for their cause by promoting the restriction of liquor retailing in their own communities. Local-option laws permitted prohibitionists to educate their neighbors on the dangers of alcohol and prevented their opponents from arguing that the antiliquor crusade was undemocratic. More important, the apparent failure of local-option legislation to curtail alcohol consumption led highlanders to accept more stringent forms of legislation, such as statewide prohibition.

The work of southern prohibitionists was ultimately successful, however, because they were able to convince most residents that alcohol manufacturing lay at the heart of the liquor problem. In western North Carolina, where distillers had historically enjoyed a broad base of support, widespread acceptance of the Bureau of Internal Revenue and the Democratic Party's abandonment of moonshiners, along with the negative portrayal of the mountain region by the national media, paved the way for a local movement against distillers following Reconstruction. By the beginning of the twentieth century, this crusade had eliminated the final obstacle confronting reformers in their fight for statewide prohibition: the belief that alcohol manufacturing was an inalienable right and an economic necessity. Ironically, distillers aided in the removal of this barrier by defying popular temperance laws in their communities. As a result, many mountain denizens increasingly blamed distillers for promoting drunkenness and violence. For them, statewide prohibition became the only logical option.

The prohibitionists' triumph in 1908 was also a result of western North Carolina's transition from a rural to an industrial economy during the nineteenth century. Perhaps nowhere did industrialization have a greater impact than in the mountain countryside. There, improved transportation, urban growth, and increased commercial farming sparked an economic and social revolution. These forces helped bridge the cultural gap that had divided mountain townspeople and their rural counterparts since the antebellum period. Adapting to a changing environment, many rural residents began to reject preindustrial drinking mores and become more receptive to the rhetoric of mostly urban prohibitionists. By the turn of the twentieth century, these men and women had embraced the temperance crusade, denouncing alcohol and those who distilled it as obstacles to economic and moral progress. The prohibition movement would have failed without the support of these rural highlanders.

The rise of prohibition in western Carolina communities demonstrated once and for all that Appalachia was not exceptional, despite the popular perception. Indeed, the same forces shaping antialcohol sentiment elsewhere in America encouraged highlanders to reject traditional drinking mores throughout the nineteenth century. That being said, the road to prohibition in Appalachia may have been more difficult than in other parts of the nation. The region's predominantly white, native-born population handicapped prohibitionists who wanted to capitalize on racism and xenophobia to build sympathy for their cause. And although the national media exaggerated the extent to which distilling took place in Appalachia, the profession remained an economic necessity for many mountain residents well into the twentieth century. Local crusaders responded by demonizing alcohol manufacturers and their rural clientele, much like southern reformers did to African Americans and northern temperance advocates did to eastern European immigrants. Their efforts made the Appalachian distiller, depicted as a violent and uncivilized man who promoted economic and moral decline, the symbol of the ills of mountain society. By eliminating that problem, reformers believed they could save the region from itself.

Prohibitionists might have gained support for their cause, but they were never able to eliminate either the demand for or the supply of alcohol. The advent of statewide prohibition in 1908 and national prohibition in 1919 only intensified North Carolinians' appetite for liquor and increased the profitability of moonshining. The struggling economy added to the problem. Like those living elsewhere in the nation, many mountain residents, unable to find employment, began to distill alcohol illegally during the 1920s and 1930s. As one Cherokee County moonshiner recalled in 1989: "Everybody was needy; half of them didn't have shoes. I finally got to where I just didn't care. Young and stout and couldn't get jobs. I'd been all around South Carolina—just hitch-hiking everywhere trying to find a job. Finally, I came back home in the fall. We'd made a crop; I'd left it with the old lady. And I started making liquor. I had to have some money."[1]

Alcohol distilling soon emerged as a well-organized criminal business, resulting in the proliferation of moonshiner violence in western North Carolina and other parts of the United States.[2] These moonshiners manufactured more liquor than ever before. In 1935, federal agents raided a house in Wilkes County, where they confiscated 7,100 gallons of liquor, the "largest inland seizure of untaxed whiskey ever made in the United States."[3]

A moonshine still in operation during the 1920s. From Horace Kephart, *Our Southern Highlanders: A Narrative of Adventure in the Southern Appalachians and a Study of Life among the Mountaineers* (New York: Macmillan, 1922), facing 120.

During the 1920s, the distilling process also underwent a dramatic transformation, as alcohol manufacturers attempted to increase their profit margin by accelerating the volume of production. Three new inventions—the "thumper" keg, the "steamer," and the "groundhog" still—aided liquor makers in their quest to boost production.[4] The discovery that they could substitute sugar for corn mash further revolutionized the distilling process, reducing the fermentation period by three-fourths and allowing moonshiners to increase their profit margin.[5] With new emphasis placed on quantity over quality, alcohol distilling was no longer a craft but a profession.

The 1920s also witnessed the collapse of the antialcohol alliance between urban and rural Americans, which had been so important in achieving prohibition just a few years earlier. Middle-class townspeople, embracing a new consumer culture that placed less value on restraint and sobriety, redefined Victorian standards of behavior and abandoned their previous support for prohibition. For them, prohibition became "a grim reminder of the moral frenzy that so many wished to forget, a ludicrous caricature of the reforming impulse, of the Yankee-Protestant notion that it is both possible and desirable to moralize private life through public action."[6] Ironically, middle-class townspeople now perceived the antialcohol crusade as an unwanted remnant of "traditional" American values, overlooking the fact that their forefathers and foremothers had been the first to champion the cause before the Civil War. Meanwhile, rural evangelicals and farmers, the last to accept prohibition, continued to defend it. They were fighting not just for temperance but for the preservation of those same "traditional" values that the urban culture wanted to eliminate. But these men and women had also forgotten why they originally embraced anti-alcohol reform: not to restore "traditional" values (which had actually accepted the consumption and manufacturing of alcohol) but to forge a new "modern" America, one that their urban counterparts had envisioned as well.

Notes

Introduction

1. *Sylvan Valley News,* May 29, 1908.
2. Austin Kerr, *Organized for Prohibition: A New History of the Anti-Saloon League* (New Haven, CT: Yale University Press, 1985); Thomas R. Pegram, *Battling Demon Rum: The Struggle for a Dry America, 1800–1933* (Chicago: Ivan R. Dee, 1998); Jack S. Blocker Jr., *American Temperance Movements: Cycles of Reform* (Boston: Twayne Publishers, 1989); Jack S. Blocker Jr., *Retreat from Reform: The Prohibition Movement in the United States, 1890–1913* (Westport, CT: Greenwood Press, 1976); Norman H. Clark, *Deliver Us from Evil: An Interpretation of American Prohibition* (New York: W. W. Norton, 1976); Richard F. Hamm, *Shaping the Eighteenth Amendment: Temperance Reform, Legal Culture, and the Polity, 1880–1920* (Chapel Hill: University of North Carolina Press, 1995); Roy Rosenzweig, *Eight Hours for What We Will: Workers and Leisure in an Industrial City, 1870–1920* (New York: Cambridge University Press, 1983); Joseph R. Gusfield, *Symbolic Crusade: Status Politics and the American Temperance Movement* (Urbana: University of Illinois Press, 1963); Madelon Powers, *Faces along the Bar: Lore and Order in the Workingman's Saloon, 1870–1920* (Chicago: University of Chicago Press, 1998).
3. For this study, the counties of western North Carolina include Alexander, Alleghany, Ashe, Buncombe, Burke, Caldwell, Catawba, Cherokee, Clay, Cleveland, Haywood, Henderson, Jackson, McDowell, Macon, Madison, Mitchell, Polk, Rutherford, Surry, Swain, Transylvania, Watauga, Wilkes, and Yancey. Residents from these counties considered themselves mountaineers, and most Americans believed that these counties constituted Appalachian North Carolina during the nineteenth and early twentieth centuries.
4. Ada F. Haynes, *Poverty in Central Appalachia: Underdevelopment and Exploitation* (New York: Garland Publishing, 1997); Ronald D. Eller, *Miners, Millhands, and Mountaineers: Industrialization of the Appalachian South, 1880–1930* (Knoxville: University of Tennessee Press, 1982); John Gaventa, *Power and Powerlessness: Quiescence and Rebellion in an Appalachian Valley* (Urbana: University of Illinois Press, 1982); David A. Corbin, *Life, Work, and Rebellion in the Coal Fields: The Southern West Virginia Miners, 1880–1922* (Urbana: University of Illinois Press, 1981); David E. Whisnant, *Modernizing the Mountaineer: People, Power, Planning in Appalachia* (Knoxville: University of Tennessee Press, 1994); Helen Matthews Lewis, Linda Johnson, and Donald Askins, eds., *Colonialism in Modern America: The Appalachian Case* (Boone, NC: Appalachian Consortium Press, 1978).
5. Dwight B. Billings and Kathleen M. Blee, *The Road to Poverty: The Making of Wealth and Hardship in Appalachia* (Cambridge: Cambridge Uni-

versity Press, 2000); Mary Beth Pudup, Dwight B. Billings, and Altina L. Waller, eds., *Appalachia in the Making: The Mountain South in the Nineteenth Century* (Chapel Hill: University of North Carolina Press, 1995); Altina L. Waller, *Feud: Hatfields, McCoys, and Social Change in Appalachia, 1860–1900* (Chapel Hill: University of North Carolina Press, 1988); Durwood Dunn, *Cades Cove: The Life and Death of a Southern Appalachia Community, 1818–1937* (Knoxville: University of Tennessee Press, 1988); Southern Mountain Research Collective, ed., "Essays in Political Economy: Toward a Class Analysis of Appalachia," *Appalachian Journal* 11 (autumn–winter, 1983–1984): 19–162.

6. For a recent discussion of stereotypes and southern Appalachia, see Dwight B. Billings, Gurney Norman, and Katherine Ledford, eds., *Confronting Appalachian Stereotypes: Back Talk from an American Region* (Lexington: University Press of Kentucky, 1999).

7. Transcript of "Another America," CBS News's *Forty-eight Hours,* December 14, 1989, 2.

8. Quoted in "Signs of the Times," *Appalachian Journal* 23 (fall 1996): 144.

9. Henry D. Shapiro, *Appalachia on Our Mind: The Southern Mountains and Mountaineers in the American Consciousness, 1870–1920* (Chapel Hill: University of North Carolina Press, 1978); Allen W. Batteau, *The Invention of Appalachia* (Tucson: University of Arizona Press, 1990); David E. Whisnant, *All That Is Native and Fine: The Politics of Culture in an American Region* (Chapel Hill: University of North Carolina Press, 1983); Whisnant, *Modernizing the Mountaineer;* Jane S. Becker, *Selling Tradition: Appalachia and the Construction of an American Folk, 1930–1940* (Chapel Hill: University of North Carolina Press, 1998); Anne Rowe, *The Enchanted Country: Northern Writers in the South, 1865–1910* (Baton Rouge: Louisiana State University Press, 1978); Richard Ohmann, *Selling Culture: Magazines, Markets, and Class at the Turn of the Century* (New York: Verso, 1996); Kevin E. O'Donnell and Helen Hollingsworth, eds., *Seekers of Scenery: Travel Writing from Southern Appalachia, 1840–1900* (Knoxville: University of Tennessee Press, 2004); Anthony Harkins, *Hillbilly: A Cultural History of an American Icon* (New York: Oxford University Press, 2004).

10. Batteau, *Invention of Appalachia,* 1.

11. Robert S. Weise, *Grasping at Independence: Debt, Male Authority, and Mineral Rights in Appalachian Kentucky, 1850–1915* (Knoxville: University of Tennessee Press, 2001), 6.

12. Ronald L. Lewis, *Transforming the Appalachian Countryside: Railroads, Deforestation, and Social Change in West Virginia, 1880–1920* (Chapel Hill: University of North Carolina Press, 1998); Eller, *Miners, Millhands, and Mountaineers;* Gaventa, *Power and Powerlessness;* Lewis, Johnson, and Askins, *Colonialism in Modern America.*

13. David C. Hsiung, *Two Worlds in the Tennessee Mountains: Exploring the Origins of Appalachian Stereotypes* (Lexington: University Press of Kentucky, 1997). In his study on tourism in western North Carolina during

the late nineteenth century, Richard Starnes also believes that local boosters, hoping to attract northern capitalists and tourists, promoted the region as the "Land of the Sky," a mystical and exotic place where urban middle-class Americans could escape from "modernity." See Richard D. Starnes, *Creating the Land of the Sky: Tourism and Society in Western North Carolina* (Tuscaloosa: University of Alabama Press, 2005).

14. Ted Ownby, *Subduing Satan: Religion, Recreation, and Manhood in the Rural South, 1865–1920* (Chapel Hill: University of North Carolina Press, 1990); Joe L. Coker, *Liquor in the Land of the Lost Cause: Southern White Evangelicals and the Prohibition Movement* (Lexington: University Press of Kentucky, 2007).

15. William A. Link, *The Paradox of Southern Progressivism, 1880–1930* (Chapel Hill: University of North Carolina Press, 1992).

1. "This Country Improves in Cultivation, Wickedness, Mills, and Still"

Epigraph: North Carolina folk saying, quoted in Joseph Earl Dabney, *Mountain Spirits: A Chronicle of Corn Whiskey from King James' Ulster Plantation to America's Appalachians and the Moonshine Life* (New York: Charles Scribner's Sons, 1974), 3.

1. McGee returned to Beaver Creek sometime after 1870. He worked as a schoolteacher there until his death in 1883. See B. B. McGee, *The Country Youth: Autobiography of B. B. McGee* (1874; reprint, North Wilkesboro, NC: Pearson Publishing Co., 1964), introduction.

2. Ibid., 46, 58–60.

3. Blocker, *American Temperance Movements,* 3–11; W. J. Rorabaugh, *The Alcoholic Republic: An American Tradition* (New York: Oxford University Press, 1979), 95–100, 232.

4. Paul Aaron and David Musto, "Temperance and Prohibition in America: A Historical Overview," in *Alcohol and Public Policy: Beyond the Shadow of Prohibition,* ed. Mark H. Moore and Dean R. Gerstein (Washington, DC: National Academy Press, 1981), 135; Rorabaugh, *Alcoholic Republic,* 68–92.

5. For scholarship on antebellum distilling, see Cratis Williams, "Moonshining in the Mountains," *North Carolina Folklore* 15 (May 1967): 11–17; Esther Kellner, *Moonshine: Its History and Folklore* (Indianapolis: Bobbs-Merrill, 1971); Jess Carr, *The Second Oldest Profession: An Informal History of Moonshining in America* (Englewood Cliffs, NJ: Prentice-Hall, 1972); David W. Maurer, *Kentucky Moonshine* (Lexington: University Press of Kentucky, 1974); Dabney, *Mountain Spirits;* Thomas P. Slaughter, *The Whiskey Rebellion: Frontier Epilogue to the American Revolution* (New York: Oxford University Press, 1986); Wilbur R. Miller, *Revenuers & Moonshiners: Enforcing Federal Liquor Law in the Mountain South, 1865–1900* (Chapel Hill: University of North Carolina Press, 1991).

6. Margaret W. Morley, *The Carolina Mountains* (Boston: Houghton Mifflin, 1913), 102–3; Ina Woestemeyer Van Noppen and John J. Van Noppen, *Western North Carolina since the Civil War* (Boone, NC: Appalachian Con-

sortium Press, 1973), 1–3; Laura Thornborough, *The Great Smoky Mountains* (New York: Thomas Y. Crowell, 1942), 1–2.

7. H. Tyler Blethen and Curtis W. Wood Jr., *From Ulster to Carolina: The Migration of the Scotch-Irish to Southwestern North Carolina,* rev. ed. (Raleigh: Division of Archives and History, North Carolina Department of Cultural Resources, 1998), 38–43.

8. Quoted in Donald Edward Davis, *Where There Are Mountains: An Environmental History of the Southern Appalachians* (Athens: University of Georgia Press, 2000), 95–96.

9. Francois Andrew Michaux, *Travels to the Westward of the Alleghany Mountains* (London: Richard Phillips, 1805), 290.

10. John C. Inscoe, *Mountain Masters, Slavery, and the Sectional Crisis in Western North Carolina* (Knoxville: University of Tennessee Press, 1989), 13, 53. For a case study detailing the settlement patterns of pioneer farmers in western North Carolina, see Edward W. Phifer, "Slavery in Microcosm: Burke County, North Carolina," *Journal of Southern History* 28 (May 1962): 140.

11. Most historians no longer view the frontier as a dividing line between uncivilized and civilized. Instead, they insist that the frontier was a place where different cultures, experiences, environments, motives, economies, and perspectives came into contact. On this frontier, people exchanged ideas, cultural traits, values, and sometimes lifestyles, thereby creating a new culture. See John Anthony Caruso, *The Appalachian Frontier: America's First Surge Westward* (Indianapolis: Bobbs-Merrill, 1959); Gregory H. Nobles, "Breaking into the Backcountry: New Approaches to the Early American Frontier, 1750–1800," *William and Mary Quarterly* 46 (1989): 641–70; and Robert D. Mitchell, ed., *Appalachian Frontiers: Settlement, Society, & Development in the Preindustrial Era* (Lexington: University Press of Kentucky, 1991).

12. Blethen and Wood, *From Ulster to Carolina,* 33.

13. Davis, *Where There Are Mountains,* 97–107 (quotation 99).

14. Historian Joseph Dabney estimates that at least a quarter of a million Ulster Scots descended on American soil between 1717 and 1776. See Dabney, *Mountain Spirits,* 40.

15. Blethen and Wood, *From Ulster to Carolina,* 29–50.

16. For a detailed study on the origins of cattle herding and Presbyterianism in western North Carolina, see ibid., 55–62.

17. No one knows for sure who discovered the distillation process. Before the birth of Christ, the Chinese and Japanese distilled rice into alcohol. Mideastern alchemists rediscovered the distillation process during the Middle Ages, disseminating it to Europe sometime before the eleventh century. See Kellner, *Moonshine,* 30–31.

18. See Dabney, *Mountain Spirits,* 34; Ray Rensi and Leo Downing, "A Touch of Mountain Dew: Art and History of Whiskey-Making in North Georgia," in *The Many Faces of Appalachia: Proceedings of the 7th Annual Appalachian Studies Conference,* ed. Sam Gray (Boone, NC: Appalachian Consortium Press, 1985), 196–97; David Hackett Fischer, *Albion's Seed: Four British Folkways in America* (New York: Oxford University Press, 1989), 729; and Wil-

liam C. Lehmann, *Scottish and Scotch-Irish Contributions to Early American Life and Culture* (Port Washington, NY: Kennikat Press, 1978), 51–64.

19. Dabney, *Mountain Spirits*, 50–51.

20. William Lenoir's distilling recipe book, box 23, folder 289, Household and Plantation Records, Lenoir Family Papers, Southern Historical Collection, Manuscripts Department, Wilson Library, University of North Carolina at Chapel Hill.

21. Kellner, *Moonshine*, 58; Maurer, *Kentucky Moonshine*, 29–32.

22. Johnson J. Hayes, *The Land of Wilkes* (Wilkesboro, NC: Wilkes County Historical Society, 1962), 77; Kellner, *Moonshine*, 56–57.

23. Dabney, *Mountain Spirits*, 67.

24. "Fresh water was needed for both the mixing and tempering of the moonshine as well as a coolant for the condensation part of the distillation procedure." Rensi and Downing, "A Touch of Mountain Dew," 200.

25. Kellner, *Moonshine*, 56; Rensi and Downing, "A Touch of Mountain Dew," 199–200.

26. John Parris, *These Storied Mountains* (Asheville, NC: Citizen-Times Publishing Co., 1972), 263–64.

27. Williams, "Moonshining in the Mountains," 12; Joseph Earl Dabney, *Mountain Spirits II: The Continuing Chronicle of Moonshine Life and Corn Whiskey, Wines, Cider, & Beers in America's Appalachians* (Lakemont, GA: Copple House Books, 1980), 51–70.

28. Distillers desired the sprouts to grow to a length of one to one and a half inches. See Williams, "Moonshining in the Mountains," 13.

29. "The added warmth of the oxidation generally cut the sprouting time in half." Rensi and Downing, "A Touch of Mountain Dew," 200.

30. "If he had a stout arm, or a stout wife or son, he might obtain two bushels of ground corn per day." Kellner, *Moonshine*, 57.

31. Williams, "Moonshining in the Mountains," 13.

32. Kellner, *Moonshine*, 58.

33. During the winter, the distiller kept the mash warm by burying it in hot manure or sawdust piles. See Dabney, *Mountain Spirits*, 4, 6, 8.

34. "A skilled distiller could tell the proper degree of fermentation by the sound in the barrel; it was at perfection when the bubbling resembled rain drumming on a roof or a slice of pork frying in the pan." Miller, *Revenuers & Moonshiners*, 32.

35. Dabney, *Mountain Spirits*, 5.

36. As children, pioneers learned from relatives that heating the still to the appropriate temperature was an important skill; some learned later by trial and error. As historian Esther Kellner explains, "The mash must cook neither too slowly nor too rapidly. If it becomes too hot, the vapor will carry too much steam, or the mash will be scorched. In cases of extreme heat, the steam can build up too fast and the still may explode." Kellner, *Moonshine*, 59.

37. Williams, "Moonshining in the Mountains," 14; Kellner, *Moonshine*, 60.

38. Kellner, *Moonshine*, 60.

39. Dabney, *Mountain Spirits,* 10.

40. Inscoe, *Mountain Masters,* 14.

41. Michael Ann Williams, *Great Smoky Mountains Folklife* (Jackson: University Press of Mississippi, 1995), 92.

42. Kellner, *Moonshine,* 55.

43. Inscoe, *Mountain Masters;* Donald L. Winters, *Tennessee Farming, Tennessee Farmers: Antebellum Agriculture in the Upper South* (Knoxville: University of Tennessee Press, 1994); Paul Salstrom, *Appalachia's Path to Dependency: Rethinking a Region's Economic History, 1730–1940* (Lexington: University Press of Kentucky, 1994); Pudup, Billings, and Waller, *Appalachia in the Making;* William A. Dunaway, *The First American Frontier: Transition to Capitalism in Southern Appalachia, 1700–1860* (Chapel Hill: University of North Carolina Press, 1996); Blethen and Wood, *From Ulster to Carolina;* Billings and Blee, *Road to Poverty;* Davis, *Where There Are Mountains;* Weise, *Grasping at Independence;* H. Tyler Blethen, "Pioneer Settlement," in *High Mountains Rising: Appalachia in Time and Place,* ed. Richard A. Straw and H. Tyler Blethen (Urbana: University of Illinois Press, 2004), 17–29.

44. James Patton, *Biography of James Patton* (Asheville, NC: n.p., 1850), 9–16.

45. H. Tyler Blethen and Curtis W. Wood Jr., "A Trader on the Carolina Frontier," in *Appalachian Frontiers,* 162.

46. Inscoe, *Mountain Masters,* 17–19, 49–51. See also Wilma Dykeman, *The French Broad* (New York: Rinehart, 1955), 137–51; Forrest McDonald and Grady McWhiney, "The Antebellum Southern Herdsman: A Reinterpretation," *Journal of Southern History* 41 (May 1975): 160; Blethen and Wood, *From Ulster to Carolina;* F. A. Sondley, *A History of Buncombe County,* 2 vols. (Asheville, NC: Advocate Print. Co., 1930), 2:665; Jinsie Underwood, *This Is Madison County* (Mars Hill, NC: Underwood, 1974), 18–19; and Kevin Barksdale, "Whiskey Distillation in Antebellum Western North Carolina," *Tuckasegee Valley Historical Review* 5 (April 1999): 8–9.

47. John Collet quoted in William P. Cummings, *North Carolina in Maps* (Raleigh, NC: Department of Archives and History, 1966), 19.

48. Eli W. Caruthers quoted in Jeffrey J. Crow, "The Whiskey Rebellion in North Carolina," *North Carolina Historical Review* 67 (January 1989): 5.

49. Francis Asbury, *The Journal of the Rev. Francis Asbury, Bishop of the Methodist Episcopal Church, from August 7, 1771 to December 7, 1815,* 3 vols. (New York: N. Bangs and T. Mason, 1821), 3:1.

50. Eli W. Caruthers quoted in Crow, "The Whiskey Rebellion in North Carolina," 5.

51. Charles Lanman, *Letters from the Alleghany Mountains* (New York: G. P. Putman, 1849), 195.

52. Dunaway, *First American Frontier;* Weise, *Grasping at Independence.*

53. Miller, *Revenuers & Moonshiners,* 28.

54. Davis, *Where There Are Mountains,* 140.

55. Ledger, 1831–1861, John Finley Papers; Pedan and Kelly Account

Book, 1835–1837, Peden and Kelly Papers; Samuel P. Sherrill Account Book, 1845–1847; Thomas Miller Daybook, 1849–1850; Samuel F. Kirby Account Book, 1785–1804; T. P. Jackson Account Book, 1820–1826; James A. Sadler Account Book, 1848–1854; Hiram Burgess Account Book, 1853–1864, all in Rare Book, Manuscript, and Special Collections Library, Duke University, Durham, NC; Strabane (N. C.) Account Book, 1821, Southern Historical Collection.

56. Corn whiskey required at least two bushels of grain for each five-gallon batch. See Davis, *Where There Are Mountains,* 140.

57. Miller Daybook. Store records also reveal the value of whiskey in the mountain marketplace compared with that of other important consumer goods. In the 1830s, a Haywood County store charged the same amount for both a gallon of whiskey and gunpowder, an essential product. See W. Clark Medford, *The Early History of Haywood County* (Waynesville, NC: privately printed, 1961), 107–8.

58. Quoted in Margaret E. Harper, *Fort Defiance and the General* (Hickory, NC: Clay Printing Co., 1976), 84.

59. Quoted in Edward William Phifer Jr., *Burke: The History of a North Carolina County, 1777–1920, with a Glimpse Beyond* (Morganton, NC: privately printed, 1977), 208.

60. Nancy Alexander, *Here Will I Dwell: The Story of Caldwell County* (Salisbury, NC: Rowan Printing, 1956), 94–95.

61. Lanman, *Letters from the Alleghany Mountains,* 153; William Wyndam Malet, *An Errand to the South in the Summer of 1862* (London: R. Bentley, 1863), 250–51.

62. In 1778, for instance, John Witherspoon from Wilkes County bequeathed both "still and mill" to his seven children. Nearly twenty years later, Burke County farmer Thomas England, who fattened his livestock on corn mash, insisted that his wife inherit "my stock of Hogs with my still." See Will of John Witherspoon, November 1, 1778, Wilkes County Records of Wills, Will Book 1; and Will of Thomas England, 1795, Burke County Record of Wills, both in State Archives, North Carolina Office of Archives and History, Raleigh.

63. Quoted in Harper, *Fort Defiance and the General,* 33–34.

64. McGee, *Country Youth,* 46, 58–60.

65. Harper, *Fort Defiance and the General,* 85.

66. Quoted in Dabney, *Mountain Spirits,* 73.

67. Henry Reid Book, 1800–1802, box 1, Benjamin Austin Papers, 1756–1803, Special Collections, Duke University.

68. See Manly Wade Wellman, *The Kingdom of Madison: A Southern Mountain Fastness and Its People* (Chapel Hill: University of North Carolina Press, 1973), 34, 158.

69. Fred M. Burnett, *This Was My Valley* (Ridgecrest, NC: Heritage Printers, 1960), 74.

70. Rorabaugh, *Alcoholic Republic,* xi.

71. Grady L. E. Carroll, ed., *Francis Asbury in North Carolina, the North*

Carolina Portions of the Journal of Francis Asbury, 2 vols. (Nashville, TN: Parthenon Press, 1964), 134, 175–76.

72. Frederick Law Olmsted, *A Journey in the Back County in the Winter of 1853–54* (New York: Mason Bros., 1860), 273; A. R. Newsome, ed., "John Brown's Journal of Travel in Western North Carolina in 1795," *North Carolina Historical Review* 11 (October 1934): 284–313.

73. Alexander, *Here Will I Dwell,* 36.

74. Wealthy Burke County banker Robert Pearson, for instance, kept bottles of champagne in his wine cellar. During the Civil War, Unionist women plundered Pearson's home, discovered the bottles of champagne, and distributed them among themselves. One of these women fled when she opened the bottle and heard the cork pop. She declared that the champagne "was pizen, put there to kill them for nobody had ever seed liquor pop that way." Quoted in John C. Inscoe and Gordon B. McKinney, *The Heart of Confederate Appalachia: Western North Carolina during the Civil War* (Chapel Hill: University of North Carolina Press, 2000), 251.

75. Ledger, 1831–1861, Finley Papers; Pedan and Kelly Account Book; Sherrill Account Book; Miller Daybook; Kirby Account Book; Jackson Account Book; Sadler Account Book; Burgess Account Book; Strabane (N. C.) Account Book.

76. Kellner, *Moonshine,* 64. Along with whiskey, brandy became popular in Henderson and Wilkes counties, where farmers distilled it from an abundance of apples and peaches and kept its price affordable. See Lanman, *Letters from the Alleghany Mountains,* 153; and Malet, *An Errand to the South,* 250–51.

77. Newsome, "John Brown's Journal of Travel," 296.

78. "Comptroller's Report, 1815. A Statement of the Revenue of North Carolina," box 4, Accounts (1731–1935), Office of State Treasurer, State Archives.

79. Guion Griffis Johnson, *Ante-Bellum North Carolina: A Social History* (Chapel Hill: University of North Carolina Press, 1937), 96. See also Hayes, *Land of Wilkes,* 26–27.

80. Lanman, *Letters from the Allegheny Mountains,* 125. For more on resort hotels, see F. A. Sondley, *Asheville and Buncombe County,* 2 vols. (Asheville, NC: Citizen Co., 1922), 2: 722; Inscoe, *Mountain Masters,* 32–34; and Underwood, *This Is Madison County,* 17–18.

81. Bill Cecil-Fronsman, *Common Whites: Class and Culture in Antebellum North Carolina* (Lexington: University Press of Kentucky, 1992), 178; Ian R. Tyrrell, "Drink and Temperance in the Old South: An Overview and Interpretation," *Journal of Southern History* 48 (1982): 506. For more on preindustrial work habits, see E. P. Thompson, "Time, Work-Discipline, and Industrial Capitalism," *Past & Present* 38 (December 1967): 56–97; and Herbert G. Gutman, "Work, Culture, and Society in Industrializing America, 1815–1919," *American Historical Review* 78 (June 1973): 531–88.

82. Frank L. Owsley, *Plain Folk of the Old South* (Baton Rouge: Louisiana State University Press, 1949), 104, 112, 116.

83. Lanman, *Letters from the Alleghany Mountains,* 115.

84. J. Jay Anderson, *Wilkes County Sketches* (1976; reprint, Wilkesboro, NC: J. J. Anderson, 1978), 12.

85. Carroll, *Francis Asbury in North Carolina,* 135.

86. H. E. Taliaferro, *Fisher's River (North Carolina): Scenes and Characters by "Skitt," "Who Was Raised Thar"* (New York: Harper and Brothers, 1859), 20–27.

87. Kemp Plummer Battle, *Memories of an Old-Time Tar Heel,* ed. William James Battle (Chapel Hill: University of North Carolina Press, 1945), 91–92.

88. A. R. Newsome, ed., "The A. S. Merrimon Journal, 1853–1854," *North Carolina Historical Review* 8 (July 1931): 329.

89. Rorabaugh, *Alcoholic Republic,* 151; Bertram Wyatt-Brown, *Southern Honor: Ethics and Behavior in the Old South* (New York: Oxford University Press, 1982), 278–80, 329–30.

90. *Asheville Messenger,* May 26, 1852.

91. Newsome, "A. S. Merrimon Journal," 306.

92. Wilbur G. Zeigler and Ben S. Grosscup, *The Heart of the Alleghanies, or Western North Carolina* (Raleigh, NC: Alfred Williams and Co., 1883), 115–16.

93. Brantley York, *The Autobiography of Brantley York,* rev. ed., ed. Charles Mathis (Jonesville, NC: Amanuensis Two, 1977), 2.

94. In 1857, Thomas Lenoir of Caldwell County noted that "people on the East Fork have become alarmed about milk sickness." See Thomas Lenoir to "My Dear Father," December 30, 1857, Thomas Lenoir Papers, Special Collections, Duke University.

95. Benjamin Earle Washburn, *A Country Doctor in the Southern Mountains* (1955; reprint, Spindale, NC: Spindale Press, 1973), 12.

96. The federal government levied taxes on imported and domestic manufactured alcohol in 1791 and 1814. Because of opposition in western North Carolina and other backcountry regions, the federal government retreated both times from collecting the liquor tax. See Crow, "The Whiskey Rebellion in North Carolina."

2. Select Men of Sober and Industrious Habits

Epigraph: From "Sign of the Sons of Temperance," transcribed by Ruth E. Jones from Alexander County on August 7, 1850. See Sue Campbell Watts Papers #4372, folder 2, Ballads, Southern Historical Collection.

1. *North Carolina Spectator and Western Advertiser,* June 11, 1831; Jason F. E. Hardy, *Second Annual Address: Delivered before the Asheville Temperance Society, on the 4th of July, 1832: With the Executive Committee's First Annual Report* (Rutherfordton, NC: Roswell Elmer Jr., Printer, 1832), 4, 9.

2. For a discussion of reform in the antebellum United States, see Ronald G. Walters, *American Reformers, 1815–1865* (New York: Hill and Wang, 1997); Douglas T. Miller, *The Birth of Modern America, 1820–1850* (New York: Pegasus, 1970); Alice Felt Tyler, *Freedom's Ferment: Phases of Amer-*

ican Social History from the Colonial Period to the Outbreak of the Civil War (Minneapolis: University of Minnesota Press, 1944); Clifford S. Griffin, *The Ferment of Reform, 1830–1860* (New York: Crowell, 1967); Teresa Anne Murphy, *Ten Hours' Labor: Religion, Reform, and Gender in Early New England* (Ithaca, NY: Cornell University Press, 1992); Henry Steele Commager, ed., *The Era of Reform, 1830–1860* (New York: Van Nostrand, 1960); and David Brion Davis, ed., *Ante-Bellum Reform* (New York: Harper and Row, 1967).

3. See John W. Quist, *Restless Visionaries: The Social Roots of Antebellum Reform in Alabama and Michigan* (Baton Rouge: Louisiana State University Press, 1998); Douglas W. Carlson, "'Drinks He to His Own Undoing': Temperance Ideology in the Deep South," *Journal of the Early Republic* 18 (winter 1998): 659–91; Ellen Eslinger, "Antebellum Liquor Reform in Lexington, Virginia: The Story of a Small Southern Town," *Virginia Magazine of History and Biography* 99 (April 1991): 163–86; Stanley K. Schultz, "Temperance Reform in the Antebellum South: Social Control and Urban Order," *South Atlantic Quarterly* 83 (summer 1984): 322–39; Tyrrell, "Drink and Temperance in the Antebellum South"; and W. J. Rorabaugh, "The Sons of Temperance in Antebellum Jasper County," *Georgia Historical Quarterly* 64 (fall 1980): 263–79.

4. Like E. P. Thompson, I consider class both a cultural construction and an objective component of the social order. As men and women of moderate economic means, middle-class professionals were not as wealthy as many large commercial farmers in the mountains or planters in the Black Belt. Some professionals did become members of the urban elite, having amassed large fortunes. But middle-class mountaineers "consider[ed] themselves above the rural yeomen and urban laboring whites," and according to Jonathan Wells, "it appears other southerners recognized the higher status that a career as a doctor, grocer, or teacher might provide." Moreover, middle-class mountain residents, like those elsewhere in the South, became a "self-conscious class" by the late antebellum period. As Wells explains, "Middle-class southerners rallied around ideas about culture that they learned from their northern correspondents and restyled them to incorporate slavery. From ideas about gender and family, to notions about the virtues of industrialization, to discomfiture with the practice of dueling, the formation of the southern middle class depended to a significant extent on cultural values that it adopted from its contacts with the North and, indeed, the rest of the world. Thus, the linguistic and ideological construction of the southern middle-class was just as important to class formation as its objective middling position in the southern social structure." It is also important to note that southerners of moderate economic means called themselves "middle class" during the antebellum period, so it is appropriate to use that term. See Jonathan Wells, *The Origins of the Southern Middle Class, 1800–1861* (Chapel Hill: University of North Carolina Press, 2004); and E. P. Thompson, *The Making of the English Working Class* (New York: Pantheon Books, 1963).

5. Historians have long been intrigued by the seeming lack of social con-

flict within white southern society during the antebellum period. Some scholars have pointed out that paternalism mediated disputes among the majority white population, while others have stressed the important role that *"Herrenvolk* democracy" played in uniting whites of all socioeconomic groups. More recent explanations for this absence of social tensions focus on kinship ties, white males' adherence to the patriarchal ideal, and notions of honor. Whatever the reasons, historians agree that most southern whites felt it necessary to maintain a united front in the face of growing northern abolition sentiment and potential slave insurrection. See Eugene D. Genovese, "Yeoman Farmers in a Slaveholders' Democracy," *Agricultural History* 49 (April 1975): 331–42; George M. Frederickson, *The Black Image in the White Mind: The Debate on Afro-American Character and Destiny* (New York: Harper and Row, 1971); Robert C. Kenzer, *Kinship and Neighborhood in a Southern Community: Orange County, North Carolina, 1849–1881* (Knoxville: University of Tennessee Press, 1987); Stephanie McCurry, *Masters of Small Worlds: Yeoman Households, Gender Relations, and the Political Culture of the Antebellum Southern Carolina Low Country* (New York: Oxford University Press, 1995); Bertram Wyatt-Brown, *The Shaping of Southern Culture: Honor, Grace, and War, 1760s–1890s* (Chapel Hill: University of North Carolina Press, 2001); Bruce Collins, *White Society in the Antebellum South* (New York: Longman House, 1985); J. William Harris, *Plain Folk and Gentry in a Slave Society: White Liberty and Black Slavery in Augusta's Hinterlands* (Middletown, CT: Wesleyan University Press, 1985); and Owsley, *Plain Folk of the Old South.*

6. Newsome, "John Brown's Journal of Travel," 304.

7. Ora Blackmun, *Western North Carolina: Its Mountains and Its People to 1880* (Boone, NC: Appalachian Consortium Press, 1977), 163.

8. Laura Siler to "Leon," September 29, 1847, Lyle and Siler Family Papers #1818, Southern Historical Collection, quoted in Laurel Horton, "Nineteenth Century Quilts in Macon County, North Carolina," in *The Many Faces of Appalachia,* 15.

9. Inscoe, *Mountain Masters,* 31.

10. Like Robert D. Mitchell, I define hamlets as having 20 to 150 residents and villages as housing 151 to 500 inhabitants. Although villages were numerically small, they functioned much like larger towns, serving as trade and communication centers for residents in the southern backcountry. In a rural context, these villages can be labeled as urban. See Robert D. Mitchell, "The Settlement Fabric of the Shenandoah Valley, 1790–1860: Pattern, Process, and Structure," in *After the Backcountry: Rural Life in the Great Valley of Virginia, 1800–1900,* ed. Kenneth E. Koons and Warren R. Hofstra (Knoxville: University of Tennessee Press, 2000), 34–47, especially 35.

11. John Inscoe, "Diversity in Antebellum Mountain Life: The Towns of Western North Carolina," in *The Many Faces of Appalachia,* 153–66; Gordon B. McKinney, "Preindustrial Jackson County and Economic Development," *Journal of the Appalachian Studies Association* 2 (1990): 1–10; Blackmun, *Western North Carolina,* 284–305; John Preston Arthur, *Western North Car-*

olina: A History from 1730 to 1913 (Raleigh, NC: Edwards and Broughton, 1914), 143–214, 491–99.

12. These ten communities were Rockford in Surry County (639 residents), Morganton in Burke County (558 residents), Rutherfordton in Rutherford County (484 residents), Asheville in Buncombe County (420 residents), Hendersonville in Henderson County (250 residents), Lenoir in Caldwell County (250 residents), Newton in Catawba County (175 residents), Waynesville in Haywood County (170 residents), Marion in McDowell County (150 residents), and Wilkesboro in Wilkes County (150 residents). Population statistics for Morganton, Rutherfordton, Asheville, Hendersonville, Lenoir, Newton, Waynesville, Marion, and Wilkesboro were taken from J. Calvin Smith, ed., *Harper's Statistical Gazetteer of the World* (New York: Harper and Brothers, 1855). Population statistics for Rockford were derived from U.S. Census Office, *The Seventh Census of the United States: 1850* (Washington, DC: Robert Armstrong, Public Printer, 1853), 308.

13. Inscoe, "Diversity in Antebellum Mountain Life," 157.

14. Inscoe, *Mountain Masters*, 53; Phifer, "Slavery in Microcosm," 140; Jason Bail Deyton, "The Toe River Valley to 1865," *North Carolina Historical Review* 24 (October 1947): 446; Gene Wilhelm Jr., "Folk Settlements in the Blue Ridge Mountains," *Appalachian Journal* 5 (winter 1978): 192–222.

15. Historians Van Beck Hall and David C. Hsiung recently discovered that "two worlds" emerged within Appalachian Virginia and Tennessee during the antebellum period. According to Hall, "one with towns and diversification, the other with farms and isolated farmers and stockmen, and the two often responded quite differently to political issues" (166). Although they unveil the political and economic issues that divided urbanizing and rural mountain residents, Hall and Hsiung overlook social issues, such as temperance reform, that sparked conflict between these two groups. See Van Beck Hall, "The Politics of Appalachian Virginia, 1790–1830," in *Appalachian Frontiers*, 166–86; and Hsiung, *Two Worlds in the Tennessee Mountains*.

16. For a discussion of how so-called outsiders used southern Appalachia to help forge a middle-class identity during the antebellum period, see Katherine E. Ledford, "'The Primitive Circle': Inscribing Class in Southern Appalachian Travel Writing, 1816–1846," *Appalachian Journal* 29 (fall 2001–winter 2002): 68–89.

17. James Graham to William A. Graham, May 20, 1840, in Joseph G. de Roulhac Hamilton and Max R. Williams, eds., *The Papers of William Alexander Graham*, 5 vols. (Raleigh: North Carolina Division of Archives and History, 1957–1973), 2:91–92.

18. Newsome, "A. S. Merrimon Journal," 313.

19. Mary Gash to "aunt," February 15, 1853, Gash Family Papers, PC 1514, North Carolina State Archives, quoted in Johnson *Ante-Bellum North Carolina*, 63.

20. *Rutherfordton Intelligencer*, March 17, 1842, April 26, 1843; Wells, *Origins of the Southern Middle Class*, 53–54; Wilkesborough Debating Society minutes, Thurmond Chatham Papers, PC 1139, North Carolina State Archives, quoted in Wells, *Origins of the Southern Middle Class*, 95.

21. Sarah Ann Gordon to Caroline L. Gordon, December 17, 1843, Gordon-Hackett Family Papers #1040, Southern Historical Collection, quoted in Wells, *Origins of the Southern Middle Class,* 105.

22. *Carolina Watchman,* July 13, 1848, January 4, 1849, April 24, 1851, April 7, 1853; M. H. G. to "cousin Ada," March 1, 1852, Mary Gash Papers, PC 59, North Carolina State Archives; *Asheville News,* February 23, 1854.

23. H. E. Colton, *Guidebook to the Scenery of Western North Carolina* (Asheville, NC: Western Advocate Office, 1860), 14–15, quoted in Inscoe, *Mountain Masters,* 33.

24. Mollie Carrie to Leander Gash, August 3, 1855, Gash Family Papers, quoted in Inscoe, "Diversity in Antebellum Mountain Life," 157.

25. Clarence W. Griffin, *The History of Old Tryon and Rutherford Counties, North Carolina, 1730–1936* (Asheville, NC: Miller Printing Co., 1937), 591; Johnson, *Ante-Bellum North Carolina,* 384.

26. Blackmun, *Western North Carolina,* 179, 184, 185.

27. For a discussion of the Great Awakening in the South and in the United States, see John B. Boles, *The Great Revival, 1787–1805: The Origins of the Southern Evangelical Mind* (Lexington: University Press of Kentucky, 1972); Donald G. Mathews, *Religion in the Old South* (Chicago: University of Chicago Press, 1977); and Richard J. Carwardine, *Evangelicals and Politics in Antebellum America* (New Haven, CT: Yale University Press, 1993).

28. "The tightly organized structure of the Presbyterian Church did not work well on the frontier. As settlers moved further away, they advanced beyond the organizational capabilities of the church." As a result, Presbyterianism was "greatly reduced after about 1810 by the rapid growth of Baptist and Methodist churches in the mountains, and there is no doubt that the absence of qualified Presbyterian clergy caused many old Scotch-Irish families to join those denominations rather than to abandon religious life altogether." Blethen and Wood, *From Ulster to Carolina,* 47–48, 55–58.

29. Anne C. Loveland, *Southern Evangelicals and the Social Order, 1800–1860* (Baton Rouge: Louisiana State University Press, 1980), 72.

30. Loyal Jones, "Mountain Religion: An Overview," in *Christianity in Appalachia: Profiles in Regional Pluralism,* ed. Bill J. Leonard (Knoxville: University of Tennessee Press, 1999), 92.

31. Blackmun, *Western North Carolina,* 183–84.

32. For further discussions of evangelicalism in southern Appalachia and elsewhere in the antebellum South, see Beth Barton Schweiger, *The Gospel Working Up: Progress and the Pulpit in Nineteenth-Century Virginia* (New York: Oxford University Press, 2000), and Deborah Vansau McCauley, *Appalachian Mountain Religion: A History* (Urbana: University of Illinois Press, 1995).

33. George Washington Paschal, *History of the North Carolina Baptists,* 2 vols. (Raleigh: North Carolina Baptist Convention, 1955), 2:492.

34. John R. Logan, *Sketches, Historical and Biographical, of the Broad River and King's Mountain Baptist Associations, from 1800 to 1882* (Shelby, NC: Babington, Roberts, 1887), 9.

35. Paschal, *History of the North Carolina Baptists*, 2:492.

36. Loveland, *Southern Evangelicals and the Social Order*, 135.

37. Paschal, *History of the North Carolina Baptists*, 2:243.

38. Logan, *Sketches, Historical and Biographical, of the Broad River and King's Mountain Baptist Associations*, 44.

39. *North Carolina Spectator and Western Advertiser*, February [?], 1832. See also Hardy, *Second Annual Address*, 4–5, 7.

40. E. H. Stillwell, ed., *Minutes of the Tuckaseegee Baptist Association, 1829–1957* (Nashville, TN: Historical Commission, Southern Baptist Convention, 1962), 6–8 (quotation on 7).

41. Logan, *Sketches, Historical and Biographical, of the Broad River and King's Mountain Baptist Associations*, 9.

42. Rorabaugh, *Alcoholic Republic*, 13.

43. *Minutes and Membership Roll of the Three Forks Baptist Church* (Boone, NC), February 1, 1798 (Raleigh: North Carolina State Archives, 1980).

44. In 1844, the Senter Primitive Baptist Church in Ashe County resolved unanimously to exclude members who repeatedly engaged in heavy drinking. Six years later, the Mount Zion Methodist Church expelled a Macon County resident for "getting drunk." See J. C. Weaver, ed., *Records of the Senter Primitive Baptist Church, Nathan's Creek, Ashe County, North Carolina* (Arlington, VA: J. C. Weaver, 1989), 17; and Mount Zion Methodist Church minutes, September 27, 1850, box 1, folder 13, Siler Family Papers, Southern Historical Collection, Wilson Library, University of North Carolina at Chapel Hill. For more examples of churches that excluded members for getting intoxicated, see Carolyn Adams, *History of Cove Creek Baptist Church, 1799–1974* (Sugar Grove, NC: Cove Creek Baptist Church, 1974), 6; *Minutes and Membership Roll of the Three Forks Baptist Church*, September 1, 1800; and Paschal, *History of the North Carolina Baptists*, 2:234–35.

45. See Globe Church (Caldwell County, NC) Record Book, 1797–1911, 22, 26, 27, 65, Southern Historical Collection, Wilson Library, University of North Carolina; and W. Earl Greene, *Meat Camp Baptist Church, 1851–1981: A History* (Boone, NC: Minor's Publishing Co., 1983), 103.

46. Wellman, *Kingdom of Madison*, 159.

47. Stephen Morgan was one such man, a Baptist minister from Buncombe County who manufactured his own brandy. See Theodore F. Davidson, *Reminiscences and Traditions of Western North Carolina* (Asheville, NC: Service Printing, 1928), 19.

48. Fred Burnett, *This Was My Valley* (Ridgecrest, NC: Heritage Printers, 1960), 16.

49. Griffin, *History of Old Tryon and Rutherford Counties*, 177–80, 586.

50. *North Carolina Spectator and Western Advertiser*, July 23, 1831.

51. Johnson, *Ante-Bellum North Carolina*, 454–55.

52. As Kerr pointed out in 1832, "a general disuse of ardent spirits . . . would be an essential improvement in farming." See *North Carolina Spectator and Western Advertiser*, February [?], March 3, 1832.

53. These men were Elijah Patton, William H. Walton, William Irvine, Pinckney Reid, Silas R. Melton, James Morrison, Samuel Andrews, Jason Carson, and Jesse Groves. See *North Carolina Spectator and Western Advertiser,* July 23, 1831. A description of these men and their professions can be found in Griffin, *History of Old Tryon and Rutherford Counties.*

54. Many mountain whites testified that the Cherokees responded favorably to Yonaguska's crusade against alcohol. See Lanman, *Letters from the Alleghany Mountains,* 106–8; John R. Finger, *The Eastern Band of Cherokees, 1819–1900* (Knoxville: University of Tennessee Press, 1984), 65–66; and Stanly E. Godbold Jr. and Mattie U. Russell, *Confederate Colonel and Cherokee Chief: The Life of William Holland Thomas* (Knoxville: University of Tennessee Press, 1990), 19–20.

55. Macon and Haywood County residents to William Thomas, January 31, 1836, roll 2, William Holland Thomas Papers, Special Collections, Duke University.

56. William H. Thomas to Hon. James Graham, October 18, 1838, quoted in John H. Wheeler, *Historical Sketches of North Carolina from 1584 to 1851 . . . with Biographical Sketches of Her Distinguished Statesmen, Jurists, Lawyers, Soldiers, Divines, Etc.* (1851; reprint, Baltimore: Genealogical Pub. Co. for Clearfield Co., 1993), 205–6.

57. Finger, *Eastern Band of Cherokees,* 66.

58. Ibid., 65–66; Godbold and Russell, *Confederate Colonel and Cherokee Chief,* 19–20.

59. Cecil-Fronsman, *Common Whites,* 191–96.

60. Daniel Jay Whitener, *Prohibition in North Carolina, 1715–1945* (Chapel Hill: University of North Carolina Press, 1946), 21.

61. Johnson, *Ante-Bellum North Carolina,* 455–56.

62. McCauley, *Appalachian Mountain Religion,* 113–18.

63. Johnson, *Ante-Bellum North Carolina,* 456.

64. *North Carolina Spectator and Western Advertiser,* May 7 (Wilkes), June 11 (Buncombe), July 23 (Rutherford), 1831.

65. Bertram Wyatt-Brown, "The Antimission Movement in the Jacksonian South: A Study in Regional Folk Culture," *Journal of Southern History* 36 (November 1970): 515.

66. Johnson, *Ante-Bellum North Carolina,* 341; Dunn, *Cades Cove,* 112.

67. Cecil-Fronsman, *Common Whites,* 199 (quotations); Johnson, *Ante-Bellum North Carolina,* 341.

68. From the beginning of alcohol reform, Primitive Baptists and "traditional" Methodists in western North Carolina perceived the temperance movement as an attack on their way of life. Several Buncombe County churches, for instance, opposed the first temperance society founded in Asheville in 1831. One minister who joined the society quickly withdrew from it, having been threatened with dismissal from his church. In Surry County in 1832, the Fischer's River Association voted to remain an antimissionary body. Six years later, the Mountain Baptist Association in Wilkes County declared nonfellowship with churches that favored missions and temperance societies. See Hardy, *Sec-*

ond Annual Address, 9–10; Van Noppen and Van Noppen, *Western North Carolina since the Civil War,* 73; and Hayes, *Land of Wilkes,* 121.

69. Stillwell, *Minutes of the Tuckaseegee Baptist Association,* 6–8.

70. Whitener, *Prohibition in North Carolina,* 29–30; Johnson, *Ante-Bellum North Carolina,* 170–72.

71. Loveland, *Southern Evangelicals and the Social Order,* 150–51. See also *Proceedings of the Fifth Annual Meeting of the Baptist State Convention of North Carolina,* 15, quoted in Paschal, *History of North Carolina Baptists,* 2:305; and *Mountain Banner,* April 9, 1850.

72. Gordon B. McKinney, "Economy and Community in Western North Carolina, 1860–1865," in *Appalachia in the Making,* 174.

73. For a discussion of the important role of the middle class in the Sons of Temperance and other societies in the United States, see Elizabeth R. Varon, *We Mean to Be Counted: White Women and Politics in Antebellum Virginia* (Chapel Hill: University of North Carolina Press, 1998); Tyrrell, "Drink and Temperance in the Old South"; Ian Tyrrell, *Sobering Up: From Temperance to Prohibition in Antebellum America, 1800–1860* (Westport, CT: Greenwood Press, 1979); Rorabaugh, *Alcoholic Republic*; Clark, *Deliver Us from Evil*; C. C. Pearson and J. Edwin Hendricks, *Liquor and Anti-Liquor in Virginia, 1619–1919* (Durham, NC: Duke University Press, 1967); Gusfield, *Symbolic Crusade*; and James B. Sellers, *The Prohibition Movement in Alabama, 1702–1943* (Chapel Hill: University of North Carolina Press, 1943).

74. Patton, *Biography of James Patton,* 23–25. One of Patton's sons and a grandson became members of the Sons of Temperance. See *Asheville News,* January 9, 1851, March 1, 1855.

75. *Asheville News,* August 24, 1854.

76. Newsome, "A. S. Merrimon Journal," 306; *Asheville News,* March 1, 1855.

77. *Raleigh Spirit of the Age,* January 9, 1852. Other middle-class residents supported the order's efforts to improve education and sponsor schools in places such as Weaverville, Taylorsville, and Wilkesboro. See *Carolina Watchman,* July 13, 1848, January 4, 1849, April 24, 1851, December 10, 1852; *Asheville News,* February 23, 1854; and Mrs. M. H. G. to "cousin Ada," July 18, 1853, Mary Gash Papers.

78. These county seats were Asheville, Rutherfordton, Shelby, Jefferson, Marion, Burnsville, Wilkesboro, Lenoir, Taylorsville, Morganton, Franklin, and Marshall. The seven non–county seat communities where residents organized divisions were Reems Creek (Buncombe County), High Brighton (Buncombe County), Sulphur Springs (Cleveland County), Helton (Ashe County), Mountain Cross (McDowell County), Old Fort (McDowell County), and Quallatown (Cherokee County). See *Asheville Spectator,* July 13, 1853; *Asheville News,* July 28, 1853; *Mountain Banner,* January 3, November 14, 1849; *Raleigh Spirit of the Age,* March 21, May 30, July 25, October 10, 1851, January 9, September 15, 1852, March 3, April 6, 1853, March 28, 1855; "Celebration of the Fourth of July in Burnsville," *Highland Messenger,* July 24, 1846, in Lloyd Bailey, ed., *News from Yancey: Articles from Area Newspa-*

pers, 1840–1900 (Burnsville, NC: Yancey Graphics, 1983), 10; and Lanman, *Letters from the Alleghany Mountains,* 107–8.

79. Two of these societies were located in Ashe County, and the other two were situated in Cherokee and Macon counties.

80. These men were H. M. Corbitt, William Albright, A. Hamby, John R. Pickett, J. W. Vandiver, W. H. Wilson, John T. Miller, A. H. Roberts, J. M. Covington, and G. W. Baxter. The occupations of these officers are from the online database Ancestry.com, *1850 United States Federal Census* (Provo, UT, 2005).

81. Two other officials in the Rutherford Sons of Temperance, J. N. Scoggins and J. P. Halford, were not listed in the 1850 census. For a list of the officers in this local division, see *Mountain Banner,* April 9, 1850. The officers in the Rutherford Sons of Temperance were typical of those living elsewhere in western North Carolina. Professionals and religious leaders from Jefferson, Shelby, and other commercial centers monopolized high office in county divisions. Even officers in the Ashe Sons of Temperance, located in rural Ashe County, included a physician, a merchant, a carpenter, and a lawyer. Whigs and Democrats alike served as officials in the Sons, suggesting that the organization was nonpartisan, although ambitious young men used it as a springboard into local politics. Future senators Augustus S. Merrimon and Robert Vance (who served as the "Worthy Patriarch" in 1851) held their first leadership positions in the Asheville Sons of Temperance. See *Raleigh Spirit of the Age,* May 30, 1851, March 3, 1852; *Asheville News,* January 8, 1851, July 28, 1853; *Asheville Messenger,* April 30, 1851; *Mountain Banner,* November 14, 1849, April 9, June 25, 1850; J. M. Gentry to Ashe Sons of Temperance, October 22, 1850, Ashe County Records, North Carolina State Archives.

82. Tyrrell, "Drink and Temperance in the Antebellum South," 493.

83. Memorial from Ashe County, N.C., to the Honorable, the General Assembly of the State of North Carolina, 1855, Petitions, box 12, Session Records, General Assembly Record Group, North Carolina State Archives; hereafter cited as General Assembly Session Records.

84. For the names of antiprohibitionists in Yancey County, see [Yancey County residents] to the Honorable, the General Assembly of North Carolina, 1852, Petitions, box 8, General Assembly Session Records. These two counties were situated in the northeastern part of western North Carolina. Both were predominantly rural and agricultural. Farmers in these two counties grew mostly corn and oats. The average size of a farm in Ashe County was 293 acres, while in Yancey County it was 303 acres. The cash value of farms in Yancey County ($614) was higher than those in Ashe County ($366). Nonetheless, these counties are economically comparable. See U.S. Census Office, *Seventh Census of the United States: 1850,* 1:318–21.

85. The remaining forty-four male petitioners in Ashe County could not be positively identified in the 1850 population or agricultural censuses. See *Agricultural and Manufacturing Census Records of Fifteen Southern States for the Years, 1850, 1860, 1870, and 1880* (Chapel Hill: Library Photographic Services, University of North Carolina, 1960–1965), microfilm, North Carolina, reel 1 (Ashe County), reel 3 (Yancey County).

86. The three mechanics were William Hawkins, George Hawk, and Aaron Johnston; the two ministers were Richard Gentry and Richard Jacks; and the two merchants were David Smith and Nathan Waugh.

87. The remaining thirty-seven male petitioners in Yancey County could not be positively identified in the 1850 population or agricultural censuses. Although the 1850 census failed to give the profession of seven of the twenty-six known petitioners, these seven men did own farms, suggesting that they were agriculturalists.

88. The average size of Ashe County farms was 545 acres. Ashe County farmers were also more likely to invest in improvements in their land. Among Yancey County antiprohibitionists, 13 percent of their land was improved, compared with 15 percent in Ashe County. If the farms of prohibitionists who were listed as professionals are excluded, the percentage of improved land in Ashe County increases to 27 percent, markedly higher than in Yancey County. See *Agricultural and Manufacturing Census Records of Fifteen Southern States,* North Carolina, reels 1 and 3.

89. These farmers were also wealthier and had larger landholdings than others in Ashe County. Whereas the average cash value of a farm in that county was $366, it was $762 for prohibitionists. The average size of a prohibitionist's farm was 545 acres, while other Ashe County farms averaged 293 acres. Antiprohibitionists were poorer and had smaller landholdings than other farmers in Yancey County; the average cash value of a farm in that county was $614, but it was only $397 for antiprohibitionists. The average size of an antiprohibitionist's farm was 217 acres, while other Yancey County farms averaged 303 acres. See ibid.

90. *Asheville News,* March 1, 1855.

91. *Raleigh Spirit of the Age,* July 25, 1851.

92. The Sons of Temperance organized such celebrations in Asheville, Lenoir, Burnsville, Sulphur Springs, Wilkesboro, Taylorsville, and Shelby. See *Carolina Watchman,* July 13, 1848; *Raleigh Spirit of the Age,* March 21, 1851, January 9, March 10, 1852, March 18, 1853; *Asheville News,* January 9, 1851, March 1, 1855; Bailey, *News From Yancey,* 10; J. M. Gentry to Brethren of Sharon Division, February 5, 1851, and J. M. Carson to Sharon Division, March 27, 1851, both in James Gordon Hackett Collection, 1806–1887, PC 112, North Carolina State Archives.

93. Rorabaugh, *Alcoholic Republic,* 194–95 (quotation on 194).

94. *North Carolina Spectator and Western Advertiser,* May 7, 1831.

95. Varon, *We Mean to Be Counted,* 31.

96. *North Carolina Spectator and Western Advertiser,* June 11, 1831.

97. *Spirit of the Age,* March 21, 1851, January 9, March 10, 1852, March 18, April 6, 1853; *Asheville News,* March 1, 1855; Bailey, *News From Yancey,* 10; J. G. Ballow to Wilkesboro Division Sons of Temperance, March 17, 1851, James Gordon Hackett Collection, 1806–1887.

98. *Raleigh Spirit of the Age,* March 21, 1851.

99. Elizabeth Avery to Isaac Theodore Avery, November 14, 1852, Avery Family Papers, privately owned, Morganton, NC.

100. Mrs. M. H. G. to "cousin Ada," July 18, 1853, Mary A. Gash Papers.

101. Varon, *We Mean to Be Counted*, 40.

102. Carroll, *Francis Asbury in North Carolina*, 134–35, 175–76; James S. Buckingham, *The Slave States of America*, vol. 2 (London: Fisher, Son and Co., 1842), 210–11.

103. Paschal, *History of the North Carolina Baptists*, 2:305.

104. George W. Featherstonhaugh, *A Canoe Voyage up the Minnay Sotor*, 2 vols. (London: R. Bentley, 1847), 2:281.

105. *Carolina Watchman*, March 29, 1849.

106. *North Carolina Argus*, January 20, 1855, quoted in Inscoe, *Mountain Masters*, 165.

107. *Raleigh Spirit of the Age*, December 8, 1852.

108. "The East and the West," *North Carolina Journal of Education* 1 (1857): 13, quoted in Inscoe, *Mountain Masters*, 139.

109. *North Carolina Standard*, September 7, 1859, quoted in Johnson, *Ante-Bellum North Carolina*, 34.

110. For a detailed discussion of western North Carolinians' fight for internal improvements during the antebellum period, see Inscoe, *Mountain Masters*, 152–76.

111. *Raleigh Spirit of the Age*, February 7, October 10, July 25, 1851, April 6, 1853.

112. As historian John Inscoe explains, "Travelers only occasionally veered from their well-beaten paths, and when they did so their encounters with the more remote local residents were sporadic and superficial." Inscoe, *Mountain Masters*, 37; see also Hsiung, *Two Worlds in the Tennessee Mountains*, 19.

113. *Raleigh Spirit of the Age*, February 7, 1851.

114. Ibid., December 15, 1852.

115. Newsome, "A. S. Merrimon Journal," 329 (first, third, and fourth quotations), 311 (second quotation).

116. [Wilkesboro Division] to James Hackett, July 15, 1850, James Gordon Hackett Collection, 1806–1887.

117. Walter Clark, ed., *State Records of North Carolina* (Raleigh, NC: P. M. Hale, 1886–1907), 23:79–80, 182–85; 24:279–80. See also House bills (October 28): Bill to Prevent Distilling Grain into Spirituous Liquor (rejected), Session of October–November 1779, General Assembly Session Records.

118. Crow, "Whiskey Rebellion in North Carolina."

119. Whitener, *Prohibition in North Carolina*, 39; Hardy, *Second Annual Address*, 3.

120. In 1837, the General Assembly raised the fine to $200. Seventeen years later, the state legislature also passed a law expelling members from the General Assembly if they were convicted of treating. See Whitener, *Prohibition in North Carolina*, 37.

121. *North Carolina Spectator and Western Advertiser*, February [?], 1832. Laws regulating the sale and consumption of alcoholic beverages had existed in North Carolina since the colonial period. In 1715, the General Assembly, hoping to restore order after the Tuscarora uprising, enacted a law that

required retailers to purchase a liquor license from the governor and made public drunkenness a crime punishable by a fine. In 1740, Governor Gabriel Johnston, largely due to public hostility against drunken disturbances at tippling houses (or grog shops), recommended that the General Assembly improve the license system. Legislators responded the next year by outlawing the tippling house and giving county courts (and justices of the peace in 1758) the authority to grant licenses to people of "Good Character." The first state law in 1779 regarding the retail of alcoholic beverages was virtually a reenactment of the colonial system. See Clark, *State Records of North Carolina,* 23:79–80, 182–85; 24:279. For a more detailed description on the genesis of state regulation of the vending and consumption of alcohol during the colonial and antebellum periods, see Whitener, *Prohibition in North Carolina,* 1–11.

122. Clark, *State Records of North Carolina,* 23:725; Hardy, *Second Annual Address,* 6; *North Carolina Spectator and Western Advertiser,* February [?], 1832; *Rutherfordton Intelligencer,* September 28, 1841; *Asheville Messenger* quoted in *Carolina Watchman,* May 13, 1852; *Raleigh Spirit of the Age,* May 11, 1853.

123. Whitener, *Prohibition in North Carolina,* 35.

124. *North Carolina Spectator and Western Advertiser,* January 14, 1832.

125. Ibid., March 3, 1832.

126. Hardy, *Second Annual Address,* 4.

127. Thomas Lenoir, temperance speech, December 25, 1843, folder 251, Lenoir Family Papers, 1763–1940, Southern Historical Collection, Wilson Library, University of North Carolina at Chapel Hill.

128. *Raleigh Spirit of the Age,* July 21, 1851, December 15, 1852.

129. Stillwell, *Minutes of the Tuckaseegee Baptist Association,* 13.

130. In 1848, the Holston Methodist Conference, which supervised churches in western North Carolina and eastern Tennessee, allowed ministers to expel members who distilled alcohol. Baptists soon followed suit. In 1850, Gabriel's Creek Church in Madison County voted not to "retain in membership persons who make, vend, or use intoxicating liquors, except for medical or mechanical purpose." The Broad River Baptist Association declared in 1853 that alcohol distilling was "immoral and injurious to the religious prosperity of the community at large, and therefore ought by all prudent ways to be discountenanced by the churches composing this body." Five years later, it adopted a sterner resolution, recommending that churches and ministers not "receive and baptize distillers of ardent spirits into the fellowship." See Mary Rowles and Hunter K. Rountree, eds., *The Diary of Augustine P. Shannon, 1848–1850* (Nashville, TN: Historical Records Survey, 1940), 48, 50; John Ammons, *Outlines of History of French Broad Association and Mars Hill College: From the Organization of the Association in 1807 to 1907, Being a Period of 100 Years* (Mars Hill, NC: Mars Hill College Press, 2001), 27; and Logan, *Sketches, Historical and Biographical, of the Broad River and King's Mountain Baptist Associations,* 82.

131. Rowles and Rountree, *Diary of Augustine P. Shannon,* 48.

132. The King's Mountain Baptist Association included churches from

Cleveland, Rutherford, and Gaston counties (as well as York County, South Carolina). See Logan, *Sketches, Historical and Biographical, of the Broad River and King's Mountain Baptist Associations,* 177–78, 180–82, 184–88 (quotations on 185).

133. These members were all prominent men, further suggesting that the group received its strongest support from the burgeoning middle class. Two of them were successful merchants and the sons of Richard Gentry, a well-to-do farmer and former clerk of the Ashe County Superior Court, who was also expelled for joining the fraternal society. The other banished congregants were Aaron Johnston, a popular minister, and merchant Nathan Waugh, who was Richard Gentry's son-in-law. See Martin Crawford, *Ashe County's Civil War: Community and Society in the Appalachian South* (Charlottesville: University Press of Virginia, 2001), 9–10.

134. Paschal, *History of the North Carolina Baptists,* 304–11; J. F. Fletcher, *A History of the Ashe County, North Carolina and New River, Virginia Baptist Associations* (Raleigh, NC: Commercial Printing Co., 1935): 24–25, 34–37, 48–49; Arthur L. Fletcher, *Ashe County: A History* (Jefferson, NC: Ashe County Research Association, 1963), 152–54; minutes of the Elk Creek Primitive Baptist Church, July 2, 1851, Elk Creek Primitive Baptist Church (Alleghany County, NC) Records, 1839–1890, #4357, Southern Historical Collection; *Raleigh Spirit of the Age,* December 15, 1852.

135. Stillwell, *Minutes of the Tuckaseegee Baptist Association,* 7–9.

136. Porte Crayon (pseudonym), "A Winter in the South," *Harper's New Monthly Magazine* 15 (November 1857): 732.

137. *Raleigh Spirit of the Age,* July 25, 1851.

138. Ibid., December 15, 1852.

139. Ibid., August 3, 1853.

140. Ibid., September 15, December 15, 1852, August 3, 1853.

141. *North Carolina Spectator and Western Advertiser,* March 3, 1832; *Raleigh Spirit of the Age,* May 11, 1853.

142. *Raleigh Spirit of the Age,* July 25, 1851.

143. Ibid., May 11, 1853.

144. Blocker, *American Temperance Movements,* 51–60.

145. Of the almost 18,000 North Carolinians who signed the prohibition memorial in 1852, 2,889 of them were from the mountains. Of those 2,889 mountain prohibitionists, 1,011 were females. See *Raleigh Spirit of the Age,* January 5, 1853. Counties included in the tally are Alexander, Ashe, Buncombe, Caldwell, Catawba, Cherokee, Cleveland, Haywood, Henderson, McDowell, Macon, Surry, and Yancey.

146. *Raleigh Spirit of the Age,* July 25, 1851, December 15, 1852, May 11, 1853; *Asheville Messenger,* April 21, May 26, 1852; *Asheville News,* January 17, 1856; memorials from Alexander, Buncombe, Burke, Caldwell, Catawba, Cleveland, Cherokee, Haywood, Henderson, Madison, Rutherford, and Wilkes counties, 1855, all in box 13, Petitions, General Assembly Session Records; memorial from Jackson County, 1855, box 12, Petitions, General Assembly Session Records.

147. Of the fourteen states that adopted prohibition laws before the Civil War, the only slave state to do so was Delaware. See Pegram, *Battling Demon Rum*, 40; and Eslinger, "Antebellum Liquor Reform in Lexington, Virginia," 164.

148. Whitener, *Prohibition in North Carolina*, 41–47 (quotations on 47).

149. [Yancey County residents] to the Honorable, the General Assembly of North Carolina, 1852, box 8, Petitions, General Assembly Session Records.

150. Crayon, "Winter in the South," 732.

151. [Yancey County residents] to the Honorable, the General Assembly of North Carolina, 1852, box 8, Petitions, General Assembly Session Records.

152. Western North Carolinians also denounced the Sons as a "company of mid-night revelers," an "arm of Romanism," a "branch of Masons," "Wolves in Sheeps' Clothing," "followers of false Prophets," and "a set of men conspiring against the liberties of the country." See *Raleigh Spirit of the Age*, July 25, 1851.

153. *Asheville News*, November 22, 1855 (first quotation), January 17, 1856 (second quotation).

154. Ibid., January 17, 1856.

155. McKinney, "Economy and Community in Western North Carolina," 177–78.

3. "Is There Any Way to Get at the Distillers?"

Epigraph: From "Moon Shine," poem recorded in *Wolfery: A Collection of Burke County Folklore* (1977).

1. *Greensboro Patriot*, March 27, 1862.

2. Jed Dannenbaum, *Drink and Disorder: Temperance Reform in Cincinnati from the Washington Revival to the WCTU* (Urbana: University of Illinois Press, 1984), 174–75; Coker, *Liquor in the Land of the Lost Cause*, 18–19; Pegram, *Battling Demon Rum*, 124.

3. William M. Robinson Jr., "Prohibition in the Confederacy," *American Historical Review* 37 (October 1931): 50–58; Mark E. Neely Jr., *Southern Rights: Political Prisoners and the Myth of Confederate Constitutionalism* (Charlottesville: University of Virginia Press, 1999), 29–42.

4. Amelia Gwyn to Sister Sallie, April 15, 1861, Lenoir Family Papers, #426, Southern Historical Collection.

5. James M. Gentry to Jonathan Faw, May 6, 1861, quoted in Inscoe and McKinney, *Heart of Confederate Appalachia*, 60.

6. Edmund W. Jones to S. F. Patterson, May 20, 1861, quoted in Inscoe and McKinney, *Heart of Confederate Appalachia*, 62.

7. Elizabeth Watson to James Watson, October 29, 1861, James Watson Papers, Special Collections, Western Carolina University.

8. [Niece] to Lizzie Lenoir, December 26, 1862, quoted in Inscoe and McKinney, *Heart of Confederate Appalachia*, 168–69.

9. R. L. Abernethy to Z. B. Vance, November 4, 1862, quoted in W. Buck Yearns and John G. Barrett, eds., *North Carolina Civil War Documentary* (Chapel Hill: University of North Carolina Press, 1980), 217–18.

10. "When the Confederacy introduced the tax-in-kind in 1863, some of the supplies collected were distributed at home rather than being sent to the front." McKinney, "Moonshiners, Law Enforcement, and Violence," 5; see also Paul D. Escott, "Poverty and Government Aid for the Poor in Confederate North Carolina," *North Carolina Historical Review* 61 (October 1984): 462–80.

11. Joseph C. Norwood to Walter Lenoir, November 17, 1863, Lenoir Family Papers, #426, Southern Historical Collection. For more examples of relief for the poor in western North Carolina and other parts of the state, see Inscoe and McKinney, *Heart of Confederate Appalachia,* 169–71; Deyton, "Toe River Valley to 1865," 463; J. Kent Coward, "The Community in Crisis," in *History of Jackson County,* ed. Max R. Williams (Sylva, NC: Jackson County Historical Association, 1987): 439; Escott, "Poverty and Governmental Aid for the Poor"; and William F. Entrekin Jr., "Poor Relief in North Carolina" (MA thesis, Duke University, 1947). On efforts elsewhere in the Confederacy, see Mary Elizabeth Massey, "Food and Drink Shortages on the Confederate Homefront," *North Carolina Historical Review* 26 (July 1949): 306–34; Mary Elizabeth Massey, *Ersatz in the Confederacy* (Baton Rouge: Louisiana State University Press, 1952); Paul D. Escott, "'Cry of the Sufferers': The Problem of Welfare in the Confederacy," *Civil War History* 23 (September 1977): 228–40; and Robinson, "Prohibition in the Confederacy."

12. James Gwyn to Joseph C. Norwood, February 12, 1862, James Gwyn Papers, #426, Southern Historical Collection.

13. *Greensboro Patriot,* March 27, 1862.

14. Logan, *Sketches, Historical and Biographical, of the Broad River and King's Mountain Baptist Associations,* 188.

15. *Ordinances of the State Convention: Published in Pursuance of a Resolution of the General Assembly [Ratified 11th February 1863]* (Raleigh, NC: W. W. Holden, 1863), 70–71.

16. *Raleigh Spirit of the Age,* June 12, 1861. See also ibid., August 28, 1861, July 28, December 22, 1862.

17. Quoted in *Marion Western Enterprise,* March 14, 1862.

18. *Raleigh Spirit of the Age,* January 8, February 5, 12, 19, March 10, 1862.

19. This legislation also outlawed distillers from using wheat, oats, peas, peanuts, rice, potatoes, sugarcane, dried fruit, and syrup to manufacture alcohol. The General Assembly added several amendments during the course of the war. "In order to enable the government better to ferret out the law breakers, it was provided in 1863 that one-half of the fine collected should be paid to the informer. Buckwheat and barley were added to the prohibited materials in 1864. In December of the same year another amendment was added which made it unlawful to use any material in the making of spirituous liquors." Whitener, *Prohibition in North Carolina,* 49–52.

20. *Raleigh Spirit of the Age,* December 8, 1862. See also *Public Laws of North Carolina, 1862–1863,* 20–21.

21. E. D. Hawkins to Zebulon Vance, February 15, 1863, in *The Papers of*

Zebulon Baird Vance, ed. Gordon B. McKinney and Richard McMurry (Frederick, MD: University Publications of America, 1987), reel 16 (microfilm ed.); hereafter citied as *Vance Papers.*

22. Phillip G. Davis, "Mountain Heritage, Mountain Promise under Siege: The Origin and Devastation of Confederate Sympathy in the North Carolina Mountains during the Civil War" (MA thesis, Wake Forest University, 1994), 135.

23. Maryann Arrowood to Zebulon Vance, November 26, 1862, *Vance Papers,* reel 20.

24. E. D. Hawkins to Zebulon Vance, February 15, 1863, ibid., reel 16.

25. *Raleigh Spirit of the Age,* March 16, 1863.

26. T. J. Bicknell to Zebulon Vance, May 7, 1863, *Vance Papers,* reel 63.

27. Jas. O. Simmons to Zebulon Vance, April 18, 1864, reel 23; M. W. Simmons to Zebulon Vance, April 18, 1864, reel 23; E. R. Norton to Zebulon Vance, September 27, 1864, reel 24; James Sloan to Zebulon Vance, January 17, 1865, reel 26; Tod R. Caldwell, et al., to Zebulon Vance, February 4, 1865, reel 26, all in *Vance Papers.*

28. J. A. Goode and J. W. Harris to Zebulon Vance, March 28, April 10, 1863, ibid., reel 16. See also petition from Caldwell County residents to the General Assembly, January 23, 1863, Petitions, General Assembly Session Records; Wm. Enloe, et al. to Zebulon Vance, May 22, 1863, *Vance Papers,* reel 17; Jessie R. Combs to Zebulon Vance, November 24, 1863, ibid., reel 20; Peter Johnson to Zebulon Vance, February 22, 1864, ibid., reel 22; memorial from Cleveland County residents to the General Assembly, December 2, 1864, Petitions, General Assembly Session Records; and S. P. Brittain to Zebulon Vance, December 5, 1864, *Vance Papers,* reel 25.

29. For a discussion of prohibition in the South during the Civil War, see Robinson, "Prohibition in the Confederacy," 50–58.

30. Zebulon Vance to James Seddon, December 31, 1863, *Vance Papers,* reel 13.

31. James Seddon to Zebulon Vance, January 12, 1864, ibid. See also Zebulon Vance to S. H. Rogers, January 22, 1864; and J. Jarratt to Zebulon Vance, October 12, 1864, ibid.

32. Zebulon Vance to James Seddon, February 6, 1865, ibid. See also Zebulon Vance to S. H. Rogers, January 16, 1865; S. H. Rogers to Zebulon Vance, January 18, 1865; and Tod R. Caldwell, et al. to Zebulon Vance, February 4, 1865, ibid.

33. A. D. Childs to Zebulon Vance, April 10, 1863, ibid., reel 17.

34. James Sloan to Zebulon Vance, January 17, 1865, ibid., reel 26.

35. Tod R. Calwell, et al. to Zebulon Vance, February 4, 1865, ibid.

36. E. D. Hawkins to Zebulon Vance, February 15, 1863, ibid., reel 16.

37. *Raleigh Spirit of the Age,* March 16, 1863.

38. Alfred W. Bell to Zebulon Vance, February 23, 1863, *Vance Papers,* reel 26.

39. William W. England to Alexander England, December 7, 1862, quoted in Inscoe and McKinney, *Heart of Confederate Appalachia,* 174.

40. R. L. Abernethy to Zebulon Vance, February 20, 1863, quoted in John G. Barrett, *The Civil War in North Carolina* (Chapel Hill: University of North Carolina Press, 1963), 188.

41. Calvin J. Cowles to Zebulon Vance, November 23, 1863, quoted in Inscoe and McKinney, *Heart of Confederate Appalachia,* 134.

42. E. D. Hawkins to Zebulon Vance, February 15, 1863, *Vance Papers,* reel 16.

43. *Raleigh Spirit of the Age,* March 16, 1863.

44. M. W. Simmons to Zebulon Vance, April 18, 1864, *Vance Papers,* reel 23; Jas. O. Simons to Zebulon Vance, April 18, 1864, quoted in Yearns and Barrett, *North Carolina Civil War Documentary,* 178.

45. E. R. Norton to Zebulon Vance, September 27, 1864, *Vance Papers,* reel 24.

46. James Sloan to Zebulon Vance, January 17, 1865, ibid., reel 26.

47. Paul D. Escott, *Many Excellent People: Power and Privilege in North Carolina, 1850–1900* (Chapel Hill: University of North Carolina Press, 1985), 59–84; McKinney, "Economy and Community in Western North Carolina," 163–84; Crawford, *Ashe County's Civil War,* 125–47; Inscoe and McKinney, *Heart of Confederate Appalachia,* 237.

48. Quoted in Glenn Tucker, *Zeb Vance: Champion of Personal Freedom* (New York: Bobbs-Merrill, 1965), 175.

49. Blackmun, *Western North Carolina,* 356–57.

50. These counties included Rutherford, Wilkes, Madison, Yancey, Watauga, Buncombe, and Clay. See Inscoe and McKinney, *Heart of Confederate Appalachia,* 269–70.

51. W. C. Tate to "My Dear Daughter," August 27, 1865, Miscellaneous Letters #516, Southern Historical Collection.

52. *Ordinances of the State Convention, 1865–1866,* 11; *Revenue Law of North Carolina, 1866,* 15.

53. Methodist Episcopal Church, South, *Journal of the North Carolina Annual Conference of the M. E. Church, South* (North Carolina: The Conference, 1883–1939), 16–17.

54. J. R. Siler, et al. to William H. Thomas, February 1866, William Holland Thomas Papers, Special Collections, Duke University.

55. Petition from Lenoir residents to the General Assembly, Petitions, 1866, General Assembly Session Records.

56. By 1868, the Friends of Temperance had organized seventeen lodges in western North Carolina. Ten of those lodges (or 59 percent) were located in county seat towns. See Levi Branson, ed., *Branson's North Carolina Business Directory* (Raleigh, NC: Branson and Jones, 1869), 165. For more on the Friends of Temperance in North Carolina, see Whitener, *Prohibition in North Carolina,* 54–55.

57. *Raleigh Sentinel,* December 18, 1865, January 25, 26, 29, February 9, 1866.

58. Journal of the House, 1866, 42–43; Journal of the Senate, 1866, 69.

59. Otto H. Olsen and Ellen Z. McGrew, eds., "Prelude to Reconstruction:

The Correspondence of State Senator Leander Sams Gash, 1866–1867, Part I," *North Carolina Historical Review* 60 (January 1983): 86.

60. Journal of the Senate, 1866, 191–98.

61. Logan, *Sketches, Historical and Biographical, of the Broad River and King's Mountain Baptist Associations,* 208.

62. Otto H. Olsen and Ellen Z. McGrew, "Prelude to Reconstruction: The Correspondence of State Senator Leander Sams Gash, 1866–1867, Part II," *North Carolina Historical Review* 60 (April 1983): 363.

63. Account Book of Isaac Jarratt, 1866, Jarratt-Puryear Family Papers, Special Collections, Duke University.

64. In 1953, Congress renamed this agency the Internal Revenue Service.

65. Miller, *Revenuers & Moonshiners,* 6–7, 44, 61–62.

66. *Congressional Globe,* 37th Cong., 2nd sess. (1862), 1194.

67. Ibid., 1306.

68. Ibid., 1304–13.

69. Ibid., 1195.

70. *Annual Report of the Commissioner of Internal Revenue, 1866,* viii. David A. Wells, head of the special revenue commission, complained in 1865 about Congress's decision to raise the liquor tax: "The immediate effect of the enactment of the first and successive rates of duty was to cause an almost entire suspension of the business of distilling which was resumed again with great activity as soon as an advance in the rate of tax in each instance became probable. The stock of whiskey and high-wines accumulated in the country under this course of procedure was without precedent; and Congress, by its refusal to make the advance in taxation, in any instance, retroactive, virtually legislated for the benefit of distillers and speculators rather than for the treasury and the government." Herbert Ferleger, *David A. Wells and the American Revenue System: 1865–1870* (Philadelphia: Porcupine Press, 1977), 67.

71. Quoted in Heather Cox Richardson, *The Greatest Nation of the Earth: Republican Economic Policies during the Civil War* (Cambridge, MA: Harvard University Press, 1997), 133.

72. *New York Times,* June 19, July 2, 1865.

73. *Annual Report of the Commissioner of Internal Revenue, 1866,* viii, xiv.

74. Alexander, Catawba, Surry, and Wilkes counties constituted part of the state's Sixth Collection District, while the remaining mountain counties fell within the Seventh Collection District.

75. The federal agency, having relied on Treasury Department clerks, received its own clerical staff. Moreover, Congress created the Office of Solicitor of Internal Revenue to oversee legal cases in each district. In 1868, the Bureau of Internal Revenue began to employ supervisors to monitor the work of local officials. These supervisors appointed "detectives," who conducted special investigations to uncover fraud. In 1872, Congress changed their title from "detective" to "agent," merging "them with the previously appointed agents. Calling them detectives had suggested spies and informers." Miller, *Revenuers & Moonshiners,* 62–63.

76. Storekeepers "were paid a flat fee per day," while gaugers "were paid according to the amount of liquor they measured." Ibid.

77. Ibid., 11.

78. According to historian Wilbur Miller, "Johnson, seeking to build a power base among federal officeholders, was more concerned with placing his friends in the revenue service than suppressing illicit distilling." Wilbur R. Miller, "The Revenue: Federal Law Enforcement in the Mountain South, 1870–1900," *Journal of Southern History* 55 (May 1989): 197.

79. *Annual Report of the Commissioner of Internal Revenue, 1866–1867*, 28.

80. When North Carolina and other southern states voted against the Fourteenth Amendment (granting African Americans citizenship) in late 1866, congressional Republicans, believing that harder measures were needed, passed a series of laws known as the Reconstruction Acts. The first of these acts, passed on March 2, 1867, divided the South into five military districts and assigned a military commander to each district to register voters (defined as all adult black males and those whites who had not supported the Confederacy). These voters would then elect a convention to adopt a new state constitution, which had to support African American suffrage and the Fourteenth Amendment. After the constitution was ratified, voters could hold state elections. From March 1867 to July 1868, North Carolina was part of the Second Military District under the command of Gen. Daniel E. Sickles and later Gen. Edwin R. S. Canby. See Richard L. Zuber, *North Carolina during Reconstruction* (Raleigh: North Carolina Division of Archives and History, 1969), 6–20.

81. Muriel Earley Sheppard, *Cabins in the Laurel* (Chapel Hill: University of North Carolina Press, 1935), 192.

82. In western North Carolina, the number of revenuers would reach 325 by the early 1870s. See Miller, *Revenuers & Moonshiners*, 44.

83. Second Military District to J. B. Weaver, April 8, 1867, Second Military District, 1867–68, Records of Military (Reconstruction) Districts, Records of the U.S. Army Continental Commands, Record Group 393, National Archives, Washington, DC; hereafter cited as Records of the Second Military District.

84. Thomas H. Adams to "Colonel," April 18, 1867, ibid.

85. E. A. Rollins to Daniel Sickles, April 17, 1867, ibid. See also J. B. Weaver to Second Military District, March 30, 1867, ibid.

86. Second Military District to James H. Wiley, May 10, 1867, ibid.

87. J. B. Weaver to E. A. Rollins, May 20, 1867, ibid.

88. *New York Times,* May 25, 1867.

89. Account Book of Isaac Jarratt, 1867, Jarratt-Puryear Papers, Special Collections, Duke University.

90. *Hendersonville Pioneer,* May 8, 1867.

91. Crow, "Whiskey Rebellion in North Carolina," 1–28; Ferleger, *Wells and the American Revenue System,* 112. For a discussion of whiskey rebellions in other parts of the United States, see Kevin T. Barksdale, "Our Rebellious Neighbors: Virginia's Border Counties during Pennsylvania's Whiskey Rebellion," *Virginia Magazine of History and Biography* 111 (January 2003): 5–32; Mary K. Tachau, "The Whiskey Rebellion in Kentucky: A Forgotten Episode

of Civil Disobedience," *Journal of the Early Republic* 2 (July 1982): 239–59; Slaughter, *Whiskey Rebellion;* and Steven R. Boyd, ed., *The Whiskey Rebellion: Past and Present Perspectives* (Westport, CT: Greenwood Press, 1985).

92. Inscoe and McKinney, *Heart of Confederate Appalachia,* 153; McKinney, "Moonshiners, Law Enforcement, and Violence," 10.

93. In 1864, Dedman sold the newspaper when local Confederates "threatened to conscript him unless he did so." See McKinney and Inscoe, *Heart of Confederate Appalachia,* 155–56, 163; and *Raleigh Spirit of the Age,* March 10, 1863.

94. Jesse Wheeler to Bureau of Internal Revenue, June 25, 1868, Very Miscellaneous, 1865–1870, Bureau of Internal Revenue Records, Record Group 58, National Archives, College Park, MD; hereafter cited as Internal Revenue Records.

95. Helper, an abolitionist and a Union soldier, fled to Illinois before the Civil War to escape fallout from his brother's controversial book *The Impending Crisis.* See H. H. Helper to Commissioner J. W. Douglass, August 25, 1869, Very Miscellaneous, 1865–1870, Internal Revenue Records.

96. During the spring and summer of 1867, food shortages continued to plague the region.

97. E. A. Rollins to Daniel Sickles, April 17, 1867, Records of the Second Military District. See also J. B. Weaver to Headquarters Second Military District, April 9, 1867, Records of the Second Military District; J. B. Weaver to E. A. Rollins, May 20, 1867, Internal Revenue Records; and J. B. Weaver to Captain J. W. [Clouis], May 23, 1867, Records of the Second Military District.

98. *New York Times,* May 25, 1867.

99. General Sickles to Headquarters Second Military District, August 22, 1867, and W. B. Royall to Lt. L. V. Caziaro, January 20, 1868, Records of the Second Military District.

100. Headquarters Second Military District to E. A. Rollins, September 17, 1867, ibid.

101. J. B. Weaver to E. A. Rollins, May 20, 1867; Jones & Payrow Detective Officers to Colonel E. W. Hinks, July 1, 1867; Thomas H. Adams, July 1867; Thomas H. Adams to "Colonel," August 12, 1867; Pinkney Rollins to Lt. Louis Caziaro, November 12, 1867; Edward B. Jennings to General Canby, December 27, 1867; and John Mulby, March 22, 1868, all in ibid.

102. Pinkney Rollins to Lt. Louis Caziaro, November 12, 1867, ibid.

103. E. A. Rollins to General Canby, November 15, 1867, ibid.

104. A. H. Guernsey, "Illicit Distilling of Liquors—Southern Mode of Making Whiskey," *Harper's Weekly* 11 (December 7, 1867): 733.

105. Edward Jennings to General Canby, December 27, 1867, Records of the Second Military District.

106. John Mulby to Second District Military Headquarters, March 22, 1868, ibid.

4. "They Tax Us and Give Us Negro Civil Rights"

Epigraph: From "Moonshine Still," sung by Frank Proffit and Pick Britches on Beaver Dam in Sugar Grove, NC, August 14, 1937. See Edna Lucille Miller,

"A Study of Folklore in Watauga County, North Carolina" (MA thesis, Georgia Peabody of College for Teachers, 1938), 178.

1. Gordon B. McKinney, *Zeb Vance: North Carolina's Civil War Governor and Gilded Age Political Leader* (Chapel Hill: University of North Carolina Press, 2004), 322.

2. Hamilton G. Ewart to Charles Devens, May 29, 1877 (microfilm, reel 2, M1345), Letters Received from the State of North Carolina, 1871–1884, Records of the Attorney General, General Records of the Department of Justice, Record Group 60, National Archives, College Park, MD; hereafter cited as Department of Justice Records.

3. O. H. Dockery to Carl Schurz, November 22, 1877, in James A. Padgett, ed., "Reconstruction Letters from North Carolina, Part III," *North Carolina Historical Review* 19 (July 1942): 299.

4. Hamilton G. Ewart to Charles Devens, May 29, 1877 (microfilm, reel 2, M1345), Department of Justice Records.

5. For a general discussion of Reconstruction, see Eric Foner, *Reconstruction: America's Unfinished Revolution, 1863–1877* (New York: Harper and Row, 1988).

6. Gordon B. McKinney, *Southern Mountain Republicans, 1865–1900* (Chapel Hill: University of North Carolina Press, 1978), 7, 44–50.

7. Eric J. Olson, "Race Relations in Asheville, North Carolina: Three Incidents, 1868–1906," in *The Appalachian Experience: Proceedings of the 6th Annual Appalachian Studies Conference,* ed. Barry Buxton (Boone, NC: Appalachian Consortium Press, 1983), 153–56, 163–64; John C. Inscoe, "Race and Racism in Nineteenth-Century Southern Appalachia," in *Appalachia in the Making,* 122–23.

8. "Home rule" meant Democratic control of state governments in the South.

9. In his 1991 book *Revenuers & Moonshiners,* Wilbur Miller notes that the issue of liquor taxation, along with African American civil rights, energized mountain politics. He observes that mountain whites, whether Republican or Conservative, opposed liquor taxation because it increased federal authority and threatened to reduce local distillers' profit margin. Miller concludes that mountain politicians sensed this growing hostility and attempted to garner support by protesting the liquor law. Gordon McKinney also concedes that reintroduction of the liquor tax and expansion of the Bureau of Internal Revenue after the Civil War intensified mountain whites' opposition to the Republican Party. Like Miller, he argues that many Carolina highlanders believed that the federal government used revenue enforcement to extend its authority. Despite this more recent scholarship, however, historians have inadequately addressed how liquor taxation affected party politics in western North Carolina during Reconstruction. Miller and McKinney, for instance, focus most of their attention on violence between revenuers and moonshiners, arguing that mountain whites resorted to extralegal retribution because they perceived revenue enforcement as a federal intrusion into their private lives. Both studies are devoid of any thorough research concerning the partisan

politics of liquor taxation. The failure to examine the political implications of liquor taxation more closely has made it impossible to understand the varied responses of regional communities to the rise of the nation-state after the Civil War. See Miller, *Revenuers & Moonshiners*, 41–44; and McKinney, "Moonshiners, Law Enforcement, and Violence," 15.

10. Radical Republicanism represented what the Democrats believed were the evils of Congressional Reconstruction: black suffrage, taxation, and expansion of federal authority.

11. The Conservative Party was renamed the Democratic Party after the 1876 election. During Reconstruction, North Carolina Conservatives supported the national Democratic Party, and their opponents called them Democrats in an attempt to capitalize on Unionists' hatred of that party. For more information on Republicans and Conservatives in North Carolina, see Joseph G. de Roulhac Hamilton, *Reconstruction in North Carolina* (New York: Columbia University, 1914); Otto H. Olsen, "Reconsidering the Scalawags," *Civil War History* 12 (December 1966): 304–15; Zuber, *North Carolina during Reconstruction*; and Inscoe and McKinney, *Heart of Confederate Appalachia*.

12. McKinney, *Southern Mountain Republicans*, 44–50.

13. Inscoe and McKinney, *Heart of Confederate Appalachia*, 271–72.

14. For election returns in these counties, see Donald R. Matthews, ed., *North Carolina Votes: General Election Returns by County* (Chapel Hill: University of North Carolina Press, 1962).

15. Alexander et al. to William L. Scott, May 31, 1871, Scott Papers, Special Collections, Duke University, quoted in Inscoe and McKinney, *Heart of Confederate Appalachia*, 272.

16. In other parts of Appalachian North Carolina, the relative absence of African Americans freed many white highlanders from the fear of "Negro domination" and allowed Republicans to retain their loyalty. Of the five mountain counties with the lowest percentage of blacks, four (Cherokee, Madison, Watauga, and Mitchell) voted Republican in the 1868 gubernatorial election. For a discussion of the role demographics played in allowing mountain Republicans to overlook their prejudices and work with blacks politically, see Gordon B. McKinney, "Southern Mountain Republicans and the Negro, 1865–1900," in *Appalachians and Race: The Mountain South from Slavery to Segregation*, ed. John C. Inscoe (Lexington: University Press of Kentucky, 2001), 205. For election returns in these counties, see Matthews, *North Carolina Votes*.

17. *Raleigh Sentinel*, November 23, 1866, November 9, 1867; *Asheville Pioneer*, September 21, 1867; Inscoe, *Mountain Masters*, 152.

18. "Even more significant," historian Paul Escott argues, "in terms of the daily lives of most North Carolinians, was the fact that the constitution abolished the old county courts and their lifetime 'squirarchy,' replacing them with five commissioners in each county elected by the people." Escott, *Many Excellent People*, 142–44.

19. Conservatives insisted that the people should not elect judges, and they wanted representation in the senate to be based on wealth rather than population. See Zuber, *North Carolina during Reconstruction*, 18.

20. R. B. Bogle to Tod Caldwell, November 16, 1868, Tod Robinson Caldwell Papers, 1801–1890, #128, Southern Historical Collection.

21. *Asheville News,* March 12, 1868.

22. *Rutherfordton Western Vindicator,* March 28, 1868.

23. *Asheville Pioneer,* May 20, 1867; McKinney, *Southern Mountain Republicans,* 46.

24. *Asheville Pioneer,* September 21, 1867.

25. Holden received 54 percent of the mountain vote, winning in Buncombe, Burke, Cherokee, Henderson, Madison, McDowell, Mitchell, Polk, Rutherford, Surry, Watauga, and Wilkes counties. Computed from Matthews, *North Carolina Votes.* For the 1868 North Carolina Constitution results, see *Tribune Almanac,* 1869, 76–77.

26. Escott, *Many Excellent People,* 145.

27. *Raleigh Sentinel,* September 9, 14, 17, 28, 1868.

28. Quoted in ibid., September 23, 1868.

29. James Gwyn to Jamie [Gwyn], February 16, 1868, James Gwyn Papers, Southern Historical Collection.

30. *Raleigh Standard,* September 15, 21, 1868.

31. Quoted in *Raleigh Daily Standard,* October 10, 1868.

32. Blackmer and McCarkle to General Canby, March 5, 1868, Records of the Second Military District.

33. William L. Scott to Rufus [Scott], November 3, 1868, William Lafayette Scott Papers, Special Collections, Duke University.

34. The men arrested for illicit distilling were Wesley Walker, Ephraim Abee, W. C. Good, John Robinson, Lewis Robinson, Amos Huffman, R. R. Caswell, and William Brittain. See J. B. Kincaid to Tod Caldwell, November 27, 1868; Tod Caldwell, November 29, 1868; D. H. Starbuck to Tod Caldwell, November 12, 1868; and Pinkney Rollins to Tod Caldwell, September 1, 1870, all in Tod Robinson Caldwell Papers, Southern Historical Collection.

35. Seymour received 51 percent of the mountain vote, winning in Alexander, Alleghany, Ashe, Buncombe, Caldwell, Catawba, Clay, Cleveland, Haywood, Jackson, Macon, Transylvania, Watauga, and Yancey counties. Computed from Matthews, *North Carolina Votes.* For U.S. Senate results, see *Tribune Almanac,* 1869, 76.

36. Ferleger, *Wells and the American Revenue System,* 112–14; Miller, *Revenuers & Moonshiners,* 40, 63; Frederic C. Howe, *Taxation and Taxes in the United States under the Internal Revenue System, 1791–1895* (New York: Thomas Y. Crowell, 1896), 139–51.

37. *Rutherfordton Western Vindicator,* November 8, 1869.

38. Most farmers in western North Carolina had five-gallon stills. It took two bushels of corn to make five gallons of whiskey. Thus, a farmer could earn $20 if he distilled two bushels of corn into whiskey. See Account Book of Isaac Jarratt, 1868–1869, Jarratt-Puryear Family Papers, Special Collections, Duke University.

39. Miller, *Revenuers & Moonshiners,* 40.

40. Testimony of D. C. Pearson, in "Testimony before the Senate Special

Committee to Investigate the Administration of the Collection of Internal Revenue in the Sixth District of North Carolina, Appointed April 21, 1882," *Senate Miscellaneous Documents,* no. 116, 47th Cong., 1st sess., 323; hereafter cited as "Sixth District of North Carolina."

41. *Atlanta Constitution,* May 19, 1880, quoted in Miller, *Revenuers & Moonshiners,* 41.

42. Edward L. Ayers, *Vengeance and Justice: Crime and Punishment in the Nineteenth Century American South* (New York: Oxford University Press, 1984), 262.

43. M. L. White, *A History of the Life of Amos Owens, the Noted Blockader, of Cherry Mountain, N.C.* (Shelby, NC: Cleveland Star Job Print, 1901), 32.

44. *Raleigh Daily Standard,* February 3, 1870, quoted in Miller, *Revenuers & Moonshiners,* 41.

45. In 1871, the price for a bushel of corn was $1.00. If a farmer legally distilled two bushels of corn into five gallons of whiskey, he could earn $7.50. See Account Book of Isaac Jarratt, 1871, Jarratt-Puryear Family Papers, Special Collections, Duke University.

46. *Raleigh Weekly Standard,* October 20, 1869.

47. Ibid., September 8, 1869.

48. *Raleigh Sentinel,* September 9, 14, 28, 1868.

49. William T. Sherman to General G. G. Meade, March 21, 1871 (microfilm, reel 14, 1723 AGO 1871); C. H. Morgan to the Adjutant General, October 22, 1871 (microfilm, reel 12, M666); Mr. Shelton, report, 1871; Secretary of War [William Worth Belknap] to Secretary of the Treasury [George S. Boutwell], June 30, 1871 (microfilm, reel 12, M666), all in Letters Received, Adjutant General's Office, Record Group 94, National Archives, Washington, DC; hereafter cited as Adjutant General's Office Records.

50. Miller, *Revenuers & Moonshiners,* 70.

51. *Asheville News,* June 24, 1869.

52. *Raleigh Standard,* October 20, 1869, June 1, 1870.

53. Miller, *Revenuers & Moonshiners,* 45.

54. Guernsey, "Illicit Distilling of Liquors," 733.

55. Miller, *Revenuers & Moonshiners,* 31.

56. John Parris, *Mountain Bred* (Asheville, NC: Citizen-Times Publishing Co., 1967), 4–6.

57. William S. Ball to C. Devens, February 23, 1878 (microfilm, reel 2, M1345), Department of Justice Records.

58. W. H. Deaver to Pinkney Rollins, March 26, 1871, Adjutant General's Office Records.

59. *Report of the Joint Select Committee to Inquire into the Condition of Affairs in the Late Insurrectionary States,* 13 vols. (Washington, DC, 1872), House Reports, 42nd Cong., 2nd sess., no. 22, North Carolina, 179; hereafter cited as *KKK Report.*

60. *Charlotte Western Democrat,* July 25, 1871.

61. *Asheville Pioneer,* January 4, 1872.

62. Ibid., February 21, 28, 1874. For brevity's sake, I have included only a few examples of moonshiners attacking revenuers. For additional cases, see Pinkney Rollins to P. W. Perry, June 17, 1871; R. F. Frank, June 23, 1870; and N. M. Manchester to Pinkney Rollins, April 1, 1871, all in Adjutant General's Office Records; *Raleigh Daily Standard*, June 3, 1869; *Rutherford Star*, January 29, 1870; *Asheville Pioneer*, April 4, 1872, February 21, March 28, April 18, 1874; J. J. Mott to S. F. Phillips, November 30, 1877; V. S. Lusk to George Williams, December 23, 1873; and Robert Dick to George Williams, November 21, 1874, all in Department of Justice Records; Jacob Wagner to Green R. Raum, February 9, 1877, and Jacob Wagner to Green R. Raum, April 5, 1877, in Bureau of Internal Revenue Records.

63. *Rutherford Star*, January 29, 1870.

64. *Asheville Pioneer*, January 4, 1872.

65. *Asheville News*, June 3, 1869.

66. As Gen. William T. Sherman had feared in the late 1860s, soldiers who fired on moonshiners were arrested and tried "for murder in state courts before justices composed of the very men against whom they [were] called upon to act." Miller, *Revenuers & Moonshiners*, 70, 74.

67. *Asheville Pioneer*, February 21, 28, October 24, 1874.

68. Robert Dick to George Williams, November 21, 1874 (microfilm, reel 2, M1345), Department of Justice Records.

69. W. H. Deaver to the Attorney General, June 21, 1877 (microfilm, reel 3, M1345), ibid.

70. V. S. Lusk to George Williams, December 23, 1873; V. S. Lusk to U.S. District Attorney, June 21, 1875; W. A. Ross and T. H. Lindsay to the Attorney General, September 29, 1875; and U.S. Marshall to the Attorney General, November 11, 1875, all in ibid. (microfilm, reel 2, M1345); *Asheville Pioneer*, September 9, October 3, 1874.

71. Miller, *Revenuers & Moonshiners*, 109–10.

72. Two works mention the connection between the Ku Klux Klan and moonshiners during Reconstruction but do not provide a detailed study of this relationship. See Allen W. Trelease, *White Terror: The Ku Klux Klan Conspiracy and Southern Reconstruction* (New York: Harper and Row, 1971), xlviii, 185, 189, 190, 239, 282, 305, 331, 340–41, 345, 357; and Miller, *Revenuers & Moonshiners*, 43–44, 53–54. For scholarship on the Reconstruction-era Ku Klux Klan, see John Hope Franklin, *Reconstruction: After the Civil War* (Chicago: University of Chicago Press, 1961); Otto H. Olsen, "The Ku Klux Klan: A Study in Reconstruction Politics and Propaganda," *North Carolina Historical Review* 39 (July 1962): 340–62; William Peirce Randel, *The Ku Klux Klan: A Century of Infamy* (London: Hamish Hamilton, 1965); Kenneth M. Stampp, *The Era of Reconstruction: 1865–1877* (New York: Alfred A. Knopf, 1965); Trelease, *White Terror*; George C. Rable, *But There Was No Peace: The Role of Violence in the Politics of Reconstruction* (Athens: University of Georgia Press, 1984); and Foner, *Reconstruction*.

73. Trelease, *White Terror*, 189–225; Olsen, "Ku Klux Klan." See also Carole Watterson Troxler, "'To Look More Closely at the Man': Wyatt Outlaw, a

Nexus of National, Local, and Personal History," *North Carolina Historical Review* 77 (October 2000): 403–33.

74. For a discussion of Klan violence against white Republicans and African Americans in western North Carolina, see Bruce E. Stewart, "'When Darkness Reigns Then Is the Hour to Strike': Moonshining, Federal Liquor Taxation, and Klan Violence in Western North Carolina, 1868–1872," *North Carolina Historical Review* 80 (October 2003): 455–56.

75. The Klan also left the same warning on the door of a local African American carpenter that night. See Bureau B. F. and A. L. to Lt. Col. George H. William, April 17, 1868, Records of the Second Military District.

76. Trelease, *White Terror,* 338, 340–42; Hamilton, *Reconstruction in North Carolina,* 462.

77. *Asheville Pioneer,* August 10, November 9, 1871; Bureau B. F. and A. L. to Lt. Col. George H. Williams, April 17, 1868, Records of the Second Military District.

78. *Asheville Pioneer,* November 9, 1871. For more examples of Klansmen attacking white Republicans and African Americans in western North Carolina during the early 1870s, see Stewart, "When Darkness Reigns," 457–58.

79. Pinkney Rollins to P. W. Perry, April 26, 1871 (microfilm, reel 14, 1723 AGO 1871), Adjutant General's Office Records. See also Pleasonton to the Secretary of War [William Worth Belknap], May 16, 1871, ibid.

80. C. C. Vest to Pinkney Rollins, May 9, 1871, M. M. Manchester to Pinkney Rollins, April, 1871, C. C. Vest to Pinkney Rollins, April 19, 1871, and Pinkney Rollins to P. W. Perry, June 17, 1871, all in ibid.; *KKK Report,* 137.

81. J. B. Eaves to Pinkney Rollins, April 20, 1871 (microfilm, reel 14, 1723 AGO 1871), Adjutant General's Office Records.

82. *Asheville Pioneer,* August 24, 1871. See also *Raleigh Daily Standard,* January 11, 1870.

83. *KKK Report,* 105, 440–41, 443.

84. Pinkney Rollins to P. W. Perry, April 26, 1871 (microfilm, reel 14, 1723 AGO 1871), Adjutant General's Office Records.

85. J. B. Eaves to Pinkney Rollins, April 20, 1871, ibid.

86. *KKK Report,* 234.

87. Ibid., 222.

88. Ibid., 403, 405; "Outlawry in North Carolina," newspaper clipping, August 14, 1871 (microfilm, reel 12, M666), Adjutant General's Office Records.

89. *Asheville Pioneer,* June 22, 1871; *Charlotte Democrat,* June 20, October 17, 1871; Trelease, *White Terror,* 348.

90. Miller, "The Revenue," 201.

91. *Raleigh Sentinel,* September 2, 1869.

92. *Asheville News,* June 24, September 3, 1869.

93. *Rutherfordton Western Vindicator,* October 11, 1869.

94. *Raleigh Sentinel,* July 1, 1870; *Rutherford Star,* March 5, 1870; McKinney, *Southern Mountain Republicans,* 47.

95. Whitener, *Prohibition in North Carolina,* 53.

96. *Rutherford Star,* July 2, 6, 1870.

97. *Raleigh Standard,* October 20, 1869.

98. *Raleigh Sentinel,* August 17, 1869.

99. Maj. C. H. Morgan, 4th Artillery, Report, June 9, 1871 (microfilm, reel 14, 1723 AGO 1871), Adjutant General's Office Records.

100. *Raleigh Sentinel,* February 29, 1872.

101. *Asheville Citizen,* September 25, 1872.

102. C. R. Thomas to James Ramsay, December 12, 1872, James G. Ramsay Papers, 1784–1955, #1568, Southern Historical Collection; Howe, *Taxation and Taxes,* 219–20.

103. *Raleigh Sentinel,* March 26, April 3, July 8, 1872.

104. Testimony of W. M. Walker, "Sixth District of North Carolina," 177.

105. *Asheville Pioneer,* February 15, March 7, 21, 1872.

106. *Raleigh Sentinel,* April 20, 1872.

107. Whitener, *Prohibition in North Carolina,* 53.

108. "Congress responded to the crisis by reforming the revenue system. In 1872, the office of assessor was abolished, and its duties were transferred to the collectors. In the same year, a law provided that gaugers would be paid by the government instead of by distillers' fees. In 1876, the supervisors were abolished, with most of their duties going to the collectors and the agents. The agents were made directly responsible to the commissioner and soon became the backbone of the system, checking up on local officials and often organizing large-scale raids on illicit distillers." Miller, *Revenuers & Moonshiners,* 66; Foner, *Reconstruction,* 566.

109. Theodore Davidson, February 14, 1875, Theodore Davidson Papers, North Carolina State Archives.

110. *Raleigh Sentinel,* March 1, 26, 1873.

111. "The vast majority of federal appointees in western North Carolina were employed in the Internal Revenue Service, with the man who was the head or collector in the region usually controlling the party organization." McKinney, *Southern Mountain Republicans,* 49.

112. J. J. Mott to J. G. Ramsay, April 9, 1874, James G. Ramsay Papers, Southern Historical Collection.

113. J. G. Ramsay to J. W. Douglas, December 4, 1874, ibid.

114. Ramsay received the support of Governor Tod R. Caldwell, Thomas Settle, D. H. Starbuck, Robert Dick, and other prominent Republicans. See Tod Caldwell to U. S. Grant, January 17, 1872; D. H. Starbuck and Thomas Settle, November 1872; Robert Dick to U. S. Grant, December 10, 1872; Richmond Pearson, November 21, 1872; Robert Dick, September 1874; and James G. Ramsay to J .W. Douglas, March 28, 1874, all in ibid.

115. A. C. Bryan to Thomas Settle, January 1, 1873, Thomas Settle Papers, 1850–1924, #3345, Southern Historical Collection.

116. George H. Brown to Thomas Settle, November 18, 1874, ibid.

117. For more examples of rank-and-file Republicans supporting Mott, see A. C. Bryan to Thomas Settle, January 1, 1873, and F. J. Dula to Thomas

Settle, June 9, 1873, ibid.; George H. Brown to W. F. Henderson, April 10, 1873; James G. Ramsay to Samuel F. Phillips, August 17, 1874; and James G. Ramsay to J. W. Douglas, December 4, 1974, all in James G. Ramsay Papers, Southern Historical Collection.

118. J. J. Mott to Thomas Settle, November 12, 1874, Thomas Settle Papers, Southern Historical Collection.

119. *Asheville Pioneer,* June 27, 1874.

120. *Asheville Citizen,* February 26, 1874.

121. *Asheville Pioneer,* February 14, 1874; *Raleigh Sentinel,* June 20, 1874.

122. *Asheville Pioneer,* August 22, 1874; *Asheville Citizen,* August 13, 1874.

123. Foner, *Reconstruction,* 313.

124. *Asheville Citizen,* July 22, August 5, 1875. See also McKinney, *Zeb Vance,* 299–300, 312–13.

125. McKinney, *Southern Mountain Republicans,* 49.

126. *Asheville Citizen,* April 29, July 15, 22, August 5, 1875.

127. Evidence suggests that most revenuers in western North Carolina were competent and honest. Nonetheless, Conservatives seized on isolated cases of fraud to criticize the Bureau of Internal Revenue. Whether or not there was a massive amount of corruption is irrelevant, however. Mountain whites opposed to the expansion of federal authority perceived revenue corruption as pervasive, thereby uniting them with the moonshiners.

128. These gaugers had visited these stills only once, even though they reported visiting them on several occasions over a period of days.

129. P. W. Perry to P. P. Pratt, June 28, 1875; W. W. Holden, Governor Brogden, D. A. Jenkins to Edward Pierrepont, June 14, 1875; J. M. Orr, June 2, 1875; V. S. Lusk, report, July 1, 1875; J. J. Mott to George Williams, 1875; Thomas Settle to George Williams, February 23, 1875; W. A. Smith to George Williams, February 26, 1875; Governor C. H. Brodgen to George Williams, January 31, 1875; and V. S. Lusk to George Williams, March 15, 1875, all in Department of Justice Records (microfilm, reel 2, M1345).

130. C. H. Brogden et al. to Geo. H. Williams, January 31, 1875, ibid.

131. V. S. Lusk to Atty. Gen. Edwards Pierrepoint, July 14, 1875, ibid.

132. Whitener, *Prohibition in North Carolina,* 79.

133. *Asheville Citizen,* February 25, 1876. See also *Blue Ridge Blade,* May 9, August 8, 1876.

134. W. S. Tate to Thomas Settle, June 14, 1876, Thomas Settle Papers, Southern Historical Collection.

135. Robert Dick to Thomas Settle, September 7, 1876, ibid.

136. A. C. Bryan to Thomas Settle, January 1, 1873, ibid.

137. *Asheville Citizen,* July 8, 1875; Howe, *Taxation and Taxes,* 220–21.

138. A bushel of corn sold for $1.00 and a gallon of whiskey retailed at $1.50 in 1875. See Account Book of Isaac Jarratt, 1875, Jarratt-Puryear Family Papers, Special Collections, Duke University.

139. Moonshiners in 1875 continued to earn a $5.50 profit on every five gallons of alcohol they produced.

140. Miller, *Revenuers & Moonshiners,* 121.

141. McKinney, *Southern Mountain Republicans,* 97.

142. J. J. Mott to F.A. Sewell, October 11, 1876, Bureau of Internal Revenue Records.

143. *New Regime,* February 12, 1876.

144. Vance won in nineteen of the twenty-three mountain counties (votes for Ashe, Catawba, and Swain were not listed). Western North Carolinians also gave 64 percent of their votes to Democratic presidential candidate Samuel Tilden. Computed from Matthews, *North Carolina Votes.*

145. Testimony of D. C. Person, "Sixth District of North Carolina," 323.

146. Testimony of J. J. Mott, ibid., 366.

5. Civilization Requires Prohibition

Epigraph: From *Blue Ridge Blade,* February 26, 1881.

1. J. J. Mott to Hon. Green B. Raum, November 12, 1877, Bureau of Internal Revenue Records.

2. Green B. Raum to John J. Mott, June 16, 1877, in "Enforcement of Internal Revenue Laws . . . Report of the Commissioner of Internal Revenue to the Secretary of the Treasury, in Reply to House Resolution of February 10, 1880, Making Inquiry for Information Tending to Explain the Necessity for Employment of Armed Men in Enforcement of the Internal Revenue Laws," *House Executive Documents* 62, 46th Cong., 2nd sess., 101.

3. Testimony of Green B. Raum, "Sixth District of North Carolina," 293.

4. Testimony of J. J. Mott, ibid., 368.

5. For more on the New South, see Galvin Wright, *Old South, New South: Revolutions in the Southern Economy since the Civil War* (New York: Basic Books, 1986); James C. Cobb, *Industrialization and Southern Society, 1877–1984* (Lexington: University Press of Kentucky, 1984); Dwight B. Billings, *Planters and the Making of the "New South": Class, Politics, and Development in North Carolina, 1865–1900* (Chapel Hill: University of North Carolina Press, 1979); Paul M. Gaston, *The New South Creed: A Study in Southern Mythmaking* (New York: Alfred A. Knopf, 1970); and C. Vann Woodward, *Origins of the New South, 1877–1913* (Baton Rouge: Louisiana State University Press, 1951).

6. Thomas L. Clingman, *Selections from the Speeches and Writings of Hon. Thomas L. Clingman of North Carolina* (Raleigh, NC: John Nichols, 1878), 124–26. See also Thomas E. Jeffrey, *Thomas Lanier Clingman: Fire Eater from the North Carolina Mountains* (Athens: University of Georgia Press, 1999), 222–24.

7. H. P. Gatchell, *Western North Carolina, Its Resources, Mineral Wealth, Climate, Salubriety, and Scenery* (Asheville, NC: E. J. Aston, 1870), quoted in Starnes, *Creating the Land of the Sky,* 25–26.

8. Ibid.

9. For a discussion of antebellum western North Carolinians' demands for a railroad, see Inscoe, *Mountain Masters,* 152.

10. *Asheville Citizen,* July 10, 1873.

11. *Lenoir Topic,* March 9, 1878.

12. By 1879, the Asheville-Spartanburg Railroad reached the community of Saluda, located in western Polk County. See Anne Osborne and Charlene Pace, *Saluda, N.C.: One Hundred Years, 1881–1981* (Saluda, NC: Holly Hill Publishers, 1981). For a detailed discussion of the construction of the WNCRR and Asheville-Spartanburg Railroad, see William H. Abrams Jr., "The Western North Carolina Railroad, 1855–1894" (MA thesis, Western Carolina University, 1976), 1–32; Allen W. Trelease, *The North Carolina Railroad, 1849–1871, and the Modernization of North Carolina* (Chapel Hill: University of North Carolina Press, 1991), 122–26; William D. Cotton, "Appalachian North Carolina: A Political Study" (PhD diss., University of North Carolina at Chapel Hill, 1954), 36–44; Blackmun, *Western North Carolina,* 377–79, 391–97; Van Noppen and Van Noppen, *Western North Carolina since the Civil War;* and Starnes, *Creating the Land of the Sky,* 24.

13. Cotton, "Appalachian North Carolina," 22–23.

14. Lee B. Weathers, *The Living Past of Cleveland County: A History* (1956; reprint, Spartanburg, SC: Reprint Company, Publishers, 1980), 181; James D. Marler, *Heritage of Cleveland County* (Shelby, NC: Cleveland County Historical Association, 1982), 162.

15. Cotton, "Appalachian North Carolina," 56–57.

16. Crawford, *Ashe County's Civil War,* 165; Fletcher, *Ashe County,* 224–25.

17. Jennifer Bauer Wilson, *Roan Mountain: A Passage of Time* (Winston-Salem, NC: John F. Blair, 1991), 75–77.

18. Crawford, *Ashe County's Civil War,* 164–65.

19. Williams, *History of Jackson County,* 614–15; John Preston Arthur, *A History of Watauga County, North Carolina, with Sketches of Prominent Families* (Richmond: Everett Waddey, 1915), 267.

20. Wellman, *Kingdom of Madison,* 112.

21. Weathers, *Living Past of Cleveland County,* 174–76; Marler, *Heritage of Cleveland County,* 162; J. G. Hollingsworth, *History of Surry County, or Annals of Northwest North Carolina* (J. G. Hollingsworth, 1935), 158–59; Phifer, *Burke,* 244; Charles Preslar Jr., *A History of Catawba County* (Salisbury, NC: Rowan Printing Co., 1954), 184–86.

22. These counties were Alexander, Yancey, Haywood, Cherokee, Caldwell, Jackson, Madison, Catawba, McDowell, Wilkes, Burke, Buncombe, Rutherford, Surry, and Cleveland. See U.S. Census Office, *The Statistics of Wealth and Industry . . . Ninth Census: 1870* (Washington, DC: Government Printing Office, 1872), 554–55, and *Report on the Manufacturers . . . Tenth Census: 1880* (Washington, DC: Government Printing Office, 1883), 159–60. Census enumerators did not record capital invested in manufacturing in 1870 and 1880 in Ashe, Clay, Graham, Macon, Mitchell, Swain, Transylvania, and Watauga counties.

23. See U.S. Census Office, *Manufacturers of the United States . . . Eighth Census: 1860* (Washington, DC: Government Printing Office, 1865), 420–35.

24. *Raleigh Observer,* October 17, 1877, quoted in Jeffrey, *Thomas Lanier Clingman,* 224.

25. Logan, *Sketches, Historical and Biographical, of the Broad River and King's Mountain Baptist Associations*, 130, 218.

26. In 1830, the per capita consumption of absolute alcohol was 3.9 gallons. Forty years later, that number had fallen to 1.3 gallons. See Rorabaugh, *Alcoholic Republic*, 232.

27. William Cowles to the North Carolina Superior Court, 1874, 1875, Alexander County Miscellaneous Records, North Carolina State Archives.

28. U.S. Census Office, *Agriculture of the United States in 1860 . . . The Eighth Census* (Washington, DC: Government Printing Office, 1864), 105–9; U.S. Census Office, *Report of the Productions of Agriculture . . . Tenth Census: 1880* (Washington, DC: Government Printing Office, 1883), 128–29.

29. *Asheville Pioneer*, June 15, 29, 1871.

30. Hayes, *Land of Wilkes*, 180–81.

31. Whitener, *Prohibition in North Carolina*, 54–55.

32. These county seats were Bakersville, Brevard, Charleston, Franklin, Hendersonville, Hickory, Jefferson, Lenoir, Marion, Marshall, Murphy, Robbinsville, Waynesville, Webster, and Wilkesboro. See *Spirit of the Age*, October 9, 1875.

33. Hollingsworth, *History of Surry County*, 158–60.

34. Robbinsville had a population of sixty-one, and Dodson had ninety-five residents. See U.S. Census Office, *Statistics of the Population of the United States at the Tenth Census* (Washington, DC: Government Printing Office, 1883), 278–85.

35. Petition from Shelby residents to the General Assembly, 1873, Petitions, General Assembly Session Records.

36. Petition from Morganton residents to the General Assembly, 1873, ibid.

37. Charles A. Israel, *Before Scopes: Evangelicalism, Education, and Evolution in Tennessee, 1870–1925* (Athens: University of Georgia Press, 2004), 79–81.

38. *William Wilson Memoir* (privately owned), 76.

39. Logan, *Sketches, Historical and Biographical, of the Broad River and King's Mountain Baptist Associations*, 218.

40. *Friend of Temperance*, August 20, 1873; York, *Autobiography of Brantley York*, 57; J. Alex Mull, *Tales of Old Burke* (Morganton, NC: News Herald Press, 1975), 101–5.

41. *Friend of Temperance*, September 24, 1873.

42. Petition from Asheville residents to the General Assembly, 1873, Petitions, General Assembly Session Records.

43. *Asheville Citizen*, February 28, 1874.

44. See petition from Ashe County residents to the General Assembly, 1873; petition from Henderson County residents to the General Assembly, 1874; and petition from Rutherfordton residents to the General Assembly, 1874, all in Petitions, General Assembly Session Records.

45. Petition from Morganton residents to the General Assembly, 1873, Petitions, General Assembly Session Records.

46. By the 1880s, Virginia, Georgia, and Mississippi relied on local-option laws to combat King Alcohol. In fact, by the late 1890s, four-fifths of Mississippi's counties would become "dry" as a result of local-option legislation. See Blocker, *American Temperance Movements*, 89.

47. I could not identify the exact locale of eight places where local option was passed, so I subtracted these places, bringing the total to 106 instead of 114. See *Laws of North Carolina* (1872–1873), 60–61, 108–9, 285–89; *Laws of North Carolina* (1873–1874), 216–25; *Laws of North Carolina* (1874–1875), 125–26, 184–85, 319–21; *Laws of North Carolina* (1876–1877), 179–80, 481–83; and *Laws of North Carolina* (1878–1879), 314–18.

48. County seats that enacted local-option laws were Asheville, Bakersville, Boone, Brevard, Burnsville, Charleston, Dobson, Franklin, Hendersonville, Jefferson, Lenoir, Marshall, Morganton, Robbinsville, Rutherfordton, Shelby, Sparta, Taylorsville, Waynesville, Webster, and Wilkesboro.

49. Five of the churches along the Buncombe Turnpike were located in Hominy Creek, Weaverville, and Leicester, all of which were in Buncombe County. Another church was located in Swannanoa in Buncombe County, which served as a major stage line connecting Asheville to the eastern part of the state. The remaining three churches were located in McDowell County, all of which were situated along the WNCRR.

50. *Friend of Temperance*, August 20, 1873.

51. Edward King, "The Great South: Among the Mountains of Western North Carolina," *Scribner's Monthly* 7 (March 1874): 524–25.

52. See petition from Morganton ladies to the General Assembly, 1873, and petition from Shelby ladies to the General Assembly, 1873, both in Petitions, General Assembly Session Records.

53. *Asheville Citizen*, November 27, 1873. See also *Friend of Temperance*, July 2, 1873.

54. *Asheville Pioneer*, February 28, 1874.

55. *Raleigh Sentinel*, April 16, 1874.

56. *Rutherfordton Star and Record*, January 16, 1875.

57. *New Regime*, February 19, 1876.

58. *Blue Ridge Blade*, February 8, 1879.

59. *Lenoir Topic*, November 24, 1877; *Hickory Piedmont Press*, December 15, 1877; *Asheville Citizen* January 2, 1879.

60. Quoted in *Asheville Citizen*, December 12, 1878.

61. Ibid., April 13, 1879.

62. *Hendersonville Independent Herald*, May 18, 1882.

63. *Asheville Citizen*, December 5, 1878.

64. Ibid., April 3, 1879.

65. J. G. de Roulhac Hamilton, ed., *The Papers of Randolph Abbott Shotwell*, 3 vols. (Raleigh: North Carolina Historical Commission, 1929–1931), 2:284.

66. Testimony of A. T. Davidson, "Sixth District of North Carolina," 434. See also testimony of A. H. Brooks, ibid., 145, and testimony of W. J. Coite, ibid., 235.

67. Miller, *Revenuers & Moonshiners*, 97–100.

68. In 1876, the federal government consolidated the Sixth and Seventh Collection Districts of North Carolina. The newly formed Sixth Collection District included the mountain counties of Wilkes, Alexander, Catawba, Ashe, Alleghany, Watauga, Yancey, Mitchell, McDowell, Burke, Caldwell, Rutherford, Cleveland, Polk, Henderson, Transylvania, Buncombe, Madison, Haywood, Jackson, Macon, Cherokee, and Clay. Surry County remained in the Fifth Collection District.

69. Testimony of Green Raum, "Sixth District of North Carolina," 291–92.

70. *Annual Report, Commissioner of Internal Revenue, 1879, House Executive Documents*, 46th Cong., 2nd sess., iv.

71. The use of federal troops to enforce the liquor law officially ended in 1879, when the Democratic-controlled Congress passed the Posse Comitatus Act. See Miller, *Revenuers & Moonshiners*, 80–81.

72. Ibid., 102–4.

73. "Enforcement of Internal Revenue Laws," 102–7; *Lenoir Topic*, January 12, 1878; *Asheville Citizen*, July 4, 1878, February 13, 1879; *Blue Ridge Blade*, September 7, December 14, 1878, April 12, May 30, September 20, 1879; *Asheville Semi-Weekly Journal*, April 2, 1879.

74. *Asheville Citizen*, February 14, 1878.

75. *Lenoir Topic*, October 19, 1878.

76. Robert Dick, March 1, 1878, Source Chronological Files: Letters Received by the Department of Justice from North Carolina, Record Group 60, Department of Justice Records. Miller, *Revenuers & Moonshiners*, 104–5.

77. *Annual Report, Commissioner of Internal Revenue, 1878, House Executive Documents*, 42nd Cong., 2nd sess., xxxiii; ibid., 1880, 46th Cong., 2nd sess., xiii.

78. J. J. Mott to G. B. Raum, June 17, 1878, in "Enforcement of Internal Revenue Laws," 105.

79. Robert Dick, March 1, 1878. For more examples of moonshine violence during the late 1870s, see J. J. Mott to G. B. Raum, October 8, December 30, 1877, July 5, 1878, April 12, 1879, all in "Enforcement of Internal Revenue Laws," 102, 103, 106, 108; *Lenoir Topic*, October 13, 1877; *Asheville Citizen*, April 25, July 4, 1878; *Blue Ridge Blade*, September 7, 1878, April 12, May 30, 1879; and "Sixth District of North Carolina," 285, 469, 472, 476, 478, 538.

80. Testimony of T. K. Davis, "Sixth District of North Carolina," 285.

81. Miller, *Revenuers & Moonshiners*, 107.

82. North Carolina's Sixth Collection District ranked fifth in the total number of officers killed and wounded in the suppression of illicit distillation in the South, behind Georgia's Second Collection District (five killed, twelve wounded), South Carolina (five killed, ten wounded), Tennessee's Second District (five killed, two wounded), and Tennessee's Fifth District (two killed, six wounded). See "Enforcement of Internal Revenue Laws," 210.

83. Ayers, *Vengeance and Justice*, 263; Miller, *Revenuers & Moonshiners*, 52–53.

84. J. J. Mott to G. B. Raum, June 17, 1878, in "Enforcement of Internal Revenue Laws," 105.

85. W. H. Chapman to J. J. Mott, April 18, 1879, ibid., 108.

86. Testimony of George Smathers, "Sixth District of North Carolina," 475.

87. Testimony of Green Raum, ibid., 292.

88. H. C. Rogers to J. J. Mott, October 26, 1878, in "Enforcement of Internal Revenue Laws," 106–7; *Asheville Citizen,* October 31, 1878.

89. *Lenoir Topic,* August 31, 1878.

90. *Asheville Citizen,* October 31, 1878.

91. Ibid., November 14, 1878.

92. *Annual Report, Attorney General, 1874, 1876, 1878, 1880.*

93. Miller, *Revenuers & Moonshiners,* 121.

94. Robert Dick to Attorney General Charles Devens, September 22, 1877, Source Chronological Files: Letters Received by the Department of Justice from North Carolina, Record Group 60, Department of Justice Records; testimony of A. T. Davidson, "Sixth District of North Carolina," 426; *Asheville Citizen,* April 19, 1877.

95. Miller, *Revenuers & Moonshiners,* 139, 181.

96. *Blue Ridge Blade,* May 9, August 8, 1876; *Lenoir Topic,* October 13, 1877; *Asheville Citizen,* January 17, 31, July 4, 1878, November 13, 20, 1879; *Asheville Semi-Weekly Journal,* April 2, 1879.

97. Testimony of J. A. Ramsey, "Sixth District of North Carolina," 100; testimony of Tyre Green, ibid., 127.

98. Testimony of M. G. Campbell, Tyre Green, A. H. Brooks, D. C. Pearson, and J. J. Mott, all in ibid., 114, 124, 150, 323, 367.

99. *Asheville Semi-Weekly Journal,* April 2, 1879.

100. Testimony of W. J. Coite, "Sixth District of North Carolina," 232.

101. Testimony of T. K. Bruner, ibid., 215.

102. Testimony of T. K. Davis, ibid., 286, 289.

103. Testimony of A. C. Avery, ibid., 441.

104. Testimony of J. J. Mott and Green Raum, ibid., 295–96, 367.

105. Miller, *Revenuers & Moonshiners,* 19–20.

106. Testimony of W. M. Walker, "Sixth District of North Carolina," 161.

107. Testimony of Tyre Green, ibid., 128. See also testimony of J. J. Mott, and D. C. Pearson, ibid., 322, 367–69.

108. "Enforcement of the Internal Revenue Laws," 211; *Annual Report, Commissioner of Internal Revenue, 1880, House Executive Documents,* 42nd Cong., 2nd sess., xxiv.

109. *Annual Report, Commissioner of Internal Revenue, 1880,* x.

110. J. J. Mott to G. B. Raum, January 16, 1880, in "Enforcement of Internal Revenue Laws," 109.

111. Testimony of M. L. McCorkle, "Sixth District of North Carolina," 457.

112. Testimony of J. A. Ramsay, ibid., 99; testimony of J. R. Henderson, ibid., 351.

113. Testimony of M. G. Campbell, ibid., 115; testimony of T. K. Davis, ibid., 286.

114. Testimony of T. K. Davis, ibid., 286. See also J. J. Mott to G. B. Raum, January 16, 1880, in "Enforcement of Internal Revenue Laws," 109.

115. For scholarship chronicling the decline of economic prosperity in southern Appalachia after the Civil War, see Waller, *Feud;* Dunn, *Cades Cove;* Weise, *Grasping at Independence;* Eller, *Miners, Millhands, and Mountaineers;* and McKinney, *Southern Mountain Republicans.*

116. Burke County experienced a 39 percent decline in farm acreage, while the size of farms in Rutherford County decreased 34 percent and those in Wilkes County farms declined 21 percent. Graham and Swain counties were not included in these census reports. See U.S. Census Office, *Statistics of Wealth and Industry . . . Ninth Census,* 359–60, and *Report of the Productions of Agriculture . . . Tenth Census,* 128–29.

117. V. S. Lusk to Attorney General, December 3, 1878, Source Chronological Files: Letters Received by the Department of Justice from North Carolina, Record Group 60, Department of Justice Records.

118. Testimony of W. M. Walker, "Sixth District of North Carolina," 158–59.

119. *Asheville Citizen,* December 12, 1878.

120. *Lenoir Topic,* June 12, 1879.

121. Testimony of J. J. Mott, "Sixth District of North Carolina," 367–68; J. J. Mott to G. B. Raum, January 31, 1879, in "Enforcement of Internal Revenue Laws," 107.

122. *Asheville Citizen,* April 3, 1879.

123. Testimony of Tyre Green, "Sixth District of North Carolina," 130.

124. *Blue Ridge Blade,* May 8, 1880.

125. "Enforcement of Internal Revenue Laws," 205.

126. Testimony of W. M. Walker, "Sixth District of North Carolina," 159–60.

127. Testimony of A. T. Davidson, ibid., 430.

128. Testimony of J. M. Leach, ibid., 276.

129. Testimony of A. C. Avery, ibid., 438. See also testimony of M. L. McCorkle, ibid., 453.

130. *New York Times,* August 1, 1881.

131. Whitener, *Prohibition in North Carolina,* 61–66.

132. *Asheville Citizen,* February 18, 1881.

133. McKinney, *Southern Mountain Republicans,* 99–108.

134. *New York Times,* February 22, March 8, 1881.

135. *Asheville Weekly Citizen,* March 10, 1881.

136. *New York Times,* March 8, 1881.

137. Zebulon Vance to Theodore Davidson, January 13, 1887, *Vance Papers.*

138. Whitener, *Prohibition in North Carolina,* 64.

139. S. V. Hoyle to Samuel Tate, January 13, 1881, Samuel McDowell Tate Papers, 1810–1918, #710, Southern Historical Collection.

140. W. S. Pearson to Samuel Tate, February 2, 1881, ibid.

141. *Laws of North Carolina* (1881), 554–58.

142. *New York Times,* June 2, 10, 1881.

143. *Statesville American,* July 2, 1881.

144. McKinney, *Zeb Vance,* 355.

145. Miller, *Revenuers & Moonshiners,* 172.

146. J. J. Mott to Green B. Raum, July 1, 1881, Miscellaneous Official Letters Received by the Commissioner of Internal Revenue, Record Group 58, Bureau of Internal Revenue, National Archives, College Park, MD.

147. Miller, *Revenuers & Moonshiners,* 171.

148. *Newton Enterprise,* July 23, 1881; *Marion Lamp Post,* July 20, 1881; *Lenoir Topic,* May 19, June 2, 9, 16, 30, July 7, 21, 1881; *Asheville Citizen,* July 21, 1881.

149. *Lenoir Topic,* June 30, 1881.

150. Ibid., July 21, 1881.

151. Ibid., July 7, 1881.

152. *Marion Lamp Post,* July 20, 1881.

153. *Lenoir Topic,* July 7, 1881.

154. Ibid., July 21, 1881.

155. Ibid., July 7, 1881.

156. *Asheville Weekly Citizen,* July 21, 1881.

157. *State Journal,* July 6, 1881.

158. *Lenoir Topic,* July 7, 1881.

159. Ibid., June 9, 1881.

160. *Asheville Weekly Citizen,* July 21, 1881.

161. *Lenoir Topic,* June 30, 1881.

162. *Asheville Weekly Citizen,* July 21, 1881.

163. *Newton Enterprise,* July 23, 1881.

164. *Asheville Weekly Citizen,* July 21, 1881.

165. A total of 48,370 North Carolina voters favored the bill. See Whitener, *Prohibition in North Carolina,* 73.

166. Thirty-three percent of highlanders favored statewide prohibition, while only 21 percent of other Tar Heels voted to pass the bill. See ibid., appendix.

167. An analysis of the four mountain counties where prohibition nearly succeeded (Cleveland, Haywood, Mitchell, and Buncombe) suggests that industrialization helped shape attitudes on alcohol reform. Haywood County had the third highest percentage increase of capital invested in manufacturing in the Carolina highlands between 1870 and 1880. Meanwhile, Buncombe, Cleveland, and Mitchell counties were among the mountain region's leaders in the total amount of money invested in industry during the decade. Of the five mountain counties that invested the most capital in manufacturing in 1880, Mitchell ranked second, Buncombe fourth, and Cleveland fifth. See U.S. Census Office, *Report on the Manufacturers . . . Tenth Census,* 159–60.

6. "These Big-Boned, Semi-Barbarian People"

Epigraph: From a western North Carolina folksong, quoted in Emma Bell Miles, *The Spirit of the Mountains* (New York: J. Pott, 1905), 148.

1. *Asheville Semi-Weekly Citizen,* January 4, 1883.

2. *Asheville Weekly Citizen,* November 13, 1889.

3. The most popular of these magazines were *Harper's Weekly, Lippincott's, Scribner's, The Living Age, The Century,* and *Appleton's Journal.* On the rise of these magazines, see Shapiro, *Appalachia on Our Mind,* and Ohmann, *Selling Culture.*

4. For more on the local color "movement," see Shapiro, *Appalachia on Our Mind;* Rowe, *Enchanted Country;* Whisnant, *All That Is Native and Fine;* and O'Donnell and Hollingsworth, *Seekers of Scenery.*

5. Harkins, *Hillbilly,* 29.

6. For a discussion of feuding and the creation of violent Appalachia, see Shapiro, *Appalachia on Our Mind;* Batteau, *Invention of Appalachia;* and Altina Waller, "Feuding in Appalachia: Evolution of a Cultural Stereotype," in *Appalachia in the Making,* 347–76.

7. Charles Lanman, "Novelties of Southern Scenery," *Appleton's Journal* (October 16–30, 1869): 257–61, 296–97, 327–29.

8. "Nineteenth-century landscape viewing in America has roots in British aristocratic traditions. The term 'picturesque' originated in eighteenth-century British aesthetic discourse. Edmund Burke's widely circulated *Philosophical Enquiry into the Origin of Our Ideas of the Sublime and Beautiful* (1757) helped to set the stage, by establishing the meanings of two related terms: 'sublime' and 'beautiful.' According to Burke, scenery that is wild, untamed, disordered, and terrifying is sublime. Scenery that is pastoral, lush, ordered, and serene is beautiful. A third term, 'picturesque,' was coined by a British cleric, William Gilpin, after Burke's treatise had circulated. In Gilpin's view, a picturesque scene contains elements both sublime and beautiful. Gilpin popularized the use of all three terms, roaming the countryside and using 'sublime,' 'beautiful,' and 'picturesque' in a series of essays to categorize specific landscape views. To Gilpin and his late eighteenth-century British adherents, a picturesque landscape was the most desirable." O'Donnell and Hollingsworth, *Seekers of Scenery,* 12.

9. Sue Rainey, *Creating Picturesque America: Monument to the Natural and Cultural Landscape* (Nashville, TN: Vanderbilt University Press, 1994), 22.

10. Paul Herman Buck, *The Road to Reunion, 1865–1900* (Boston: Little, Brown, 1937); Rowe, *Enchanted Country;* O'Donnell and Hollingsworth, *Seekers of Scenery.*

11. H. E. Colton, "A Farm on the French Broad," *Appleton's Journal* 4 (December 17, 1870): 737–38; H. E. Colton, "Mountain Island," *Appleton's Journal* 5 (January 17, 1871): 15–18; H. E. Colton, "Reems's Creek and the Old Mill," *Appleton's Journal* 5 (February 4, 1871): 135–37.

12. Christian Reid, *The Land of the Sky; or Adventures in Mountain Byways* (New York: D. Appleton, 1890), 22, 33–40.

13. For additional "scenic entrepreneur" works on the Carolina highlands, see Jehu Lewis, "The Grandfather of North Carolina," *Lakeside Monthly* 10 (September 1873): 218–24; Constance Fenimore Woolson, "The French Broad," *Harper's Monthly* 50 (April 1875): 617–36; and George Dimmock, "A Trip to Mt. Mitchell in North Carolina," *Appalachia* 1 (June 1877), 141–51.

14. Reid, *Land of the Sky,* 7.

15. David Hunter Strother, "The Mountains," *Harper's Magazine* 44 (May 1872): 800.

16. King, "The Great South," 521.

17. Rebecca Harding Davis, "Qualla," *Lippincott's Monthly Magazine* 16 (November 1875): 577. See also other works by Rebecca Harding Davis: "The Rose of Carolina," *Scribner's Monthly* 8 (October 1874): 723–26; "The Yares of the Black Mountains," *Lippincott's Monthly Magazine* 16 (July 1875): 35–47; and "A Night in the Mountains," *Appleton's Journal* 3 (July–December 1877), 505–10.

18. Woolson, "The French Broad," 630.

19. James Klotter, "The Black South and White Appalachia," *Journal of American History* 66 (March 1980): 832–49; Shapiro, *Appalachia on Our Mind*; Whisnant, *All That Is Native and Fine.*

20. Louise Coffin Jones, "In the Backwoods of Carolina," *Lippincott's Monthly Magazine* 24 (December 1879): 756.

21. Guernsey, "Illicit Distilling of Liquors," 733; A. H. Guernsey, "Hunting for Stills," *Harper's Weekly* 11 (December 21, 1867): 811.

22. *New York Times,* July 21, 1878. See also *New York Times,* March 15, July 19, October 27, 1877, July 19, December 22, 1878.

23. Ibid., February 2, 1880.

24. "The Moonshine Man: A Peep into His Haunts and Hiding Places," *Harper's Weekly* 21 (October 20, 1877): 821–22.

25. Constance Fenimore Woolson, "Up in the Blue Ridge," *Appleton's Journal* 5 (July–December 1878): 104–25.

26. *New York Times,* July 19, 21, December 22, 1878, February 2, July 5, 1880, May 25, July 23, 25, 1881.

27. See *Washington Post,* May 8, July 29, September 3, 1878; *National Police Gazette,* July 20, September 21, November 2, 1878; *Christian Union,* November 27, 1878; *Atlanta Daily Constitution,* August 3, 11, 17, 27, October 1, 1878; and *New York Times,* March 14, 15, 16, 19, July 15, 27, August 18, 20, 23, 25, 27, 28, 29, September 3, 29, November 2, 20, 27, 1878.

28. Edward B. Crittenden, *The Entwined Lives of Miss Gabrielle Austin, Daughter of the Late Rev. Ellis C. Austin, and of Redmond, the Outlaw, Leader of the North Carolina "Moonshiners"* (Philadelphia: Barclay & Co., 1879), 58, 63. In 1881, Redmond refuted the contents of this story. See R. A. Cobb, *The True Life of Maj. Richard Redmond, the Notorious and Famous Moonshiner, of Western North Carolina, Who Was Born in Swain County, N.C., in the Year 1855, and Arrested April 7th, 1881* (Raleigh, NC: Edwards, Broughton, and Co., 1881).

29. "Law and Moonshine," *Harper's Weekly* 24 (August 23, 1879): 667. See also "Moonshiners," *Harper's Weekly* 22 (November 2, 1878): 875; and "Moonshiners," *Harper's New Monthly Magazine* 59 (March 1879): 380–90.

30. Louise Coffin Jones, "In the Highlands of North Carolina," *Lippincott's Monthly Magazine* 32 (October 1883): 385.

31. "Studies in the South," *Atlantic Monthly* 49 (January 1882): 90.

32. Donald Baines, "Among the Moonshiners," *Dixie* 1 (August 1885): 10.

33. See also Rebecca Harding Davis, "By-Paths in the Mountains, III," *Harper's New Monthly Magazine* 61 (September 1880): 532–47; Sherwood Bonner, "Jack and the Mountain Pink," *Harper's Weekly* (January 29, 1881): 75–77; Sherwood Bonner, "The Case of Eliza Bleylock," *Harper's Weekly* (March 5, 1881): 155–57; George W. Atkinson, *After the Moonshiners, by One of the Raiders. A Book of Thrilling* (Wheeling, WV: Frew and Campbell Steam, Book and Job Printers, 1881); Jones, "In the Highlands of North Carolina," 385; Charles Dudley Warner, "On Horseback," *Atlantic Monthly* 56 (July 1885), 195–96; Morgan Bates and Elwyn A. Barron, *A Mountain Pink: Realistic Description among the Moonshiners of North Carolina, a Romantic Drama* (Milwaukee: Riverside Printing Co., 1885); "Home of the Moonshiners," *Harper's Weekly* 30 (October 23, 1886): 687–88; and Charles Dudley Warner, "Comments on Kentucky," *Harper's New Monthly Magazine* 78 (January 1889): 269–71.

34. James Lane Allen, "Through Cumberland Gap on Horseback," *Harper's New Monthly Magazine* 73 (June 1886): 60.

35. See Atkinson, *After the Moonshiners,* 15, 28, 32; Davis, "By-Paths in the Mountains, III," 533; "Home of the Moonshiners," 687–88; "Studies in the South," 91; Warner, "Comments on Kentucky," 270–71; Allen, "Through Cumberland Gap on Horseback," 66; and *New York Times,* February 2, 1880.

36. Baines, "Among the Moonshiners," 14.

37. Klotter, "Black South and White Appalachia," 832–49. See also Waller, "Feuding in Appalachia," 349, 361.

38. Klotter, "Black South and White Appalachia"; Nina Silber, *The Romance of Reunion: Northerners and the South, 1865–1900* (Chapel Hill: University of North Carolina Press, 1993), 143–58. See also Nina Silber, "'What Does America Need So Much as Americans?' Race and Northern Reconciliation with Southern Appalachia, 1870–1890," in *Appalachians and Race,* 245–58.

39. Van Noppen and Van Noppen, *Western North Carolina since the Civil War,* 251.

40. Starnes, *Creating the Land of the Sky,* 34.

41. *Asheville Citizen,* November 15, 1883, November 13, 1889; Joan Langley and Wright Langley, *Yesterday's Asheville* (Miami, FL: E. A. Seemann, 1975), 34.

42. *Asheville Semi-Weekly Citizen,* March 18, 1882.

43. Ibid., September 6, 1882.

44. *Morganton Mountaineer,* July 9, 1884.

45. For a discussion of the WNCRR and other railways, see Van Noppen and Van Noppen, *Western North Carolina since the Civil War,* 253–68; Starnes, *Creating the Land of the Sky,* 24–25; Abrams, "Western North Carolina Railroad."

46. *Charleston News and Courier,* July 21, 1886.

47. *Asheville Semi-Weekly Citizen,* July 1, 1882.

48. *Morganton Mountaineer,* July 2, 1884.

49. *Lenoir Topic,* April 18, 1883, quoted in Cotton, "Appalachian North Carolina," 64.

50. *Morganton Mountaineer,* March 31, 1883.

51. The fourteen counties that had a railroad before 1886 and experienced an increase in capital investment in manufacturing were Rutherford, Buncombe, Macon, Cleveland, Haywood, Clay, Caldwell, Catawba, Surry, Madison, Jackson, McDowell, Burke, and Henderson. Alleghany and Transylvania counties experienced an increase in capital investment in manufacturing but did not have access to a rail line. Swain and Graham counties were not included in the 1870 manufacturing census. See State Board of Agriculture, *Hand-Book of North Carolina, with Map of the State* (Raleigh, NC: P. M. Hale, State Printer and Binder, 1886); U.S. Census Office, *Report on the Manufacturers . . . Tenth Census: 1880,* 159–60; and U.S. Census Office, *Report on the Manufacturing Industries . . . Eleventh Census: 1890* (Washington, DC: Government Printing Office, 1895), 540–43.

52. These six counties were Ashe, Watauga, Wilkes, Alexander, Yancey, and Cherokee. The two counties that experienced a decrease in capital investment in manufacturing but had access to a rail line were Mitchell and Polk. See State Board of Agriculture, *Hand-Book of North Carolina;* State Board of Agriculture, *North Carolina and its Resources* (Winston, NC: M. I. & J. C. Stewart, Public Printers and Binders, 1896); U.S. Census Office, *Report on the Manufacturers . . . Tenth Census;* and U.S. Census Office, *Report on the Manufacturing Industries . . . Eleventh Census,* 540–43.

53. Starnes, *Creating the Land of the Sky,* 42–53.

54. *Asheville Citizen,* March 18, 1882, November 22, 1883; February 23, 1884; *Asheville Semi-Weekly Citizen,* July 1, September 6, 13, 1882; *Lenoir Topic,* July 4, 1883.

55. Preslar, *History of Catawba County,* 359; Weathers, *Living Past of Cleveland County,* 175–77, 182–83; Hollingsworth, *History of Surry County,* 159–60; Phifer, *Burke,* 238–45, 250; *Asheville Citizen,* September 18, 1881, February 15, 1882; *Lenoir Topic,* January 17, July 4, 1883, September 17, 1884; *Morganton Mountaineer,* August 11, November 14, 1883, April 30, July 9, 1884.

56. Marler, *Heritage of Cleveland County,* 158.

57. See U.S. Census Office, *Report on the Productions of Agriculture . . . Tenth Census,* 128–29; and U.S. Census Office, *Report on the Statistics of Agriculture . . . Eleventh Census: 1890* (Washington, DC: Government Printing Office, 1895), 168, 170.

58. Quoted in Phifer, *Burke,* 225–26.

59. *Lenoir Topic,* February 25, 1885.

60. Whenever possible, I derived population statistics from the 1880 and 1890 U.S. censuses. However, to formulate statistics for all the county seats, I also used several editions of *Branson's North Carolina Business Directory.* I derived population figures for Hayesville, Robbinsville, Columbus, Charleston, Boone, Burnsville, Bakersville, and Dodson from the 1884 and 1890 editions; for Taylorsville and Rutherfordton from the 1878 and 1890 editions; for

Sparta from the 1884 edition of *Branson's* and the 1890 U.S. census; and for Shelby from the 1880 U.S. census and the 1890 edition of *Branson's*.

61. Populations of non–county seat towns can be found in the 1889 edition of *Branson's North Carolina Business Directory*.

62. Starnes, *Creating the Land of the Sky*, 74.

63. *Asheville Semi-Weekly Citizen*, April 8, September 6, 1882, January 4, 1883.

64. Ibid., October 25, 1884.

65. *Lenoir Topic*, January 21, 1885. See also *Hendersonville Independent Herald*, May 18, 1882.

66. *Asheville Citizen*, November 14, 1878, August 30, 1879. See also *Asheville Citizen*, February 19, 27, 1879.

67. Cobb, *True Life of Maj. Richard Redmond*, iv. See also Crittenden, *Entwined Lives*.

68. *Asheville Citizen*, February 28, 1884. See also Zeigler and Grosscup, *Heart of the Alleghenies*.

69. *Asheville Citizen*, January 2, 1880.

70. *Rutherford Mountain Banner*, August 12, 1881.

71. *Lenoir Topic*, March 17, 1886.

72. *Asheville Citizen*, November 22, 1883.

73. See *Asheville Citizen*, November 4, 1885; *Hickory Western Carolinian*, September 30, 1887; *Highlands Blue Ridge Enterprise*, December 4, 1884; *Morganton Star*, March 27, 1885, August 15, 22, 1889; and *Lenoir Topic*, October 24, 1883, March 12, 1884, December 9, 1885.

74. *Lenoir Topic*, March 17, 1886.

75. *Highlands Blue Ridge Enterprise*, December 4, 1884.

76. S. T. Kelsey to D. D. Davies, February 26, 1885, box 97, Year Files, Department of Justice Records.

77. *Hickory Western Carolinian*, September 30, 1887.

78. *Morganton Star*, July 18, 1889.

79. Quoted in Cotton, "Appalachian North Carolina," 517.

80. *Lenoir Topic*, July 8, 22, 1885.

81. *Morganton Star*, January 11, 1889.

7. "Afloat on the Tide of Improvement"

Epigraph: From "The Drunkard's Last Drink," Appalachian folksong, quoted in Florence Cope Bush, *Dorie: Woman of the Mountains* (Knoxville: University of Tennessee Press, 1992), 17.

1. *North Wilkesboro Semi-Weekly Hustler*, March 13, 1900.

2. Ellen Myers, "The Mountain Whites of the South," *American Missionary* 39 (January 1885), quoted in Richard B. Drake, ed., "Documents Relating to the Mission to Appalachia," *Appalachian Notes* 3 (1975): 36–38.

3. Between 1885 and 1895, Presbyterians founded thirty-one missionary schools in the mountain region. Ten years later, that number had increased to sixty-five, with an enrollment of 8,478 students. The Protestant Episcopal Church

followed suit in 1889, starting a mission in the Ragged Mountains of Virginia. During the early 1890s, the Methodist Episcopal Church, North, also began mission work in the mountains. By 1908, the Episcopal dioceses of North Carolina, Tennessee, Kentucky, and West Virginia had established schools and churches in their highland districts. See Shapiro, *Appalachia on Our Mind,* 55–56; Richard Drake, "The Mission School Era in Southern Appalachia: 1880–1940," *Appalachian Notes* 6 (1978): 4; Ernest Trice Thompson, *Presbyterian Missions in the Southern United States* (Richmond, VA: Presbyterian Committee of Publication, 1934), 224–28; Elizabeth R. Hooker, *Religion in the Highlands: Native Churches and Missionary Enterprises in the Southern Appalachian Area* (New York: Home Missions Council, 1933), 199–202; and Samuel H. Thompson, *The Highlanders of the South* (New York: Eaton and Mains, 1910), 66–67.

4. Shapiro, *Appalachia on Our Mind,* 54–55; Van Noppen and Van Noppen, *Western North Carolina since the Civil War,* 159; Arthur, *Western North Carolina,* 439.

5. Jacqueline Burgin Painter, *The Season of Dorland-Bell: History of an Appalachian Mission School* (Boone, NC: Appalachian Consortium Press, 1996), 16–17; Shapiro, *Appalachia on Our Mind,* 55; Samuel Tyndale Wilson, *The Southern Mountaineers* (New York: Presbyterian Home Missions, 1906), 130; *Bryson City Times,* April 3, 1896.

6. Conrad Ostwalt and Phoebe Pollitt, "The Salem School and Orphanage: White Missionaries, Black School," in *Appalachians and Race,* 235–58; Wellman, *Kingdom of Madison,* 115–17; Clifford R. Lovin, "Religion," in *History of Jackson County,* 261; Van Noppen and Van Noppen, *Western North Carolina since the Civil War,* 80–81; Wilson, *Southern Mountaineers,* 130–31, 162; Edward Marshall Craig, *Highways and Byways of Appalachia: A Study of the Work of the Synod of Appalachia of the Presbyterian Church in the United States* (Kingsport, TN: Kingsport Press, 1927), 36–41, 74–78; Fletcher, *Ashe County,* 174–75; H. Paul Douglas, *Christian Reconstruction in the South* (Boston: Pilgrim Press, 1909), 356–58; R. P. Smith, *Some Results of the Mission Work in Western North Carolina* (Asheville, NC: Home Mission Committee of the Asheville Presbytery, 1905), 7–14; David E. Whisnant, "Susan G. Chester and the Log Cabin Settlement: First Social Settlement Institution in the Southern Mountains," 15–16, David Eugene Whisnant Papers, #4326, Southern Historical Collection; Michael C. Hardy, *A Short History of Old Watauga County* (Boone, NC: Parkway Publishers, 2005), 112; Fletcher, *Ashe County,* 179–80; *Morganton Herald,* January 5, 1899.

7. Starnes, *Creating the Land of the Sky,* 151–52; Becker, *Selling Tradition,* 63–66; Allen H. Eaton, *Handicrafts of the Southern Highlands* (New York: Russell Sage Foundation, 1937), 64–68; Frances Goodrich, *Mountain Homespun* (New Haven, CT: Yale University Press, 1931), 21–23.

8. Whisnant, "Susan G. Chester and the Log Cabin Settlement," 17; *Asheville Weekly Citizen,* April 14, June 16, July 14, 1892.

9. Whisnant, "Susan G. Chester and the Log Cabin Settlement," 7–8.

10. *Philadelphia Church Standard,* June 17, 1893; Whisnant, "Susan G. Chester and the Log Cabin Settlement," 7–8, 12–13, 15–26.

11. "Report from the Mountain Schools," *American Missionary* 44 (June 1890): 184; "Among the Great Smoky Mountains," *American Missionary* 45 (March 1891): 96; "Seeking in the Wilderness," *American Missionary* 45 (March 1891): 99; "From the Mountains," *American Missionary* 48 (June 1894): 235; Miss Kate C. La Grange, "Big Creek Seminary, Tenn.," *American Missionary* 53 (October 1899): 124; Mrs. D. L. Pierson, "The Mountaineers of Madison County, N.C." *Missionary Review of the World* 10 (November 1897): 825.

12. Pierson, "Mountaineers of Madison County, N.C.," 824–25; see also Waller, "Feuding in Appalachia," 347–76.

13. Mary Murfree, "The Mountaineers at Hoho-Hebee Falls," *Harper's Weekly* 37 (September 23, 30, 1893); Will Allen Dromgoole, *Spurrier with the Wildcats and Moonshiners* (Nashville, TN: University Press, 1892); William M. Brewer, "Moonshining in Georgia," *Cosmopolitan* 12 (June 1897): 127–34; Francis Lynde "The Moonshiners of Fact," *Lippincott's Magazine* 57 (January 1896): 66–76; Emil O. Peterson, "A Glimpse of the Moonshiners," *Chautauquan* 26 (November 1897): 178–82; B. G. McFall, *Among the Moonshiners, or, A Drunkard's Legacy: A Temperance Drama in Three Acts* (Clyde, OH: Ames, 1897); Bernard Francis Moore, *The Moonshiner's Daughter: A Play of Mountain Life in Three Acts* (Boston: Walter H. Baker, 1898); Will Allen Dromgoole, *A Moonshiner's Son* (Philadelphia: Penn Publishing Co., 1898); "North Carolina Romance," *New York Times,* December 25, 1898; C. W. Waite, *Among the Moonshiners* (New York: F. T. Neely, 1899); J. C. L. Harris, "A True Story of Life among the Moonshiners of the Blue Ridge," *Raleigh News and Observer,* January 19, 1899; Samuel G. Blythe, "Raiding Moonshiners" *Munsey's Magazine* 25 (June 1901): 418–24; Leonidas Hubbard Jr., "The Moonshiner at Home" *Atlantic Monthly* 90 (August 1902): 234–41.

14. Margaret Johann, "A Little Moonshiner," *Christian Observer* 85 (July 21, 1897): 700–701.

15. "A Mountain Evangelist," *American Missionary* 45 (March 1891): 94; "Horse Needed," *American Missionary* 48 (March 1894): 135; "From the Mountains," 235; La Grange, "Big Creek Seminary," 124.

16. Mac E. Davis, *Home Mission Experiences in the Mountains of North Carolina* (Richmond, VA: Whittet and Shepperson, 1903), 9–13; *Asheville Semi-Weekly Citizen,* February 12, 1901.

17. J. T. Wilds, "The Mountain Whites of the South," *Missionary Review* 12 (December 1895): 923; *Waynesville Courier,* March 5, 1897; Robert F. Campbell, *Mission Work among the Mountain Whites in Asheville Presbytery, North Carolina* (Asheville, NC: Citizen Co., 1899), 1; *Lenoir Topic,* March 23, 1892; *Morganton Herald,* April 27, 1899.

18. *Waynesville Chronicle,* April 29, 1891, April 14, 1892; *Morganton Herald,* April 28, 1892; *Franklin Press,* March 4, 1891; *Lenoir Topic,* September 17, 1890, September 23, 1891, August 23, 1893; July 24, 1895, January 17, 1898; *Lenoir Semi-Weekly News,* July 3, 1900.

19. Cornelius Miller Pickens, July 5, 1892, Rev. Cornelius Miller Pickens Diary, 1892–1901, Special Collections, Duke University.

20. Campbell, *Mission Work among the Mountain Whites*, 5.

21. *Lenoir Topic*, March 23, 1892.

22. *North Wilkesboro News*, September 19, 1895; *Lenoir Topic*, August 21, October 23, 1895; *Franklin Press*, January 23, 1901; *Raleigh News and Observer*, February 22, 1903; *Lenoir News*, December 6, 1907; *Morganton News-Herald*, November 21, 1907; *Waynesville Courier*, January 16, May 21, 1908.

23. For more on the Woman's Christian Temperance Union, see Link, *Paradox of Southern Progressivism*; Jonathan Zimmerman, *Distilling Democracy: Alcohol Education in America's Public Schools, 1880–1925* (Lawrence: University Press of Kansas, 1999); Anne Firor Scott, *The Southern Lady from Pedestal to Politics, 1880–1930* (Chicago: University of Chicago Press, 1970); Jean F. Friedman, *The Enclosed Garden: Women and Community in the Evangelical South* (Chapel Hill: University of North Carolina Press, 1985); Barbara Leslie Epstein, *The Politics of Domesticity: Women, Evangelicalism, and Temperance in Nineteenth-Century America* (Middleton, CT: Wesleyan University, 1981); Carol Mattingly, *Well-Tempered Women: Nineteenth-Century Temperance Rhetoric* (Carbondale: Southern Illinois University Press, 1998); and Ruth Bordin, *Women and Temperance: The Quest for Power and Liberty, 1873–1900* (Philadelphia: Temple University Press, 1981).

24. J. D. Eggleston, *Asheville and Vicinity* (Atlanta, GA: Franklin Printing and Publishing Co., 1896), 23.

25. *Blue Ridge Enterprise*, February 15, 1883; *Hickory Press and Carolinian*, November 17, 1887; *Tuckaseige Democrat*, July 16, 1890, September 23, 1891, February 21, April 23, May 30, 1895; *Asheville Weekly Citizen*, December 13, 1891, June 16, July 14, August 18, 1892; *Hickory Western Carolinian*, September 23, 1887; *Wilkesboro Chronicle*, April 30, June 4, 1896; *Asheville Semi-Weekly Citizen*, April 16, 1901.

26. *Blue Ridge Enterprise*, February 15, 1883.

27. *Tuckaseige Democrat*, September 23, 1891.

28. *Asheville Weekly Citizen*, July 14, 1892; *Wilkesboro Chronicle*, April 30, 1896; *Tuckaseige Democrat*, July 16, 1890.

29. Petitions of the WCTU in regard to regulating instruction in public schools, January–March 1887, Petitions, General Assembly Session Records.

30. *Laws of North Carolina* (1891), 154. The law also stipulated that teachers were required to pass an examination on these subjects, and failure to teach them was cause for dismissal. For a discussion of the WCTU's campaign for scientific temperance instruction, see Zimmerman, *Distilling Democracy*.

31. *Wilkesboro Chronicle*, October 7, 1903.

32. See Robert P. Porter, *Report on Population of the United States at the Eleventh Census: 1890, Part I* (Washington, DC: Government Printing Office, 1895), 33–34; Francis A. Walker, *The Statistics of the Population of the United States at the Ninth Census: 1870, Volume I* (Washington, DC: Government Printing Office, 1872), 549–50; and Henry K. Carroll, *Report on Statistics of Churches in the United States at the Eleventh Census: 1890* (Washington, DC: Government Printing Office, 1894), 74–75.

33. In western North Carolina, 255 churches, schools, and industrial facilities enacted local option between 1881 and 1890. I was unable to determine the exact location of 80 of them. Between 1871 and 1880, 27 percent of locales that enacted local option in western North Carolina were in non–county seats or communities with fewer than 100 residents. See *Laws of North Carolina* (1872–1873), 60–61, 108–9, 285–89; *Laws of North Carolina* (1873–1874), 216–25; *Laws of North Carolina* (1874–1875), 125–26, 184–85, 319–21; *Laws of North Carolina* (1876–1877), 179–80, 481–83; *Laws of North Carolina* (1881), 442–49; *Laws of North Carolina* (1883), 263–68, 443, 470; *Laws of North Carolina* (1885), 193–94; and *Laws of North Carolina* (1889), 356–60, 442–43.

34. Graham County is not included. See U.S. Census Office, *Report on the Manufacturing Industries . . . Eleventh Census*, 540–43; and U.S. Census Office, *Twelfth Census . . . 1900 . . . Manufacturers, Part II: States and Territories* (Washington, DC: U.S. Census Office, 1902), 664–66.

35. County seats grew 41 percent. See William R. Merriam, *Twelfth Census of the United States, 1900: Population, Part I* (Washington DC: U.S. Census Office, 1901), 286–95. I derived the population of Webster from the 1896 edition of *Branson's North Carolina Business Directory*. When calculating the total population of county seats in 1890, I did not include Robbinsville.

36. Population of non–county seat towns can be found in *Branson's North Carolina Business Directory, 1896*, and Merriam, *Twelfth Census of the United States*, 286–95.

37. These commercial centers served not only as marketplaces for goods but also as points where rural culture intersected with the larger currents of the outside world. Edward Ayers, *The Promise of the New South: Life after Reconstruction* (New York: Oxford University Press, 1992), 55–109. See also Darrett B. Rutman and Anita H. Rutman, "The Village South," in *Small Worlds, Large Questions: Explorations in Early American Social History, 1600–1850* (Charlottesville: University Press of Virginia, 1994), 231–72.

38. Salstrom, *Appalachia's Path to Dependency*, 20–41; Billings and Blee, *Road to Poverty*, 178–87, 199–200; J. S. Otto, "The Decline of Forest Farming in Southern Appalachia," *Journal of Forest History* 27 (January 1983): 18–26.

39. For a discussion of mine, lumber, and other industrial workers in southern Appalachia, see Eller, *Miners, Millhands, and Mountaineers*; Ronald L. Lewis, *Black Coal Miners in America: Race, Class and Community Conflict, 1780–1980* (Lexington: University Press of Kentucky, 1987); Waller, *Feud*; Corbin, *Life, Work, and Rebellion in the Coal Fields*; and Crandall A. Shifflett, *Coal Towns: Life, Work, and Culture in Company Towns of Southern Appalachia, 1880–1960* (Knoxville: University of Tennessee Press, 1991).

40. Van Noppen and Van Noppen, *Western North Carolina since the Civil War*, 276; Wellman, *Kingdom of Madison*, 110; Zeigler and Grosscup, *Heart of the Alleghenies*; Sondley, *History of Buncombe County*, 727–34.

41. These counties were Swain, Haywood, Jackson, and Yancey. See U.S. Census Office, *Report on the Productions of Agriculture . . . Tenth Census*, 300–302, and *Report on the Statistics of Agriculture . . . Eleventh Census*, 444–45.

42. Farmers grew large amounts of cotton in Catawba, Cleveland, Polk, and Rutherford counties. See U.S. Census Office, *Report on Statistics of Agriculture . . . Eleventh Census,* 395.

43. *Lenoir Topic,* October 22, 1890.

44. U.S. Census Office, *Report on the Productions of Agriculture . . . Tenth Census,* 300–302; U.S. Census Office, *Twelfth Census . . . 1900 . . . Agriculture, Part I: Farms, Live Stock, and Animal Products* (Washington, DC: U.S. Census Office, 1902), 464–66.

45. *Lenoir Topic,* June 23, 1893.

46. *Tuckaseige Democrat,* October 14, 1891.

47. *Lenoir Topic,* July 16, 1890. For additional examples, see *Morganton Herald,* April 2, 1891, April 28, 1892; *Tuckaseige Democrat,* February 5, August 20, November 26, 1890, July 15, 22, September 9, 1891, April 16, 1892; *Lenoir Topic,* March 26, April 30, 1890, March 16, 1892, February 5, 1896; *Bryson City Times,* December 18, 1896; and *Asheville Weekly Citizen,* April 7, 1892.

48. For a discussion of the Southern Farmers' Alliance in North Carolina and other parts of the South, see Lala Carr Steelman, *The North Carolina Farmers' Alliance: A Political History, 1887–1893* (Greenville, NC: East Carolina University Publications, 1985); Ayers, *Promise of the New South;* Robert C. McMath Jr., *Populist Vanguard: A History of the Southern Farmers' Alliance* (Chapel Hill: University of North Carolina Press, 1975); Lawrence Goodwyn, *The Democratic Promise: The Populist Moment in America* (New York: Oxford University Press, 1976); and Michael Schwartz, *Radical Protest and Social Structure: The Southern Farmers' Alliance and Cotton Tenancy, 1880–1890* (New York: Academic Press, 1976).

49. By the late 1890s, the cash value of farms in western North Carolina had dropped 17 percent, while farm acreage plummeted 22 percent. For a more in-depth discussion of the impact of these forces on southern farmers, see Steven A. Hahn, *The Roots of Southern Populism: Yeomen Farmers and the Transformation of the Georgia Upcountry, 1850–1890* (New York: Oxford University Press, 1983).

50. These counties were Madison, Burke, Caldwell, Jackson, Macon, Yancey, Wilkes, Catawba, Buncombe, Cherokee, Swain, Henderson, Haywood, Rutherford, Cleveland, and Ashe. See *Hickory Mercury,* December 2, 1891; *Tuckaseige Democrat,* February 12, April 9, November 26, 1890; *Wilkesboro Chronicle,* April 22, May 20, 1891; *Lenoir Topic,* July 24, 1889, March 26, 1890, November 4, 1891; *Morganton Star,* April 11, 1889; *Swain County Herald,* April 18, May 16, 30, June 13, July 18, September 19, 1889; *Hickory Western Carolinian,* September 9, 1887; and Steelman, *North Carolina Farmers' Alliance,* 63, 260.

51. William F. Holmes, "The Southern Farmers' Alliance: The Georgia Experience," *Georgia Historical Quarterly* 72 (winter 1988): 629; McMath, *Populist Vanguard.*

52. *Swain County Herald,* September 19, 1889; *Lenoir Topic,* February 26, 1890, November 4, 1891; *Tuckaseige Democrat,* February 12, 1890.

53. In this case, western North Carolinians were not exceptional. Most farmers elsewhere in the South also embraced capitalism. See Bruce E. Stewart, "The Urban-Rural Dynamic of the Southern Farmers' Alliance: Relations Between Athens Merchants and Clarke County Farmers, 1888–1891," *Georgia Historical Quarterly* 84 (summer 2005): 155–84.

54. *Hickory Mercury,* December 2, 1891.

55. *Lenoir Topic,* July 2, 1890.

56. *Swain County Herald,* June 27, 1889; *Tuckaseige Democrat,* January 14, 1891; *Lenoir Topic,* August 13, 1890, March 13, 1891.

57. *Lenoir Topic,* July 27, 1892.

58. *Tuckaseige Democrat,* July 9, 1890.

59. *Lenoir Topic,* March 13, 1891.

60. See chapter 5.

61. Israel, *Before Scopes,* 81.

62. James Floyd Fletcher, "The Story of a Mountain Missionary: Rev. James Floyd Fletcher," Fletcher Papers, North Carolina State Archives.

63. *Hickory Press and Carolinian,* November 17, December 8, 1887.

64. For a more in-depth discussion of the impact these phenomena had on encouraging evangelicals to broaden their churches' authority to include all the surrounding society, see Israel, *Before Scopes,* 79–84.

65. *Asheville Citizen,* November 19, 1891.

66. Meat Camp Baptist Church minutes (1885), 105; minutes of the Catawba River Baptist Association (1882), 9; minutes of the Brushy Mountain Association (1882), 7; minutes of the Green River Association (1881), 7; minutes of the Brier Creek Association (1881), 7; Fletcher, *History of Ashe County, North Carolina and New River, Virginia Baptist Associations,* 75, 102, 106.

67. Ownby, *Subduing Satan,* 167–73, 206–8.

68. In western North Carolina, 407 churches, schools, towns, and industrial facilities enacted local option between 1891 and 1899. I was unable to determine the exact location of 149 of them. See *Laws of North Carolina* (1891), 345–50; *Laws of North Carolina* (1893), 297–300, 328–29, 414–15; *Laws of North Carolina* (1895), 452–54; *Laws of North Carolina* (1897), 579–82, 596–98; and *Laws of North Carolina* (1899), 417–18, 879–84.

8. "Wilt Thou Send the Revenues Down upon the Distillers"

Epigraph: From *Waynesville Courier,* April 23, 1908.

1. "The bill passed the Senate by a vote of 45 with none voting in opposition, and the House by a vote of 82 to 3. Those voting against it in the House were Albright of Surry, Grant of Davie, Republicans, and Morton of New Hanover, Democrat." See Whitener, *Prohibition in North Carolina,* 162.

2. Wellman, *Kingdom of Madison,* 161–63.

3. *North Wilkesboro Hustler,* June 13, 1902.

4. Ibid., May 22, 1908.

5. *New York Times,* January 14, 1898.

6. Hamm, *Shaping the Eighteenth Amendment,* 123–29; Blocker, *Retreat from Reform,* 68–93; Pegram, *Battling Demon Rum,* 109–10.

7. For a more detailed discussion of the strategy of "local gradualism" and prohibitionists' successful use of it, see Ann-Marie E. Szymanski, *Pathways to Prohibition: Radicals, Moderates, and Social Movement Outcomes* (Durham, NC: Duke University Press, 2003).

8. Blocker, *American Temperance Movements,* 107.

9. McKinney, *Southern Mountain Republicans,* 98.

10. *New York Times,* July 16, 1882.

11. McKinney, *Southern Mountain Republicans,* 98–99, 120.

12. *Asheville News,* December 20, 1882. Vance received 69 percent of the mountain vote in 1880 and 56 percent of the mountain vote in 1882.

13. R. M. Furman to Zebulon Baird Vance, January 20, 1882, W. S. Pearson to Zebulon Baird Vance, January 23, 1882, J. C. Brown to Zebulon Baird Vance, July 3, 1882, all in *Vance Papers,* reel 8; W. H. H. Cowles to Zebulon Baird Vance, July 3, 1882, ibid., reel 5.

14. G. M. Mathes to Zebulon Baird Vance, February 2, 1882, ibid., reel 5.

15. Testimony of W. C. Morrison, W. H. Kestler, J. N. Summers, J. S. Leonard, and A. C. Avery, all in "Sixth District of North Carolina," 8, 53, 90, 110, 442.

16. Testimony of J. J. Mott, ibid., 362–95.

17. Testimony of Green Raum, ibid., 293.

18. McKinney, *Zeb Vance,* 358.

19. Miller, *Revenuers & Moonshiners,* 145.

20. *Blue Ridge Blade,* July 10, 1880.

21. Testimony of D. C. Pearson, "Sixth District of North Carolina," 323.

22. J. C. Wills to Zebulon Baird Vance, February 18, 1884, *Vance Papers,* reel 8.

23. Miller, *Revenuers & Moonshiners,* 148.

24. *Mountain Banner,* July 14, 1882; *Morganton Mountaineer,* August 8, 1883, February 13, July 2, 1884; *Ashville Semi-Weekly Citizen,* December 16, 1882, June 13, 1883.

25. Quoted in *Asheville Weekly Citizen,* December 20, 1883.

26. *Morganton Mountaineer,* January 30, 1884.

27. *Mountain Banner,* April 25, 1884.

28. Miller, *Revenuers & Moonshiners,* 149.

29. C. Dowd to Zebulon Baird Vance, July 8, September 2, November 21, 1885; John A. Richardson to Zebulon Baird Vance, July 1, 1885, H. H. Helper to Zebulon Baird Vance, February 16, 1885, E. P. Jones to Zebulon Baird Vance, March 30, 1885, all in *Vance Papers,* reel 5; Robert Vance to Zebulon Baird Vance, October 23, 1885, M. W. Ransom to Zebulon Baird Vance, 1885, ibid., reel 9.

30. Gordon B. McKinney, "Moonshiners, Law Enforcement, and Violence: Legitimacy and Community in Western North Carolina, 1862–1882" (paper presented at the annual meeting of the Southern Historical Association, New Orleans, November 1995), 15.

31. McKinney, *Zeb Vance*, 373.

32. *Lenoir Topic*, July 8, 1885.

33. See Hamilton Erwin to Samuel Tate, March 18, 1885; W. W. Stringfield to Samuel Tate, March 19, 1885; Bob Newland to Samuel Tate, March 31, 1885; C. Dowd to Samuel Tate, March 31, 1885; A. A. Shuford to Samuel Tate, April 3, 1885; A. J. Hugh to Samuel Tate, April 6, 1885; and M. N. Kimsey to Samuel Tate, May 1, 1885, all in Tate Papers, Southern Historical Collection.

34. S. T. Kelsey to D. D. Davies, February 26, 1885, box 97, Year Files, Department of Justice Records.

35. T. B. Coward to Thomas B. Keogh, March 26, 1885, ibid. For additional reports on the so-called Moccasin War, see D. D. Davies to A. H. Garland, March 5, 1885; Thomas B. Keogh to A. H. Garland, March 13, 1885; D. D. Davies to Jas. E. Boyd, March 16, 1885; H. C. Goodell to Thomas B. Keogh, March 20, 1885, ibid.

36. For more on the "Moccasin War," see Randolph P. Shaffner, *Heart of the Blue Ridge: Highlands, NC* (Highlands, NC: Faraway Publishing, 2001), 205–12.

37. Joseph Miller to A. H. Garland, April 9, 1885, box 97, Year Files, Department of Justice Records. See also Joseph Miller to A. H. Garland, May 15, 1885; Joseph Miller to A. H. Garland, May 22, 1885; D. Settle to Joseph Miller, May 16, 1885; and T. B. Coward to D. Settle, September 28, 1885, ibid.

38. *Annual Report, Commissioner of Internal Revenue, 1884, 1885*.

39. *Annual Report, Attorney General, 1884, 1886*.

40. C. Dowd to Joseph Miller, December 11, 1886, Letters Received, Internal Revenue Records.

41. *Lenoir Topic*, March 18, 1885.

42. *Morganton Star*, May 1, 1885.

43. Ibid., August 28, October 16, 1885. See also *Lenoir Topic*, April 8, 1885, and J. W. Wilson to Zebulon Baird Vance, March 3, 1884, *Vance Papers*, reel 5.

44. Quoted in *Morganton Star*, July 10, 1885.

45. *Lenoir Topic*, May 20, 1885.

46. Kerr, *Organized for Prohibition*, 41–42.

47. Paul E. Isaac, *Prohibition and Politics: Turbulent Decades in Tennessee, 1885–1920* (Knoxville: University of Tennessee Press, 1965), 61; James D. Ivy, *No Saloon in the Valley: The Southern Strategy of Texas Prohibitionists in the 1880s* (Waco, TX: Baylor University Press, 2003), 27, 28, 36; Pearson and Hendricks, *Liquor and Anti-Liquor in Virginia*, 174; Sellers, *Prohibition Movement in Alabama*, 84.

48. *State Chronicle*, December 17, 1885, quoted in Whitener, *Prohibition in North Carolina*, 81.

49. *Salisbury Watchman*, quoted in *Lenoir Topic*, December 23, 1885.

50. *Lenoir Topic*, December 23, 1885.

51. Whitener, *Prohibition in North Carolina*, 83.

52. W. T. Blackwell to Zebulon Baird Vance, May 21, 1888, *Vance Papers,* reel 23; *Hickory Press and Carolinian,* May 17, 1888. For additional examples, see *Lenoir Topic,* May 12, 1886, February 29, July 4, 1888; *Alexander County Journal,* June 28, July 19, 1888; *Morganton Star,* January 25, 1889; *Asheville Citizen,* July 26, August 12, September 16, 1888, November 14, 1889; *Hickory Western Carolinian,* September 16, October 7, 21, 1887; and *Hickory Press and Carolinian,* May 31, August 2, October 25, 1888.

53. Whitener, *Prohibition in North Carolina,* 85.

54. Quoted in *State Chronicle,* December 17, 1885.

55. *Hickory Western Carolinian,* September 16, 1887. For additional examples of mountain Democrats embracing local option to offset the appeal of the Prohibitionist Party, see *Hickory Press and Carolinian,* April 5, May 31, August, 2, October 25, 1888; *Lenoir Topic,* December 23, 1885, March 3, 1886, October 3, 1888; and *Mountain Star,* January 25, 1889.

56. Whitener, *Prohibition in North Carolina,* 87.

57. For a discussion of tourism in western North Carolina, see Starnes, *Creating the Land of the Sky.*

58. Hardy, *Short History of Old Watauga County,* 98–99.

59. *Asheville Weekly Citizen,* June 16, September 22, 29, 1892; *Lenoir Weekly News,* October 8, 1907; *Morganton News-Herald,* October 10, 1907; J. C. Pritchard, *The Moral and Intellectual Development of the People of Western North Carolina* (1907), and J. C. Pritchard, "Judge J. C. Pritchard on Prohibition: His Great Speech at Wilmington, North Carolina to a Packed House on March 14, 1908," Duke University Papers, North Carolina State Archives. Townspeople in Morganton, Wilkesboro, and Hickory also remained hesitant to enact local option during the 1890s, warning that it would damage the economic interests of their communities. See Whitener, *Prohibition in North Carolina,* 96–97; *Morganton Herald,* May 7, 1891, May 9, 1895; and *Wilkesboro Chronicle,* May 7, 1896.

60. See *Laws of North Carolina* (1891), 345–50; *Laws of North Carolina* (1893), 297–300, 328–29, 414–15; *Laws of North Carolina* (1895), 452–54; *Laws of North Carolina* (1897), 579–82, 596–98; and *Laws of North Carolina* (1899), 417–18, 879–84.

61. Whitener, *Prohibition in North Carolina,* 87.

62. *Morganton Herald,* May 4, 11, 1899; *Asheville Weekly Citizen,* June 16, 1892; *Lenoir Topic,* February 6, 1895; *Wilkesboro Chronicle,* April 23, 1896.

63. *Morganton Herald,* April 2, 1891.

64. *Hickory Mercury,* March 9, 1892; *Lenoir Topic,* April 23, July 9, 1890, July 22, August 19, 1896; *Asheville Weekly Citizen,* April 21, May 26, 1892; *North Wilkesboro News,* September 28, 1893, November 22, 1894; *Wilkesboro Chronicle,* July 30, 1896.

65. *Lenoir Topic,* July 24, 1889.

66. *New York Times,* July 25, 1890.

67. Sarah M. Blalock to Hon. Landon Green, January 11, 1897, Petitions (Liquor), January–March 1897, General Assembly Session Records; *Morganton Herald,* August 3, 1899.

68. U.S. Census Office, *Report on the Productions of Agriculture . . . Tenth Census,* 128–29, 300–302; *Report on the Statistics of Agriculture . . . Eleventh Census,* 168, 170; and Twelfth Census . . . 1900 . . . *Agriculture: Part I,* 290–91.

69. Miller, *Revenuers & Moonshiners,* 166.

70. Joseph S. Jones Daybook, 1875–1900, Special Collections, Duke University; Miller *Revenuers & Moonshiners,* 28.

71. Miller, *Revenuers & Moonshiners,* 172.

72. *New York Times,* April 14, 1895.

73. *New York Tribune,* January 25, 1896.

74. Miller, *Revenuers & Moonshiners,* 168. For specific examples of liquor law enforcement in western North Carolina during the 1890s, see *New York Times,* March 22, 1891, December 14, 1892, July 22, 1894; *North Wilkesboro News,* September 28, 1893, December 6, 1894, January 17, June 6, July 11, 1895; *Wilkesboro Chronicle,* February 18, March 4, April 1, 1891, June 18, November 12, 1896; *Morganton Herald,* March 26, 1891, May 23, 1895; *Asheville Weekly Citizen,* February 28, 1892; *Tuskaseige Democrat,* March 7, September 19, October 31, 1895; *Franklin Press,* March 13, 1895; *Lenoir Topic,* July 1, 1896, January 26, 1898; and *Waynesville Courier,* February 26, 1897.

75. *Annual Report, Commissioner of Internal Revenue* (Washington, DC: Government Printing Office, 1890–1896), 17 (1890), 16 (1891), 15 (1892), 18 (1893), 17 (1894), 19 (1895), 27 (1896).

76. *Morganton News-Herald,* February 27, 1902.

77. William F. Holmes, "Moonshiners and Whitecaps in Alabama, 1893," *Alabama Review* 24 (January 1981): 31–49; William F. Holmes, "Moonshining and Collective Violence: Georgia, 1889–1895," *Journal of American History* 67 (December 1980): 589–611; William F. Holmes, "Whitecapping and Agrarian Violence in Mississippi, 1902–1906," *Journal of Southern History* 25 (May 1969): 165–85.

78. *Wilkesboro Chronicle,* March 25, July 1, 1891. See also ibid., March 17, 1892.

79. Ibid., February 21, 28, March 7, 28, June 6, 1895; *North Wilkesboro News,* March 7, 1895.

80. *Wilkesboro Chronicle,* March 28, 1895.

81. Bailey, *News from Yancey,* 65, 68–72, 78.

82. *Wilkesboro Chronicle,* March 7, 1895.

83. *North Wilkesboro News,* April 4, 1895. See also *Tuckaseige Democrat,* October 31, 1895.

84. *Moravian Falls Yellow-Jacket,* November 1895.

85. Bailey, *News from Yancey,* 70.

86. *Marion Messenger,* February 11, 1898.

87. *Hickory Mercury,* September 8, 1897; *Charlotte Observer,* January 22, 1899.

88. *Laws of North Carolina* (1893), 300.

89. Ibid. (1899), 738.

90. In western North Carolina, 369 churches, schools, towns, and indus-

trial facilities enacted antidistiller local-option laws between 1893 and 1903. I was unable to determine the exact location of 160 of them. See *Laws of North Carolina* (1893), 299, 414–15; *Laws of North Carolina* (1897), 579–82; *Laws of North Carolina* (1901), 761–69; and *Laws of North Carolina* (1903), 275–76, 477–83.

91. These counties were Cherokee (1899), Jackson (1899), Madison (1901), Ashe (1901), Yancey (1901), Clay (1901), Polk (1905), Watauga (1905), Burke (1907), Catawba (1907), McDowell (1907), Madison (1907), Cherokee (1907), and Macon (1907). See *Laws of North Carolina* (1899), 737–38, 841; *Laws of North Carolina* (1901), 438, 548, 556, 746; *Laws of North Carolina* (1905), 499–500; and *Laws of North Carolina* (1907), 57–58, 121–23, 188, 266–69, 456–58.

92. Whitener, *Prohibition in North Carolina,* 116; John Evans Eubanks, *Ben Tillman's Baby: The Dispensary System of South Carolina, 1892–1915* (Augusta, GA: n.p., 1950); Michael Joseph Buseman, "One Trade, Two Worlds: Politics, Conflict, and Illicit Liquor Trade in White County, Georgia and Pickens County, South Carolina, 1894–1895" (MA thesis, University of Georgia, 2002); Francis Butler Simkins, *Pitchfork Ben Tillman: South Carolinian* (Baton Rouge: Louisiana State University Press, 1944).

93. Quoted in *Chatham Record,* May 9, 1895.

94. *Morganton Herald,* January 24, 1895.

95. Quoted in *Morganton Herald,* January 17, 1895.

96. Quoted in *Morganton Herald,* February 7, 1895.

97. *Marion Messenger,* January 22, 1897.

98. *Laws of North Carolina* (1895), 310, 545.

99. Whitener, *Prohibition in North Carolina,* 118.

100. Quoted in *Raleigh News and Observer,* February 14, 1897.

101. *Asheville Citizen,* February 26, 1897.

102. *Morganton Herald,* April 18, 1895.

103. Whitener, *Prohibition in North Carolina,* 118–19.

104. *Laws of North Carolina* (1897), 592–95; *Laws of North Carolina* (1899), 649–50, 744–49; *Laws of North Carolina* (1901), 577–78; *Laws of North Carolina* (1905), 63.

105. Quoted in *Lenoir Topic,* February 6, 1895.

106. *Rutherfordton Sun,* April 16, 1903. See also ibid., January 15, April 9, April 30, 1903; *Morganton News-Herald,* May 7, 1903; and *Wilkesboro Chronicle,* January 12, 1905, January 9, 1908.

107. *Rutherfordton Sun,* April 30, 1903.

108. Ibid., April 6, 1905.

109. *Waynesville Courier,* January 12, 1903.

110. *Lenoir Weekly News,* March 13, 1903. See also *North Wilkesboro Hustler,* June 13, 1902.

111. Pritchard, "Judge J. C. Pritchard on Prohibition," 7.

112. *Wilkesboro Chronicle,* January 21, 1903. For examples of Wilkes County residents' disapproval of moonshining, see *Wilkesboro Chronicle,* May 17, October 19, 1905.

113. Quoted in *Rutherfordton Sun*, February 9, 1903.

114. Whitener, *Prohibition in North Carolina*, 140.

115. *Wilkesboro Chronicle*, October 18, 1905.

116. Whitener, *Prohibition in North Carolina*, 108.

117. S. M. McCall, "Address of S. M. McCall upon the Evils of Prohibition to the Patriotic Voters of Caldwell County, N.C., during the Campaign between Patriotism and Fanaticism; Prior to May 26, 1908" (Syracuse, NY: Photo Mount Pamphlet Binder, Gaylord Bros. Makers, 1908), 5.

118. [Wilkes County citizens] to the Honorable, the General Assembly of North Carolina, 1903, Petitions, box 18, General Assembly Session Records.

119. McCall, "Address of S. M. McCall upon the Evils of Prohibition," 6.

120. Hamm, *Shaping the Eighteenth Amendment*, 92–119, 155–74.

121. *Chicago Tribune*, September 25, 1886, quoted in Hamm, *Shaping the Eighteenth Amendment*, 113.

122. *Rutherfordton Sun*, July 30, 1903.

123. *Asheville Semi-Weekly Citizen*, April 26, 1903.

124. *Wilkesboro Chronicle*, March 25, 1903.

125. *Lenoir Weekly News*, September 22, 1905.

126. *Wilkesboro Chronicle*, May 24, 1905.

127. *Waynesville Courier*, May 28, 1908.

128. Quoted in *Raleigh News and Observer*, May 30, 1908.

129. Whereas 75 percent of mountain men approved of statewide prohibition in 1908, 58 percent of those living elsewhere in North Carolina voted in favor of the proposed law. See Whitener, *Prohibition in North Carolina*, appendix.

130. Ibid.

131. *Jackson County Journal*, May 22, 29, 1908.

132. "On January 10, 1919, the North Carolina Senate ratified the Eighteenth Amendment unanimously, without a roll call, and the House, on January 14, by the vote of ninety-three to ten, seventeen members being absent or not voting. North Carolina was the twenty-eighth state to ratify." Whitener, *Prohibition in North Carolina*, 182.

Conclusion

1. Williams, *Great Smoky Mountains Folklife*, 104–5.

2. For examples, see *Bryson City Times*, October 29, November 5, 1920, May 20, August 5, 1921, March 17, May 19, 1922, July 9, 1926; *Asheville Citizen*, October 28, December 11, 1920, November 24, 1927; *Asheville Times*, May 17, 1921; Chas. J. Beck to Hon. S. R. Brame, April 22, 1921, Horace Kephart Papers, Special Collections, Western Carolina University; Sheppard, *Cabins in the Laurel*, 193–98; Dykeman, *French Broad*, 294–303; Hardy, *Short History of Old Watauga County*, 164; and Wellman, *Kingdom of Madison*, 164–67.

3. Dabney, *Mountain Spirits*, 136.

4. The "thumper" keg eliminated "the time-consuming second distilling

step. The thumper, usually fifty gallons in size, is placed between the cooking pot and condenser, and filled with beer. Hot vapors sent bubbling up from the pot through the thumper beer produce a second distillation in the keg along with a rhythmic thumping sound. The resulting whiskey is thus double distilled on only one run. Next, a new type of still was put into operation—a 'steamer,' which enabled the illicit distillers to boost production tremendously. The steamer sends hot vapors through one or a series of pots of fresh beer, providing very efficient distillations. Many of the early steamers were 'stack steamers'—two or three metal drums welded together. In some isolated areas, the groundhog still came onto the scene—giant metal cylinders that enabled a man to produce two or three hundred gallons of whiskey a day and to ferment and distill in the same giant pot." Ibid., 110.

5. As historian Joseph Dabney has explained, "For only $5 worth of sugar—100 pounds worth—the moonshiner could turn out ten gallons of high proof 'shine, selling for $20 to $40 a gallon, or for a total of $200 to $400." Illicit distillers also began to dilute their homemade brew with water and sometimes attempted to speed up fermentation by using carbide, "which heated the mash but left a deadly chemical residue." Ibid., 110, 111.

6. Richard Hofstadter, *The Age of Reform: From Bryan to F.D.R.* (New York: Alfred A. Knopf, 1955), 287. See also John C. Burnham, *Bad Habits: Drinking, Smoking, Taking Drugs, Gambling, Sexual Misbehavior, and Swearing in American History* (New York: New York University Press, 1993); Lynn Dumenil, *The Modern Temper: American Culture and Society in the 1920s* (New York: Hill and Wang, 1995); Robert H. Wiebe, *Self-Rule: A Cultural History of American Democracy* (Chicago: University of Chicago Press, 1995); Willa Cather, *Not under Forty* (New York: Alfred A. Knopf, 1936); William E. Leuchtenburg, *The Perils of Prosperity, 1914–1932* (Chicago: University of Chicago Press, 1958); Geoffrey Perrett, *America in the Twenties: A History* (New York: Simon and Schuster, 1982); Warren I. Susman, *Culture as History: The Transformation of American Society in the Twentieth Century* (New York: Pantheon Books, 1984).

Bibliography

Unpublished Manuscript Collections

Anderson, John. Papers. North Carolina State Archives, Raleigh.

Archdale, John. Papers. North Carolina State Archives, Raleigh.

Arledge, Grant. Papers. Southern Historical Collection, University of North Carolina, Chapel Hill.

Austin, Benjamin, and Henry Reid. Papers. Rare Book, Manuscript, and Special Collections Library, Duke University, Durham.

Avery, Alphonso Calhoun. Papers. Southern Historical Collection, University of North Carolina, Chapel Hill.

Aycock, Charles Brantley. Collection. North Carolina State Archives, Raleigh.

Bailey, Joseph William. Papers. Rare Book, Manuscript, and Special Collections Library, Duke University, Durham.

Beckham, William. Account Book. Rare Book, Manuscript, and Special Collections Library, Duke University, Durham.

Biggerstaff Family Papers. North Carolina State Archives, Raleigh.

Buncombe County Record of Wills. North Carolina State Archives, Raleigh.

Burgess, Hiram. Account Book. Rare Book, Manuscript, and Special Collections Library, Duke University, Durham.

Burke County Record of Wills. North Carolina State Archives, Raleigh.

Burton, Robert. Papers. Southern Historical Collection, University of North Carolina, Chapel Hill.

Caldwell, Tod. Papers. Southern Historical Collection, University of North Carolina, Chapel Hill.

Campbell, John Charles, and Olive Dame. Papers. Southern Historical Collection, University of North Carolina, Chapel Hill.

Cathey, Col. Joseph. Daybook. North Carolina State Archives, Raleigh.

Cathey, Joseph. Papers. North Carolina State Archives, Raleigh.

Clinard, L. N. Papers. North Carolina State Archives, Raleigh.

Comptroller's Report, 1805: A Statement of Revenue of North Carolina. North Carolina State Archives, Raleigh.

Coulter, John Ellis. Papers. Southern Historical Collection, University of North Carolina, Chapel Hill.

County Records. Counties of Alexander, Ashe, Caldwell, Cherokee, Cleveland, Madison, McDowell. North Carolina State Archives, Raleigh.

Cox, Talton T. Papers. Rare Book, Manuscript, and Special Collections Library, Duke University, Durham.

Davidson, Theodore F. Papers. North Carolina State Archives, Raleigh.

Davis, Orin Datus. Papers. Southern Historical Collection, University of North Carolina, Chapel Hill.

Duke University Library Papers. North Carolina State Archives, Raleigh.

Elk Creek Primitive Baptist Church Records. Southern Historical Collection, University of North Carolina, Chapel Hill.

Estes, William. Papers. Special Collections, Western Carolina University, Cullowhee.

Finley, John. Papers. Rare Book, Manuscript, and Special Collections Library, Duke University, Durham.

Fletcher, James Floyd. Papers. North Carolina State Archives, Raleigh.

Gardner, Oliver Max. Papers. Southern Historical Collection, University of North Carolina, Chapel Hill.

Gash, Leander S. Papers. North Carolina State Archives, Raleigh.

Gash, Mary A. Papers. North Carolina State Archives, Raleigh.

Gash Family Papers. North Carolina State Archives, Raleigh.

Gwyn, James. Papers. Southern Historical Collection, University of North Carolina, Chapel Hill.

Hackett, James Gordon. Collection. North Carolina State Archives, Raleigh.

Hanbury, William R., and Company. North Carolina State Archives, Raleigh.

Hawkins, Marmaduke James. Papers. North Carolina State Archives, Raleigh.

Hedrick, Benjamin Sherwood. Papers. Rare Book, Manuscript, and Special Collections Library, Duke University, Durham.

Holden, William Woods. Papers. Rare Book, Manuscript, and Special Collections Library, Duke University, Durham.

Jackson, T. P. Account Book. Rare Book, Manuscript, and Special Collections Library, Duke University, Durham.

Jarratt-Puryear Family Papers. Rare Book, Manuscript, and Special Collections Library, Duke University, Durham.

Jones, Joseph S. Daybook. Rare Book, Manuscript, and Special Collections Library, Duke University, Durham.

Kephart, Horace. Papers. Special Collections, Western Carolina University, Cullowhee.

Kirby, Samuel F. Account Book. Rare Book, Manuscript, and Special Collections Library, Duke University, Durham.

Lenoir, Thomas. Papers. Rare Book, Manuscript, and Special Collections Library, Duke University, Durham.

Lenoir Family Papers. Southern Historical Collection, University of North Carolina, Chapel Hill.

Lusk, Virgil S. Papers. North Carolina State Archives, Raleigh.

McMurry, M., and C. G. Accounts. North Carolina State Archives, Raleigh.

Miller, Robert Johnston. Papers. North Carolina State Archives, Raleigh.

Miller, Thomas. Daybook. Rare Book, Manuscript, and Special Collections Library, Duke University, Durham.

Miscellaneous Letters. Southern Historical Collection, University of North Carolina, Chapel Hill.

Mitchell, Robert. Account Book. North Carolina State Archives, Raleigh.

Morrison, Theodore Davidson. Papers. Southern Historical Collection, University of North Carolina, Chapel Hill.

Patton, James, and Andrew Erwin. Account Book. North Carolina State Archives, Raleigh.

Peden and Kelly Papers. Rare Book, Manuscript, and Special Collections Library, Duke University, Durham.

Pickens, Cornelias Miller. Diary. Rare Book, Manuscript, and Special Collections Library, Duke University, Durham.

Polk and Yeatman Family Papers. Southern Historical Collection, University of North Carolina, Chapel Hill.

Ramsay, James G. Papers. Southern Historical Collection, University of North Carolina, Chapel Hill.

Reed, Austin. Papers. Rare Book, Manuscript, and Special Collections Library, Duke University, Durham.

Rollins, Pinkney. Papers. Rare Book, Manuscript, and Special Collections Library, Duke University, Durham.

Sadler, James A. Account Book. Rare Book, Manuscript, and Special Collections Library, Duke University, Durham.

Scott, William Lafayette. Papers. Rare Book, Manuscript, and Special Collections Library, Duke University, Durham.

Settle, Thomas. Papers. Southern Historical Collection, University of North Carolina, Chapel Hill.

Sharpe, Eli. Papers. Southern Historical Collection, University of North Carolina, Chapel Hill.

Sherrill, Samuel P. Account Book. Rare Book, Manuscript, and Special Collections Library, Duke University, Durham.

Shotwell Family Papers. Southern Historical Collection, University of North Carolina, Chapel Hill.

Siler, Jacob. Papers. Southern Historical Collection, University of North Carolina, Chapel Hill.

Smith, J. L. Ledgers. North Carolina State Archives, Raleigh.

Smyth, J. C. Journal. North Carolina State Archives, Raleigh.

Strabane (N.C.) Account Book. Southern Historical Collection, University of North Carolina, Chapel Hill.

Sutton, Maude Minish. Papers. Southern Historical Collection, University of North Carolina, Chapel Hill.

Tate, Samuel McDowell. Papers. Southern Historical Collection, University of North Carolina, Chapel Hill.

Thomas, William Holland. Papers. Rare Book, Manuscript, and Special Collections Library, Duke University, Durham.

Thomas, William Holland. Papers. Special Collections, Western Carolina University, Cullowhee.

Unidentified Merchant Journal (Haywood County). North Carolina State Archives, Raleigh.

Walker, A., and A. T. Account Book. Southern Historical Collection, University of North Carolina, Chapel Hill.

Walser, Zeb Vance. Papers. Southern Historical Collection, University of North Carolina, Chapel Hill.

Watson, James. Papers. Special Collections, Western Carolina University, Cullowhee.
Watts, Sue Campbell. Papers. Southern Historical Collection, University of North Carolina, Chapel Hill.
Waugh and Finley Daybooks. North Carolina State Archives, Raleigh.
Webb, E. Y. Papers. Southern Historical Collection, University of North Carolina, Chapel Hill.
Whisnant, David Eugene. Papers. Southern Historical Collection, University of North Carolina, Chapel Hill.
White, W. A. Papers. Rare Book, Manuscript, and Special Collections Library, Duke University, Durham.
Wilkes County Record of Wills. North Carolina State Archives, Raleigh.
Williams, Cratis Dearl. Papers. William Leonard Eury Collection, Special Collections, Appalachian State University, Boone, NC.
Wilson, William. Memoir. Privately owned.

Government Documents

Adjutant General's Office, Record Group 94. National Archives, Washington, DC.
Agricultural and Manufacturing Census Records of Fifteen Southern States for the Years, 1850, 1860, 1870, 1880. Chapel Hill: Library Photographic Services, University of North Carolina, 1960–1965.
Annual Report of the Attorney General (usually *House Executive Documents* 6 for each year).
Annual Report of the Commissioner of Internal Revenue (usually *House Executive Documents* 4 for each year).
Bureau of Internal Revenue, Record Group 58. National Archives, College Park, MD.
Carroll, Henry K. *Report on Statistics of Churches in the United States at the Eleventh Census: 1890.* Washington, DC: Government Printing Office, 1894.
Clark, Walter. *The State Records of North Carolina.* Raleigh, NC: P. M. Hale, 1886–1907.
Congressional Globe.
Department of Justice, Record Group 21. National Archives, Atlanta, GA.
Department of Justice, Record Group 60. National Archives, College Park, MD.
"Enforcement of Internal Revenue Laws. . . . Report of the Commissioner of Internal Revenue to the Secretary of the Treasury, in Reply to House Resolution of February 10, 1880, Making Inquiry for Information Tending to Explain the Necessity for Employment of Armed Men in Enforcement of the Internal Revenue Law." *House Executive Documents* 62, 46th Cong., 2nd sess. (1880).
General Assembly State Records, 1852–1908. North Carolina State Archives, Raleigh.
Journal of the House, 1866. North Carolina State Archives, Raleigh.

Journal of the Senate, 1866. North Carolina State Archives, Raleigh.

Laws of North Carolina, 1871–1908.

Merriam, William R. *Twelfth Census of the United States, 1900: Population, Part I.* Washington, DC: U.S. Census Office, 1901.

Ordinances of the State Convention: Published in Pursuance of a Resolution of the General Assembly [Ratified 11th February 1863]. Raleigh, NC: W. W. Holden, 1863.

Porter, Robert P. *Report on the Population of the United States at the Eleventh Census: 1890.* Washington, DC: Government Printing Office, 1895.

Public Laws of North Carolina, 1862–1863, 1881.

Records of U.S. Army Continental Commands, Record Group 393. National Archives, Washington, DC.

Revenue Law of North Carolina, 1866.

"Salaries of Revenue Officers." *Senate Executive Documents* 23, 46th Cong., 1st sess. (1879).

State Board of Agriculture. *Hand-Book of North Carolina, with Map of the State.* Raleigh, NC: P. M. Hale, State Printer and Binder, 1886.

———. *North Carolina and Its Resources.* Winston, NC: M. I. and J. C. Stewart, Public Printers and Binders, 1896.

"Testimony before the Senate Special Committee to Investigate the Administration of the Collection of Internal Revenue in the Sixth District of North Carolina, Appointed April 21, 1882." *Senate Miscellaneous Documents* 116, 47th Cong., 1st sess. (1882).

U.S. Census Office. *Aggregate Amount of Each Description of Persons within the United States of America, and the Territories thereof . . . 1810.* Washington, DC: 1811.

———. *A Statement of the Arts and Manufacturers of the United States . . . 1810 . . .* Philadelphia: 1814.

———. *Compendium of the Enumeration of the Inhabitants and Statistics of the United States . . . Sixth Census. . . .* Washington, DC: 1841.

———. *The Seventh Census of the United States: 1850.* Washington, DC: Robert Armstrong, Public Printer, 1853.

———. *Agriculture of the United States in 1860 . . . The Eighth Census.* Washington, DC: Government Printing Office, 1864.

———. *Manufacturers of the United States . . . Eighth Census.* Washington, DC: Government Printing Office, 1865.

———. *A Compendium of the Ninth Census: 1870.* Washington, DC: Government Printing Office, 1872.

———. *The Statistics of Wealth and Industry . . . Ninth Census: 1870.* Washington, DC: Government Printing Office, 1872.

———. *Statistics of the Population of the United States at the Tenth Census.* Washington, DC: Government Printing Office, 1883.

———. *Report of the Productions of Agriculture . . . Tenth Census: 1880.* Washington, DC: Government Printing Office, 1883.

———. *Report on the Manufacturers . . . Tenth Census: 1880.* Washington, DC: Government Printing Office, 1883.

———. *Report on the Manufacturing Industries . . . Eleventh Census: 1890.* Washington, DC: Government Printing Office, 1895.

———. *Report on the Statistics of Agriculture . . . Eleventh Census: 1890.* Washington, DC: Government Printing Office, 1895.

———. *Twelfth Census . . . 1900 . . . Agriculture, Part I: Farms, Live Stock, and Animal Products.* Washington, DC: U.S. Census Office, 1902.

———. *Twelfth Census . . . 1900 . . . Manufacturers, Part II: States and Territories.* Washington, DC: U.S. Census Office, 1902.

U.S. Congress. Joint Selection Committee. *The Condition of Affairs in the Late Insurrectionary States.* 42nd Cong., 2nd sess. (1872).

Walker, Francis A. *The Statistics of the Population of the United States at the Ninth Census: 1870.* Washington, DC: Government Printing Office, 1872.

Primary and Secondary Sources

Aaron, Paul, and David Musto. "Temperance and Prohibition in America: A Historical Overview." In *Alcohol and Public Policy: Beyond the Shadow of Prohibition,* ed. Mark H. Moore and Dean R. Gerstein, 127–81. Washington, DC: National Academy Press, 1981.

Abernathy, Arthur Talmage. *Moonshine Being Appalachia's Arabian Nights.* Asheville, NC: Dixie Publishing Co., 1924.

Abrams, William H., Jr. "The Western North Carolina Railroad, 1855–1894." MA thesis, Western Carolina University, 1976.

Adams, Carolyn. *History of Cove Creek Baptist Church, 1799–1974.* Sugar Grove, NC: Cove Creek Baptist Church, 1974.

Alduino, Frank. "Prohibition in Tampa." *Tampa Bay History* 9 (January 1987): 17–28.

Alexander, Nancy. *Here Will I Dwell: The Story of Caldwell County.* Salisbury, NC: Rowan Printing, 1956.

Allen, James L. "Mountain Passes of the Cumberland." *Harper's New Monthly Magazine* 81 (September 1890): 561–76.

———. "Through Cumberland Gap on Horseback." *Harper's New Monthly Magazine* 73 (June 1886): 50–66.

Allen, W. C. *The Annals of Haywood County, North Carolina.* Spartanburg, SC: Reprint Co., Publishers, 1977.

Allison, Thomas R. *Moonshine Memories.* Montgomery, AL: NewSouth Books, 2001.

Ammons, John. *Outlines of History of French Broad Association and Mars Hill College: From the Organization of the Association in 1807 to 1907, Being a Period of 100 Years.* Mars Hill, NC: Mars Hill College Press, 2001.

Anderson, J. Jay. *Wilkes County Sketches.* Wilkesboro, NC: Anderson, 1978.

Arthur, John P. *A History of Watauga County, North Carolina, with Sketches of Prominent Families.* Richmond: Everett Waddey, 1915.

———. *Western North Carolina: A History from 1730 to 1913.* Raleigh, NC: Edwards and Broughton, 1914.

Asbury, Francis. *The Journal of the Rev. Francis Asbury, Bishop of the Meth-*

odist Episcopal Church, from August 7, 1771 to December 7, 1815. 3 vols. New York: N. Bangs and T. Mason, 1821.

Ashe, Samuel D'Court. *History of North Carolina.* Vol. 2. Raleigh, NC: Edwards and Broughton, 1925.

Atkinson, George Wesley. *After the Moonshiners, by One of the Raiders.* Wheeling, WV: Frew and Campbell Steam, Book and Job Printers, 1881.

Avery, Alphonso Calhoun. *Burke County History.* 1890.

Ayers, Edward. *The Promise of a New South: Life after Reconstruction.* New York: Oxford University Press, 1992.

———. *Vengeance and Justice: Crime and Punishment in the Nineteenth-Century American South.* New York: Oxford University Press, 1984.

Bailey, Fred A. *Class and Tennessee's Confederate Generation.* Chapel Hill: University of North Carolina Press, 1989.

Bailey, Jody, and Robert S. McPherson. "'Practically Free from the Taint of the Bootlegger': A Closer Look at Prohibition in Southeastern Utah." *Utah Historical Quarterly* 57 (April 1989): 150–64.

Bailey, Josiah William. "The Political Treatment of the Drink Evil." *South Atlantic Quarterly* 6 (1907): 109–24.

Bailey, Lloyd, ed. *News from Yancey: Articles from Area Newspapers, 1840–1900.* Burnsville, NC: Yancey Graphics, 1983.

Baines, Donald A. "Among the Moonshiners." *Dixie* 1 (August 1885): 9–14.

Barksdale, Kevin. "Our Rebellious Neighbors: Virginia's Border Counties during Pennsylvania's Whiskey Rebellion." *Virginia Magazine of History and Biography* 111 (January 2003): 5–32.

———. "Whiskey Distillation in Antebellum Western North Carolina." *Tuckasegee Valley Historical Review* 5 (April 1999): 1–14.

Barrett, John G. *The Civil War in North Carolina.* Chapel Hill: University of North Carolina Press, 1963.

Barrick, Mac E. "Memories of a Moonshiner." *Pennsylvania Folklife* 26 (January 1976): 18–24.

Bates, Morgan, and Elwyn A. Barron. *A Mountain Pink: Realistic Description among the Moonshiners of North Carolina, a Romantic Drama.* Milwaukee: Riverside Printing Co., 1885.

Batteau, Allen W. *The Invention of Appalachia.* Tucson: University of Arizona Press, 1990.

Battle, Kemp Plummer. *Memories of an Old-Time Tar Heel.* Chapel Hill: University of North Carolina Press, 1945.

Becker, Jane S. *Selling Tradition: Appalachia and the Construction of an American Folk, 1930–1940.* Chapel Hill: University of North Carolina Press, 1998.

Billings, Dwight B. *Planters and the Making of the "New South": Class, Politics, and Development in North Carolina, 1865–1900.* Chapel Hill: University of North Carolina Press, 1979.

Billings, Dwight B., and Kathleen M. Blee. *Road to Poverty: The Making of Wealth and Hardship in Appalachia.* Cambridge: Cambridge University Press, 2000.

Billings, Dwight B., Gurney Norman, and Katherine Ledford, eds. *Confronting Appalachian Stereotypes: Back Talk from an American Region.* Lexington: University Press of Kentucky, 1999.

Blackmun, Ora. *A Spire in the Mountains.* Asheville, NC: First Presbyterian Church, 1970.

———. *Western North Carolina: Its Mountains and Its People to 1880.* Boone, NC: Appalachian Consortium Press, 1977.

Blakey, Leonard S. *The Sale of Liquor in the South: The History of the Development of a Normal Social Restraint in Southern Commonwealths.* Columbia University Studies in History, Economics, and Public Law 51, no. 127. New York: Columbia University Press, 1912.

Blethen, H. Tyler. "Pioneer Settlement." In *High Mountains Rising: Appalachia in Time and Place,* ed. Richard A. Straw and H. Tyler Blethen, 17–29. Urbana: University of Illinois Press, 2004.

Blethen, H. Tyler, and Curtis W. Wood Jr. *From Ulster to Carolina: The Migration of the Scotch-Irish to Southwestern North Carolina.* Rev. ed. Raleigh: North Carolina Division of Archives and History, 1998.

———. "The Pioneer Experience to 1851." In *The History of Jackson County,* ed. Max R. Williams, 67–100. Sylva, NC: Jackson County Historical Association, 1987.

———. "A Trader on the Western Carolina Frontier." In *Appalachian Frontiers: Settlement, Society, and Development in the Preindustrial Era,* ed. Robert D. Mitchell, 150–65. Lexington: University Press of Kentucky, 1992.

Blevins, Brooks R. "The Strike and the Still: Anti-Radical Violence and the Ku Klux Klan in the Ozarks." *Arkansas Historical Quarterly* 52 (October 1993): 405–25.

Blocker, Jack S., Jr. *American Temperance Movements: Cycles of Reform.* Boston: Twayne Publishers, 1989.

———. *Retreat from Reform: The Prohibition Movement in the United States, 1890–1913.* Westport, CT: Greenwood Press, 1976.

Blythe, Samuel G. "Raiding Moonshiners." *Munsey's Magazine* 25 (June 1901): 418–24.

Bogue, Jesse Parker. "Violence and Oppression in North Carolina during Reconstruction, 1865–1873." PhD diss., University of North Carolina at Chapel Hill, 1973.

Boles, John B. *The Great Revival, 1787–1805: The Origins of the Southern Evangelical Mind.* Lexington: University Press of Kentucky, 1972.

Bonner, Sherwood. "The Case of Eliza Bleylock." *Harper's Weekly* (March 5, 1881): 155–58.

———. "Jack and the Mountain Pink." *Harper's Weekly* (January 29, 1881): 75–77.

Bordin, Ruth. *Women and Temperance: The Quest for Power and Liberty, 1873–1900.* Philadelphia: Temple University Press, 1981.

Bott, Donna. *Amazing Grace, 1845–1995: A History of Grace Episcopal Church, Morganton, North Carolina & of the Missions of Burke County.* Morganton, NC: Grace Episcopal Church, 1997.

Boyd, Steven R., ed. *The Whiskey Rebellion: Past and Present Perspectives.* Westport, CT: Greenwood Press, 1985.

Branson, Levi. *Branson's North Carolina Business Directory.* Raleigh, NC: Branson and Jones, 1867–1896.

Brewer, William M. "Moonshining in Georgia." *Cosmopolitan* 12 (June 1897): 127–34.

Browder, Nathaniel C. *The Cherokee Indians and Those Who Came After: Notes for a History of Cherokee County North Carolina, 1835–1860.* Hayesville, NC: Browder, 1973.

———. *The William Thomas Prestwood Enciphered Diary, 1808–1859.* Raleigh, NC: Nathaniel C. Browder, 1983.

Brown, Margaret Lynn. *The Wild East: A Biography of the Great Smoky Mountains.* Gainesville: University Press of Florida, 2000.

Buck, Paul Herman. *The Road to Reunion, 1865–1900.* Boston: Little, Brown, 1937.

Buckingham, James S. *The Slave States of America.* Vol. 2. London: Fisher, Son and Co., 1842.

Burnett, Fred M. *This Was My Valley.* Ridgecrest, NC: Heritage Printers, 1960.

Burnham, John C. *Bad Habits: Drinking, Smoking, Taking Drugs, Gambling, Sexual Misbehavior, and Swearing in American History.* New York: New York University Press, 1993.

Buseman, Michael Joseph. "One Trade, Two Worlds: Politics, Conflict, and Illicit Liquor Trade in White County, Georgia and Pickens County, South Carolina, 1894–1895." MA thesis, University of Georgia, 2002.

Bush, Florence Cope. *Dorie: Woman of the Mountains.* Knoxville: University of Tennessee Press, 1992.

Buxton, Barry M. *A Village Tapestry: The History of Blowing Rock.* Boone, NC: Appalachian Consortium Press, 1989.

Calhoon, Bruce W. "Presbyterian Home Missions in Southern Appalachia." *Tuckasegee Valley Historical Review* 10 (spring 2004): 9–22.

Campbell, John C. *The Southern Highlander and His Homeland.* New York: Russell Sage Foundation, 1921.

Campbell, Robert F. *Mission Work among the Mountain Whites in Asheville Presbytery, North Carolina.* Asheville, NC: Citizen Co., 1899.

Cannon, James. *History of the Southern Methodist Missions.* Nashville, TN: Cokesbury Press, 1926.

Carlson, Douglas W. "'Drinks He to His Own Undoing': Temperance Ideology in the Deep South." *Journal of the Early Republic* 18 (winter 1998): 659–91.

Carr, Jess. *The Second Oldest Profession: An Informal History of Moonshining in America.* Englewood Cliffs, NJ: Prentice-Hall, 1972.

Carroll, Grady L. E., ed. *Francis Asbury in North Carolina, the North Carolina Portions of the Journal of Francis Asbury.* Nashville, TN: Parthenon Press, 1964.

Caruso, John Anthony. *The Appalachian Frontier: America's First Surge Westward.* Indianapolis: Bobbs-Merrill, 1959.

Carwardine, Richard J. *Evangelicals and Politics in Antebellum America*. New Haven, CT: Yale University Press, 1993.

Cash, W. J. *The Mind of the South*. New York: Alfred A. Knopf, 1941.

Cather, Willa. *Not under Forty*. New York: Alfred A. Knopf, 1936.

Cathey, Cornelius O. *Agriculture in North Carolina before the Civil War*. Raleigh: North Carolina Division of Archives and History, 1974.

Caudill, Harry M. *Night Comes to the Cumberlands: A Biography of a Depressed Region*. Boston: Little, Brown, 1962.

Cecil-Fronsman, Bill. *Common Whites: Class and Culture in Antebellum North Carolina*. Lexington: University Press of Kentucky, 1992.

Clark, Norman H. *Deliver Us from Evil: An Interpretation of American Prohibition*. New York: W. W. Norton, 1976.

Clingman, Thomas L. *Selections from the Speeches and Writings of Hon. Thomas L. Clingman of North Carolina*. Raleigh, NC: John Nichols, 1878.

Cobb, James C. *Industrialization and Southern Society, 1877–1984*. Lexington: University Press of Kentucky, 1984.

Cobb, R. A. *The True Life of Maj. Richard Redmond, the Notorious Outlaw and Famous Moonshiner of Western North Carolina, Who Was Born in Swain County, N.C., in the Year 1855, and Arrested April 7th, 1881*. Raleigh, NC: Edwards, Broughton, 1881.

Cofer, Richard. "Bootleggers in the Backwoods: Prohibition and the Depression in Hernando County." *Tampa Bay History* 1 (January 1979): 17–23.

Coker, Joe L. *Liquor in the Land of the Lost Cause: Southern White Evangelicals and the Prohibition Movement*. Lexington: University Press of Kentucky, 2007.

Collins, Bruce. *White Society in the Antebellum South*. New York: Longman House, 1985.

Colton, H. E. "A Farm on the French Broad." *Appleton's Journal* 4 (December 17, 1870): 737–38.

———. *Guidebook to the Scenery of Western North Carolina*. Asheville, NC: Western Advocate Office, 1860.

———. "Mountain Island." *Appleton's Journal* 5 (January 17, 1871): 15–18.

———. "Reems's Creek and the Old Mill." *Appleton's Journal* 5 (February 4, 1871): 135–37.

Commager, Henry Steele, ed. *The Era of Reform, 1830–1860*. New York: Van Nostrand, 1960.

Cooke, John Esten. "Moonshiners." *Harper's New Monthly Magazine* 58 (February 1879): 380–90.

Cooper, Horton. *History of Avery County, North Carolina*. Asheville, NC: Biltmore Press, 1964.

Cooper, Leland R., and Mary Lee Cooper. *The People of the New River: Oral Histories from the Ashe, Alleghany, and Watauga Counties of North Carolina*. Jefferson, NC: McFarland, 2001.

Corbin, David Alan. *Life, Work, and Rebellion in the Coal Fields: The Southern West Virginia Miners, 1880–1922*. Urbana: University of Illinois Press, 1981.

Corbitt, David L. *The Formation of the North Carolina Counties, 1663–1943.* Raleigh: North Carolina Division of Archives and History, 1950.

Cotton, William D. "Appalachian North Carolina: A Political Study, 1860–1899." PhD diss., University of North Carolina at Chapel Hill, 1954.

Coward, J. Kent. "The Community in Crisis." In *History of Jackson County,* ed. Max R. Williams, 433–68. Sylva, NC: Jackson County Historical Association, 1987.

Craig, Edward Marshall. *Highways and Byways of Appalachia: A Study of the Work of the Synod of Appalachia of the Presbyterian Church in the United States.* Kingsport, TN: Kingsport Press, 1927.

Crawford, Martin. *Ashe County's Civil War: Community and Society in the Appalachian South.* Charlottesville: University Press of Virginia, 2001.

Crayon, Porte [David Hunter Strother]. "A Winter in the South" *Harper's New Monthly Magazine* 15 (November 1857): 721–40.

Cresswell, Stephen. *Mormons & Cowboys, & Moonshiners & Klansmen: Federal Law Enforcement in the South & West, 1870–1893.* Tuscaloosa: University of Alabama Press, 1991.

Crittenden, Edward. *The Entwined Lives of Miss Gabrielle Austin, Daughter of the Late Rev. Ellis C. Austin, and of Redmond, the Outlaw, Leader of the North Carolina "Moonshiners."* Philadelphia: Barclay, 1879.

Crow, Jeffrey J. "The Whiskey Rebellion in North Carolina." *North Carolina Historical Review* 67 (January 1989): 1–28.

Culpepper, Linda Parramore. *Under Their Own Vine and Fig Tree: The History of Mud Creek Missionary Baptist Church, East Flat Rock, Henderson County, North Carolina, 1867–2002.* Special Collections, Western Carolina University, 2002.

Cummings, Lawrence Edward. "Moonshining as a Deviant Occupation." MA thesis, University of Georgia, 1974.

Cummings, William P. *North Carolina in Maps.* Raleigh: North Carolina Division of Archives and History, 1966.

Cunningham, Rodger. *Apples on the Flood: The Southern Mountain Experience.* Knoxville: University of Tennessee Press, 1987.

Dabney, Joseph Earl. *Mountain Spirits: A Chronicle of Corn Whiskey from King James' Ulster Plantation to America's Appalachians and the Moonshine Life.* New York: Charles Scribner's Sons, 1974.

———. *Mountain Spirits II: The Continuing Chronicle of Moonshine Life and Corn Whiskey, Wines, Cider & Beers in America's Appalachians.* Lakemont, GA: Copple House Books, 1980.

Daily, Douglas C. "The Elections of 1872 in North Carolina." *North Carolina Historical Review* 40 (summer 1963): 338–60.

Dannenbaum, Jed. *Drink and Disorder: Temperance Reform in Cincinnati from the Washington Revival to the WCTU.* Urbana: University of Illinois Press, 1984.

Davidson, Allen T. "Reminiscences of Western North Carolina." *Lyceum* 1 (January 1891).

Davidson, Theodore F. *Reminiscences and Traditions of Western North Carolina.* Asheville, NC: Service Printing, 1928.

Davis, David Brion, ed. *Ante-Bellum Reform.* New York: Harper and Row, 1967.

Davis, Donald Edward. *Where There Are Mountains: An Environmental History of the Southern Appalachians.* Athens: University of Georgia Press, 2000.

Davis, Mac E. *Home Mission Experiences in the Mountains of North Carolina.* Richmond, VA: Whittet and Shepperson, 1903.

Davis, Phillip G. "Mountain Heritage, Mountain Promise under Siege: The Origin and Devastation of Confederate Sympathy in the North Carolina Mountains during the Civil War." MA thesis, Wake Forest University, 1994.

Davis, Rebecca Harding. "By-Paths in the Mountains, III." *Harper's New Monthly Magazine* 61 (September 1880): 532–47.

———. "A Night in the Mountains." *Appleton's Journal* 3 (July–December 1877): 505–10.

———. "Qualla." *Lippincott's Monthly Magazine* 16 (November 1875): 576–86.

———. "The Rose of Carolina." *Scribner's Monthly* 8 (October 1874): 723–26.

———. "The Yares of the Black Mountains." *Lippincott's Monthly Magazine* 16 (July 1875): 35–47.

Davis, Robert S. "The Night Riders of Pickens County." *North Georgia Journal* 4 (June 1987): 22–24.

———. "The North Georgia Moonshine War of 1876–1877." *North Georgia Journal* 6 (autumn 1989): 42–45.

Deyton, Jason Basil. "The Toe River Valley to 1865." *North Carolina Historical Review* 24 (October 1947): 423–66.

Dimmock, George. "A Trip to Mr. Mitchell in North Carolina." *Appalachia* 1 (June 1877): 141–51.

Douglas, H. Paul. *Christian Reconstruction in the South.* Boston: Pilgrim Press, 1909.

Downard, William C. *Dictionary of the History of the American Brewing and Distilling Industries.* Westport, CT: Greenwood, 1980.

Drake, Richard B. "Documents Relating to the Mission to Appalachia." *Appalachian Notes* 3 (1975): 34–38.

———. "The Mission School Era in Southern Appalachia, 1880–1940." *Appalachian Notes* 6 (1978): 1–9.

———. "Slavery and Antislavery in Appalachia." *Appalachian Heritage* 14 (winter 1986): 25–33.

Dromgoole, Will Allen. *A Moonshiner's Son.* Philadelphia: Penn Publishing Co., 1898.

———. *Spurrier with the Wildcats and Moonshiners.* Nashville, TN: University Press, 1892.

Dumenil, Lynn. *The Modern Temper: American Culture and Society in the 1920s.* New York: Hill and Wang, 1995.

Dunaway, Wilma A. *The First American Frontier: Transition to Capitalism in*

Southern Appalachia, 1700–1860. Chapel Hill: University of North Carolina Press, 1996.

Dunn, Durwood. *Cades Cove: The Life and Death of a Southern Appalachian Community, 1818–1937.* Knoxville: University of Tennessee Press, 1988.

Dykeman, Wilma. *The French Broad.* New York: Rinehart, 1955.

Eaton, Allen H. *Handicrafts of the Southern Highlands.* New York: Russell Sage Foundation, 1937.

Eaton, Clement. *The Freedom-of-Thought Struggle in the Old South.* New York: Harper and Row, 1964.

Edmonds, Helen G. *The Negro and Fusion Politics in North Carolina: 1894–1901.* Chapel Hill: University of North Carolina Press, 1951.

Eggleston, J. D. *Asheville and Vicinity.* Atlanta, GA: Franklin Printing and Publishing Co., 1896.

Eller, Ronald D. *Miners, Millhands, and Mountaineers: Industrialization of the Appalachian South, 1880–1930.* Knoxville: University of Tennessee Press, 1982.

Entrekin, William F., Jr. "Poor Relief in North Carolina." MA thesis, Duke University, 1947.

Epstein, Barbara Leslie. *The Politics of Domesticity: Women, Evangelicals, and Temperance in Nineteenth-Century America.* Middleton, CT: Wesleyan University, 1981.

Escott, Paul D. "'Cry of the Sufferers': The Problem of Welfare in the Confederacy." *Civil War History* 23 (September 1977): 228–40.

———. *Many Excellent People: Power and Privilege in North Carolina, 1850–1900.* Chapel Hill: University of North Carolina Press, 1985.

———. "Poverty and Government Aid for the Poor in Confederate North Carolina." *North Carolina Historical Review* 61 (October 1984): 462–80.

Eslinger, Ellen. "Antebellum Liquor Reform in Lexington, Virginia: The Story of a Small Southern Town." *Virginia Magazine of History and Biography* 99 (April 1991): 163–86.

Eubanks, John Evans. *Ben Tillman's Baby: The Dispensary System of South Carolina, 1892–1915.* Augusta, GA: n.p., 1950.

Featherstonhaugh, George W. *A Canoe Voyage up the Minnay Sotor.* 2 vols. London: R. Bentley, 1847.

Ferleger, Herbert. *David A. Wells and the American Revenue System, 1865–1870.* Philadelphia: Porcupine Press, 1977.

Finger, John R. *The Eastern Band of Cherokees, 1819–1900.* Knoxville: University of Tennessee Press, 1984.

Fisher, David Hackett. *Albion's Seed: Four British Folkways in America.* New York: Oxford University Press, 1989.

Fletcher, Arthur L. *Ashe County: A History.* Jefferson, NC: Ashe County Research Association, 1963.

Fletcher, J. F. *A History of the Ashe County, North Carolina and New River, Virginia Baptist Associations.* Raleigh, NC: Commercial Printing Co., 1935.

Foner, Eric. *Reconstruction: America's Unfinished Revolution.* New York: Harper and Row, 1988.

Fossett, Mildred B. *History of McDowell County.* Marion, NC: McDowell County American Revolution Bicentennial Commission Heritage Committee, 1976.

Fox, John, Jr. "The Southern Mountaineer." *Scribner's Magazine* 29 (April–May 1901): 387–99, 556–70.

Franklin, John Hope. *Reconstruction: After the Civil War.* Chicago: University of Chicago Press, 1961.

Frederickson, George M. *The Black Image in the White Mind: The Debate on Afro-American Character and Destiny.* New York: Harper and Row, 1971.

Friedman, Jean F. *The Enclosed Garden: Women and Community in the Evangelical South.* Chapel Hill: University of North Carolina Press, 1985.

Frost, William G. "Our Contemporary Ancestors in the Southern Mountains." *Atlantic Monthly* 83 (March 1899): 311–19.

Gaston, Paul M. *The New South Creed: A Study in Southern Mythmaking.* New York: Alfred A. Knopf, 1970.

Gatchell, H. P. *Western North Carolina, Its Resources, Mineral Wealth, Climate, and Salubriety.* Asheville, NC: E. J. Aston, 1870.

Gaventa, John. *Power and Powerlessness: Quiescence and Rebellion in an Appalachian Valley.* Urbana: University of Illinois Press, 1980.

Genovese, Eugene D. "Yeoman Farmers in a Slaveholders' Democracy." *Agricultural History* 49 (April 1975): 331–42.

Gielow, Martha S. *Old Andy the Moonshiner.* New York: Fleming H. Revell Co., 1909.

Gillette, William. *Retreat from Reconstruction, 1869–1879.* Baton Rouge: Louisiana State University Press, 1979.

Globe Baptist Church Records. Chapel Hill: Photographic Services, University of North Carolina Library, 1976.

Godbold, Stanly E., Jr., and Mattie U. Russell. *Confederate Colonel and Cherokee Chief: The Life of William Holland Thomas.* Knoxville: University of Tennessee Press, 1990.

Goodrich, Frances. *Mountain Homespun.* New Haven, CT: Yale University Press, 1931.

Goodwyn, Lawrence. *The Democratic Promise: The Populist Moment in America.* New York: Oxford University Press, 1976.

Gray, Sam, ed. *The Many Faces of Appalachia: Exploring a Region's Diversity.* Boone, NC: Appalachian Consortium Press, 1985.

Greene, W. Earl. *Meat Camp Baptist Church, 1851–1981: A History.* Boone, NC: Minor's Publishing Co., 1983.

Griffin, Clarence W. *Centennial History of Pleasant Grove Methodist Church, 1838–1938.* Forest City, NC: Pleasant Grove Centennial Committee, 1938.

———. *The History of Old Tryon and Rutherford Counties, 1730–1930.* Asheville, NC: Miller Printing Co., 1937.

Griffin, Clifford S. *The Ferment of Reform, 1830–1860.* New York: Crowell, 1967.

Guernsey, A. H. "Hunting for Stills." *Harper's Weekly* 11 (December 21, 1867): 811.

———. "Illicit Distilling of Liquors—Southern Mode of making Whiskey." *Harper's Weekly* 11 (December 7, 1867): 773.

Gusfield, Joseph R. *Symbolic Crusade: Status Politics and the American Temperance Movement*. Urbana: University of Illinois Press, 1963.

Gutman, Herbert G. "Work, Culture, and Society in Industrializing America, 1815–1919." *American Historical Review* 78 (June 1973): 531–88.

Hahn, Steven A. *The Roots of Southern Populism: Yeomen Farmers and the Transformation of the Georgia Backcountry, 1850–1900*. New York: Oxford University Press, 1983.

Hall, Joseph S. *Smoky Mountain Folks and Their Lore*. Asheville, NC: Great Smoky Mountains Natural History Association, 1960.

Hall, Van Beck. "The Politics of Appalachian Virginia, 1790–1830." In *Appalachian Frontiers: Settlement, Society, and Development in the Preindustrial Era*, ed. Robert D. Mitchell, 166–86. Lexington: University Press of Kentucky, 1991.

Hamilton, Joseph G. de Roulhac. *Reconstruction in North Carolina*. New York: Columbia University, 1914.

———, ed. *The Papers of Randolph Abbott Shotwell*. Vols. 2 and 3. Raleigh: North Carolina Historical Commission, 1929–1931.

Hamilton, Joseph G. de Roulhac, and Max R. Williams, eds. *The Papers of William Alexander Graham*, 5 vols. Raleigh: North Carolina Division of Archives and History, 1957–1973.

Hamm, Richard F. *Shaping the Eighteenth Amendment: Temperance Reform, Legal Culture, and the Polity, 1880–1920*. Chapel Hill: University of North Carolina Press, 1995.

Hancock, H. Irving. *Fighting the Cowards, or, Among the Moonshiners*. New York: Street and Smith, 1904.

Hardy, Jason F. E. *Second Annual Address: Delivered before the Asheville Temperance Society, on the 4th of July, 1832: With the Executive Committee's First Annual Report*. Rutherfordton, NC: Roswell Elmer Jr., Printer, 1832.

Hardy, Michael C. *A Short History of Old Watauga County*. Boone, NC: Parkway Publishers, 2005.

Harkins, Anthony. *Hillbilly: A Cultural History of an American Icon*. New York: Oxford University Press, 2004.

Harper, Margaret E. *Fort Defiance and the General*. Hickory, NC: Clay Printing Co., 1976.

Harris, J. William. *Plain Folk and Gentry in a Slave Society: White Liberty and Black Slavery in Augusta's Hinterlands*. Middletown, CT: Wesleyan University Press, 1985.

Harris, William C. *William Woods Holden: Firebrand of North Carolina Politics*. Baton Rouge: Louisiana State University Press, 1987.

Hartt, Rollin Lynde. "The Mountaineers: Our Own Lost Tribes." *Century Magazine* 95 (January 1918): 395–404.

Harvey, Will Wallace. "A Strange Land and Peculiar People." *Lippincott's Magazine* 12 (October 1873): 429–38.

Hatch, Elvin. "The Margins of Civilization: Progressives and Moonshiners in the Late 19th-Century Mountain South." *Appalachian Journal: A Regional Studies Review* 32 (fall 2004): 68–99.

Hayes, Johnson J. *The Land of Wilkes*. Wilkesboro, NC: Wilkes County Historical Society, 1962.

Haylor, Nicole, ed. *Sound Wormy: Memoir of Andrew Gennett, Lumberman*. Athens: University of Georgia Press, 2002.

Haynes, Ada F. *Poverty in Central Appalachia: Underdevelopment and Exploitation*. New York: Garland Publishing, 1997.

Hickerson, Thomas Felix. *Echoes of Happy Valley*. Durham, NC: Seeman Printery, 1962.

Hicks, George L. *Appalachian Valley*. New York: Holt, Rinehart and Winston, 1976.

History of Alleghany County, 1859 through 1976, Sparta, North Carolina. Sparta, NC: Alleghany County Historical Committee, 1976.

Hofstadter, Richard. *The Age of Reform: From Bryan to F.D.R.* New York: Alfred A. Knopf, 1955.

Hollingsworth, J. G. *History of Surry County, or Annals of Northwest North Carolina*. J. G. Hollingsworth, 1935.

Holmes, William F. "Moonshiners and Whitecaps in Alabama, 1893." *Alabama Review* 24 (January 1981): 31–49.

———. "Moonshining and Collective Violence: Georgia, 1889–1895." *Journal of American History* 67 (December 1980): 589–611.

———. "The Southern Farmers' Alliance: The Georgia Experience." *Georgia Historical Quarterly* 72 (winter 1988): 627–52.

———. "Whitecapping, Agrarian Violence in Mississippi, 1902–1906." *Journal of Southern History* 25 (May 1969): 165–85.

"Home of the Moonshiners." *Harper's Weekly* 30 (October 23, 1886): 687–88.

Hooker, Elizabeth R. *Religion in the Highlands: Native Churches and Missionary Enterprises in the Southern Appalachian Area*. New York: Home Missions Council, 1933.

Horton, Laurel. "Nineteenth Century Quilts in Macon County, North Carolina." In *The Many Faces of Appalachia: Proceedings of the 7th Annual Appalachian Studies Conference*, ed. Sam Gray, 11–22. Boone, NC: Appalachian Consortium Press, 1985.

Hostra, Warren R., and Robert D. Mitchell. "Town and Country in Backcountry Virginia: Winchester and the Shenandoah Valley, 1730–1800." *Journal of Southern History* 59 (November 1993): 619–46.

Houch, John. *Ashe County*. Charleston, SC: Arcadia, 2000.

Howe, Frederic C. *Taxation and Taxes in the United States under the Internal Revenue System, 1791–1895*. New York: Thomas Y. Crowell, 1896.

Hsiung, David C. *Two Worlds in the Tennessee Mountains: Exploring the Origins of Appalachian Stereotypes*. Lexington: University Press of Kentucky, 1997.

Hu, Tun Yuan. *The Liquor Tax in the United States, 1791–1947: A History of the Internal Revenue Taxes Imposed on Distilled Spirits by the Federal Government.* New York: Graduate School of Business, Columbia University, 1950.

Hubbard, Leonidas, Jr. "The Moonshiner at Home." *Atlantic Monthly* 90 (August 1902): 234–41.

Inscoe, John C. "Diversity in Antebellum Mountain Life: The Towns of Western North Carolina." In *The Many Faces of Appalachia: Proceedings of the 7th Annual Appalachian Studies Conference,* ed. Sam Gray, 153–68. Boone, NC: Appalachian Consortium Press, 1985.

———. *Mountain Masters, Slavery, and the Sectional Crisis in Western North Carolina.* Knoxville: University of Tennessee Press, 1989.

———. "Race and Racism in Nineteenth-Century Southern Appalachia." In *Appalachia in the Making: The Mountain South in the Nineteenth Century,* ed. Mary Beth Pudup, Dwight B. Billings, and Altina L. Waller, 103–31. Chapel Hill: University of North Carolina Press, 1995.

———, ed. *Appalachians and Race: The Mountain South from Slavery to Segregation.* Lexington: University Press of Kentucky, 2001.

Inscoe, John C., and Gordon B. McKinney. *The Heart of Confederate Appalachia: Western North Carolina in the Civil War.* Chapel Hill: University of North Carolina Press, 2000.

Isaac, Paul E. *Prohibition and Politics: Turbulent Decades in Tennessee, 1885–1920.* Knoxville: University of Tennessee Press, 1965.

Israel, Charles A. *Before Scopes: Evangelicalism, Education, and Evolution in Tennessee, 1870–1925.* Athens: University of Georgia Press, 2004.

Ivy, James D. *No Saloon in the Valley: The Southern Strategy of Texas Prohibitionists in the 1880s.* Waco, TX: Baylor University Press, 2003.

Jeffrey, Thomas E. *Thomas Lanier Clingman: Fire Eater from the North Carolina Mountains.* Athens: University of Georgia Press, 1999.

Johann, Margaret. "A Little Moonshiner." *Christian Observer* 85 (July 21, 1897): 700–701.

Johnson, Guion G. *Ante-Bellum North Carolina: A Social History.* Chapel Hill: University of North Carolina Press, 1937.

Johnston, Frontis W., ed. *The Papers of Zebulon Baird Vance.* Vol. 1, *1843–1862.* Raleigh: North Carolina Department of Archives and History, 1963.

Jolley, Daniel Wayne. "The Ku Klux Klan in Rutherford County, 1870–1871." MA thesis, University of North Carolina at Chapel Hill, 1974.

Jones, Louise Coffin. "In the Backwoods of Carolina." *Lippincott's Monthly Magazine* 24 (December 1879): 747–56.

———. "In the Highlands of North Carolina." *Lippincott's Monthly Magazine* 32 (October 1883): 378–86.

Jones, Loyal. "Mountain Religion: An Overview." In *Christianity in Appalachia: Profiles in Regional Pluralism,* ed. Bill J. Leonard, 91–102. Knoxville: University of Tennessee Press, 1999.

Kelley, William D. *Abolish the Whiskey Ring.* Sanford, NC: Microfilming Corporation of America, 1979.

Kellner, Esther. *Moonshine: Its History and Folklore.* Indianapolis: Bobbs-Merrill, 1971.

Kellner, Kenneth W. "What Is Distinctive about the Scotch-Irish?" In *Appalachian Frontiers: Settlement, Society, and Development in the Preindustrial Era,* ed. Robert D. Mitchell, 69–86. Lexington: University Press of Kentucky, 1991.

Kenzer, Robert C. *Kinship and Neighborhood in a Southern Community: Orange County, North Carolina, 1849–1881.* Knoxville: University of Tennessee Press, 1987.

Kephart, Horace. *Our Southern Highlanders.* New York: Outing Publishing Co., 1913.

———. "Roving with Kephart: The Sport of Still Hunting (Moonshine Stills)." *All Outdoors* (September 1919): 490–91.

Kerr, K. Austin. *Organized for Prohibition: A New History of the Anti-Saloon League.* New Haven, CT: Yale University Press, 1985.

Key, V. O. *Southern Politics in State and Nation.* New York: Random House, 1949.

King, Edward. "The Great South: Among the Mountains of Western North Carolina." *Scribner's Monthly* 7 (March 1874): 513–44.

Kirby, Jack T. *Darkness at the Dawning: Race and Reform in the Progressive South.* Philadelphia: J. B. Lippincott, 1972.

Klotter, James. "The Black South and White Appalachia." *Journal of American History* 66 (March 1980): 832–49.

Kulikoff, Allan. "The Transition to Capitalism in Rural America." *William and Mary Quarterly* 46 (January 1989): 120–44.

Langley, Joan, and Wright Langley. *Yesterday's Asheville.* Miami, FL: E. A. Seemann, 1975.

Lanman, Charles. *Letters from the Alleghany Mountains.* New York: G. P. Putnam, 1849.

———. "Novelties of Southern Scenery." *Appleton's Journal* (October 16–30, 1869): 257–61, 296–97, 327–29.

Lasley, R. T., ed. *Burke County Tales.* Conover, NC: Hometown Memories, 1995.

"Law and Moonshine." *Harper's Weekly* 24 (August 23, 1879): 667.

Ledford, Katherine E. "'The Primitive Circle': Inscribing Class in Southern Appalachian Travel Writing, 1816–1846." *Appalachian Journal* 29 (fall 2001–winter 2002): 68–89.

Lehmann, William C. *Scottish and Scotch-Irish Contributions to Early American Life and Culture.* Port Washington, NY: Kennikat Press, 1978.

Leonard, Bill J., ed. *Christianity in Appalachia: Profiles in Regional Pluralism.* Knoxville: University of Tennessee Press, 1999.

Leuchtenburg, William E. *The Perils of Prosperity, 1914–32.* Chicago: University of Chicago Press, 1958.

Lewis, Helen, Linda Johnson, and Donald Askins, eds. *Colonialism in Modern America: The Appalachian Case.* Boone, NC: Appalachian Consortium Press, 1978.

Lewis, Jehu. "The Grandfather of North Carolina." *Lakeside Monthly* 10 (September 1873): 218–24.

Lewis, Ronald L. "Beyond Isolation and Homogeneity: Diversity and the History of Appalachia." In *Confronting Appalachian Stereotypes: Back Talk from an American Region,* ed. Dwight B. Billings, Gurney Norman, and Katherine Ledford, 21–43. Lexington: University Press of Kentucky, 1999.

———. *Black Coal Miners in America: Race, Class and Community Conflict, 1780–1980.* Lexington: University Press of Kentucky, 1987.

———. *Transforming the Appalachian Countryside: Railroads, Deforestation, and Social Change in West Virginia, 1880–1920.* Chapel Hill: University of North Carolina Press, 1998.

Link, Arthur S. "The Progressive Movement in the South, 1870–1914." *North Carolina Historical Review* 23 (April 1946): 172–95.

Link, William A. *The Paradox of Southern Progressivism, 1880–1930.* Chapel Hill: University of North Carolina Press, 1992.

Logan, John R. *Sketches, Historical and Biographical, of the Broad River and King's Mountain Baptist Associations, from 1800–1882.* Shelby, NC: Babington, Roberts, 1887.

Loveland, Anne C. *Southern Evangelicals and the Social Order, 1800–1860.* Baton Rouge: Louisiana State University Press, 1980.

Lovin, Clifford R. "Religion." In *The History of Jackson County,* ed., Max R. Williams, 255–80. Sylva, NC: Jackson County Historical Association, 1987.

Lynde, Francis. "The Moonshiners of Fact." *Lippincott's Magazine* 57 (January 1896): 66–76.

Malet, William W. *An Errand to the South in the Summer of 1862.* London: R. Bentley, 1863.

Marler, James D. *Heritage of Cleveland County.* Shelby, NC: Cleveland County Historical Association, 1982.

Martin, Edgar W. *The Standard of Living in 1860: American Consumption Levels on the Eve of the Civil War.* Chicago: University of Chicago Press, 1942.

Mason, Robert L. *The Lure of the Great Smokies.* Boston: Houghton Mifflin, 1927.

Massey, Mary Elizabeth. *Ersatz in the Confederacy.* Baton Rouge: Louisiana State University Press, 1952.

———. "Food and Drink Shortages on the Confederate Homefront." *North Carolina Historical Review* 26 (July 1949): 306–34.

Mast, A. Clyde. *History of Watauga County, North Carolina.* Boone, NC: A. Clyde Mast, 1976.

Mathews, Donald G. *Religion in the Old South.* Chicago: University of Chicago Press, 1977.

Matthews, Donald R., ed. *North Carolina Votes: General Election Returns by County.* Chapel Hill: University of North Carolina Press, 1962.

Mattingly, Carol. *Well-Tempered Women: Nineteenth-Century Temperance Rhetoric.* Carbondale: Southern Illinois University Press, 1998.

Maurer, David W. *Kentucky Moonshine.* Lexington: University Press of Kentucky, 1974.

McCall, S. M. "Address of S. M. McCall upon the Evils of Prohibition to the Patriotic Voters of Caldwell County, N.C., during the Campaign between Patriotism and Fanaticism; Prior to May 26, 1908." Syracuse, NY: Photo Mount Pamphlet Binder, Gaylord Bros. Makers, 1908.

McCauley, Deborah Vansau. *Appalachian Mountain Religion: A History.* Urbana: University of Illinois Press, 1995.

McCurry, Stephanie. *Masters of Small Worlds: Yeoman Households, Gender Relations, and the Political Culture of the Antebellum Southern Carolina Low Country.* New York: Oxford University Press, 1995.

McDonald, Forrest, and Grady McWhiney. "The Antebellum Southern Herdsman: A Reinterpretation." *Journal of Southern History* 41 (May 1975): 147–66.

McFall, B. G. *Among the Moonshiners, or, A Drunkard's Legacy: A Temperance Drama in Three Acts.* Clyde, OH: Ames, 1897.

McGee, Bluford Bartlett. *The Country Youth: Autobiography of B. B. McGee.* Edited by James Larkin Pearson. 1874. Reprint, North Wilkesboro, NC: Pearson Publishing Co., 1964.

McGonan, Richard. *Government Regulation of the Alcohol Industry: The Search for Revenue and the Common Good.* Westport, CT: Quorom Books, 1997.

McKelway, Alexander J. "The Dispensary in North Carolina." *Outlook* 61 (April 8, 1899): 820–22.

———. "State Prohibition in North Carolina." *Outlook* 89 (June 6, 1908): 271–72.

McKenzie, Robert Tracy. *One South or Many? Plantation Belt and Upcountry in Civil War Era Tennessee.* Cambridge: Cambridge University Press, 1994.

McKinney, Gordon B. "Economy and Community in Western North Carolina, 1860–1865." In *Appalachia in the Making: The Mountain South in the Nineteenth Century,* ed. Mary Beth Pudup, Dwight B. Billings, and Altina L. Waller, 163–84. Chapel Hill: University of North Carolina Press, 1995.

———. "Moonshiners, Law Enforcement, and Violence: Legitimacy and Community in Western North Carolina, 1862–1882." Paper presented at the annual meeting of the Southern Historical Association, New Orleans, LA, November 1995.

———. "Preindustrial Jackson County and Economic Development." *Journal of the Appalachian Studies Association* 2 (1990): 1–10.

———. *Southern Mountain Republicans, 1865–1900.* Chapel Hill: University of North Carolina Press, 1978.

———. "Southern Mountain Republicans and the Negro, 1865–1900." In *Appalachians and Race: The Mountain South from Slavery to Segregation,* ed. John C. Inscoe, 199–219. Lexington: University Press of Kentucky, 2001.

———. *Zeb Vance: North Carolina's Civil War Governor and Gilded Age Political Leader.* Chapel Hill: University of North Carolina Press, 2004.

————, ed. "The Klan in the Southern Mountains: The Lusk-Shotwell Controversy." *Appalachian Journal* 8 (winter 1981): 89–104.

McKinney, Gordon B., and Richard M. McMurry, eds. *The Papers of Zebulon Vance.* Microfilm ed. Frederick, MD: University Publications of America, 1987.

McMath, Robert C., Jr. *Populist Vanguard: A History of the Southern Farmers' Alliance.* Chapel Hill: University of North Carolina Press, 1975.

Medford, W. Clark. *The Early History of Haywood County.* Waynesville, NC: Privately printed, 1961.

————. *Great Smoky Mountain Stories and Sun over Ol' Starlin.* Waynesville, NC: Miller Printing Co., 1966.

————. *The Middle History of Haywood County.* Waynesville, NC: Miller Printing Co., 1968.

Methodist Episcopal Church, South. *Journal of the North Carolina Annual Conference of the M. E. Church, South.* North Carolina: The Conference, 1883–1939.

Michaux, Francois Andrew. *Travels to the Westward of the Alleghany Mountains.* London: Richard Phillips, 1805.

Miles, Emma B. *The Spirit of the Mountains.* 1905. Reprint, Knoxville: University of Tennessee Press, 1975.

Miller, Douglas T. *The Birth of Modern America, 1820–1850.* New York: Pegasus, 1970.

Miller, Edna Lucille. "A Study of Folklore in Watauga County, North Carolina." MA thesis, George Peabody College for Teachers, 1938.

Miller, Wilbur R. "The Revenue: Federal Law Enforcement in the Mountain South, 1870–1900." *Journal of Southern History* 55 (May 1989): 195–216.

————. *Revenuers & Moonshiners: Enforcing Federal Liquor Law in the Mountain South, 1865–1900.* Chapel Hill: University of North Carolina Press, 1991.

Minutes, Three Forks Baptist Church, 1790–1895. Wilkes County, NC: Three Forks Baptist Church, 1895.

Mitchell, Robert D. "The Settlement Fabric of the Shenandoah Valley, 1790–1860: Pattern, Process, and Structure." In *After the Backcountry: Rural Life in the Great Valley of Virginia, 1800–1900,* ed. Kenneth E. Koons and Warren R. Hofstra, 34–47. Knoxville: University of Tennessee Press, 2000.

————, ed. *Appalachian Frontiers: Settlement, Society, & Development in the Preindustrial Era.* Lexington: University Press of Kentucky, 1991.

Montell, William L. *Killings: Folk Justice in the Upper South.* Lexington: University Press of Kentucky, 1986.

"The Moonshine Man: A Peep into His Haunts and Hiding Places." *Harper's Weekly* 21 (October 20, 1877): 820–22.

"Moonshiners." *Harper's New Monthly Magazine* 59 (March 1879): 380–90.

"Moonshiners." *Harper's Weekly* 22 (November 2, 1878): 875.

Moore, Bernard Francis. *The Moonshiner's Daughter: A Play of Mountain Life in Three Acts.* Boston: Walter H. Baker, 1898.

Morgan, Norma Dillingham. *Flat Creek Baptist Church Minutes, Weaverville, North Carolina, 1883–1931.* Mars Hill, NC: Southern Appalachian Center, Mars Hill College, 1986.

Morley, Margaret W. *The Carolina Mountains.* Boston: Houghton Mifflin, 1913.

Mull, J. Alex. *Tales of Old Burke.* Morganton, NC: News Herald Press, 1975.

Murfree, Mary. "The Moonshiners at Hoho-Hebee Falls." In *The Phantoms of the Foot-Bridge and Other Stories.* New York: Harper and Brothers, 1895.

Murphy, Teresa Anne. *Ten Hours' Labor: Religion, Reform, and Gender in Early New England.* Ithaca, NY: Cornell University Press, 1992.

Nash, Steven E. "Presidential Reconstruction in Western North Carolina." MA thesis, Western Carolina University, 2001.

Neely, Mark E., Jr. *Southern Rights: Political Prisoners and the Myth of Confederate Constitutionalism.* Charlottesville: University of Virginia Press, 1999.

Newsome, A. R. "Twelve North Carolina Counties in 1810–1811." *North Carolina Historical Review* 5 (October 1928): 413–46.

———, ed. "John Brown's Journal of Travel in Western North Carolina in 1795." *North Carolina Historical Review* 11 (October 1934): 284–313.

———. "The A. S. Merrimon Journal, 1853–1854." *North Carolina Historical Review* 8 (July 1931): 300–330.

Nobles, Gregory H. "Breaking into the Backcountry: New Approaches to the Early American Frontier, 1750–1800." *William and Mary Quarterly* 46 (1989): 641–70.

Noblitt, Philip T. *A Mansion in the Mountains: The Story of Moses and Bertha Cone and Their Blowing Rock Manor.* Boone, NC: Parkway Publishers, 1996.

O'Donnell, Kevin E., and Helen Hollingsworth, eds. *Seekers of Scenery: Travel Writing from Southern Appalachia, 1840–1900.* Knoxville: University of Tennessee Press, 2004.

Ohmann, Richard. *Selling Culture: Magazines, Markets, and Class at the Turn of the Century.* New York: Verso, 1996.

Olmsted, Frederick Law. *The Cotton Kingdom.* New York: Mason Bros., 1861.

———. *A Journey in the Back Country in the Winter of 1853–54.* New York: Mason Bros., 1860.

Olsen, Otto H. "The Ku Klux Klan: A Study in Reconstruction Politics and Propaganda." *North Carolina Historical Review* 39 (July 1962): 340–62.

———. "North Carolina: An Incongruous Presence." In *Reconstruction and Redemption in the South,* ed. Otto H. Olsen, 156–201. Baton Rouge: Louisiana State University Press, 1980.

———. "Reconsidering the Scalawags." *Civil War History* 12 (December 1966): 304–15.

Olsen, Otto H., and Ellen Z. McGrew, eds. "Prelude to Reconstruction: The Correspondence of State Senator Leander S. Gash, 1866–1867, Part I." *North Carolina Historical Review* 60 (January 1983): 37–88.

———. "Prelude to Reconstruction: The Correspondence of State Senator Leander S. Gash, 1866–1867, Part II." *North Carolina Historical Review* 60 (April 1983): 333–66.

Olson, Eric J. "Race Relations in Asheville, North Carolina: Three Incidents, 1868–1906." In *The Appalachian Experience: Proceedings of the 6th Annual Appalachian Studies Conference,* ed. Barry M. Buxton, 153–68. Boone, NC: Appalachian Consortium Press, 1983.

Osborne, Anne, and Charlene Pace. *Saluda, N.C.: One Hundred Years, 1881–1981.* Saluda, NC: Holly Hill Publishers, 1981.

Ostwalt, Conrad, and Phoebe Pollitt. "The Salem School and Orphanage: White Missionaries, Black School." In *Appalachians and Race: The Mountain South from Slavery to Segregation,* ed. John C. Inscoe, 235–44. Lexington: University Press of Kentucky, 2001.

Otto, John Solomon. "The Decline of Forest Farming in Southern Appalachia." *Journal of Forest History* 27 (January 1983): 18–26.

———. "'Hillbilly Culture': The Appalachian Mountain Folk in History and Popular Culture." *Southern Quarterly* 24 (spring 1986): 25–34.

Ownby, Ted. *Subduing Satan: Religion, Recreation, and Manhood in the Rural South, 1865–1900.* Chapel Hill: University of North Carolina Press, 1990.

Owsley, Frank L. *Plain Folk of the Old South.* Baton Rouge: Louisiana State University Press, 1949.

Padgett, Guy. *A History of Clay County, North Carolina.* Hayesville, NC: Clay County Bicentennial Committee, 1976.

Padgett, James A., ed. "Reconstruction Letters from North Carolina, Part III." *North Carolina Historical Review* 19 (July 1942): 333–66.

Painter, Jacqueline Burgin. *The Season of Dorland-Bell: History of an Appalachian Mission School.* Boone, NC: Appalachian Consortium Press, 1996.

Paludan, Phillip S. *Victims: A True Story of the Civil War.* Knoxville: University of Tennessee Press, 1981.

Parris, John. *Mountain Bred.* Asheville, NC: Citizen-Times Publishing Co., 1967.

———. *My Mountains, My People.* Asheville, NC: Citizen-Times Publishing Co., 1957.

———. *Roaming the Mountains.* Asheville, NC: Citizen-Times Publishing Co., 1955.

———. *These Storied Mountains.* Asheville, NC: Citizen-Times Publishing Co., 1972.

Paschal, George Washington. *History of the North Carolina Baptists.* 2 vols. Raleigh: North Carolina Baptist Convention, 1955.

Patton, James. *Biography of James Patton.* Asheville, NC: n.p., 1850.

Patton, James W., ed. "Glimpses of North Carolina in the Writing of Northern and Foreign Travelers, 1783–1860." *North Carolina Historical Review* 45 (July 1968): 298–323.

Patton, Sadie Smathers. *Sketches of Polk County History.* Spartanburg, SC: Reprint Co., Publishers, 1976.

———. *The Story of Henderson County.* Asheville, NC: Miller Printing Co., 1947.

Pearson, C. C., and J. Edwin Hendricks. *Liquor and Anti-Liquor in Virginia, 1619–1919.* Durham, NC: Duke University Press, 1967.

Peattie, Roderick, ed. *The Great Smokies and the Blue Ridge: The Story of the Southern Appalachians.* New York: Vanguard Press, 1943.

Pederson, Lee. "The Randy Sons of Nancy Whisky." *American Speech* 52 (1977): 112–21.

Pegram, Thomas R. *Battling Demon Rum: The Struggle for a Dry America.* Chicago: Ivan R. Dee, 1998.

Pendleton, Charles S. "Illicit Whiskey-Making." *Tennessee Folklore Society Bulletin* 12 (March 1946): 1–16.

Perrett, Geoffrey. *America in the Twenties: A History.* New York: Simon and Schuster, 1982.

Peterson, Emil O. "A Glimpse of the Moonshiners." *Chautauquan* 26 (November 1897): 178–82.

Phifer, Edward W. "Slavery in Microcosm: Burke County, North Carolina." *Journal of Southern History* 28 (May 1962): 137–65.

Phifer, Edward W., Jr. *Burke: The History of a North Carolina County, 1777–1920, with a Glimpse Beyond.* Morganton, NC: privately published, 1977.

———. *Burke County: A Brief History.* Raleigh: North Carolina Division of Archives and History, 1979.

Pierce, Daniel S. *The Great Smokies: From Natural Habitat to National Park.* Knoxville: University of Tennessee Press, 2000.

Pierson, Mrs. D. L. "The Mountaineers of Madison County, North Carolina." *Missionary Review of the World* (November 1897): 821–31.

Powers, Madelon. *Faces along the Bar: Lore and Order in the Workingman's Saloon, 1870–1920.* Chicago: University of Chicago Press, 1998.

Preslar, Charles J., Jr., ed. *A History of Catawba County.* Salisbury, NC: Rowan Printing Co., 1954.

Price, Theodore H., and Richard Spillane. "The Commissioner of Internal Revenue as a Policeman." *Outlook* 120 (November 27, 1918): 498, 503–5.

Pudup, Mary Beth, Dwight B. Billings, and Altina L. Waller, eds. *Appalachia in the Making: The Mountain South in the Nineteenth Century.* Chapel Hill: University of North Carolina Press, 1995.

Quist, John W. *Restless Visionaries: The Social Roots of Antebellum Reform in Alabama and Michigan.* Baton Rouge: Louisiana State University Press, 1998.

Rable, George C. *But There Was No Peace: The Role of Violence in the Politics of Reconstruction.* Athens: University of Georgia Press, 1984.

Raine, James Watt. *The Land of Saddle-Bags: A Study of the Mountain People of Appalachia.* 1924. Reprint, Lexington: University Press of Kentucky, 1997.

Rainey, Sue. *Creating Picturesque America: Monument to the Natural and Cultural Landscape.* Nashville, TN: Vanderbilt University Press, 1994.

Randel, William Peirce. *The Ku Klux Klan: A Century of Infamy.* London: Hamish Hamilton, 1965.

Raper, Horace W. *William Woods Holden: North Carolina's Political Enigma.* Chapel Hill: University of North Carolina Press, 1985.

Ray, J. E. *Our Danger Signal.* Asheville, NC: Asheville Printing Co., 1892.

Reasons Why the Tax on Distilled Spirits Should Be Reduced. Pamphlet, 1897.

Reeves, Thomas W. "History of Haywood County." MA thesis, Duke University, 1937.

Reid, Christian. *The Land of the Sky; or Adventures in Mountain By-ways* (New York: D. Appleton, 1890).

Rensi, Ray, and Leo Downing. "A Touch of Mountain Dew: Art and History of Whiskey-Making in North Georgia." In *The Many Faces of Appalachia: Proceedings of the 7th Annual Appalachian Studies Conference,* ed. Sam Gray, 195–204. Boone, NC: Appalachian Consortium Press, 1985.

Richardson, Heather Cox. *The Greatest Nation on the Earth: Republican Economic Policies during the Civil War.* Cambridge, MA: Harvard University Press, 1997.

Robinson, William M., Jr. "Prohibition in the Confederacy." *American Historical Review* 37 (October 1931): 50–58.

Rorabaugh, W. J. *The Alcoholic Republic: An American Tradition.* New York: Oxford University Press, 1979.

———. "The Sons of Temperance in Antebellum Jasper County." *Georgia Historical Quarterly* 64 (fall 1980): 263–79.

Rosenzweig, Roy. *Eight Hours for What We Will: Workers and Leisure in an Industrial City, 1870–1920.* New York: Cambridge University Press, 1983.

Rowe, Anne. *The Enchanted Country: Northern Writers in the South, 1865–1910.* Baton Rouge: Louisiana State University Press, 1978.

Rowles, Mary, and Hunter K. Rountree, eds. *The Diary of Augustine P. Shannon, 1848–1850.* Nashville, TN: Historical Records Survey, 1940.

Rutman, Darrett B., and Anita H. Rutman. "The Village South." In *Small Worlds, Large Questions: Explorations in Early American Social History, 1600–1850,* ed. Darrett B. Rutman and Anita H. Rutman, 231–72. Charlottesville: University Press of Virginia, 1994.

Said, Edward. *Orientalism.* New York: Pantheon, 1978.

Salmon, Emily J. "Thicker'in Huckleberries: Moonshiners and Revenuers in Franklin County, 1900–1930." *Virginia Cavalcade* 41 (July 1992): 132–43.

Salstrom, Paul. *Appalachia's Path to Dependency: Rethinking a Region's Economic History, 1730–1940.* Lexington: University Press of Kentucky, 1994.

Schultz, Stanley K. "Temperance Reform in the Antebellum South: Social Control and Urban Order." *South Atlantic Quarterly* 83 (summer 1984): 323–39.

Schwartz, Michael. *Radical Protest and Social Structure: The Southern Farmers' Alliance and Cotton Tenancy, 1880–1890.* New York: Academic Press, 1976.

Schweiger, Beth Barton. *The Gospel Working Up: Progress and the Pulpit in Nineteenth-Century Virginia.* New York: Oxford University Press, 2000.

Scomp, Henry D. *King Alcohol in the Realm of King Cotton: A History of the*

Liquor Traffic and of the Temperance Movement in Georgia from 1733 to 1887. Atlanta: Blakely, 1888.

Scott, Anne Firor. *The Southern Lady from Pedestal to Politics, 1880–1930.* Chicago: University of Chicago Press, 1970.

Sellers, James Benson. *The Prohibition Movement in Alabama, 1702 to 1943.* Chapel Hill: University of North Carolina Press, 1943.

Shaffner, Randolph P. *Heart of the Blue Ridge: Highlands, North Carolina.* Highlands, NC: Faraway Publishing, 2001.

Shapiro, Henry D. *Appalachia on Our Mind: The Southern Mountains and Mountaineers in the American Consciousness, 1870–1920.* Chapel Hill: University of North Carolina Press, 1978.

Sheppard, Muriel E. *Cabins in the Laurel.* Chapel Hill: University of North Carolina Press, 1935.

Sherman, Mandel, and Thomas R. Henry. *Hollow Folk.* New York: Thomas Y. Crowell, 1933.

Shifflett, Crandall A. *Coal Towns: Life, Work, and Culture in Company Towns of Southern Appalachia, 1880–1960.* Knoxville: University of Tennessee Press, 1991.

Silber, Nina. *The Romance of Reunion: Northerners and the South, 1865–1900.* Chapel Hill: University of North Carolina Press, 1993.

———. "'What Does America Need So Much as Americans?' Race and Northern Reconciliation with Southern Appalachia, 1870–1890." In *Appalachians and Race: The Mountain South from Slavery to Segregation,* ed. John C. Inscoe, 245–58. Lexington: University Press of Kentucky, 2001.

Simkins, Francis Butler. *Pitchfork Ben Tillman: South Carolinian.* Baton Rouge: Louisiana State University Press, 1944.

Slaughter, Thomas P. *The Whiskey Rebellion: Frontier Epilogue to the American Revolution.* New York: Oxford University Press, 1986.

Smith, C. D. *A Brief History of Macon County, North Carolina.* Franklin, NC: Franklin Press, 1891.

Smith, Gavin D. *The Secret Still: Scotland's Clandestine Whiskey Makers.* Edinburgh: Birlinn, 2002.

Smith, J. Calvin, ed. *Harper's Statistical Gazetteer of the World.* New York: Harper and Brothers, 1855.

Smith, J. Wesley. *The Mountaineers; or, Bottled Sunshine for Blue Mondays.* Nashville, TN: Publishing House of the Methodist Episcopal Church, South, 1902.

Smith, R. P. *Some Results of the Mission Work in Western North Carolina.* Asheville, NC: Home Mission Committee of the Asheville Presbytery, 1905.

Sondley, F. A. *Asheville and Buncombe County.* 2 vols. Asheville, NC: Citizen Co., 1922.

———. *A History of Buncombe County.* 2 vols. Asheville, NC: Advocate Print. Co., 1930.

Southern Mountain Research Collective, ed. "Essays in Political Economy: Toward a Class Analysis of Appalachia." *Appalachian Journal* 11 (autumn–winter 1983–1984): 19–162.

Spalding, Arthur W. *Men of the Mountains*. Nashville, TN: Southern Publishing Association, 1915.

Stampp, Kenneth M. *The Era of Reconstruction, 1865–1877*. New York: Alfred A. Knopf, 1965.

Starnes, Richard D. *Creating the Land of the Sky: Tourism and Society in Western North Carolina*. Tuscaloosa: University of Alabama Press, 2005.

———. "'Rule of the Rebs': White Supremacy, the Lost Cause, and the White Social Memory in Reconstruction North Carolina, 1865–1871." MA thesis, Western Carolina University, 1994.

Steelman, Joseph F. "The Progressive Era in North Carolina, 1884–1917." PhD diss., University of North Carolina at Chapel Hill, 1955.

Steelman, Lala Carr. *The North Carolina Farmers' Alliance: A Political History, 1887–1893*. Greenville, NC: East Carolina University Publications, 1985.

Stewart, Bruce E. "Attacking Red-Legged Grasshoppers: Moonshiners, Violence, and the Politics of Federal Liquor Taxation in Western North Carolina, 1865–1876." *Appalachian Journal: A Regional Studies Review* 32 (fall 2004): 26–48.

———. "Select Men of Sober and Industrious Habits: Alcohol Reform and Social Conflict in Antebellum Appalachia." *Journal of Southern History* 73 (May 2007): 289–322.

———. "'This Country Improves in Cultivation, Wickedness, Mills and Still': Drinking and Distilling in Antebellum Western North Carolina." *North Carolina Historical Review* 83 (October 2006): 447–78.

———. "The Urban-Rural Dynamic of the Southern Farmers' Alliance: Relations between Athens Merchants and Clarke County Farmers, 1888–1891." *Georgia Historical Quarterly* 84 (summer 2005): 155–84.

———. "'When Darkness Reigns Then Is the Hour to Strike': Moonshining, Federal Liquor Taxation, and Klan Violence in Western North Carolina, 1868–1872." *North Carolina Historical Review* 80 (October 2003): 453–74.

Stillwell, E. H. ed. *Minutes of the Tuckaseegee Baptist Association, 1829–1957*. Nashville, TN: Historical Commission, Southern Baptist Convention, 1962.

Straw, Richard A., and H. Tyler Blethen, eds. *High Mountains Rising: Appalachia in Time and Place*. Urbana: University of Illinois Press, 2004.

Strother, David Hunter. "The Mountains." *Harper's Monthly* (December 1871–June 1872): 659–76, 801–15; (July–November 1872): 21–35, 347–61, 502–16, 801–16; (December 1872–June 1873): 669–81; (July–November 1873): 821–32; (December 1873–June 1874): 156–68; (July–November 1874): 475–86.

"Studies in the South." *Atlantic Monthly* 49 (January 1882): 82–91.

Susman, Warren I. *Culture as History: The Transformation of American Society in the Twentieth Century*. New York: Pantheon Books, 1984.

Szymanski, Ann-Marie E. *Pathways to Prohibition: Radicals, Moderates, and Social Movement Outcomes*. Durham, NC: Duke University Press, 2003.

Tachau, Mary K. "The Whiskey Rebellion in Kentucky: A Forgotten Episode of Civil Disobedience." *Journal of the Early Republic* 2 (July 1982): 239–59.

Taliaferro, H. E. *Fisher's River (North Carolina): Scenes and Characters.* New York: Harper and Brothers, 1859.

Taylor, Joe Gray. *Eating, Drinking, and Visiting in the South: An Informal History.* Baton Rouge: Louisiana State University Press, 1982.

Thomasson, Lillian Franklin. *Swain County: Early History and Educational Development.* Bryson City, NC: author, 1965.

Thompson, E. P. *The Making of the English Working Class.* New York: Pantheon Books, 1963.

———. "Time, Work-Discipline, and Industrial Capitalism." *Past & Present* 38 (December 1967): 56–97.

Thompson, Ernest Trice. *Presbyterian Missions in the Southern United States.* Richmond, VA: Presbyterian Committee of Publication, 1934.

Thompson, Samuel H. *The Highlanders of the South.* New York: Eaton and Mains, 1910.

Thompson, Tommy R. "The Image of Appalachian Kentucky in American Popular Magazines." *Register of the Kentucky Historical Society* 91 (April 1993): 176–202.

Thornborough, Laura. *The Great Smoky Mountains.* New York: Thomas Y. Crowell, 1942.

Tinsley, Jim Bob. *The Land of Waterfalls: Transylvania County, North Carolina.* Brevard, NC: J. B. and D. Tinsley, 1988.

Tomkinson, Laura E. *Twenty Years' History of the Woman's Home Missionary Society of the Methodist Episcopal Church, 1880–1900.* Cincinnati: Woman's Home Missionary Society of the Methodist Episcopal Church, 1903.

Trelease, Allen W. *The North Carolina Railroad, 1849–1871, and the Modernization of North Carolina.* Chapel Hill: University of North Carolina Press, 1991.

———. *White Terror: The Ku Klux Klan Conspiracy and Southern Reconstruction.* New York: Harper and Row, 1971.

Troxler, Carole Watterson, "'To Look More Closely at the Man': Wyatt Outlaw, a Nexus of National, Local, and Personal History." *North Carolina Historical Review* 77 (October 2000): 403–33.

Tucker, Glenn. *Zeb Vance: Champion of Personal Freedom.* New York: Bobbs-Merrill, 1965.

Tyler, Alice Felt. *Freedom's Ferment: Phases of American Social History from the Colonial Period to the Outbreak of the Civil War.* Minneapolis: University of Minnesota Press, 1944.

Tyrrell, Ian R. "Drink and Temperance in the Old South: An Overview and Interpretation." *Journal of Southern History* 48 (1982): 485–510.

———. *Sobering Up: From Temperance to Prohibition in Antebellum America, 1800–1860.* Westport, CT: Greenwood Press, 1979.

Underwood, Jinsie. *This Is Madison County.* Mars Hill, NC: Underwood, 1974.

Van Noppen, Ina W., and John J. Van Noppen. *Western North Carolina since the Civil War.* Boone, NC: Appalachian Consortium Press, 1973.

Varon, Elizabeth R. *We Mean to Be Counted: White Women and Politics in Antebellum Virginia.* Chapel Hill: University of North Carolina Press, 1998.

Waite, C. W. *Among the Moonshiners.* New York: F. T. Neely, 1899.

Walker, Samuel. *Popular Justice: A History of American Criminal Justice.* New York: Oxford University Press, 1980.

Waller, Altina L. *Feud: Hatfields, McCoys, and Social Change in Appalachia, 1860–1900.* Chapel Hill: University of North Carolina Press, 1988.

———. "Feuding in Appalachia: Evolution of a Cultural Stereotype." In *Appalachia in the Making: The Mountain South in the Nineteenth Century,* ed. Mary Beth Pudup, Dwight B. Billings, and Altina L. Waller, 347–76. Chapel Hill: University of North Carolina Press, 1995.

Walters, Ronald G. *American Reformers, 1815–1865.* New York: Hill and Wang, 1997.

Walton, Thomas George. *Sketches of the Pioneers in Burke County History.* Easley, SC: Southern Historical Press, 1894.

Warner, Charles D. "Comments on Kentucky." *Harper's New Monthly Magazine* 78 (January 1889): 255–71.

———. "On Horseback." *Atlantic Monthly* 56 (July–October 1885): 88–100, 194–207, 388–98, 540–54.

———. *On Horseback: A Tour in Virginia, North Carolina and Tennessee.* Boston: Houghton Mifflin, 1888.

Washburn, Benjamin Earle. *A Country Doctor in the South Mountains.* 1955. Reprint, Spindale, NC: Spindale Press, 1973.

Washburn, W. D. *Secrets on the Mountain.* Hickory, NC: Tarheel Press, 2002.

Watson, Alan D. "Ordinaries in Colonial Eastern North Carolina." *North Carolina Historical Review* 45 (January 1968): 67–83.

Weathers, Lee Beam. *The Living Past of Cleveland County.* 1956. Reprint, Spartanburg, SC: Reprint Co., Publishers, 1980.

Weaver, James H. *Memoirs of James H. Weaver.* Hickory, NC, 1910.

Weaver, Jeffrey Craig, ed. *Records of the Big Helton Baptist Church, 1840–1980: Helton Township, Ashe County, North Carolina.* Arlington, VA: J. C. Weaver, 1989.

———. *Records of the Senter Primitive Baptist Church, Nathan's Creek, Ashe County, North Carolina.* Arlington, VA: J. C. Weaver, 1989.

Weise, Robert S. *Grasping at Independence: Debt, Male Authority, and Mineral Rights in Appalachian Kentucky, 1850–1915.* Knoxville: University of Tennessee Press, 2001.

Weller, Jack E. *Yesterday's People: Life in Contemporary Appalachia.* Lexington: University of Kentucky Press, 1965.

Wellman, Manly Wade. *The Kingdom of Madison: A Southern Mountain Fastness and Its People.* Chapel Hill: University of North Carolina Press, 1973.

Wells, Jonathan Daniel. *The Origins of the Southern Middle Class, 1800–1861.* Chapel Hill: University of North Carolina Press, 2004.

Wheeler, John H. *Historical Sketches of North Carolina from 1584 to 1851.* 1851. Reprint, Baltimore: Genealogical Pub. Co. for Clearfield Co., 1993.

Whisnant, David E. *All That Is Native and Fine: The Politics of Culture in an American Region.* Chapel Hill: University of North Carolina Press, 1983.

———. *Modernizing the Mountaineer: People, Power, and Planning in Appalachia.* Knoxville: University of Tennessee Press, 1994.

Whitaker, Walter C. *The Southern Highlands and Highlanders.* Hartford, CT: Church Missions Publications, 1916.

White, M. L. *A History of the Life of Amos Owens, the Noted Blockader, of Cherry Mountain, N.C.* Shelby, NC: Cleveland Star Job Print, 1901.

White, William E. *A History of Alexander County, North Carolina.* Taylorsville, NC: Alexander County Historical Society, 1926.

Whitener, Daniel J. "North Carolina Prohibition Election of 1881 and Its Aftermath." *North Carolina Historical Review* 11 (April 1934): 71–93.

———. *Prohibition in North Carolina, 1715–1945.* Chapel Hill: University of North Carolina Press, 1946.

Wiebe, Robert H. *Self-Rule: A Cultural History of American Democracy.* Chicago: University of Chicago Press, 1995.

Wilhelm, Gene, Jr. "Folk Settlements in the Blue Ridge Mountains." *Appalachian Journal* 5 (winter 1978): 192–222.

Wilkinson, Alec. *Moonshine: A Life in Pursuit of White Liquor.* New York: Random House, 1985.

Williams, Cratis D. "Moonshining in the Mountains." *North Carolina Folklore* 15 (May 1967): 11–17.

———. "The Southern Mountaineer in Fact and Fiction." PhD diss., New York University, 1961.

Williams, John Alexander. *Appalachia: A History.* Chapel Hill: University of North Carolina Press, 2002.

Williams, Max, ed. *History of Jackson County.* Sylva, NC: Jackson County Historical Association, 1987.

Williams, Michael Ann. *Great Smoky Mountains Folklife.* Jackson: University Press of Mississippi, 1995.

Williamson, J. W. *Hillbillyland: What the Movies Did to the Mountains and What the Mountains Did to the Movies.* Chapel Hill: University of North Carolina Press, 1995.

———. *Southern Mountaineers in Silent Films: Plot Synopses of Movies About Moonshining, Feuding and Other Mountain Topics, 1904–1929.* Jefferson, NC: McFarland, 1994.

Willis, Lee L. "Creating a Lost Cause: Prohibition and Confederate Memory in Apalachicola, Florida." *Southern Studies* 7 (fall–winter 2005): 55–74.

Wilson, Jennifer Bauer. *Roan Mountain: A Passage of Time.* Winston-Salem, NC: John F. Blair, 1991.

Wilson, Samuel T. *The Southern Mountaineers.* New York: Presbyterian Home Missions, 1906.

Wiltse, Henry M. *The Moonshiners.* Chattanooga, TN: Times Printing, 1895.

Winters, Donald L. *Tennessee Farming, Tennessee Farmers: Antebellum Agri-*

culture in the Upper South. Knoxville: University of Tennessee Press, 1994.

Wolfery: A Collection of Burke County Folklore. 1977.

Woodward, C. Vann. *Origins of the New South, 1877–1913.* Baton Rouge: Louisiana State University Press, 1951.

Woolson, Constance Fenimore. "The French Broad." *Harper's Monthly* 50 (April 1875): 617–36.

———. "Up in the Blue Ridge." *Appleton's Journal* 5 (July–December 1878): 104–25.

Wright, Galvin. *Old South, New South: Revolutions in the Southern Economy since the Civil War.* New York: Basic Books, 1986.

Wyatt-Brown, Bertram. "The Antimission Movement in the Jacksonian South: A Study in Regional Folk Culture." *Journal of Southern History* 36 (November 1970): 501–29.

———. *The Shaping of Southern Culture: Honor, Grace, and War, 1760s–1890s.* Chapel Hill: University of North Carolina Press, 2001.

———. *Southern Honor: Ethics and Behavior in the Old South.* New York: Oxford University Press, 1982.

Yearns, W. Buck, and John C. Barrett, eds. *North Carolina War Documentary.* Chapel Hill: University of North Carolina Press, 1980.

York, Brantley. *The Autobiography of Brantley York.* Rev. ed. Edited by Charles Mathis. Jonesville, NC: Amanuensis Two, 1977.

Zeigler, Wilbur G., and Ben Grosscup. *The Heart of the Alleghenies, or Western North Carolina.* Raleigh, NC: Alfred Williams and Co., 1883.

Zimmerman, Jonathan. *Distilling Democracy: Alcohol Education in America's Public Schools, 1880–1925.* Lawrence: University Press of Kansas, 1999.

Zuber, Richard L. *North Carolina during Reconstruction.* Raleigh: North Carolina Division of Archives and History, 1969.

Index

Lightning Source UK Ltd.
Milton Keynes UK
UKOW041559150313

207721UK00002B/12/P